Advance Praise for
100 Great Poets of the English Language

"This is an excellent selection of poems, with just the right balance of tradition and surprise."

Christian Wiman
Poet, critic, and editor of POETRY

"Remarkable for its range and selectivity, this excellent introduction to lyric poetry could well become, for readers of all sorts, a lifelong companion."

Robert Shaw
Mount Holyoke College

"A rich collection which combines old favorites with thoughtful and surprising new selections and reflects a keen sense of the lineage of poetry. This will be an inspiring book for classes, as well as for the individual reader seeking a potent mix."

Diane Thiel
Poet

"This little collection has the same specific gravity as gold. Limiting ourselves to 100 popular and important poets is a great idea. I believe this anthology or one like it should grace the shelves of every literate home."

Paul Guajardo
University of Houston

Dana Gioia is a poet, critic, and teacher. Born in Los Angeles, he attended Stanford and Harvard before taking a detour into business. After years of writing and reading late in the evenings after work, he quit a corporate vice presidency to write. He has published three collections of poetry, *Daily Horoscope* (1986), *The Gods of Winter* (1991), and *Interrogations at Noon* (2001), several anthologies, and an influential study of poetry's place in contemporary America, *Can Poetry Matter?* (1992). With X. J. Kennedy, he coedited *An Introduction to Fiction*, *An Introduction to Poetry*, and *Literature*. He has also published literary translations from Italian, German, and Latin. Gioia has taught at Johns Hopkins, Sarah Lawrence, Wesleyan (Connecticut), Mercer, and Colorado College. He is also the cofounder of the summer poetry conference at West Chester University in Pennsylvania and served as a commentator on literature for British Broadcasting Corporation. He currently lives in Washington, D.C., where he serves as Chairman of the National Endowment for the Arts.

100 Great Poets of the English Language

Edited by

Dana Gioia

with

Dan Stone

New York • San Francisco • Boston
London • Toronto • Sydney • Tokyo • Singapore • Madrid
Mexico City • Munich • Paris • Cape Town • Hong Kong • Montreal

Vice President, Editor-In-Chief: Joseph P. Terry
Executive Marketing Manager: Ann Stypuloski
Production Manager: Eric Jorgensen
Project Coordination, Text Design, and Electronic Page Makeup: Pre-Press Company, Inc.
Senior Cover Design Manager/Designer: Nancy Danahy
Cover Photo: © Photographers Choice/Getty Images, Inc.
Senior Manufacturing Buyer: Alfred C. Dorsey
Printer and Binder: RR Donnelley & Sons Company
Cover Printer: Phoenix Color Corp.

For permission to use copyrighted material, grateful acknowledgment is made to the copyright holders on pp. 545–550, which are hereby made part of this copyright page.

Library of Congress Cataloging-in-Publication Data
100 great poets of the English language / edited by Dana Gioia.
p. cm.
Includes bibliographical references and index.
ISBN 0-321-19867-0
1. English poetry. 2. American poetry. I. Title: One hundred great poets of the English language. II. Gioia, Dana.

PR1175.A137155 2004
821.008--dc22

2003067620

Visit us at http://www.ablongman.com.

ISBN 0-321-19867-0

12345678910—DOH—07060504

Contents

Preface

"Poetry is life distilled."
—*Gwendolyn Brooks*

The purpose of this book is twofold. First, it hopes to introduce the reader to the pleasure, enlightenment, and consolation of poetry. Second, it attempts to outline the development of English-language poetry from the Middle Ages to the present by presenting the high points of its artistic achievement. "The purpose of poetry," Wallace Stevens claimed, "is to contribute to man's happiness." Pleasure, therefore, is always at the heart of the poetic impulse. Without experiencing the pleasure of poetry, a reader cannot appreciate the true nature of the art.

Poetry helps one understand—intuitively and emotionally as well as intellectually—what it means to be alive by embodying even the starkest message in delight. It is not a matter of being witty or amusing, though poems can be funny. Instead, in poetry the very way a thing is said must give pleasure. As Seamus Heaney has remarked, "Poetry cannot afford to lose its fundamentally self-delighting inventiveness, its joy in being a process of language as well as a representation of things in the world." The editor of this anthology has been unbending in his insistence that every poem—no matter how tragic or profound, experimental or heartfelt—follows the pleasure principle. Art has no enemy so deadly as dullness.

This anthology also rests on the belief that poetry is not primarily an intellectual art. Although poems can be powerful means of expressing ideas, they communicate differently from philosophy or other types of analytical writing. "Prose is for ideas, verse for visions," claimed the playwright Henrik Ibsen, acknowledging the mysterious ways in which poetry communicates. Poetry speaks to the fullness of our humanity—our intellect, emotions, imagination, intuition, memory, and physical being. Thought plays an important part in our humanity, but it by no means constitutes the majority of what we know and feel in life. The strength of poetry is that it refuses to separate us into our separate human faculties. It insists on addressing us as complete and complex beings. There is no theoretical substitute for experiencing poetry. "We learn what poetry is," wrote T. S. Eliot, "—if we ever learn—by reading it."

Poetry is also the most concise, compressed, and intense of literary forms. It communicates in short, expressive bursts of energy that arrest attention and settle in the memory. "Prose wanders around with a lantern and laboriously schedules and verifies the details and particulars of a valley and its frame of crags and peaks," wrote Mark Twain, "then Poetry comes, and lays bare the whole landscape with a single splendid flash." The "flash" that Twain describes is the powerful lyrical effect poetry offers—its sudden, overpowering, visionary impact. Poetry's effect is physical as well as mental. "If I read a book [and] it makes my whole body so cold no fire ever can warm me," remarked Emily Dickinson, "I know *that* is poetry. If I feel physically as if the top of my head were taken off, I know *that* is poetry. These are the only ways I know it."

This is not a scholarly anthology, though the editor has tried to provide accurate texts and biographical data. Instead, the book tries to present in accessible and enjoyable terms the broad sweep and development of English-language poetry from its early origins in medieval Anglo-Saxon culture to its cosmopolitan present. The poets have been presented in chronological order. Dates for the first book publication and/or the composition date of the selection are printed below each poem. Although there are sometimes significant gaps of time between individual writers, a historical arrangement allows the reader to see, at least in general terms, the development of literary styles and thematic concerns. It also suggests the complex, fascinating, and often unpredictable ways in which poets influence one another. There is no doubt, for example, that John Milton shaped William Blake's sense of poetry and the poet's role, but what the younger poet took from his master was transformed in utterly original ways. An anthology allows a curious reader to observe many such cases of influence.

The scope of the book is international with poets drawn from three continents, but it emphasizes the development of poetry in Britain, Ireland, and the United States. Although it includes some poets from Australia, Canada, and the Caribbean, there was no room in this compact volume to trace the full development of English poetry across the world. The book's broad historical coverage—twelve centuries—and its limited number of authors prevented full representation of contemporary postcolonial verse in English. Given the restrictions, it seemed more useful to provide adequate historical representation of British, Irish, and American poetry. For reasons of space and focus, especially in the contemporary era, many fine poets have been omitted who have a legitimate claim on the book.

The editor also wishes to include a few surprises and discoveries rather than merely repeating some familiar roll call of the poetic great. It seemed a worthy enterprise to introduce American readers to distinguished foreign writers like A. D. Hope, Earle Birney, and Charles Causley as well as earlier masters like Mary Sidney Wroth, Aphra Behn, and Coventry Patmore. Will everyone be pleased? Of course not. An anthology, the editor has come to believe, is a book that omits your favorite poem. The unavoidable fate of any anthologist is to leave out nearly as many wonderful things as he or she includes. The only defense is by making what remains in the book indisputably excellent. Only the reader can judge whether I have succeeded in that attempt.

DANA GIOIA

100 Great Poets of the English Language

Beowulf is the oldest surviving epic poem in British literature. Although its authorial history is unknown, it is generally assumed to have been composed sometime between the eighth and eleventh centuries. Certain Christian elements in the poem's largely pagan narrative have led some scholars to assume that the original text was revised by a later copyist. The manuscript for Beowulf *exists in only one copy, written in Old English probably dating from around 1000* AD. *It is held in the British Museum, London. Donated to England by Sir Robert Cotton in 1700, the manuscript was damaged and nearly destroyed by fire in 1731.* Beowulf *is written in Anglo-Saxon alliterative stress meter: the line is built on four strong stresses, with either three alliterative stresses, or alliterative pairs.*

Beowulf Poet—Anonymous

from Beowulf*

Grendel Attacks

Each day, one evil dweller in darkness
spitefully suffered the din from that hall
where Hrothgar's men made merry with mead.
Harp-strings would sound, and the song of the scop
would recount the tales told of time past: 5
whence mankind had come, and how the Almighty
had fashioned flat land, fair to behold,
surrounded with water. The worker of wonders
lifted and lit the sun and moon
for Earth's dwellers; He filled the forests 10
with branches and blooms; He breathed life
into all kinds of creatures.

So the king's thanes
gathered in gladness; then crime came calling,
a horror from hell, hideous Grendel,
wrathful rover of borders and moors, 15
holder of hollows, haunter of fens.
He had lived long in the homeland of horrors,
born to the band whom God had banished
as kindred of Cain, thereby requiting
the slayer of Abel. Many such sprang 20

*The translation used here is by Alan Sullivan and Timothy Murphy.

from the first murderer: monsters and misfits,
elves and ill-spirits, also those giants
whose wars with the Lord earned them exile.

After nightfall he nosed around Heorot,
saw how swordsmen slept in the hall, *25*
unwary and weary with wine and feasting,
numb to the sorrows suffered by men.
The cursed creature, cruel and remorseless,
swiftly slipped in. He seized thirty thanes
asleep after supper, shouldered away *30*
what trophies he would, and took to his lair
pleased with the plunder, proud of his murders.

When daylight dawned on the spoils of slaughter,
the strength of the fiend was readily seen.
The feast was followed by fits of weeping, *35*
and cries of outrage rose in the morning.
Hrothgar the strong sank on his throne,
helpless and hopeless beholding the carnage,
the trail of the terror, a trouble too wrathful,
a foe too ferocious, too steadfast in rage, *40*
ancient and evil. The evening after
he murdered again with no more remorse,
so fixed was his will on that wicked feud.
Henceforth the fearful were easily found
elsewhere, anywhere far from the fiend, *45*
bedding in barns, for the brutal hall-thane
was truly betokened by terrible signs,
and those who escaped stayed safer afar.

So wrath fought alone against rule and right;
one routed many; the mead-hall stood empty. *50*
Strongest of Spear-Danes, Hrothgar suffered
this fell affliction for twelve winters' time.
As his woes became known widely and well,
sad songs were sung by the sons of men:
how season on season, with ceaseless strife, *55*
Grendel assailed the Scylding's sovereign.
The monster craved no kinship with any,
no end to the evil with wergeld owed;
nor might a king's council have reckoned
on quittance come from the killer's hand. *60*

The dark death-shadow daunted them all,
lying in ambush for old and young,
secretly slinking and stalking by night.
No man knows where on the misty moor
the heathen keepers of hell-runes° wander. *65*

So over and over the loathsome ogre
mortally menaced mankind with his crimes.
Raiding by night, he reigned in the hall,
and Heorot's high adornments were his,
but God would not grant throne-gifts to gladden *70*
a scourge who spurned the Sovereign of Heaven.

Stricken in spirit, Hrothgar would often
closet his council to ponder what plan
might be deemed best by strong-minded men.
Sometimes the elders swore before altars *75*
of old war-idols, offering prayers
for the soul-slayer to succor their people.°
Such was their habit, the hope of heathens:
with hell in their hearts, they were lost to the Lord.
Their inmost minds knew not the Almighty; *80*
they never would worship the world's true protector.
Sorry is he who sears his soul,
afflicted by flames he freely embraced.
No cheer for the chastened! No change in his fate!
But happy is he whom heaven welcomes, *85*
and after his death-day he dwells with the Father.

65 *hell-runes:* By rendering the Old English *helrunan,* which means "those adept in the mysteries of hell," as "heathen keepers of hell-runes," the translators are taking the liberty of suggesting that "demons" such as Grendel are familiar with runes—the letters of the early Germanic alphabet.
77 *to succor their people:* In their fear, the Danes resume heathen practices. In Christian belief, the pagan gods were transformed into devils.

Battle with Grendel

Cunningly creeping, a spectral stalker
slunk through the gloom. The bowmen were sleeping
who ought to have held the high-horned house,
all except one, for the Lord's will
now became known: no more would the murderer *5*
drag under darkness whomever he wished.

Anger was wakeful, watching the enemy;
hot-hearted Beowulf was bent upon battle.

Then from the moor under misty hillsides,
Grendel came gliding girt with God's anger. *10*
The man-scather sought someone to snatch
from the high hall. He crept under clouds
until he caught sight of the king's court
whose gilded gables he knew at a glance.
He often had haunted Hrothgar's house; *15*
but he never found, before or after,
hardier hall-thanes or harder luck.
The joyless giant drew near the door,
which swiftly swung back at the touch of his hand
though bound and fastened with forge-bent bars. *20*
The building's mouth had been broken open,
and Grendel entered with ill intent.
Swollen with fury, he stalked over flagstones
and looked round the manse where many men lay.
An unlovely light most like a flame *25*
flashed from his eyes, flared through the hall
at young soldiers dozing shoulder to shoulder,
comradely kindred. The cruel creature laughed
in his murderous mind, thinking how many
now living would die before the day dawned, *30*
how glutted with gore he would guzzle his fill.
It was not his fate to finish the feast
he foresaw that night.

Soon the Stalwart,
Hygelac's kinsman, beheld how the horror,
not one to be idle, went about evil. *35*
For his first feat he suddenly seized
a sleeping soldier, slashed at the flesh,
bit through bones and lapped up the blood
that gushed from veins as he gorged on gobbets.
Swiftly he swallowed those lifeless limbs, *40*
hands and feet whole; then he headed forward
with open palm to plunder the prone.
One man angled up on his elbow:
the fiend soon found he was facing a foe
whose hand-grip was harder than any other *45*
he ever had met in all Middle-Earth.

Cravenly cringing, coward at heart,
he longed for a swift escape to his lair,
his bevy of devils. He never had known
from his earliest days such awful anguish. *50*

The captain, recalling his speech to the king,
straightaway stood and hardened his hold.
Fingers fractured. The fiend spun round;
the soldier stepped closer. Grendel sought
somehow to slip that grasp and escape, *55*
flee to the fens; but his fingers were caught
in too fierce a grip. His foray had failed;
the harm-wreaker rued his raid on Heorot.
From the hall of the Danes a hellish din
beset every soldier outside the stronghold, *60*
louder than laughter of ale-sodden earls.
A wonder it was the wine-hall withstood
this forceful affray without falling to earth.
That beautiful building was firmly bonded
by iron bands forged with forethought *65*
inside and out. As some have told it,
the struggle swept on and slammed to the floor
many mead-benches massive with gold.
No Scylding elders ever imagined
that any would harm their elk-horned hall, *70*
raze what they wrought, unless flames arose
to enfold and consume it. Frightful new sounds
burst from the building, unnerved the North-Danes,
each one and all who heard those outcries
outside the walls. Wailing in anguish, *75*
the hellish horror, hateful to God,
sang his dispair, seized by the grip
of a man more mighty than any then living.

That shielder of men meant by no means
to let the death-dealer leave with his life, *80*
a life worthless to anyone elsewhere.
Then the young soldiers swung their old swords
again and again to save their guardian,
their kingly comrade, however they could.
Engaging with Grendel and hoping to hew him *85*
from every side, they scarcely suspected

that blades wielded   by worthy warriors
never would cut   to the criminal's quick.
The spell was spun   so strongly about him
that the finest iron   of any on earth,   *90*
the sharpest sword-edge   left him unscathed.
Still he was soon   to be stripped of his life
and sent on a sore   sojourn to Hell.
The strength of his sinews   would serve him no more;
no more would he menace   mankind with his crimes,   *95*
his grudge against God,   for the high-hearted kinsman
of King Hygelac   had hold of his hand.
Each found the other   loathsome in life;
but the murderous man-bane   got a great wound
as tendons were torn,   shoulder shorn open,   *100*
and bone-locks broken.   Beowulf gained
glory in war;   and Grendel went off
bloody and bent   to the boggy hills,
sorrowfully seeking   his dreary dwelling.
Surely he sensed   his life-span was spent,   *105*
his days upon days;   but the Danes were grateful:
their wish was fulfilled   after fearsome warfare.

Wise and strong-willed,   the one from afar
had cleansed Heorot,   hall of Hrothgar.
Great among Geats,   he was glad of his night-work   *110*
ending the evil,   his fame-winning feat,
fulfilling his oath   to aid the East Danes,
easing their anguish,   healing the horror
they suffered so long,   no small distress.
As token of triumph,   the troop-leader hung   *115*
the shorn-off shoulder   and arm by its hand:
the grip of Grendel   swung from the gable!

Beowulf's Burial

There the king's kinsmen   piled him a pyre,
wide and well-made   just as he willed it.
They hung it with helmets,   shields and mail-shirts,
then laid in its midst   their beloved lord,
renowned among men.   Lamenting their loss,   *5*

his warriors woke   the most woeful fire
to flare on the bluff.   Fierce was the burning,
woven with weeping,   and wood-smoke rose
black over the blaze,   blown with a roar.
The fire-wind faltered   and flames dwindled,   *10*
hot at their heart   the broken bone-house.
Sunken in spirit   at Beowulf's slaying,
the Geats gathered   grieving together.
Her hair wound up,   a woebegone woman
sang and resang   her dirge of dread,   *15*
foretelling a future   fraught with warfare,
kinfolk sundered,   slaughter and slavery
even as Heaven   swallowed the smoke.

High on the headland   they heaped his grave-mound
which seafaring sailors   would spy from afar.   *20*
Ten days they toiled   on the scorched hilltop,
the cleverest men   skillfully crafting
a long-home built   for the bold in battle.
They walled with timbers   the trove they had taken,
sealing in stone   the circlets and gems,   *25*
wealth of the worm-hoard   gotten with grief,
gold from the ground   gone back to Earth
as worthless to men   as when it was won.
Then sorrowing swordsmen   circled the barrow,
twelve of his earls   telling their tales,   *30*
the sons of nobles   sadly saluting
deeds of the dead.   So dutiful thanes
in liege to their lord   mourn him with lays
praising his peerless   prowess in battle
as it is fitting   when life leaves the flesh.   *35*
Heavy-hearted   his hearth-companions
grieved for Beowulf,   great among kings,
mild in his mien,   most gentle of men,
kindest to kinfolk   and keenest for fame.

***Geoffrey Chaucer** (c. 1340–1400) was born into a middle-class merchant family. Though little is known about his early education, we know he learned Latin, French, and Italian. At 15 he served as a page for the Countess of Ulster. He received a suit of livery when he was 17 years old, and in 1359 entered military service during the Hundred Years War between England and France. He was taken prisoner in France. The next year the king paid a 16-pound ransom for Chaucer's freedom. Returning to Engand, he married in 1365 a relative of John of Gaunt, who patronized the poet for much of his life. Chaucer rejoined the army in 1370, and was stationed in Italy. He saw hard times for the last years of his life—his wife died in 1387, and he suffered from significant financial stress, which the king partly relieved. During this difficult period, however, Chaucer wrote* The Canterbury Tales, *his unfinished masterpiece. At a time when many British writers used Latin or French, Chaucer wrote in English, specifically the speech of his adopted London. His poetry helped establish English as the vernacular for serious literature. He was buried in the Chapel of St. Benedict in Westminster Abbey as the first tenant of Poet's Corner.*

Geoffrey Chaucer

from The Canterbury Tales

from The General Prologue

Whan that April with his showres soote°
The droughte of March hath perced to the roote,
And bathed every veine in swich licour,°
Of which vertu° engendred is the flowr;
Whan Zephyrus° eek° with his sweete breeth *5*
Inspired hath in every holt and heeth°
The tendre croppes, and the yonge sonne
Hath in the Ram° his halve cours yronne,
And smale fowles maken melodye
That sleepen al the night with open yë°— *10*

1 *soote*: sweet. 3 *swich licour*: such liquid. 4 *Of which vertu*: by whose strength. 5 *Zephyrus*: In Roman mythology Zephyrus was the demigod of the west wind, herald of warmer weather; *eek*: also. 6 *holt and heeth*: wood and field. 8 *Ram*: the zodiac sign Aries. 10 *yë*: eye.

So priketh hem Nature in hir corages°—
Thanne longen folk to goon on pilgrimages,
And palmeres° for to seeken straunge strondes°
To ferne halwes, couthe° in sondry londes;
And specially from every shires ende *15*
Of Engelond to Canterbury they wende,°
The holy blisful martyr° for to seeke
That hem hath holpen° whan that they were seke.°
Bifel that in that seson on a day,
In Southwerk° at the Tabard as I lay, *20*
Redy to wenden on my pilgrimage
To Canterbury with ful devout corage,
At night was come into that hostelrye
Wel nine and twenty in a compaignye
Of sondry folk, by aventure yfalle *25*
In felaweshipe, and pilgrimes were they alle
That toward Canterbury wolden ride.
The chambres° and the stables weren wide,
And wel we weren esed° at the beste.
And shortly, whan the sonne was to reste, *30*
So hadde I spoken with hem everichoon
That I was of hir felaweshipe anoon,
And made forward° erly for to rise,
To take oure way ther as I you devise.°
But nathelees, whil I have time and space,° *35*
Er that I ferther in this tale pace,°
Me thinketh it accordant to resoun
To telle you al the condicioun°
Of eech of hem, so as it seemed me,
And whiche they were, and of what degree,° *40*
And eek in what array that they were inne:
And at a knight thanne wol I first biginne.

• • •

11 *corages*: hearts, spirits. 13 *palmeres*: Pilgrims who had traveled to the Holy Land; *strondes*: shores. 14 *ferne halwes, couthe*: far-off shrines, known . . . 16 *wende*: go. 17 *martyr*: St. Thomas Becket, murdered in Canterbury Cathedral in 1170. 18 *holpen*: helped; *seke*: sick. 20 *Southwerk*: a suburb of London south of the Thames and the traditional starting point for the pilgrimage to Canterbury in Kent, it was notorious as a center of gambling and prostitution. The Tabard Inn was an actual public house at the time, named for the shape of its sign which resembled the coarse, sleeveless outer garment worn by members of the lower classes, monks, and foot soldiers alike. 28 *chambres*: guestrooms. 29 *esed*: accommodated. 33 *made forward*: agreed. 34 *devise*: relate. 35 *space*: opportunity. 36 *pace*: proceed. 38 *condicioun*: circumstances. 40 *degree*: social status.

from The Wife of Bath's Prologue

Experience, though noon auctoritee°
Were in this world, is right ynough for me
To speke of wo that is in mariage:
For lordinges,° sith I twelf yeer was of age—
Thanked be God that is eterne on live— *5*
Housbondes at chirche dore I have had five
(If I so ofte mighte han wedded be),
And alle were worthy men in hir° degree.
But me was told, certain, nat longe agoon is,
That sith that Crist ne wente nevere but ones° *10*
To wedding in the Cane of Galilee,°
That by the same ensample taughte he me
That I ne sholde wedded be but ones.
Herke eek, lo, which a sharp word for the nones,°
Biside a welle, Jesus, God and man, *15*
Spak in repreve° of the Samaritan:°
"Thou hast yhad five housbondes," quod he,
"And that ilke° man that now hath thee
Is nat thyn housbonde." Thus saide he certain.
What that he mente therby I can nat sayn, *20*
But that I axe why that the fifthe man
Was noon housbonde to the Samaritan?
How manye mighte she han in mariage?
Yit herde I nevere tellen in myn age
Upon this nombre diffinicioun. *25*
Men may divine° and glosen° up and down,
But wel I woot,° expres,° withouten lie,
God bad us for to wexe° and multiplye:
That gentil text can I wel understonde.
　　Eek wel I woot he saide that myn housbonde *30*
Sholde lete° fader and moder and take to me,
But of no nombre mencion made he—

1 *though noon auctoritee*: even if no written authority validates the speaker's opinion. **4** *lordinges*: gentlemen. **8** *hir*: their. **10** *ones*: once. **11** *Cane of Galilee*: Cana, where Jesus performed his first miracle at a wedding feast (John 2.1). **14** *for the nones*: for the purpose. **16** *repreve*: reproof; *Samaritan*: The story of Jesus and the Samaritan woman is related in John 4.6 ff. **18** *ilke*: same. **26** *divine and glosen*: guess and interpret. **27** *woot, expres*: know, manifestly. **28** *wexe*: increase. **31** *lete*: leave.

Of bigamye or of octogamye:
Why sholde men thanne speke of it vilainye?°
  Lo, here the wise king daun° Salomon: *35*
I trowe° he hadde wives many oon,
As wolde God it leveful° were to me
To be refresshed half so ofte as he.
Which yifte° of God hadde he for alle his wives!
No man hath swich that in this world alive is. *40*
God woot° this noble king, as to my wit,°
The firste night hadde many a merye fit
With eech of hem, so wel was him on live.
Blessed be God that I have wedded five,
Of whiche I have piked° out the beste, *45*
Bothe of hir nether purs and of hir cheste.°
Diverse° scoles maken parfit° clerkes,
And diverse practikes in sondry werkes
Maken the werkman° parfit sikerly:°
Of five housbondes scoleying° am I. *50*
Welcome the sixte whan that evere he shal!
For sith I wol nat keepe me chast in al,
Whan myn housbonde is fro the world agoon,
Som Cristen man shal wedde me anoon.
For thanne th'Apostle° saith that I am free *55*
To wedde, a Goddes half,° where it liketh° me.
He said that to be wedded is no sinne:
Bet° is to be wedded than to brinne.°
What rekketh° me though folk saye vilainye
Of shrewed° Lamech° and his bigamye? *60*
I woot wel Abraham was an holy man,
And Jacob eek, as fer as evere I can,°
And eech of hem hadde wives mo than two,
And many another holy man also.
  Where can ye saye in any manere age *65*
That hye God defended° mariage

34 *vilainye*: as churlish. **35** *daun*: Lord. **36** *trowe*: believe. **37** *leveful*: lawful. **39** *Which yifte*: what a gift. **41** *woot*: knows; *wit*: understanding. **45** *piked*: picked. **46** *cheste*: money chest, with a pun on body parts. **47** *Diverse*: different; *parfit*: accomplished. **49** *werkman*: craftsman; *sikerly*: surely. **50** *scoleying*: studying. **55** *Apostle*: St. Paul, in Romans 7.2. **56** *a Goddes half*: from God's perspective; *liketh*: please. **58** *Bet*: better; *brinne*: burn (in hell). **59** *rekketh*: do I care. **60** *shrewed*: cursed; *Lamech*: the earliest bigamist in the Bible (Genesis 4.19). **62** *can*: know. **66** *defended*: prohibited.

By expres word? I praye you, telleth me.
Or where comanded he virginitee?
I woot as wel as ye, it is no drede,°
Th'Apostle, whan he speketh of maidenhede,° *70*
He saide that precept° therof hadde he noon:
Men may conseile a womman to be oon,°
But conseiling nis no comandement.
He putte it in oure owene juggement.
For hadde God comanded maidenhede, *75*
Thanne hadde he dampned° wedding with the deede;
And certes, if ther were no seed ysowe,
Virginitee, thanne wherof sholde it growe?
Paul dorste nat comanden at the leeste
A thing of which his maister yaf no heeste.° *80*
The dart° is set up for virginitee:
Cacche whoso may, who renneth° best lat see.
But this word is nought take of every wight,°
But ther as God list° yive it of his might.
I woot wel that th'Apostle was a maide,° *85*
But nathelees, though that he wroot or saide
He wolde that every wight were swich as he,
Al nis but° conseil to virginitee;
And for to been a wif he yaf me leve
Of indulgence; so nis it no repreve *90*
To wedde me if that my make° die,
Withouten excepcion° of bigamye—
Al were it good no womman for to touche
(He mente as in his bed or in his couche,
For peril is bothe fir and tow t'assemble° *95*
Ye knowe what this ensample may resemble).
This al and som,° he heeld virginitee
More parfit than wedding in freletee.°
(Freletee clepe° I but if° that he and she
Wolde leden al hir lif in chastitee). *100*
I graunte it wel, I have noon envye
Though maidenhede preferre° bigamye:

69 *drede*: doubt. 70 *maidenhede*: virginity. 71 *precept*: command. 72 *oon*: single. 76 *dampned*: condemned. 80 *heeste*: commandment. 81 *dart*: prize. 82 *renneth*: runs. 83 *take of every wight*: required of every person. 84 *list*: pleases. 85 *maide*: virgin. 88 *Al nis but*: It is only. 91 *make*: mate. 92 *excepcion*: legal objection. 95 *fir and tow t'assemble*: to bring together fire and flax. 97 *al and som*: all told. 98 *in freletee*: due to weakness. 99 *clepe*: call; *if*: except.102 *preferre*: supasses.

It liketh hem to be clene in body and gost.°
Of myn estaat° ne wol I make no boost;
For wel ye knowe, a lord in his houshold *105*
Ne hath nat every vessel al of gold:
Some been of tree,° and doon hir lord servise.
God clepeth° folk to him in sondry wise,
And everich hath of God a propre yifte,
Som this, som that, as him liketh shifte.° *110*
Virginitee is greet perfeccioun,
And continence eek with devocioun,
But Crist, that of perfeccion is welle,°
Bad nat every wight° he sholde go selle
Al that he hadde and yive it to the poore, *115*
And in swich wise folwe° him and his fore:°
He spak to hem that wolde live parfitly°—
And lordinges, by youre leve, that am nat I.
I wol bistowe the flour of al myn age
In th'actes and in fruit of mariage. *120*
Telle me also, to what conclusioun°
Were membres maad of generacioun
And of so parfit wis a wrighte ywrought?°
Trusteth right wel, they were nat maad for nought.
Glose whoso wol, and saye bothe up and down *125*
That they were maked for purgacioun
Of urine, and oure bothe thinges smale
Was eek to knowe a femele from a male,
And for noon other cause—saye ye no?
Th'experience woot wel it is nought so. *130*
So that the clerkes be nat with me wrothe,°
I saye this, that they maked been for bothe—
That is to sayn, for office° and for ese°
Of engendrure,° ther we nat God displese.
Why sholde men elles in hir bookes sette *135*
That man shal yeelde° to his wif hir dette?°
Now wherwith sholde he make his payement
If he ne used his sely° instrument?

103 *gost*: soul. **104** *estaat*: condition. **107** *tree*: wood. **108** *clepeth*: calls. **110** *as him liketh shifte*: as it pleases him to provide. **113** *welle*: source. **114** *wight*: person. **116** *folwe*: follow; *fore*: footsteps. **117** *parfitly*: perfectly. **121** *conclusioun*: end. **123** *And of so parfit wis a wrighte ywrought?* And created by so perfectly wise a Creator? **131** *wrothe*: angry. **133** *office*: use; *ese*: pleasure. **134** *engendrure*: procreation. **136** *yeelde*: pay; *dette*: marriage debt. **138** *sely*: innocent.

Thanne were they maad upon a creature
To purge urine, and eek for engendrure. *140*
 But I saye nought that every wight is holde,°
That hath swich harneis° as I to you tolde,
To goon and usen hem in engendrure:
Thanne sholde men take of chastitee no cure.°
Crist was a maide and shapen as a man, *145*
And many a saint sith that the world bigan,
Yit lived they evere in parfit° chastitee.
I nil envye no virginitee:
Lat hem be breed° of pured° whete seed,
And lat us wives hote° barly breed— *150*
And yit with barly breed, Mark telle can,
Oure Lord Jesu refresshed many a man.
In swich estaat as God hath cleped° us
I wol persevere: I nam nat precious.°
In wifhood wol I use myn instrument *155*
As freely° as my Makere hath it sent.
If I be daungerous,° God yive me sorwe:°
Myn housbonde shal it han both eve and morwe,°
Whan that him list come forth and paye his dette.
An housbonde wol I have, I wol nat lette,° *160*
Which shal be bothe my dettour and my thral,°
And have his tribulacion withal
Upon his flessh whil that I am his wif.
I have the power during al my lif
Upon his propre° body, and nat he: *165*
Right thus th'Apostle tolde it unto me,
And bad oure housbondes for to love us weel.
Al this sentence° me liketh everydeel.

• • •

[c. 1375–1400]

141 *holde*: bound. **142** *harneis*: equipment. **144** *cure*: heed. **147** *parfit*: perfect. **149** *breed*: bread; *pured*: refined. **150** *hote*: be called. **153** *cleped*: called. **154** *nam nat precious*: am not fussy. **156** *freely*: generously. **157** *daungerous*: withholding; *sorwe*: sorrow. **158** *morwe*: morning. **160** *lette*: forgo. **161** *thral*: slave. **165** *propre*: own. **168** *sentence*: interpretation.

Merciless Beauty*

Your ÿen° two wol slee° me sodenly;
I may the beautee of hem° not sustene,°
So woundeth hit thourghout my herte kene.°

And but° your word wo! helen° hastily
My hertes wounde, while that hit is grene,° *5*
  Your ÿen two wol slee me sodenly;
  I may the beautee of hem not sustene.

Upon my trouthe° I sey you feithfully
That ye ben of my lyf and deeth the quene;
For with my deeth the trouthe° shal be sene. *10*
  Your ÿen two wol slee me sodenly;
  I may the beautee of hem not sustene,
  So woundeth it thourghout my herte kene.

*This poem is one of a group of three roundels, collectively titled "Merciles Beaute." A roundel (or rondel) is an English form consisting of 11 to 14 lines.

1 *ÿen*: eyes; *slee*: slay. **2** *hem*: them; *sustene*: resist. **3** *So woundeth . . . kene*: So deeply does it wound me through the heart. **4** *but*: unless; *helen*: heal. **5** *grene*: new. **8** *trouthe*: word. **10** *trouthe*: truth.

***Sir Thomas Wyatt** (1503–1542) was the first major lyric poet of the English language. He is credited with having introduced the sonnet and other foreign forms and meters into his native tongue. Wyatt was born in Kent in southeast England, the elder son of Henry Wyatt, who was later knighted. Presented at court when he was just 13, Wyatt began his formal studies at St. John's College, Cambridge, and was married before graduating. The couple had a daughter and a son, but the marriage fell apart when Wyatt accused his young wife of infidelity. Wyatt traveled to France and Rome on diplomatic missions, and he served as chief ewer at the coronation of Anne Boleyn. Amidst rumors that he was Queen Anne's lover, Wyatt was briefly imprisoned in the Tower of London when Queen Anne was brought to trial and executed for adultery in 1536. Soon back in royal favor, Wyatt was knighted in 1537 and sent on missions to Spain, France, and Flanders. He was elected a Member of Parliament in 1542, but, having been sent to accompany a Spanish envoy from Falmouth to London, died in Dorset of a fever that October.*

Sir Thomas Wyatt

My Lute Awake!

My lute awake! perform the last
Labour that thou and I shall waste,
And end that I have now begun;
For when this song is sung and past,
My lute be still, for I have done. *5*

As to be heard where ear is none,
As lead to grave in marble stone,
My song may pierce her heart as soon;
Should we then sigh, or sing, or moan?
No, no, my lute, for I have done. *10*

The rocks do not so cruelly
Repulse the waves continually,
As she my suit and affection,
So that I am past remedy:
Whereby my lute and I have done. *15*

Proud of the spoil that thou hast got
Of simple hearts thorough love's shot,
By whom, unkind, thou hast them won,
Think not he hath his bow forgot,
Although my lute and I have done. *20*

Vengeance shall fall on thy disdain,
That makest but game on earnest pain;
Think not alone under the sun
Unquit to cause thy lovers plain,
Although my lute and I have done. *25*

Perchance thee lie withered and old,
The winter nights that are so cold,
Plaining in vain unto the moon;
Thy wishes then dare not be told;
Care then who list, for I have done. *30*

And then may chance thee to repent
The time that thou hast lost and spent

To cause thy lovers sigh and swoon;
Then shalt thou know beauty but lent,
And wish and want as I have done. *35*

Now cease, my lute! this is the last
Labour that thou and I shall waste,
And ended is that we begun;
Now is this song both sung and past:
My lute, be still, for I have done. *40*

[1557]

They Flee from Me

They flee from me, that sometime did me seek,
With naked foot stalking in my chamber.
I have seen them, gentle, tame, and meek,
That now are wild, and do not remember
That sometime they put themselves in danger *5*
To take bread at my hand; and now they range,
Busily seeking with a continual change.

Thanked be Fortune it hath been otherwise,
Twenty times better; but once in special,
In thin array, after a pleasant guise, *10*
When her loose gown from her shoulders did fall,
And she me caught in her arms long and small,
And therewith all sweetly did me kiss
And softly said, "Dear heart, how like you this?"

It was no dream, I lay broad waking. *15*
But all is turned, thorough my gentleness,
Into a strange fashion of forsaking;
And I have leave to go, of her goodness,
And she also to use newfangleness.
But since that I so kindely am served, *20*
I fain would know what she hath deserved.

[1557]

Stand Whoso List

Stand whoso list° upon the slipper° top
    Of court's estates, and let me here rejoice;
And use me quiet without let or stop,°
    Unknown in court, that hath such brackish joys:
        In hidden place, so let my days forth pass, *5*
    That when my years be done, withouten noise,
        I may die aged after the common trace.°
For him death gripeth right hard by the crope°
        That is much known of other; and of himself, alas,
        Doth die unknown, dazed with dreadful face. *10*

[c. 1557]

1 *list*: likes; *slipper*: slippery. 3 *stop*: hindrance. 7 *trace*: way. 8 *crope*: throat.

Whoso List to Hunt

Whoso list to hunt, I know where is an hind,
    But as for me, alas, I may no more;
    The vain travail hath wearied me so sore,
    I am of them that furthest come behind.
Yet may I by no means my wearied mind *5*
    Draw from the deer, but as she fleeth afore
    Fainting I follow; I leave off therefore,
    Since in a net I seek to hold the wind.
Who list her hunt, I put him out of doubt,
    As well as I, may spend his time in vain. *10*
    And graven with diamonds in letters plain,
There is written her fair neck round about,
    "*Noli me tangere,*° for Caesar's I am,
    And wild for to hold, though I seem tame."

[1557]

13 *Noli me tangere:* Latin for "you are not allowed to touch me." Although used here in a secular context, these are also the words Christ spoke to Mary Magdalene in the garden after the resurrection.

***Edmund Spenser** (c. 1552–1599) was born in London, and attended Pembroke Hall in Cambridge. The young man first met royalty in 1579 when he began serving the Earl of Leicester. He was befriended by the Earl's nephew, Sir Philip Sidney, and became involved in a literary group, the Areopagus, headed by Sidney. Spenser was already at work on what would become his two masterpieces,* The Shepeardes Calender *(published in 1579) and, though left unfinished,* The Faerie Queene, *a long allegorical poem intended to be an English national epic (six books were published in 1596). His* Amoretti *(1595) ranks among the great sonnet sequences in English. In 1580 Spenser accompanied Arthur Grey, the new Lord Deputy of Ireland, to Dublin as his private secretary. Among his most impressive properties, Spenser had been granted Kilcolman Castle, which included 3000 acres. He took up residence there for more than a decade until Irish rebels burned the castle in 1598, soon after Spenser had been named sheriff of county Cork. It is rumored that he lost a child in the fire, as well as large unpublished sections of* The Faerie Queene. *Devastated, he returned to England and died only a few months later. Spenser was greatly revered at death, and buried in Westminster Abbey.*

Edmund Spenser

The rolling wheele*

The rolling wheele that runneth often round,
The hardest steele in tract of time doth teare;
And drizling drops that often doe redound,
The firmest flint doth in continuance weare.
Yet cannot I with many a dropping teare 5
And long intreaty soften her hard hart,
That she will once vouchsafe my plaint to heare,
Or looke with pitty on my payneful smart.
But when I pleade, she bids me play my part,
And when I weep, she sayes teares are but water: 10
And when I sigh, she sayes I know the art,
And when I waile, she turnes hir selfe to laughter.
So doe I weepe, and wayle, and pleade in vaine,
Whiles she as steele and flint doth still remayne.

[1595]

*from *Amoretti*, Sonnet #18

Like as a huntsman*

Like as a huntsman, after weary chase,
Seeing the game from him escaped away,
Sits down to rest him in some shady place,
With panting hounds beguilëd of their prey,
So after long pursuit and vain assay, *5*
When I all weary had the chase forsook,
The gentle deer returned the self-same way,
Thinking to quench her thirst at the next brook.
There she, beholding me with milder look,
Sought not to fly, but fearless still did bide: *10*
Till I in hand her yet half trembling took,
And with her own good will her firmly tied.
Strange thing, me seemed, to see a beast so wild,
So goodly won, with her own will beguiled.

[1595]

*from *Amoretti*, Sonnet #67

One day I wrote her name*

One day I wrote her name upon the strand,
But came the waves and washèd it away:
Agayne I wrote it with a second hand,
But came the tyde, and made my paynes his pray.
"Vayne man," sayd she, "that doest in vaine assay, *5*
A mortall thing so to immortalize,
For I my selve shall lyke to this decay,
And eek my name bee wypèd out lykewize."
"Not so," quod I, "let baser things devize
To dy in dust, but you shall live by fame: *10*
My verse your vertues rare shall eternize,
And in the hevens wryte your glorious name.
Where whenas death shall all the world subdew,
Our love shall live, and later life renew."

[1595]

*from *Amoretti*, Sonnet #75

Prothalamion

Calme was the day, and through the trembling ayre,
Sweete breathing Zephyrus did softly play
A gentle spirit, that lightly did delay
Hot Titans beames, which then did glyster fayre:
When I whom sullein care, *5*
Through discontent of my long fruitlesse stay
In Princes Court, and expectation vayne
Of idle hopes, which still doe fly away,
Like empty shaddowes, did aflict my brayne,
Walkt forth to ease my payne *10*
Along the shoare of silver streaming Thames,
Whose rutty Bancke, the which his River hemmes,
Was paynted all with variable flowers,
And all the meades adornd with daintie gemmes,
Fit to decke maydens bowres, *15*
And crowne their Paramours,
Against the Bridal day, which is not long:
  Sweete Thames runne softly, till I end my Song.

There, in a Meadow, by the Rivers side,
A flocke of Nymphes I chauncèd to espy, *20*
All lovely Daughters of the Flood thereby,
With goodly greenish locks all loose untyde,
As each had bene a Bride,
And each one had a little wicker basket,
Made of fine twigs entraylèd curiously, *25*
In which they gathered flowers to fill their flasket:
And with fine Fingers, cropt full feateously
The tender stalkes on hye.
Of every sort, which in that Meadow grew,
They gathered some; the Violet pallid blew, *30*
The little Dazie, that at evening closes,
The virgin Lillie, and the Primrose trew,
With store of vermeil Roses,
To decke their Bridegromes posies,
Against the Bridal day, which was not long: *35*
  Sweete Thames runne softly, till I end my Song.

With that, I saw two Swannes of goodly hewe,
Come softly swimming downe along the Lee;
Two fairer Birds I yet did never see:
The snow which doth the top of Pindus° strew, *40*
Did never whiter shew,
Nor Jove himselfe when he a Swan would be
For love of Leda, whiter did appeare:
Yet Leda was they say as white as he,
Yet not so white as these, nor nothing neare; *45*
So purely white they were,
That even the gentle streame, the which them bare,
Seemed foule to them, and bad his billowes spare
To wet their silken feathers, least they might
Soyle their fayre plumes with water not so fayre, *50*
And marre their beauties bright,
That shone as heavens light,
Against their Bridal day, which was not long:
Sweete Thames runne softly, till I end my Song.

Eftsoones the Nymphes, which now had Flowers their fill, *55*
Ran all in haste, to see that silver brood,
As they came floating on the Christal Flood.
Whom when they sawe, they stood amazèd still,
Their wondring eyes to fill,
Them seemed they never saw a sight so fayre, *60*
Of Fowles so lovely, that they sure did deeme
Them heavenly borne, or to be that same payre
Which through the Skie draw Venus silver Teeme,
For sure they did not seeme
To be begot of any earthly Seede, *65*
But rather Angels or of Angels breede:
Yet were they bred of Somers-heat they say,
In sweetest Season, when each Flower and weede
The earth did fresh aray,
So fresh they seemed as day, *70*
Even as their Bridal day, which was not long:
Sweete Thames runne softly, till I end my Song.

Then forth they all out of their baskets drew,
Great store of Flowers, the honour of the field,
That to the sense did fragrant odours yeild, *75*
All which upon those goodly Birds they threw,
And all the Waves did strew,

40 *Pindus:* rugged mountain range of northwest Greece.

That like old Peneus° Waters they did seeme,
When downe along by pleasant Tempes shore
Scattred with Flowres, through Thessaly they streeme, *80*
That they appeare through Lillies plenteous store,
Like a Brydes Chamber flore:
Two of those Nymphes, meane while, two Garlands bound,
Of freshest Flowres which in that Mead they found,
The which presenting all in trim Array, *85*
Their snowie Foreheads therewithall they crownd,
Whil'st one did sing this Lay,
Prepared against that Day,
Against their Bridal day, which was not long:
Sweete Thames runne softly, till I end my Song. *90*

Ye gentle Birdes, the worlds faire ornament,
And heavens glorie, whom this happie hower
Doth leade unto your lovers blisfull bower,
Joy may you have and gentle hearts content
Of your loves couplement: *95*
And let faire Venus, that is Queene of love,
With her heart-quelling Sonne upon you smile,
Whose smile they say, hath vertue to remove
All Loves dislike, and friendships faultie guile
For ever to assoile. *100*
Let endlesse Peace your steadfast hearts accord,
And blessed Plentie wait upon your bord,
And let your bed with pleasures chast abound,
That fruitfull issue may to you afford,
Which may your foes confound, *105*
And make your joyes redound,
Upon your Bridal day, which is not long:
Sweete Thames run softly, till I end my Song.

So ended she; and all the rest around
To her redoubled that her undersong, *110*
Which said, their bridale daye should not be long.
And gentle Eccho from the neighbour ground,
Their accents did resound.
So forth those joyous Birdes did passe along,
Adowne the Lee, that to them murmurde low, *115*
As he would speake, but that he lackt a tong
Yeat did by signes his glad affection show,
Making his streame run slow.

78 *Peneus:* a Greek river god. A river in Thessaly bears his name.

And all the foule which in his flood did dwell
Gan flock about these twaine, that did excell *120*
The rest, so far, as Cynthia doth shend
The lesser starres. So they enrangèd well,
Did on those two attend,
And their best service lend,
Against their Bridal day, which was not long: *125*
Sweete Thames run softly, till I end my song.

At length they all to mery London came,
To mery London, my most kyndly Nurse,
That to me gave this Lifes first native sourse:
Though from another place I take my name, *130*
An house of auncient fame.
There when they came, whereas those bricky towres,
The which on Thames brode agèd backe doe ryde,
Where now the studious Lawyers have their bowers
There whylome wont the Templer Knights to byde, *135*
Till they decayd through pride:
Next whereunto there standes a stately place,
Where oft I gaynèd giftes and goodly grace
Of that great Lord, which therein wont to dwell,
Whose want too well now feeles my freendles case: *140*
But Ah here fits not well
Olde woes but joyes to tell
Against the Bridal day, which is not long:
Sweete Thames runne softly, till I end my Song.

Yet therein now doth lodge a noble Peer, *145*
Great Englands glory and the Worlds wide wonder,
Whose dreadfull name, late through all Spaine did thunder,
And Hercules two pillors standing neere,
Did make to quake and feare:
Faire branch of Honor, flower of Chevalrie, *150*
That fillest England with thy triumphs fame,
Joy have thou of thy noble victorie,
And endlesse happinesse of thine owne name
That promiseth the same:
That through thy prowesse and victorious armes, *155*
Thy country may be freed from forraine harmes:
And great Elisaes glorious name may ring
Through al the world, fild with thy wide Alarmes,

Which some brave muse may sing
To ages following, 160
Upon the Bridal day, which is not long:
Sweete Thames runne softly, till I end my Song.

From those high Towers, this noble Lord issuing,
Like Radiant Hesper when his golden hayre
In th'Ocean billowes he hath Bathèd fayre, 165
Descended to the Rivers open vewing,
With a great traine ensuing.
Above the rest were goodly to bee seene
Two gentle Knights of lovely face and feature
Beseeming well the bower of anie Queene, 170
With gifts of wit and ornaments of nature,
Fit for so goodly stature:
That like the twins of Jove they seemed in sight,
Which decke the Bauldricke of the Heavens bright.
They two forth pacing to the Rivers side, 175
Received those two faire Brides, their Loves delight,
Which at th'appointed tyde,
Each one did make his Bride,
Against their Bridal day, which is not long:
Sweete Thames runne softly, till I end my Song. 180

[1596]

Sir Philip Sidney *(1554–1586) was the perfect model of the poet-gentleman, involved deeply in politics, diplomacy, and literature. He was born to a noble family in Kent, England, and began studies at Christ Church, Oxford, at the age of 13, but due to the plague left before receiving his degree. Sidney traveled extensively in his youth—visiting Germany, Austria, Italy, and Poland—and was knighted in 1582. He was married the following year to the daughter of Sir Francis Walsingham. After voicing strong support for the English involvement in the wars of the Protestant Dutch against their Spanish rulers, Sidney was sent to the Netherlands as governor of Flushing, a Dutch town that had been given to the Queen as thanks for her aid. Fighting beside his uncle, Earl of Leicester, Sidney commanded troops in Flanders. He died from wounds suffered in the battle at Zutphen. His lifelong friend, poet and biographer Fulke Greville, claimed that Sidney had* *heroically lent part of his protective armor to another soldier, leaving himself vulnerable. Although his works existed only in manuscript during his lifetime, he was well known as a poet and critic. He is remembered today for his critical work* The Defence of Poesie *(1595). His* Astrophil and Stella *(published posthumously in 1591) was the first great sonnet sequence in English.*

Sir Philip Sidney

Loving in truth, and fain in verse my love to show*

Loving in truth, and fain in verse my love to show,
That she dear she might take some pleasure of my pain,
Pleasure might cause her read, reading might make her know,
Knowledge might pity win, and pity grace obtain,
    I sought fit words to paint the blackest face of woe: *5*
Studying inventions fine, her wits to entertain,
Oft turning others' leaves, to see if thence would flow
Some fresh and fruitful showers upon my sunburned brain.
    But words came halting forth, wanting Invention's stay;
Invention, Nature's child, fled stepdame Study's blows: *10*
And others' feet still seemed but strangers in my way.
Thus, great with child to speak, and helpless in my throes,
    Biting my truant pen, beating myself for spite:
    "Fool," said my Muse to me, "look in thy heart, and write."

*from *Astrophil and Stella*, Sonnet #1

With how sad steps, Oh Moon, thou climb'st the skies*

With how sad steps, Oh Moon, thou climb'st the skies,
    How silently, and with how wan a face!

*from *Astrophil and Stella*, Sonnet #31

What, may it be that even in heav'nly place
That busy archer his sharp arrows tries?
Sure, if that long-with-love-acquainted eyes *5*
Can judge of love, thou feel'st a lover's case;
I read it in thy looks: thy languished grace,
To me that feel the like, thy state descries.
Then even of fellowship, Oh Moon, tell me,
Is constant love deemed there but want of wit? *10*
Are beauties there as proud as here they be?
Do they above love to be loved, and yet
Those lovers scorn whom that love doth possess?
Do they call virtue there ungratefulness?

Come sleep, Oh sleep, the certain knot of peace*

Come sleep, Oh sleep, the certain knot of peace,
The baiting place of wit, the balm of woe,
The poor man's wealth, the prisoner's release,
Th' indifferent judge between the high and low;
With shield of proof shield me from out the prease *5*
Of those fierce darts Despair at me doth throw;
Oh make in me those civil wars to cease;
I will good tribute pay, if thou do so.
Take thou of me smooth pillows, sweetest bed,
A chamber deaf to noise and blind to light, *10*
A rosy garland and a weary head;
And if these things, as being thine by right,
Move not thy heavy grace, thou shalt in me,
Livelier than elsewhere, Stella's image see.

[1591]

*from *Astrophil and Stella*, Sonnet #39

Leave Me, O Love

Leave me, O love which reachest but to dust,
And thou, my mind, aspire to higher things.
Grow rich in that which never taketh rust:
Whatever fades but fading pleasure brings.
Draw in thy beams, and humble all thy might 5
To that sweet yoke where lasting freedoms be;
Which breaks the clouds and opens forth the light
That doth both shine and give us sight to see.
O take fast hold; let that light be thy guide
In this small course which birth draws out to death, 10
And think how evil becometh him to slide
Who seeketh heaven and comes of heavenly breath.
Then farewell, world! thy uttermost I see:
Eternal Love, maintain thy life in me.

[1598]

My True Love Hath My Heart*

My true love hath my heart, and I have his,
By just exchange, one for the other given.
I hold his dear, and mine he cannot miss,
There never was a better bargain driven.
His heart in me keeps me and him in one, 5
My heart in him his thoughts and senses guides;
He loves my heart, for once it was his own,
I cherish his, because in me it bides.
His heart his wound receivèd from my sight,
My heart was wounded with his wounded heart; 10
For as from me on him his hurt did light,
So still methought in me his hurt did smart.
Both equal hurt, in this change sought our bliss,
My true love hath my heart and I have his.

[1590]

*This is one of the verse sequences connected by a prose narrative in the work titled *Arcadia*.

Born just two months before Shakespeare, ***Christopher Marlowe*** *(1564–1593) was the "bad boy" genius of Elizabethan literature. Although he produced a number of lasting plays and poems, he died at the young age of 29. Marlowe was born the son of a shoemaker in Canterbury, England. He attended college on a scholarship that required him to study for the ministry. When the university threatened to withhold Marlowe's degree for unknown reasons, the Queen's Privy Council intervened on his behalf. (Marlowe seems to have taken part in a secret espionage mission overseas, winning the good graces of the Crown.) During the six years between his graduation from Cambridge and his shadowy death, Marlowe wrote many successful plays, including* Doctor Faustus *and* The Jew of Malta. *He was the writer who first transformed the previously utilitarian medium of blank verse into powerful poetic form. He began one major poem, the unfinished* Hero and Leander. *He was also busy with a number of criminal activities in these years, including counterfeiting and violent brawls, and was often in trouble with the law. Marlowe was stabbed to death by Ingram Friser under mysterious circumstances in a Deptford tavern. There is much speculation as to whether his murder had been set up by someone who wanted Marlowe dead, or was merely the result of a drunken scuffle.*

Christopher Marlowe

Elegia V

Corinnae concubitus

In summer's heat, and mid-time of the day,
To rest my limbs upon a bed I lay;
One window shut, the other open stood,
Which gave such light as twinkles in a wood,
Like twilight glimpse at setting of the sun, *5*
Or night being past, and yet not day begun.
Such light to shamefast maidens must be shown,
Where they may sport and seem to be unknown.
Then came Corinna in a long loose gown,
Her white neck hid with tresses hanging down, *10*
Resembling fair Semiramis going to bed,
Or Lais of a thousand wooers sped.
I snatch'd her gown; being thin, the harm was small,
Yet striv'd she to be cover'd therewithal,

And striving thus as one that would be cast, 15
Betray'd herself, and yielded at the last.
Stark naked as she stood before mine eye,
Not one wen in her body could I spy.
What arms and shoulders did I touch and see,
How apt her breasts were to be press'd by me! 20
How smooth a belly under her waist saw I,
How large a leg, and what a lusty thigh!
To leave the rest, all lik'd me passing well;
I cling'd her naked body, down she fell.
Judge you the rest, being tir'd she bade me kiss; 25
Jove send me more such afternoons as this.

[1594]

The Passionate Shepherd to His Love

Come live with me and be my love,
And we will all the pleasures prove
That valleys, groves, hills, and fields,
Woods, or steepy mountain yields.

And we will sit upon the rocks, 5
Seeing the shepherds feed their flocks,
By shallow rivers to whose falls
Melodious birds sing madrigals.

And I will make thee beds of roses
And a thousand fragrant posies, 10
A cap of flowers, and a kirtle
Embroidered all with leaves of myrtle;

A gown made of the finest wool
Which from our pretty lambs we pull;
Fair lined slippers for the cold, 15
With buckles of the purest gold;

A belt of straw and ivy buds,
With coral clasps and amber studs:
And if these pleasures may thee move,
Come live with me, and be my love. *20*

The shepherds' swains shall dance and sing
For thy delight each May morning:
If these delights thy mind may move,
Then live with me and be my love.

[1600]

from The Tragical History of Doctor Faustus

(Act 5, scene 1*)

FAUSTUS: Was this the face that launched a thousand ships,
And burnt the topless towers of Ilium?
Sweet Helen, make me immortal with a kiss.
Her lips suck forth my soul: see where it flies.
Come, Helen, come, give me my soul again. *5*
Here will I dwell, for heaven is in those lips,
And all is dross that is not Helena.
I will be Paris, and for love of thee
Instead of Troy shall Wittenberg° be sacked,
And I will combat with weak Menelaus,° *10*
And wear thy colours on my plumed crest.
Yea, I will wound Achilles in the heel,
And then return to Helen for a kiss.
Oh, thou art fairer than the evening's air,
Clad in the beauty of a thousand stars. *15*
Brighter art thou than flaming Jupiter,
When he appeared to hapless Semele:°
More lovely than the monarch of the sky,
In wanton Arethusa's° azure arms,
And none but thou shalt be my paramour. *20*

• • •

*Faustus is addressing Helen of Troy, the legendary beauty.

9 *Wittenberg:* German city on the Elbe River. **10** *Menelaus:* King of Sparta and husband of Helen. **17** *Semele:* with Zeus (or Jupiter), gave birth to Bacchus. **19** *Arethusa:* a greek nymph associated with fountains and springs.

(Act 5, scene 2)

• • •

FAUSTUS: Ah Faustus,
Now hast thou but one bare hour to live,
And then thou must be damned perpetually.
Stand still, you ever-moving spheres of heaven,
That time may cease and midnight never come. *5*
Fair nature's eye, rise, rise again, and make
Perpetual day. Or let this hour be but
A year, a month, a week, a natural day,
That Faustus may repent and save his soul.
O lente, lente, currite noctis equi.° *10*
The stars move still, time runs, the clock will strike.
The devil will come, and Faustus must be damned.
Oh, I'll leap up to my God: who pulls me down?
See, see, where Christ's blood streams in the firmament.
One drop would save my soul, half a drop. Ah, my Christ! *15*
Ah, rend not my heart for naming of my Christ!
Yet will I call on him. Oh, spare me, Lucifer!
Where is it now? 'Tis gone:
And see where God stretcheth out his arm,
And bends his ireful brows. *20*
Mountains and hills, come, come, and fall on me,
And hide me from the heavy wrath of God.
No, no. Then will I headlong run into the earth.
Earth, gape! Oh no, it will not harbour me.
You stars that reigned at my nativity, *25*
Whose influence hath allotted death and hell,
Now draw up Faustus like a foggy mist
Into the entrails of yon labouring cloud,
That when you vomit forth into the air
My limbs may issue from your smoky mouths, *30*
So that my soul may but ascend to heaven.
[*The watch strikes.*]
Ah! half the hour is past,
'Twill all be past anon.
Oh God, if thou wilt not have mercy on my soul,
Yet, for Christ's sake whose blood hath ransomed me, *35*
Impose some end to my incessant pain.
Let Faustus live in hell a thousand years,

10 O *lente... equi:* "O run slowly, slowly, horses of the night" (Latin).

A hundred thousand, and at last be saved.
Oh, no end is limited to damned souls.
Why wert thou not a creature wanting soul? 40
Or why is this immortal that thou hast?
Ah, Pythagoras'° *metempsychosis,*° were that true
This soul should fly from me, and I be changed
Unto some brutish beast.
All beasts are happy, for when they die 45
Their souls are soon dissolved in elements,
But mine must live still to be plagued in hell.
Cursed be the parents that engendered me!
No, Faustus, curse thyself, curse Lucifer,
That hath deprived thee of the joys of heaven. 50
[*The clock strikes twelve.*]
Oh, it strikes, it strikes! Now body turn to air,
Or Lucifer will bear thee quick to hell.
Oh soul, be changed into little water drops
And fall into the ocean, ne'er be found.
[*Thunder. Enter the* DEVILS.]
My God, my God, look not so fierce on me. 55
Adders and serpents, let me breathe awhile.
Ugly hell, gape not, come not, Lucifer!
I'll burn my books. Ah, Mephistophilis!
[*Thunder and lightning.*]

[1616]

42 *Pythagoras:* Greek philosopher and mathematician (c. 6th century BC); **metempsychosis:** reincarnation.

William Shakespeare *(1564–1616) was born in Stratford-upon-Avon, one of eight children of John Shakespeare, a glovemaker and tradesman, and Mary Arden, an affluent farmer's daughter. At age 18 he married Anne Hathaway, a woman eight years his senior and three months pregnant. They had three children together. Following a gap in our historical record referred to as his "lost years," Shakespeare moved to London and was already writing plays and acting by 1590. When the theaters were closed in 1593 because of the plague, the playwright wrote two narrative poems,* Venus and Adonis *(1592) and* The Rape of Lucrece *(1593–1594), and probably began writing his richly textured sonnets. One hundred and fifty-four of his sonnets and*

38 plays have survived. Shakespeare became a shareholder in the Lord Chamberlain's Men, often playing before the court of Queen Elizabeth.The company established the Globe Theatre, and later reorganized as the King's Men for King James. Shakespeare published his sonnets, though he did not live to see his plays published in 1623. As the most performed and read works of any playwright in the world, Shakespeare's plays are staged and adapted for film and television every year, among them Richard III *(c. 1592),* Romeo and Juliet *(c. 1594), and* Othello *(c. 1604).*

William Shakespeare

When daisies pied and violets blue*

When daisies pied and violets blue
　And lady-smocks° all silver-white
And cuckoo-buds° of yellow hue
　Do paint the meadows with delight,
The cuckoo then, on every tree, *5*
Mocks married men; for thus sings he,
　　　　　　"Cuckoo,
Cuckoo, cuckoo!"—O word of fear,°
Unpleasing to a married ear!

When shepherds pipe on oaten straws, *10*
　And merry larks are ploughmen's clocks,
When turtles tread,° and rooks, and daws,
　And maidens bleach their summer smocks,
The cuckoo then, on every tree,
Mocks married men; for thus sings he, *15*
　　　　　　"Cuckoo,
Cuckoo, cuckoo!"—O word of fear,
Unpleasing to a married ear!

[1598]

*From *Love's Labour's Lost*; This song and "When icicles hang by the wall," delivered by Spring and Winter respectively, conclude the play.

2 *lady-smocks*: also named cuckoo-flowers. 3 *cuckoo-buds*: buttercups. 8 O *word of fear*: because it sounds like *cuckold*, a man whose wife has deceived him. 12 *turtles tread*: turtledoves mate.

When icicles hang by the wall*

When icicles hang by the wall,
    And Dick the shepherd blows his nail,
And Tom bears logs into the hall,
    And milk comes frozen home in pail,
When blood is nipped and ways° be foul, *5*
    Then nightly sings the staring owl:
            "Tu-whit, to-who!"
            A merry note,
While greasy Joan doth keel° the pot.

When all aloud the wind doth blow, *10*
    And coughing drowns the parson's saw,°
And birds sit brooding in the snow,
    And Marian's nose looks red and raw,
When roasted crabs° hiss in the bowl,
    Then nightly sings the staring owl: *15*
            "Tu-whit, to-who!"
            A merry note,
While greasy Joan doth keel the pot.

[1598]

*from *Love's Labour's Lost*

5 *ways*: roads. **9** *keel*: cool, as by skimming or stirring. **11** *parson's saw*: old saw, platitutde. **14** *crabs*: crab apples.

Shall I compare thee to a summer's day?*

Shall I compare thee to a summer's day?
Thou art more lovely and more temperate.
Rough winds do shake the darling buds of May,
And summer's lease hath all too short a date.

*Sonnet #18

Sometime too hot the eye of heaven shines, 5
And often is his gold complexion dimmed;
And every fair° from fair sometimes declines,
By chance, or nature's changing course, untrimmed.
But thy eternal summer shall not fade,
Nor lose possession of that fair thou ow'st;° 10
Nor shall death brag thou wand'rest in his shade,
When in eternal lines to time thou grow'st.
So long as men can breathe or eyes can see,
So long lives this, and this gives life to thee.

[1609]

7 *fair*: fair one. 10 *ow'st*: ownest, have.

When, in disgrace with Fortune and men's eyes*

When, in disgrace with Fortune and men's eyes,
I all alone beweep my outcast state,
And trouble deaf heaven with my bootless° cries,
And look upon myself and curse my fate,
Wishing me like to one more rich in hope, 5
Featured like him, like him with friends possessed,
Desiring this man's art, and that man's scope,
With what I most enjoy contented least,
Yet in these thoughts myself almost despising,
Haply° I think on thee, and then my state, 10
Like to the lark at break of day arising
From sullen earth, sings hymns at heaven's gate;
For thy sweet love rememb'red such wealth brings
That then I scorn to change my state with kings.

[1609]

*Sonnet #29

3 *bootless*: futile. 10 *Haply*: luckily.

When to the sessions of sweet silent thought*

When to the sessions of sweet silent thought
I summon up remembrance of things past,
I sigh the lack of many a thing I sought,
And with old woes new wail my dear time's waste:
Then can I drown an eye, unused to flow, *5*
For precious friends hid in death's dateless night,
And weep afresh love's long since canceled woe,
And moan th' expense of many a vanished sight:
Then can I grieve at grievances foregone,
And heavily from woe to woe tell o'er *10*
The sad account of fore-bemoanèd moan,
Which I new pay as if not paid before.
    But if the while I think on thee, dear friend,
    All losses are restored and sorrows end.

[1609]

*Sonnet #30

Not marble nor the gilded monuments*

Not marble nor the gilded monuments
Of princes, shall outlive this powerful rhyme;
But you shall shine more bright in these contents
Than unswept stone, besmeared with sluttish time.
When wasteful war shall statues overturn, *5*
And broils root out the work of masonry,
Nor Mars his sword nor war's quick fire shall burn
The living record of your memory.
'Gainst death and all-oblivious enmity
Shall you pace forth; your praise shall still find room *10*

*Sonnet #116

Even in the eyes of all posterity
That wear this world out to the ending doom.
So, till the judgment that yourself arise,
You live in this, and dwell in lovers' eyes.

[1609]

That time of year thou mayst in me behold*

That time of year thou mayst in me behold
When yellow leaves, or none, or few, do hang
Upon those boughs which shake against the cold,
Bare ruined choirs where late the sweet birds sang.
In me thou see'st the twilight of such day 5
As after sunset fadeth in the west,
Which by-and-by black night doth take away,
Death's second self that seals up all in rest.
In me thou see'st the glowing of such fire
That on the ashes of his youth doth lie, 10
As the deathbed whereon it must expire,
Consumed with that which it was nourished by.
This thou perceiv'st, which makes thy love more strong,
To love that well which thou must leave ere long.

[1609]

*Sonnet #73

Let me not to the marriage of true minds*

Let me not to the marriage of true minds
Admit impediments; love is not love
Which alters when it alteration finds,
Or bends with the remover to remove.

*Sonnet #116

O, no, it is an ever-fixèd mark° 5
That looks on tempests and is never shaken;
It is the star° to every wand'ring bark,
Whose worth's unknown, although his height be taken.
Love's not Time's fool, though rosy lips and cheeks
Within his bending sickle's compass° come; 10
Love alters not with his brief hours and weeks
But bears it out even to the edge of doom.°
If this be error and upon me proved,
I never writ, nor no man ever loved.

[1609]

5 *ever-fixèd mark*: a sea-mark like a beacon or a lighthouse that provides mariners with safe bearings. 7 *the star*: presumably the North Star, which gave sailors the most dependable bearing at sea. 10 *compass*: range. 12 *edge of doom*: either the brink of death or—taken more generally—Judgment Day.

My mistress' eyes are nothing like the sun*

My mistress' eyes are nothing like the sun;
Coral is far more red than her lips' red;
If snow be white, why then her breasts are dun;
If hairs be wires, black wires grow on her head.
I have seen roses damasked red and white, 5
But no such roses see I in her cheeks;
And in some perfumes is there more delight
Than in the breath that from my mistress reeks.
I love to hear her speak, yet well I know
That music hath a far more pleasing sound; 10
I grant I never saw a goddess go:
My mistress, when she walks, treads on the ground.
And yet, by heaven, I think my love as rare
As any she,° belied with false compare.

[1609]

*Sonnet #130

14 *she*: woman.

When my love swears that she is made of truth*

When my love swears that she is made of truth,
I do believe her, though I know she lies,
That she might think me some untutored youth,
Unlearnèd in the world's false subtleties.
Thus vainly thinking that she thinks me young, *5*
Although she knows my days are past the best,
Simply I credit her false-speaking tongue;
On both sides thus is simple truth suppressed.
But wherefore says she not she is unjust?
And wherefore say not I that I am old? *10*
Oh, love's best habit is in seeming trust,
And age in love loves not to have years told.
  Therefore I lie with her and she with me,
  And in our faults by lies we flattered be.

[1609]

*Sonnet #138

Poor soul, the center of my sinful earth*

Poor soul, the center of my sinful earth,
Fooled by these rebel powers that thee array,
Why dost thou pine within and suffer dearth,
Painting thy outward walls so costly gay?
Why so large cost, having so short a lease, *5*
Dost thou upon thy fading mansion spend?
Shall worms, inheritors of this excess,
Eat up thy charge? Is this thy body's end?
Then, soul, live thou upon thy servant's loss,
And let that pine to aggravate thy store; *10*

*Sonnet #146

Buy terms divine in selling hours of dross;
Within be fed, without be rich no more.
So shalt thou feed on death, that feeds on men,
And death once dead, there's no more dying then.

[1609]

Fear No More the Heat o' the Sun*

Fear no more the heat o' the sun,
Nor the furious winter's rages;
Thou thy worldly task hast done,
Home art gone, and ta'en thy wages:
Golden lads and girls all must, *5*
As chimney-sweepers, come to dust.

Fear no more the frown o' the great;
Thou art past the tyrant's stroke;
Care no more to clothe and eat;
To thee the reed is as the oak: *10*
The scepter, learning, physic, must
All follow this, and come to dust.

Fear no more the lightning flash,
Nor the all-dreaded thunder stone;
Fear not slander, censure rash; *15*
Thou hast finished joy and moan:
All lovers young, all lovers must
Consign to thee, and come to dust.

[1609–10]

*from *Cymbeline*, Act 4, scene 2

Ariel's Song*

Full fathom five thy father lies;
  Of his bones are coral made;
Those are pearls that were his eyes:
  Nothing of him that doth fade,
But doth suffer a sea change *5*
Into something rich and strange.
Sea nymphs hourly ring his knell.
  Ding-dong.
Hark! now I hear them—*Ding-dong, bell.*

[1611–12]

*From *The Tempest*; The spirit Ariel has sung this song to Ferdinand, prince of Naples, who mistakenly thinks his father is drowned.

***John Donne** (1572–1631), one of the major poets of the Metaphysical school, was born in London into a prosperous Roman Catholic family. He entered Oxford at age 12, and transferred to Cambridge three years later but could not take a degree because of his Catholicism. He had already completed much of his influential religious and love poetry when he worked as secretary to Sir Thomas Egerton in 1598. Donne wrote* Biathanatos *in 1608 (published in 1646), which argued for justifiable suicide. He secretly married Lady Egerton's niece, Ann More, for which he was fired from his position and briefly imprisoned. Converting to Anglicanism, Donne was ordained a priest in 1615, and his wife, with whom he had had twelve children, died in 1617, leaving him devastated. His religious doubts and convictions were explored deeply in his "Holy Sonnets" (published in 1633 in* Songs and Sonnets*). He was made deacon of St. Paul's Cathedral in London in 1621, and his powerfully elegant sermons were widely attended. His* Devotions *(1624) provided Hemingway with the title of his classic novel,* For Whom the Bell Tolls. *Few of Donne's poems were published in his lifetime, and his verse waited until the twentieth century for full critical appreciation.*

John Donne

A Valediction: Forbidding Mourning*

As virtuous men pass mildly away,
    And whisper to their souls to go,
Whilst some of their sad friends do say
    The breath goes now, and some say no:

So let us melt, and make no noise, *5*
    No tear-floods, nor sigh-tempests move;
'Twere profanation of our joys
    To tell the laity° our love.

Moving of th' earth° brings harms and fears;
    Men reckon what it did and meant; *10*
But trepidation of the spheres,°
    Though greater far, is innocent.°

Dull sublunary lovers' love
    (Whose soul is sense) cannot admit
Absence, because it doth remove *15*
    Those things which elemented° it.

But we, by a love so much refined
    That ourselves know not what it is,
Inter-assurèd of the mind,°
    Care less, eyes, lips, and hands to miss. *20*

Our two souls, therefore, which are one,
    Though I must go, endure not yet
A breach, but an expansiòn,
    Like gold to airy thinness beat.°

*According to Donne's biographer Izaak Walton, Donne's wife received this poem as a gift before the poet departed on a journey to France.

8 *laity*: common people. **9** *Moving of th' earth*: earthquake. **11** *spheres*: in Ptolemaic astronomy, the concentric spheres surrounding the earth. The trepidation or motion of the ninth sphere was thought to change the date of the equinox. **12** *innocent*: harmless.
16 *elemented*: constituted. **19** *Inter-assurèd of the mind*: each sure in mind that the other is faithful.
24 *gold to airy thinness beat*: gold is so malleable that, if beaten to the thickness of gold leaf (1/250,000 of one inch), one ounce of gold would cover 250 square feet.

If they be two, they are two so *25*
As stiff twin compasses are two:
Thy soul, the fixed foot, makes no show
To move, but doth, if th' other do.

And though it in the center sit,
Yet when the other far doth roam, *30*
It leans and harkens after it,
And grows erect as that comes home.

Such wilt thou be to me, who must,
Like th' other foot, obliquely run;
Thy firmness makes my circle just,° *35*
And makes me end where I begun.

[1611]

35 *just*: perfect.

The Ecstasy

Where, like a pillow on a bed,
A pregnant bank swelled up to rest
The violet's reclining head,
Sat we two, one another's best.
Our hands were firmly cèmented *5*
With a fast balm, which thence did spring.
Our eye-beams twisted, and did thread
Our eyes upon one double string;
So to'intergraft our hands, as yet
Was all the means to make us one; *10*
And pictures in our eyes to get
Was all our propagation.
As 'twixt two equal armies, Fate
Suspends uncertain victory,
Our souls (which to advance their state, *15*
Were gone out) hung 'twixt her and me.
And whilst our souls negotiate there,
We like sepulchral statues lay;
All day the same our postures were,
And we said nothing all the day. *20*
If any, so by love refined

That he soul's language understood,
And by good love were grown all mind,
Within convenient distance stood,
He (though he knew not which soul spake, 25
Because both meant, both spake the same)
Might thence a new concoction take,
And part far purer than he came.
This ecstasy doth unperplex,
We said, and tell us what we love; 30
We see by this it was not sex;
We see we saw not what did move;
But as all several souls contain
Mixture of things, they know not what,
Love these mixed souls doth mix again, 35
And makes both one, each this and that.
A single violet transplant,
The strength, the colour, and the size
(All which before was poor, and scant)
Redoubles still, and multiplies. 40
When love, with one another so
Interinanimates two souls,
That abler soul, which thence doth flow,
Defects of loneliness controls.
We then, who are this new soul, know, 45
Of what we are composed, and made,
For, th' atomies of which we grow,
Are souls, whom no change can invade.
But O alas, so long, so far
Our bodies why do we forbear? 50
They're ours, though they're not we; we are
Th' intelligences, they the spheres.
We owe them thanks because they thus,
Did us to us at first convey,
Yielded their forces, sense, to us, 55
Nor are dross to us, but allay.
On man heaven's influence works not so
But that it first imprints the air,
So soul into the soul may flow,
Though it to body first repair. 60
As our blood labors to beget
Spirits as like souls as it can,

Because such fingers need to knit
    That subtle knot which makes us man:
So must pure lovers' souls descend *65*
    To affections, and to faculties
Which sense may reach and apprehend;
    Else a great Prince in prison lies.
To our bodies turn we then, that so
    Weak men on love revealed may look; *70*
Love's mysteries in souls do grow,
    But yet the body is his book.
And if some lover, such as we,
    Have heard this dialogue of one,
Let him still mark us; he shall see *75*
    Small change when we're to bodies gone.

[1633]

The Flea

Mark but this flea, and mark in this
How little that which thou deny'st me is;
It sucked me first, and now sucks thee,
And in this flea our two bloods mingled be;
Thou know'st that this cannot be said *5*
A sin, nor shame, nor loss of maidenhead,
    Yet this enjoys before it woo,
    And pampered swells with one blood made of two,
    And this, alas, is more than we would do.

Oh stay, three lives in one flea spare, *10*
Where we almost, yea more than married are.
This flea is you and I, and this
Our marriage bed, and marriage temple is;
Though parents grudge, and you, we're met
And cloistered in these living walls of jet. *15*
    Though use° make you apt to kill me,
    Let not to that, self-murder added be,
    And sacrilege, three sins in killing three.

16 *use*: custom.

Cruel and sudden, hast thou since
Purpled thy nail in blood of innocence? 20
Wherein could this flea guilty be,
Except in that drop it sucked from thee?
Yet thou triumph'st, and say'st that thou
Find'st not thyself, nor me, the weaker now;
'Tis true; then learn how false, fears be; 25
Just so much honor, when thou yield'st to me,
Will waste, as this flea's death took life from thee.

[1633]

The Good-Morrow

I wonder, by my troth, what thou and I
Did, till we loved? were we not weaned till then?
But sucked on country pleasures, childishly?
Or snorted° we in the Seven Sleepers' den?
'Twas so; but° this, all pleasures fancies be. 5
If ever any beauty I did see,
Which I desired, and got, 'twas but a dream of thee.

And now good-morrow to our waking souls,
Which watch not one another out of fear;
For love, all love of other sights controls, 10
And makes one little room an everywhere.
Let sea-discoverers to new worlds have gone,
Let maps to others, worlds on worlds have shown,
Let us possess one world, each hath one, and is one.

My face in thine eye, thine in mine appears, 15
And true plain hearts do in the faces rest;
Where can we find two better hemispheres,
Without sharp North, without declining West?
Whatever dies was not mixed equally;
If our two loves be one, or, thou and I 20
Love so alike that none do slacken, none can die.

[1633]

4 *snorted*: snored. 5 *but*: except for.

Song

Go and catch a falling star,
    Get with child a mandrake root,
Tell me where all past years are,
    Or who cleft the Devil's foot,
Teach me to hear mermaids singing, *5*
    Or to keep off envy's stinging,
        And find
        What wind
Serves to advance an honest mind.

If thou be'st borne to strange sights, *10*
    Things invisible to see,
Ride ten thousand days and nights,
    Till age snow white hairs on thee,
Thou, when thou return'st, wilt tell me
    All strange wonders that befell thee, *15*
        And swear
        Nowhere
Lives a woman true, and fair.

If thou findst one, let me know,
    Such a pilgrimage were sweet— *20*
Yet do not, I would not go,
    Though at next door we might meet;
Though she were true, when you met her,
    And last, till you write your letter,
        Yet she *25*
        Will be
False, ere I come, to two, or three.

[1633]

Song

Sweetest love, I do not goe,
    For wearinesse of thee,
Nor in hope the world can show
    A fitter Love for mee;
        But since that I *5*

Must dye at last, 'tis best,
To use my selfe in jest
Thus by fain'd deaths to dye;

Yesternight the Sunne went hence,
And yet is here to day, 10
He hath no desire nor sense,
Nor halfe so short a way:
Then feare not mee,
But beleeve that I shall make
Speedier journeyes, since I take 15
More wings and spurres then hee.

O how feeble is mans power,
That if good fortune fall,
Cannot adde another houre,
Nor a lost houre recall! 20
But come bad chance,
And wee joyne to'it our strength,
And wee teach it art and length,
It selfe o'r us to'advance.

When thou sigh'st, thou sigh'st not winde, 25
But sigh'st my soule away,
When thou weep'st, unkindly kinde,
My lifes blood doth decay.
It cannot bee
That thou lov'st mee, as thou say'st, 30
If in thine my life thou waste,
Thou art the best of mee.

Let not thy divining heart
Forethinke me any ill,
Destiny may take thy part, 35
And may thy feares fulfill;
But thinke that wee
Are but turn'd aside to sleepe;
They who one another keepe
Alive, ne'r parted bee. 40

[1633]

from Holy Sonnets

Batter my heart, three-personed God

Batter my heart, three-personed God, for You
As yet but knock, breathe, shine, and seek to mend.
That I may rise and stand, o'erthrow me, and bend
Your force to break, blow, burn, and make me new.
I, like an usurped town to another due, *5*
Labor to admit You, but Oh! to no end.
Reason, Your viceroy in me, me should defend,
But is captived, and proves weak or untrue.
Yet dearly I love You, and would be lovèd fain,
But am betrothed unto Your enemy; *10*
Divorce me, untie or break that knot again;
Take me to You, imprison me, for I,
Except You enthrall me, never shall be free,
Nor ever chaste, except You ravish me.

[1610; 1633]

Death be not proud

Death be not proud, though some have callèd thee
Mighty and dreadful, for thou art not so;
For those whom thou think'st thou dost overthrow
Die not, poor death, nor yet canst thou kill me.
From rest and sleep, which but thy pictures be, *5*
Much pleasure, then from thee much more must flow,
And soonest our best men with thee do go,
Rest of their bones, and soul's delivery.
Thou art slave to fate, chance, kings, and desperate men,
And dost with poison, war, and sickness dwell, *10*
And poppy, or charms can make us sleep as well,
And better than thy stroke; why swell'st thou then?
One short sleep past, we wake eternally,
And death shall be no more; death, thou shalt die.

[c. 1610; 1633]

At the round earth's imagined corners

At the round earth's imagined corners, blow
Your trumpets, angels; and arise, arise
From death, you numberless infinities
Of souls, and to your scattered bodies go;
All whom the flood did, and fire shall, o'erthrow, *5*
All whom war, dearth, age, agues, tyrannies,
Despair, law, chance hath slain, and you whose eyes
Shall behold God, and never taste death's woe.
But let them sleep, Lord, and me mourn a space;
For, if above all these, my sins abound, *10*
'Tis late to ask abundance of Thy grace
When we are there. Here on this lowly ground,
Teach me how to repent; for that's as good
As if Thou hadst sealed my pardon with Thy blood.

[1633]

Poet and playwright **Ben Jonson** *(1572–1637) was born in London. His father having died before Ben's birth and his mother remarried, Jonson worked as a bricklayer for his stepfather and fought against the Spanish in Flanders while a young man. In 1594 he married Anne Lewis, and began working as an actor and playwright the following year. It was a turbulent and controversial career from the start. Jonson was imprisoned for his biting satires, most notably for* Eastward Ho! *(1605), for which he and his collaborator George Chapman were sent to the Tower of London. Jonson killed a fellow actor in a duel in 1598 and narrowly escaped execution by pleading benefit of clergy, but he was branded a felon and lost his property. After converting to Roman Catholicism—and returning again to the Church of England more than a decade later—Jonson traveled to France as a tutor to Sir Walter Raleigh's son. He also visited William Drummond of Hawthornden, Scotland, who famously recorded their conversations. Though the title did not yet exist, Jonson became, in effect, England's first poet laureate when James I awarded him a pension. Some of Jonson's most famous dramatic works include* Volpone *(1605–1606),* The Alchemist *(1610), and* Bartholomew Fair *(1614). He was a friend—and competitor—to fellow dramatist William Shakespeare. A stroke in 1628 left him an invalid until his death in London nine years later.*

Ben Jonson

Slow, Slow, Fresh Fount*

Slow, slow, fresh fount, keep time with my salt tears;
Yet slower yet, oh faintly, gentle springs;
List to the heavy part the music bears,
Woe weeps out her division° when she sings.
Droop herbs and flowers, 5
Fall grief in showers;
Our beauties are not ours;
Oh, I could still,
Like melting snow upon some craggy hill,
Drop, drop, drop, drop, 10
Since nature's pride is now a withered daffodil.

[1600]

*From *Cynthia's Revels*; The nymph Echo sings this lament over the youth Narcissus in Jonson's play *Cynthia's Revels*. In mythology, Nemesis, goddess of vengeance, to punish Narcissus for loving his own beauty, caused him to pine away and then transformed him into a narcissus (another name for a daffodil, line 11).

4 *division*: a part in a song.

On My First Son

Farewell, thou child of my right hand,° and joy.
My sin was too much hope of thee, loved boy;
Seven years thou wert lent to me, and I thee pay,
Exacted by thy fate, on the just day.°
Oh, could I lose all father° now. For why 5
Will man lament the state he should envỳ?—
To have so soon 'scaped world's and flesh's rage,
And, if no other misery, yet age.
Rest in soft peace, and asked, say, "Here doth lie
Ben Jonson his best piece of poetry,"° 10

1 *child of my right hand*: Jonson's son was named Benjamin; this translates the Hebrew name. 4 *the just day*: the very day. The boy had died on his seventh birthday. 5 *father*: fatherhood. 10 *poetry*: Jonson uses the word *poetry* here reflecting its Greek root *poiesis*, which means creation.

For whose sake henceforth all his vows be such
As what he loves may never like° too much.

[1603]

12 *like*: thrive.

Still to Be Neat*

Still to be neat, still to be dressed,
As you were going to a feast;
Still to be powdered, still perfumed;
Lady, it is to be presumed,
Though art's hid causes are not found, 5
All is not sweet, all is not sound.

Give me a look, give me a face
That makes simplicity a grace;
Robes loosely flowing, hair as free;
Such sweet neglect more taketh me 10
Then all th' adulteries of art.
They strike mine eyes, but not my heart.

[1609]

*from *Epicene, or the Silent Woman*

Come, my Celia*

Come, my Celia, let us prove,°
While we can, the sports of love;
Time will not be ours forever;
He at length our good will sever.
Spend not then his gifts in vain. 5
Suns that set may rise again;
But if once we lose this light,
'Tis with us perpetual night.

*From *Volpone;* Jonson's poem is a free translation from a Latin poem by Catullus.

1 *prove*: experience.

Why should we defer our joys?
Fame and rumor are but toys. *10*
Cannot we delude the eyes
Of a few poor household spies,
Or his easier ears beguile,
So removèd by our wile?
'Tis no sin love's fruit to steal; *15*
But the sweet thefts to reveal,
To be taken, to be seen,
These have crimes accounted been.

[1616]

Song to Celia

Drink to me only with thine eyes,
  And I will pledge with mine;
Or leave a kiss but in the cup,
  And I'll not ask for wine.
The thirst that from the soul doth rise *5*
  Doth ask a drink divine;
But might I of Jove's nectar sup,
  I would not change for thine.

I sent thee late a rosy wreath,
  Not so much honoring thee *10*
As giving it a hope that there
  It could not withered be.
But thou thereon didst only breathe,
  And sent'st it back to me;
Since when it grows, and smells, I swear, *15*
  Not of itself but thee.

[1616]

The childhood of **Mary Sidney Wroth** *(1587?–1653?) was spent in Penshurst, England, and in the Netherlands, where her father became governor of Flushing after his brother Sir Philip Sidney died. She had many other powerful and famous relatives—Mary Herbert was her aunt, and her mother was first cousin to Sir Walter Raleigh. By her twelfth* *birthday Wroth had already attracted suitors. She was finally married to Sir Robert Wroth, though it was clear that she had fallen in love with her cousin, William Herbert. Wroth's husband died in 1614, only a month after the birth of her first child, leaving behind considerable debt that plagued Wroth for the rest of her life. During her widowhood she had a long love affair with Herbert, which resulted in two illegitimate children. Her poems were published in* Pamphilia to Amphilanthus *(1621) under her own name, which broke with tradition—women were expected not to publish or to do so anonymously. Wroth was the first Englishwoman to write a sonnet sequence, a dramatic comedy, and a prose romance. No literary works survive from her last thirty years. Even the exact date of her death is uncertain.*

Mary Sidney Wroth

from Pamphilia to Amphilanthus

When night's blacke Mantle

When night's blacke Mantle could most darknesse prove,
  And sleepe (deaths Image) did my senses hyre
  From Knowledge of my selfe, then thoughts did move
  Swifter then those, most swiftnesse neede require;
In sleepe, a Chariot drawne by wing'd Desire *5*
  I saw, where sate bright *Venus* Queene of Love,
  And at her feete her Sonne, still adding Fire
  To burning hearts, which she did hold above,
But one heart flaming more than all the rest
  The Goddesse held, and put it to my breast, *10*
  Dear Sonne, now shut said she: thus must we winne;
He her obeyd, and martyr'd my poore heart,
  I waking hop'd as dreames it would depart,
  Yet since, O me, a Lover I have beene.

[1621]

Am I thus conquer'd?

Am I thus conquer'd? have I lost the powers
That to withstand, which joyes to ruine me?
Must I bee still while it my strength devoures
And captive leads me prisoner bound, unfree?
Love first shall leave mens fant'sies to them free, *5*
Desire shall quench loves flames, Spring hate sweet showres,
Love shall loose all his Darts, have sight, and see
His shame, and wishings hinder happy houres;
Why should we not Loves purblinde charmes resist?
Must we be servile, doing what he list? *10*
No, seeke some host to harbour thee: I flye
Thy Babish tricks, and freedome doe professe;
But O, my hurt makes my lost heart confesse
I love, and must, so farewell liberty.

[1621]

In This Strange Labyrinth*

In this strange labyrinth how shall I turn?
Ways are on all sides while the way I miss;
If to the right hand, there in love I burn;
Let me go forward, therein danger is;
If to the left, suspicion hinders bliss, *5*
Let me turn back, shame cries I ought return
Nor faint though crosses with my fortunes kiss.
Stand still is harder, although sure to mourn;
Thus let me take the right, or left hand way;
Go forward, or stand still, or back retire; *10*
I must these doubts endure without allay
Or help, but travail find for my best hire;
Yet that which most my troubled sense doth move
Is to leave all, and take the thread of love.

[1621]

*This sonnet comes from Wroth's *Urania* (1621), which offered the first significant English sonnet sequence by a woman. The labyrinth of the title was the maze built by Minos to trap the young men and women sacrificed to the Minotaur. King Minos's daughter, Ariadne, saved her beloved Theseus by giving him a skein of thread to guide his way through the labyrinth. (See the final line of the sonnet.)

You Blessed Stars

You blessed stars which does heaven's glory show,
And at your brightness make our eyes admire;
Yet envy not, though I on earth below
Enjoy a sight which moves in me more fire.
I do confess such beauty breeds desire, *5*
You shine, and clearest light on us bestow,
Yet does a sight on earth more warmth inspire
Into my loving soul, his grace to know.
Clear, bright and shining as you are, is this
Light of my joy, fixed steadfast, nor will move *10*
His light from me, nor I change from his love,
But still increase, as th'height of all my bliss.
His sight gives life unto my love-ruled eyes,
My love content, because in his, love lies.

[1621]

Robert Herrick *(1592–1674) was born in London the seventh child to a wealthy goldsmith. His father fell to his death from the their home's fourth-floor window when Herrick was still a baby. Since his father had written his will two days prior, suicide was suspected, yet the Crown allowed the family to keep the valuable estate, despite existing laws punishing suicide. Herrick probably received a traditional education until being apprenticed at age 16 to his uncle, a goldsmith who owned vast amounts of land and had been knighted. Leaving the apprenticeship six years later, Herrick began studies at St. John College in Cambridge as a fellow commoner. He later transferred to Trinity College to study law, and there received his Masters. In 1620 he moved to London where he met Ben Jonson, who became his poetic mentor. In 1623 he was ordained as priest in the Church of England. Serving as an army chaplain for the Duke of Buckingham in 1627, he survived a failed attack on the French at Île de Ré. The Crown awarded him with the vicarage of Dean Prior, and Herrick settled in a remote village in Devonshire in 1630, where he lived off and on for most of his life. Herrick published only one immense collection of poems during his lifetime,* Hesperides: Or, The Works Both Humane & Divine of Robert Herrick Esq. *(1648).*

Robert Herrick

Corinna's Going A-Maying

Get up! get up for shame! the blooming morn
Upon her wings presents the god unshorn.
  See how Aurora throws her fair
  Fresh-quilted colors through the air;
  Get up, sweet slug-a-bed, and see *5*
  The dew bespangling herb and tree.
Each flower has wept and bowèd toward the east
Above an hour since, yet you not dressed;
  Nay, not so much as out of bed?
  When all the birds have matins said, *10*
  And sung their thankful hymns, 'tis sin,
  Nay, profanation to keep in,
Whenas a thousand virgins on this day
Spring, sooner than the lark, to fetch in May.

Rise, and put on your foliage, and be seen *15*
To come forth, like the springtime, fresh and green,
  And sweet as Flora.° Take no care
  For jewels for your gown or hair;
  Fear not; the leaves will strew
  Gems in abundance upon you; *20*
Besides, the childhood of the day has kept,
Against you come, some orient pearls unwept;
  Come and receive them while the light
  Hangs on the dew-locks of the night,
  And Titan on the eastern hill *25*
  Retires himself, or else stands still
Till you come forth. Wash, dress, be brief in praying;
Few beads are best when once we go a-Maying.

Come, my Corinna, come; and, coming, mark
How each field turns a street, each street a park *30*
  Made green and trimmed with trees; see how
  Devotion gives each house a bough

17 *Flora*: goddess of flowers.

Or branch; each porch, each door ere this,
An ark, a tabernacle is,
Made up of whitethorn neatly interwove, *35*
As if here were those cooler shades of love.
Can such delights be in the street
And open fields, and we not see 't?
Come, we'll abroad; and let's obey
The proclamation made for May, *40*
And sin no more, as we have done, by staying;
But, my Corinna, come, let's go a-Maying.

There's not a budding boy or girl this day
But is got up and gone to bring in May;
A deal of youth, ere this, is come *45*
Back, and with whitethorn laden home.
Some have dispatched their cakes and cream
Before that we have left to dream;
And some have wept, and wooed, and plighted troth,
And chose their priest, ere we can cast off sloth. *50*
Many a green-gown has been given,
Many a kiss, both odd and even;
Many a glance, too, has been sent
From out the eye, love's firmament;
Many a jest told of the keys betraying *55*
This night, and locks picked; yet we're not a-Maying.

Come, let us go while we are in our prime,
And take the harmless folly of the time.
We shall grow old apace, and die
Before we know our liberty. *60*
Our life is short, and our days run
As fast away as does the sun;
And, as a vapor or a drop of rain
Once lost, can ne'er be found again;
So when or you or I are made *65*
A fable, song, or fleeting shade,
All love, all liking, all delight
Lies drowned with us in endless night.
Then while time serves, and we are but decaying,
Come, my Corinna, come, let's go a-Maying. *70*

[1648]

Delight in Disorder

A sweet disorder in the dress
Kindles in clothes a wantonness.
A lawn about the shoulders thrown
Into a fine distraction;
An erring lace, which here and there *5*
Enthralls the crimson stomacher;
A cuff neglectful, and thereby
Ribbons to flow confusedly;
A winning wave, deserving note,
In the tempestuous petticoat; *10*
A careless shoestring, in whose tie
I see a wild civility;
Do more bewitch me than when art
Is too precise in every part.

[1648]

Upon Julia's Clothes

Whenas in silks my Julia goes,
Then, then, methinks, how sweetly flows
That liquefaction of her clothes.

Next, when I cast mine eyes and see
That brave vibration each way free, *5*
O how that glittering taketh me!

[1648]

To Anthea, Who May Command Him Anything

Bid me to live, and I will live
    Thy Protestant to be;
Or bid me love, and I will give
    A loving heart to thee.

A heart as soft, a heart as kind, 5
  A heart as sound and free,
As in the whole world thou canst find,
  That heart Ile give to thee.

Bid that heart stay, and it will stay,
  To honour thy Decree; 10
Or bid it languish quite away,
  And't shall doe so for thee.

Bid me to weep, and I will weep,
  While I have eyes to see;
And having none, yet I will keep 15
  A heart to weep for thee.

Bid me despaire, and Ile despaire,
  Under that *Cypresse* tree;
Or bid me die, and I will dare
  E'en Death, to die for thee. 20

Thou art my life, my love, my heart,
  The very eyes of me;
And hast command of every part,
  To live and die for thee.

[1648]

To the Virgins, to Make Much of Time

Gather ye rose-buds while ye may,
  Old Time is still a-flying;
And this same flower that smiles today,
  Tomorrow will be dying.

The glorious lamp of heaven, the sun, 5
  The higher he's a-getting,
The sooner will his race be run,
  And nearer he's to setting.

That age is best which is the first,
    When youth and blood are warmer; 10
But being spent, the worse, and worst
    Times still succeed the former.

Then be not coy, but use your time,
    And while ye may, go marry;
For having lost but once your prime, 15
    You may for ever tarry.

[1648]

***George Herbert** (1593–1633) was born in Wiltshire, England, into an aristocratic family. He began writing poems while studying at Trinity College, Cambridge, where he was elected Public Orator of the college in 1620; he worked closely with the royal court for five years and served in Parliament. Herbert left political life in 1627 to enter the priesthood for the Church of England, desiring to retire to a quiet country parish. He was ordained in 1630 and served as rector in his hometown of Bemerton. Herbert's poetry, which was deeply religious and would later earn him recognition as one of the major Metaphysical poets, was never published during his lifetime. While on his deathbed, Herbert sent his work to a friend, Nicholas Ferrar, who published the poems as* The Temple: Sacred Poems and Private Ejaculations *(1633). Though a master of poetic meter, some of Herbert's poems, such as "Easter Wings" and "The Altar," are remembered for their original use of visual effects—their shapes reflect their subject matter. Richly complex and original, Herbert's religious verse influenced later poets, such as Henry Vaughan.*

George Herbert

Affliction [IV]

Broken in pieces all asunder,
        Lord, hunt me not,
        A thing forgot,
Once a poore creature, now a wonder,

A wonder tortur'd in the space 5
Betwixt this world and that of grace.

My thoughts are all a case of knives,
Wounding my heart
With scatter'd smart,
As watring pots give flowers their lives. 10
Nothing their furie can controll,
While they do wound and pink my soul.

All my attendants are at strife,
Quitting their place
Unto my face; 15
Nothing performs the task of life;
The elements are let loose to fight,
And while I live, trie out their right.

Oh help, my God! let not their plot
Kill them and me, 20
And also thee,
Who art my life; dissolve the knot,
As the sunne scatters by his light
All the rebellions of the night.

Then shall those powers, which work for grief, 25
Enter thy pay,
And day by day
Labour thy praise, and my relief;
With care and courage building me,
Till I reach heav'n, and much more, thee. 30

[1633]

The Collar

I struck the board and cried, "No more;
I will abroad!
What? shall I ever sigh and pine?
My lines and life are free, free as the road,
Loose as the wind, as large as store. 5
Shall I be still in suit?

Have I no harvest but a thorn
To let me blood, and not restore
What I have lost with cordial fruit?
Sure there was wine 10
Before my sighs did dry it; there was corn
Before my tears did drown it.
Is the year only lost to me?
Have I no bays to crown it,
No flowers, no garlands gay? All blasted? 15
All wasted?
Not so, my heart; but there is fruit,
And thou hast hands.
Recover all thy sigh-blown age
On double pleasures; leave thy cold dispute 20
Of what is fit and not. Forsake thy cage,
Thy rope of sands,
Which petty thoughts have made, and made to thee
Good cable, to enforce and draw,
And be thy law, 25
While thou didst wink and wouldst not see.
Away! take heed;
I will abroad.
Call in thy death's-head there; tie up thy fears.
He that forbears 30
To suit and serve his need,
Deserves his load."
But as I raved and grew more fierce and wild
At every word,
Methought I heard one calling, *Child!* 35
And I replied, *My Lord.*

[1633]

Easter Wings

Lord, who createdst man in wealth and store,°
Though foolishly he lost the same,
Decaying more and more
Till he became
Most poor; 5
With thee
Oh, let me rise
As larks, harmoniously,
And sing this day thy victories;
Then shall the fall further the flight in me. 10

My tender age in sorrow did begin;
And still with sicknesses and shame
Thou didst so punish sin,
That I became
Most thin. 15
With thee
Let me combine,
And feel this day thy victory;
For if I imp° my wing on thine,
Affliction shall advance the flight in me. 20

[1633]

1 *store*: abundance. **19** *imp*: graft, a term from falconry.

Love (III)

Love bade me welcome; yet my soul drew back,
Guilty of dust and sin.
But quick-eyed Love, observing me grow slack
From my first entrance in,
Drew nearer to me, sweetly questioning 5
If I lacked anything.

"A guest," I answered, "worthy to be here";
Love said, "You shall be he."
"I, the unkind, ungrateful? Ah, my dear,

I cannot look on Thee." *10*
Love took my hand, and smiling did reply,
"Who made the eyes but I?"

"Truth, Lord, but I have marred them; let my shame
Go where it doth deserve."
"And know you not," says Love, "who bore the blame?" *15*
"My dear, then I will serve."
"You must sit down," says Love, "and taste My meat."
So I did sit and eat.

[1633]

The Pulley

When God at first made man,
Having a glass of blessings standing by—
Let us (said he) pour on him all we can;
Let the world's riches, which dispersèd lie,
Contract into a span.° *5*

So strength first made a way,
Then beauty flowed, then wisdom, honor, pleasure;
When almost all was out, God made a stay,
Perceiving that, alone of all His treasure,
Rest in the bottom lay. *10*

For if I should (said he)
Bestow this jewel also on My creature,
He would adore My gifts instead of Me,
And rest in Nature, not the God of Nature;
So both should losers be. *15*

Yet let him keep the rest,
But keep them with repining restlessness;
Let him be rich and weary, that at least,
If goodness lead him not, yet weariness
May toss him to My breast. *20*

[1633]

5 *span*: the distance between the tips or thumb and pinkie.

Born in London to a scrivener who composed music, ***John Milton*** *(1608–1674) was educated by his mother for the ministry from an early age. Late nights of study harmed his eyes considerably when he was still a boy, leading to blindness later in life. A brilliant scholar and intellectual, Milton wrote poetry in both English and Latin. He attended Christ's College, Cambridge, and traveled to Italy in the late 1630s, where he met Galileo. In 1642 Milton married Mary Powell, a girl 16 years his junior. They had four children together, though she died shortly after giving birth to their third daughter. The poet's second wife also died due to complications in childbirth. Milton was deeply involved in the religious and political disputes of his time—supporting the antimonarchical republican regime of the Puritans. He became Oliver Cromwell's "Secretary for Foreign Tongues" and endorsed the execution of King Charles in 1649. By 1651 Milton was completely blind and dictated correspondence to several secretaries, including the young Andrew Marvell. Forced from his comfortable post during the Restoration in 1660, Milton finally turned his attention to writing the poem that would become the greatest epic in the English language,* Paradise Lost *(1667). He married for a third time, and published* Paradise Regained *and* Samson Agonistes *(both 1671) before his death.*

John Milton

On Shakespeare

1630

What needs my Shakespeare for his honored bones
The labor of an age in pilèd stones?
Or that his hallowed reliques should be hid
Under a star-ypointing pyramid?
Dear son of Memory, great heir of Fame, *5*
What need'st thou such weak witness of thy name?
Thou in our wonder and astonishment
Hast built thyself a livelong monument.
For whilst, to th' shame of slow-endeavoring art,
Thy easy numbers flow, and that each heart *10*
Hath from the leaves of thy unvalued book
Those Delphic° lines with deep impression took,

12 *Delphic:* mysterious and prophetic—in reference to the ancient oracle who lived in the Greek city of Delphi.

Then thou, our fancy of itself bereaving,
Dost make us marble with too much conceiving,
And so sepùlchred in such pomp dost lie 15
That kings for such a tomb would wish to die.

[1632]

Lycidas

In this monody the author bewails a learned friend, unfortunately drowned in his passage from Chester on the Irish seas, 1637. And by occasion foretells the ruin of our corrupted clergy, then in their height.

Yet once more, O ye laurels, and once more
Ye myrtles brown, with ivy° never sere,
I come to pluck your berries harsh and crude,
And with forced fingers rude,
Shatter your leaves before the mellowing year. 5
Bitter constraint, and sad occasion dear,
Compels me to disturb your season due;
For Lycidas is dead, dead ere his prime,
Young Lycidas, and hath not left his peer.
Who would not sing for Lycidas? He knew 10
Himself to sing, and build the lofty rhyme.
He must not float upon his watery bier
Unwept, and welter to the parching wind,
Without the meed° of some melodious tear.
Begin then, sisters of the sacred well° 15
That from beneath the seat of Jove doth spring,
Begin, and somewhat loudly sweep the string.
Hence with denial vain, and coy excuse;
So may some gentle Muse
With lucky words favor my destined urn, 20
And as he passes turn,
And bid fair peace be to my sable shroud.

1–2 *laurels, myrtles, ivy*: plants associated with poetic inspiration. **14** *meed*: reward. **15** *sisters of the sacred well*: refers to the Nine Muses, who lived near the two sacred springs on Mount Helicon.

For we were nursed upon the selfsame hill,
Fed the same flock, by fountain, shade, and rill.
    Together both, ere the high lawns appeared *25*
Under the opening eyelids of the morn,
We drove afield, and both together heard
What time the grayfly winds her sultry horn,
Battening our flocks with the fresh dews of night,
Oft till the star that rose at evening bright *30*
Toward Heaven's descent had sloped his westering wheel.
Meanwhile the rural ditties were not mute,
Tempered to th' oaten flute,°
Rough satyrs danced, and fauns with cloven heel
From the glad sound would not be absent long, *35*
And old Damaetas loved to hear our song.
    But O the heavy change, now thou art gone,
Now thou art gone, and never must return!
Thee, shepherd, thee the woods and desert caves,
With wild thyme and the gadding vine o'ergrown, *40*
And all their echoes mourn.
The willows and the hazel copses green
Shall now no more be seen,
Fanning their joyous leaves to thy soft lays.
As killing as the canker° to the rose, *45*
Or taint-worm to the weanling herds that graze,
Or frost to flowers that their gay wardrobe wear,
When first the white thorn blows;
Such, Lycidas, thy loss to shepherd's ear.
    Where were ye, nymphs, when the remorseless deep *50*
Closed o'er the head of your loved Lycidas?
For neither were ye playing on the steep,
Where your old Bards, the famous Druids° lie,
Nor on the shaggy top of Mona° high,
Nor yet where Deva° spreads her wizard stream; *55*
Ay me! I fondly dream—
Had ye been there—for what could that have done?
What could the Muse herself that Orpheus bore,°

33 *oaten flute*: panpipes, an instrument played by shepherds. 45 *canker*: a parasitic worm.
53 *Druids*: Celtic poet-kings. 54 *Mona*: the island of Anglesey. 55 *Deva*: the river Dee in Cheshire, England. 58 *Muse herself that Orpheus bore*: The Muse of epic poetry, Calliope, was Orpheus' mother.

The Muse herself, for her inchanting son
Whom universal Nature did lament, *60*
When by the rout that made the hideous roar,
His gory visage down the stream was sent,
Down the swift Hebrus to the Lesbian shore?°
　Alas! What boots it with uncessant care
To tend the homely slighted shepherd's trade, *65*
And strictly meditate the thankless Muse?
Were it not better done as others use,
To sport with Amaryllis in the shade,
Or with the tangles of Neaera's° hair?
Fame is the spur that the clear spirit doth raise *70*
(That last infirmity of noble mind)
To scorn delights, and live laborious days;
But the fair guerdon° when we hope to find,
And think to burst out into sudden blaze,
Comes the blind Fury° with th' abhorrèd shears, *75*
And slits the thin spun life. "But not the praise,"
Phoebus° replied, and touched my trembling ears;
"Fame is no plant that grows on mortal soil,
Nor in the glistering foil
Set off to th' world, nor in broad rumor lies, *80*
But lives and spreads aloft by those pure eyes,
And perfect witness of all-judging Jove;
As he pronounces lastly on each deed,
Of so much fame in Heaven expect thy meed."
　O fountain Arethuse,° and thou honored flood, *85*
Smooth-sliding Mincius,° crowned with vocal reeds,
That strain I heard was of a higher mood.
But now my oat proceeds,
And listens to the herald of the sea
That came in Neptune's° plea. *90*
He asked the waves, and asked the felon winds,
"What hard mishap hath doomed this gentle swain?"
And questioned every gust of rugged wings
That blows from off each beakèd promontory;

61–63 *the rout . . . to the Lesbian shore*: Orpheus was beheaded by a mob, or rout, of women. His head was thrown into the river Hebrus. **68–69** *Amaryllis, Neaera*: traditional names for beautiful shepherdesses. **73** *guerdon*: reward. **75** *blind Fury*: Atropos, one of the three Fates, cuts the thread of life with scissors. **77** *Phoebus*: Apollo, god of poetic inspiration. **85** *Arethuse*: Arethusa was a nymph who transformed into a fountain after fleeing an enamored river god. **86** *Mincius:* the river of Virgil's hometown, Mantua. **90** *Neptune:* in Greek, Poseidon; the god of water.

They knew not of his story, 95
And sage Hippotades° their answer brings,
That not a blast was from his dungeon strayed,
The air was calm, and on the level brine,
Sleek Panope° with all her sisters played.
It was that fatal and perfidious bark 100
Built in th' eclipse, and rigged with curses dark,
That sunk so low that sacred head of thine.
    Next Camus,° reverend sire, went footing slow,
His mantle hairy, and his bonnet sedge,
Inwrought with figures dim, and on the edge 105
Like to that sanguine flower inscribed with woe.
"Ah! who hath reft," quoth he, "my dearest pledge?"
Last came and last did go
The pilot of the Galilean lake,
Two massy keys he bore of metals twain 110
(The golden opes, the iron shuts amain).
He shook his mitered locks, and stern bespake:
"How well could I have spared for thee, young swain,
Enow° of such as for their bellies' sake,
Creep and intrude, and climb into the fold! 115
Of other care they little reckoning make,
Than how to scramble at the shearers' feast,
And shove away the worthy bidden guest.
Blind mouths! That scarce themselves know how to hold
A sheep-hook, or have learned aught else the least 120
That to the faithful herdsman's art belongs!
What reeks it them? What need they? They are sped;
And when they list, their lean and flashy songs
Grate on their scrannel° pipes of wretched straw.
The hungry sheep look up, and are not fed, 125
But swoln with wind, and the rank mist they draw,
Rot inwardly, and foul contagion spread,
Besides what the grim wolf with privy paw
Daily devours apace, and nothing said.
But that two-handed engine at the door 130
Stands ready to smite once, and smite no more."
    Return, Alpheus,° the dread voice is past,

96 *Hippotades*: or Aeolus, god of the winds. **99** *Panope*: sea nymph. **103** *Camus*: god of the river Cam, or river Granta. **114** *Enow*: archaic plural form of "enough." **124** *scrannel*: variant of "scrawny." **132** *Alpheus*: a river in southern Greece.

That shrunk thy streams; return, Sicilian muse,
And call the vales, and bid them hither cast
Their bells and flowerets of a thousand hues. *135*
Ye valleys low where the mild whispers use,
Of shades and wanton winds, and gushing brooks,
On whose fresh lap the swart star sparely looks,
Throw hither all your quaint enameled eyes,
That on the green turf suck the honeyed showers, *140*
And purple all the ground with vernal flowers.
Bring the rathe° primrose that forsaken dies,
The tufted crow-toe, and pale jessamine,
The white pink, and the pansy freaked with jet,
The glowing violet, *145*
The musk-rose, and the well attired woodbine,
With cowslips wan that hang the pensive head,
And every flower that sad embroidery wears;
Bid amaranthus° all his beauty shed,
And daffadillies fill their cups with tears, *150*
To strew the laureate hearse where Lycid lies.
For so to interpose a little ease,
Let our frail thoughts dally with false surmise.
Ay me! Whilst thee the shores and sounding seas
Wash far away, where'er thy bones are hurled, *155*
Whether beyond the stormy Hebrides,°
Where thou perhaps under the whelming tide
Visit'st the bottom of the monstrous world;
Or whether thou, to our moist vows denied,
Sleep'st by the fable of Bellerus° old, *160*
Where the great vision of the guarded mount
Looks toward Namancos and Bayona's hold;
Look homeward angel now, and melt with ruth;
And, O ye dolphins, waft the hapless youth.
    Weep no more, woeful shepherds, weep no more, *165*
For Lycidas your sorrow is not dead,
Sunk though he be beneath the watery floor,
So sinks the day-star in the ocean bed,
And yet anon repairs his drooping head,
And tricks his beams, and with new-spangled ore, *170*

142 *rathe*: archaic word meaning "early." **149** *amaranthus*: an imaginary, perpetually-blooming flower. **156** *Hebrides*: islands off the Scottish coast. **160** *Bellerus*: the fabled giant who is buried at The Land's End, Cornwall.

Flames in the forehead of the morning sky;
So Lycidas sunk low, but mounted high,
Through the dear might of him that walked the waves,
Where other groves, and other streams along,
With nectar pure his oozy locks he laves, *175*
And hears the unexpressive nuptial song,
In the blest kingdoms meek of joy and love.
There entertain him all the saints above,
In solemn troops and sweet societies
That sing, and singing in their glory move, *180*
And wipe the tears forever from his eyes.
Now, Lycidas, the shepherds weep no more;
Henceforth thou art the genius of the shore,
In thy large recompense, and shalt be good
To all that wander in that perilous flood. *185*
    Thus sang the uncouth swain to th' oaks and rills,
While the still morn went out with sandals gray;
He touched the tender stops of various quills,
With eager thought warbling his Doric° lay;
And now the sun had stretched out all the hills, *190*
And now was dropped into the western bay;
At last he rose, and twitched his mantle blue;
Tomorrow to fresh woods, and pastures new.

[1637]

189 *Doric*: referring to an ancient Greek style of architecture noted for its simplicity.

When I Consider How My Light Is Spent

When I consider how my light is spent,
    Ere half my days in this dark world and wide,
    And that one talent which is death to hide
    Lodged with me useless, though my soul more bent
To serve therewith my Maker, and present *5*
    My true account, lest He returning chide;
    "Doth God exact day-labor, light denied?"
    I fondly° ask. But Patience, to prevent

8 *fondly*: foolishly.

That murmur, soon replies, "God doth not need
Either man's work or His own gifts. Who best 10
Bear His mild yoke, they serve Him best. His state
Is kingly. Thousands at His bidding speed,
And post o'er land and ocean without rest;
They also serve who only stand and wait."

[1655?]

Methought I Saw My Late Espousèd Saint

Methought I saw my late espousèd saint
Brought to me like Alcestis° from the grave,
Whom Jove's great son to her glad husband gave,
Rescued from Death by force, though pale and faint.
Mine, as whom washed from spot of child-bed taint 5
Purification in the Old Law did save,
And such, as yet once more I trust to have
Full sight of her in heaven without restraint,
Came vested all in white, pure as her mind.
Her face was veiled; yet to my fancied sight 10
Love, sweetness, goodness, in her person shined
So clear as in no face with more delight.
But O, as to embrace me she inclined,
I waked, she fled, and day brought back my night.

[1658?]

2 *Aclestis*: In classical mythology, Alcestis gave her life to save that of her ill husband. Jupiter's son Hercules rescued her from the Underworld.

Born in Northampton, England, **Anne Bradstreet** *(1612–1672) never attended school but did receive an excellent education from her father, Thomas Dudley, a steward to the Earl of Lincoln, and private tutors. When she was 18 she emigrated to America with her parents and her husband, Simon Bradstreet; for many years they endured the adverse conditions typical of the struggling colony. Settling in Massachusetts, both her husband and father eventually became colonial governors. Anne gave* *birth to eight children. The responsibility of raising a large family—as well as the traditional, socially limited position of women—made writing poetry difficult. In 1650 a collection of her verse,* The Tenth Muse Lately Sprung Up in America, *was compiled and published in London without her knowledge. It was the first book of poetry ever published by an American, and as a result Bradstreet is often considered the "first poet of the New World." A posthumous volume appeared with her corrections and additions,* Several Poems *(1678). A fire in 1666 destroyed her home, her library, and many unpublished manuscripts.*

Anne Bradstreet

The Author to Her Book

Thou ill-formed offspring of my feeble brain,
Who after birth didst by my side remain,
Till snatched from thence by friends, less wise than true,
Who thee abroad, exposed to public view,
Made thee in rags, halting to th' press to trudge, 5
Where errors were not lessened (all may judge).
At thy return my blushing was not small,
My rambling brat (in print) should mother call,
I cast thee by as one unfit for light,
The visage was so irksome in my sight; 10
Yet being mine own, at length affection would
Thy blemishes amend, if so I could.
I washed thy face, but more defects I saw,
And rubbing off a spot still made a flaw.
I stretched thy joints to make thee even feet, 15
Yet still thou run'st more hobbling than is meet;
In better dress to trim thee was my mind,
But nought save homespun cloth i' th' house I find.
In this array 'mongst vulgars may'st thou roam.
In critic's hands beware thou dost not come, 20
And take thy way where yet thou art not known;
If for thy father asked, say thou hadst none;
And for thy mother, she alas is poor,
Which caused her thus to send thee out of door.

[1678]

Before the Birth of One of her Children

All things within this fading world hath end,
Adversity doth still our joys attend;
No ties so strong, no friends so dear and sweet,
But with death's parting blow is sure to meet.
The sentence past is most irrevocable, *5*
A common thing, yet oh inevitable;
How soon, my dear, death may my steps attend,
How soon't may be thy lot to lose thy friend;
We both are ignorant, yet love bids me
These farewell lines to recommend to thee, *10*
That when that knot's untied that made us one,
I may seem thine, who in effect am none.
And if I see not half my days that's due,
What nature would, God grant to yours and you;
The many faults that well you know I have, *15*
Let be interr'd in my oblivion's grave;
If any worth or virtue were in me,
Let that live freshly in thy memory,
And when thou feel'st no grief, as I no harms,
Yet love thy dead, who long lay in thine arms; *20*
And when thy loss shall be repaid with gains,
Look to my little babes, my dear remains.
And if thou love thy self, or loved'st me,
These O protect from step-dame's injury.
And if chance to thine eyes shall bring this verse, *25*
With some sad sighs honor my absent Hearse;°
And kiss this paper for thy love's dear sake,
Who with salt tears this last farewell did take.

[1678]

26 *Hearse*: corpse.

To My Dear and Loving Husband

If ever two were one, then surely we.
If ever man were loved by wife, then thee;
If ever wife was happy in a man,
Compare with me ye women if you can.
I prize thy love more than whole mines of gold, *5*
Or all the riches that the East doth hold.
My love is such that rivers cannot quench,
Nor ought but love from thee give recompense.
Thy love is such I can no way repay;
The heavens reward thee manifold, I pray. *10*
Then while we live, in love let's so persever,
That when we live no more we may live ever.

[1678]

***Andrew Marvell** (1621–1678) was born in Holderness, Yorkshire, England, the son of a minister, and grew up in Hull. He was sent to Trinity College, Cambridge, at the age of 12, earning a BA in 1639. After both his parents died, Marvell traveled Europe for four years, learning languages and supposedly avoiding the civil war at home. He worked as a tutor for the children of influential politicians through the 1650s, then was appointed Latin secretary to the Council of State (a post previously held by his friend John Milton). Two years later, in 1659, Marvell was elected to Parliament representing Hull, and remained so until his death. (He used his official influence to have Milton freed from imprisonment due to his outspoken and poetic support of Cromwell.) Marvell visited many European countries, often on diplomatic business, and is thought to have taken part in several espionage missions. His sharp political satires were well known—many were so racy that he had to publish them anonymously—though his lyric poetry, including such classics as "To His Coy Mistress" and "Upon Appleton House," went virtually unnoticed for centuries. He died suddenly of fever.*

Andrew Marvell
The Definition of Love

My love is of a birth as rare
As 'tis, for object, strange and high;
It was begotten by Despair
Upon Impossibility.

Magnanimous Despair alone *5*
Could show me so divine a thing,
Where feeble Hope could ne'er have flown
But vainly flapped its tinsel wing.

And yet I quickly might arrive
Where my extended soul is fixed; *10*
But Fate does iron wedges drive,
And always crowds itself betwixt.

For Fate with jealous eye does see
Two perfect loves, nor lets them close;
Their union would her ruin be, *15*
And her tyrannic power depose.

And therefore her decrees of steel
Us as the distant poles have placed
(Though Love's whole world on us doth wheel),
Not by themselves to be embraced, *20*

Unless the giddy heaven fall,
And earth some new convulsion tear,
And, us to join, the world should all
Be cramped into a planisphere.°

As lines, so loves oblique may well *25*
Themselves in every angle greet;
But ours, so truly parallel,
Though infinite, can never meet.

Therefore the love which us doth bind,
But Fate so enviously debars, *30*

24 *planisphere*: a flat sphere.

Is the conjunction of the mind,
And opposition of the stars.

[1681]

The Garden

How vainly men themselves amaze
To win the palm, the oak, or bays,°
And their incessant labors see
Crowned from some single herb, or tree,
Whose short and narrow-vergèd shade *5*
Does prudently their toils upbraid;
While all flowers and all trees do close
To weave the garlands of repose!

Fair Quiet, have I found thee here,
And Innocence, thy sister dear? *10*
Mistaken long, I sought you then
In busy companies of men.
Your sacred plants, if here below,
Only among the plants will grow;
Society is all but rude *15*
To this delicious solitude.

No white nor red was ever seen
So amorous as this lovely green.
Fond° lovers, cruel as their flame,
Cut in these trees their mistress' name; *20*
Little, alas, they know or heed
How far these beauties hers exceed!
Fair trees, wheresoe'er your barks I wound,
No name shall but your own be found.

When we have run our passion's heat, *25*
Love hither makes his best retreat.
The gods, that mortal beauty chase,
Still in a tree did end their race;°
Apollo hunted Daphne so,

2 *the palm, the oak, or bays*: These trees represent the wreaths traditionally used respectively to crown victorious athletes, politicians, and poets. **19** *Fond*: foolish. **28** *in a tree did end their race*: When the god Apollo pursued the nymph Daphne to ravish her, she was changed into a laurel tree.

Only that she might laurel grow; 30
And Pan did after Syrinx speed,
Not as a nymph, but for a reed.

What wondrous life is this I lead!
Ripe apples drop about my head;
The luscious clusters of the vine 35
Upon my mouth do crush their wine;
The nectarine and curious peach
Into my hands themselves do reach;
Stumbling on melons, as I pass,
Insnared with flowers, I fall on grass. 40

Meanwhile the mind, from pleasure less,
Withdraws into its happiness;
The mind, that ocean where each kind
Does straight its own resemblance find;
Yet it creates, transcending these, 45
Far other worlds and other seas,
Annihilating all that's made
To a green thought in a green shade.

Here at the fountain's sliding foot,
Or at some fruit tree's mossy root, 50
Casting the body's vest aside,
My soul into the boughs does glide;
There, like a bird, it sits and sings,
Then whets and combs its silver wings,
And, till prepared for longer flight, 55
Waves in its plumes the various light.

Such was that happy garden-state,
While man there walked without a mate;
After a place so pure and sweet,
What other help could yet be meet! 60
But 'twas beyond a mortal's share
To wander solitary there;
Two paradises 'twere in one
To live in paradise alone.

How well the skillful gardener drew 65
Of flowers and herbs this dial new,
Where, from above, the milder sun
Does through a fragrant zodiac run;

And as it works, th' industrious bee
Computes its time as well as we! 70
How could such sweet and wholesome hours
Be reckoned but with herbs and flowers?

[1650]

The Mower Against Gardens

Luxurious man, to bring his vice in use,
  Did after him the world seduce,
And from the fields the flowers and plants allure,
  Where Nature was most plain and pure.
He first enclosed within the gardens square 5
  A dead and standing pool of air,
And a more luscious earth for them did knead,
  Which stupefied them while it fed.
The pink grew then as double as his mind;
  The nutriment did change the kind. 10
With strange perfumes he did the roses taint;
  And flowers themselves were taught to paint.
The tulip white did for complexion seek,
  And learned to interline its cheek;
Its onion root they then so high did hold, 15
  That one was for a meadow sold;
Another world was searched through oceans new,
  To find the Marvel of Peru;
And yet these rarities might be allowed
  To man, that sovereign thing and proud, 20
Had he not dealt between the bark and tree,
  Forbidden mixtures there to see.
No plant now knew the stock from which it came;
  He grafts upon the wild the tame,
That the uncertain and adulterate fruit 25
  Might put the palate in dispute.
His green seraglio° has its eunuchs too,
  Lest any tyrant him outdo;

27 *seraglio:* a large harem, typically Muslim.

And in the cherry he does Nature vex,
    To procreate without a sex. *30*
'Tis all enforced, the fountain and the grot,
    While the sweet fields do lie forgot,
Where willing Nature does to all dispense
    A wild and fragrant innocence;
And fauns and fairies do the meadows till *35*
    More by their presence than their skill.
Their statues polished by some ancient hand,
    May to adorn the gardens stand;
But, howsoe'er the figures do excel,
    The Gods themselves with us do dwell. *40*

[1681]

To His Coy Mistress

Had we but world enough and time,
This coyness, lady, were no crime.
We would sit down, and think which way
To walk, and pass our long love's day.
Thou by the Indian Ganges' side *5*
Shoudst rubies find; I by the tide
Of Humber° would complain. I would
Love you ten years before the flood,
And you should, if you please, refuse
Till the conversion of the Jews.° *10*
My vegetable love should grow
Vaster than empires and more slow;
An hundred years should go to praise
Thine eyes, and on thy forehead gaze;
Two hundred to adore each breast, *15*
But thirty thousand to the rest;
An age at least to every part,
And the last age should show your heart.
For, lady, you deserve this state,
Nor would I love at lower rate. *20*

7 *Humber*: a river that flows by Marvell's childhood town of Hull. 10 *conversion of the Jews*: an event that, according to St. John the Divine, is to take place just before the end of the world.

But at my back I always hear
Time's wingèd chariot hurrying near;
And yonder all before us lie
Deserts of vast eternity.
Thy beauty shall no more be found; *25*
Nor, in thy marble vault, shall sound
My echoing song; then worms shall try
That long-preserved virginity,
And your quaint honor turn to dust,
And into ashes all my lust; *30*
The grave's a fine and private place,
But none, I think, do there embrace.

Now therefore, while the youthful hue
Sits on thy skin like morning dew,
And while thy willing soul transpires *35*
At every pore with instant fires,
Now let us sport us while we may,
And now, like amorous birds of prey,
Rather at once our time devour
Than languish in his slow-chapped° power. *40*
Let us roll all our strength and all
Our sweetness up into one ball,
And tear our pleasures with rough strife
Thorough° the iron gates of life;
Thus, though we cannot make our sun *45*
Stand still, yet we will make him run.

[1681]

40 *slow-chapped*: slow-jawed. **44** *Thorough*: through.

Born in Brecknockshire, Wales, **Henry Vaughan** *(1622–1695) was the son of a Welsh gentleman. He and his twin brother entered Jesus College, Oxford, at the age of 16. While his brother finished his degree (Thomas Vaughan later became a distinguished philosopher fascinated with magic, mysticism, and alchemy), Henry quit his studies to pursue a career in law. After some time in London, he returned to Wales at the start of the civil war in 1642. He served a short stint as clerk to a chief justice, and reportedly enlisted to fight for the Royalists. He began publishing his poems, which largely consisted of translations and religious works, during the*

1640s. In 1646 Vaughan married Catherine Wise, with whom he had a son and three daughters. His wife subsequently died—as did Vaughan's twin—and Vaughan married her younger sister in 1655. They also had a son and three daughters. Vaughan developed a strong religious faith after reading George Herbert, and published Silex Scintillans *in 1650 and 1655; the selections here come from that visionary work. Although there is no known record of a medical degree, Vaughan practiced medicine for much of his later life. He died in Wales.*

Henry Vaughan

The Retreat

Happy those early days! when I
Shined in my angel infancy.
Before I understood this place
Appointed for my second race,
Or taught my soul to fancy aught 5
But a white, celestial thought;
When yet I had not walked above
A mile or two from my first love,
And looking back, at that short space,
Could see a glimpse of His bright face; 10
When on some gilded cloud or flower
My gazing soul would dwell an hour,
And in those weaker glories spy
Some shadows of eternity;
Before I taught my tongue to wound 15
My conscience with a sinful sound,
Or had the black art to dispense
A several sin to every sense,
But felt through all this fleshly dress
Bright shoots of everlastingness. 20

O, how I long to travel back,
And tread again that ancient track!
That I might once more reach that plain
Where first I left my glorious train,
From whence th' enlightened spirit sees 25
That shady city of palm trees.
But, ah! my soul with too much stay
Is drunk, and staggers in the way.
Some men a forward motion love;

But I by backward steps would move, *30*
And when this dust falls to the urn,
In that state I came, return.

[1650]

The World

I saw Eternity the other night
Like a great *Ring* of pure and endless light,
All calm, as it was bright,
And round beneath it, Time in hours, days, years
Driv'n by the spheres *5*
Like a vast shadow mov'd, in which the world
And all her train were hurl'd;
The doting Lover in his queintest strain
Did their Complain,
Neer him, his Lute, his fancy, and his flights, *10*
Wits sour delights.
With gloves, and knots the silly snares of pleasure
Yet his dear Treasure
All scatter'd lay, while he his eys did pour
Upon a flow'r. *15*

The darksome States-man hung with weights and woe
Like a thick midnight-fog mov'd there so slow
He did nor stay, nor go;
Condemning thoughts (like sad Ecclipses) scowl
Upon his soul, *20*
And Clouds of crying witnesses without
Pursued him with one shout.
Yet dig'd the Mole, and lest his ways be found
Workt under ground,
Where he did Clutch his prey, but one did see *25*
That policie,
Churches and altars fed him, Perjuries
Were gnats and flies,
It rain'd about him bloud and tears, but he
Drank them as free. *30*

The fearfull miser on a heap of rust
Sate pining all his life there, did scarce trust
His own hands with the dust,

Yet would not place one peece above, but lives
In feare of theeves. 35
Thousands there were as frantick as himself
And hug'd each one his pelf,
The down-right Epicure plac'd heav'n in sense
And scornd pretence
While others slipt into a wide Excesse 40
Said little lesse;
The weaker sort slight, triviall wares Inslave
Who think them brave,
And poor, despised truth sate Counting by
Their victory. 45

Yet some, who all this while did weep and sing,
And sing, and weep, soar'd up into the *Ring*,
But most would use no wing.
O fools (said I,) thus to prefer dark night
Before true light, 50
To live in grots, and caves, and hate the day
Because it shews the way,
The way which from this dead and dark abode
Leads up to God,
A way where you might tread the Sun, and be 55
More bright than he.
But as I did their madnes so discusse
One whisper'd thus,
This Ring the Bride-groome did for none provide
But for his bride. 60

John Cap. 2. ver. 16, 17

All that is in the world, the lust of the flesh, the lust of the Eys, and the pride of life, is not of the father, but is of the world.

And the world passeth away, and the lusts thereof, but he that doth the will of God abideth for ever.

[1650]

Peace

My soul, there is a country
Far beyond the stars,
Where stands a wingèd sentry

All skillful in the wars;
There, above noise and danger, *5*
Sweet Peace sits crown'd with smiles,
And One born in a manger
Commands the beauteous files.
He is thy gracious friend.
And—O my soul awake!— *10*
Did in pure love descend,
To die here for thy sake.
If thou canst get but thither,
There grows the flower of Peace,
The rose that cannot wither, *15*
Thy fortress and thy ease.
Leave, then, thy foolish ranges,
For none can thee secure,
But One who never changes,
Thy God, thy life, thy cure. *20*

[1655]

They Are All Gone into the World of Light!

They are all gone into the world of light!
And I alone sit lingering here;
Their very memory is fair and bright,
And my sad thoughts doth clear.

It glows and glitters in my cloudy breast *5*
Like stars upon some gloomy grove,
Or those faint beams in which this hill is dressed
After the sun's remove.

I see them walking in an air of glory,
Whose light doth trample on my days; *10*
My days, which are at best but dull and hoary,
Mere glimmering and decays.

O holy hope, and high humility,
High as the heavens above!

These are your walks, and you have showed them me 15
To kindle my cold love.

Dear, beauteous death! the jewel of the just,
Shining nowhere but in the dark;
What mysteries do lie beyond thy dust,
Could man outlook that mark! 20

He that hath found some fledged bird's nest may know
At first sight if the bird be flown;
But what fair well or grove he sings in now,
That is to him unknown.

And yet, as angels in some brighter dreams 25
Call to the soul when man doth sleep,
So some strange thoughts transcend our wonted themes,
And into glory peep.

If a star were confined into a tomb,
Her captive flames must needs burn there; 30
But when the hand that locked her up gives room,
She'll shine through all the sphere.

O Father of eternal life, and all
Created glories under Thee!
Resume Thy spirit from this world of thrall 35
Into true liberty!

Either disperse these mists, which blot and fill
My perspective still as they pass;
Or else remove me hence unto that hill
Where I shall need no glass. 40

[1655]

The prominent dramatist of his day, ***John Dryden*** *(1631–1700) was born in Northamptonshire, England, into a family of Puritan gentry. He studied at the King's School under Richard Busby, then matriculated at Trinity College, Cambridge. Dryden inherited an estate when his father died, and likely worked in London as secretary to his cousin Sir Gilbert Pickering for a few years. In 1663 he married Lady Elizabeth, Sir Robert Howard's sister. Dryden wrote plays prolifically, and struck up rivalries with many* *of his contemporaries. The King's Company commissioned him to write many plays for them, although he soon tired of this arrangement and longed to spend more time on poetry. His appointment as Poet Laureate in 1668 and Historiographer Royal two years later provided the means necessary to focus more on his verse. His masterpieces are generally considered to be two long poems—*Absalom and Achitophel *(1681), a narrative based on the Old Testament but written with political implications for Dryden's time, and* Mac Flecknoe *(1682), a literary satire. He lost both his offices in 1688 when William III took power, and was forced to return to the theater to make a living. Late in life he converted to Catholicism and produced many translations. Noted as a critic as well as a poet and playwright, he died in London.*

John Dryden

Mac Flecknoe

*Or a satire upon the true-blue protestant poet, T. S.**

All human things are subject to decay,
And when fate summons, monarchs must obey.
This Flecknoe found, who, like Augustus, young
Was called to empire, and had governed long;
In prose and verse, was owned, without dispute, *5*
Through all the realms of Nonsense, absolute.
This aged prince, now flourishing in peace,
And blest with issue of a large increase,
Worn out with business, did at length debate
To settle the succession of the state; *10*
And, pondering which of all his sons was fit
To reign, and wage immortal war with wit,
Cried: "'Tis resolved; for nature pleads that he
Should only rule, who most resembles me.
Sh____ alone my perfect image bears, *15*
Mature in dullness from his tender years;
Sh____ alone, of all my sons, is he
Who stands confirmed in full stupidity.
The rest to some faint meaning make pretense,

*T.S. was the poet Thomas Shadwell, who had once been Dryden's friend but became his enemy.

But Sh____ never deviates into sense. 20
Some beams of wit on other souls may fall,
Strike through, and make a lucid interval;
But Sh____'s genuine night admits no ray,
His rising fogs prevail upon the day.
Besides, his goodly fabric fills the eye, 25
And seems designed for thoughtless majesty;
Thoughtless as monarch oaks that shade the plain,
And, spread in solemn state, supinely reign.
Heywood and Shirley were but types of thee,
Thou last great prophet of tautology. 30
Even I, a dunce of more renown than they,
Was sent before but to prepare thy way;
And, coarsely clad in Norwich drugget, came
To teach the nations in thy greater name.
My warbling lute, the lute I whilom strung, 35
When to King John of Portugal I sung,
Was but the prelude to that glorious day,
When thou on silver Thames didst cut thy way,
With well-timed oars before the royal barge,
Swelled with the pride of thy celestial charge; 40
And big with hymn, commander of a host,
The like was ne'er in Epsom blankets tossed.
Methinks I see the new Arion sail,
The lute still trembling underneath thy nail.
At thy well-sharpened thumb from shore to shore 45
The treble squeaks for fear, the basses roar;
Echoes from Pissing Alley Sh____ call,
And Sh____ they resound from Aston Hall.
About thy boat the little fishes throng,
As at the morning toast that floats along. 50
Sometimes, as prince of thy harmonious band,
Thou wield'st thy papers in thy threshing hand.
St. André's feet ne'er kept more equal time,
Not ev'n the feet of thy own *Psyche's* rhyme;
Though they in number as in sense excel; 55
So just, so like tautology, they fell,
That, pale with envy, Singleton forswore
The lute and sword, which he in triumph bore,
And vowed he ne'er would act Villerius more."
Here stopped the good old sire, and wept for joy 60

In silent raptures of the hopeful boy.
All arguments, but most his plays, persuade,
That for anointed dullness he was made.
    Close to the walls which fair Augusta bind
(The fair Augusta much to fears inclined), *65*
An ancient fabric raised to inform the sight,
There stood of yore, and Barbican it hight;
A watchtower once; but now, so fate ordains,
Of all the pile an empty name remains.
From its old ruins brothel houses rise, *70*
Scenes of lewd loves, and of polluted joys,
Where their vast courts the mother-strumpets keep,
And, undisturbed by watch, in silence sleep.
Near these a Nursery erects its head,
Where queens are formed, and future heroes bred; *75*
Where unfledged actors learn to laugh and cry,
Where infant punks their tender voices try,
And little Maximins the gods defy.
Great Fletcher never treads in buskins here,
Nor greater Jonson dares in socks appear; *80*
But gentle Simkin just reception finds
Amidst this monument of vanished minds;
Pure clinches the suburbian Muse affords,
And Panton waging harmless war with words.
Here Flecknoe, as a place to fame well known, *85*
Ambitiously designed his Sh____'s throne;
For ancient Dekker prophesied long since,
That in this pile would reign a mighty prince,
Born for a scourge of wit, and flail of sense;
To whom true dullness should some *Psyches* owe, *90*
But worlds of *Misers* from his pen should flow;
Humorists and *Hypocrites* it should produce,
Whole Raymond families, and tribes of Bruce.
    Now Empress Fame had published the renown
Of Sh____'s coronation through the town. *95*
Roused by report of Fame, the nations meet,
From near Bunhill, and distant Watling Street.
No Persian carpets spread the imperial way,
But scattered limbs of mangled poets lay;
From dusty shops neglected authors come, *100*
Martyrs of pies, and relics of the bum.

Much Heywood, Shirley, Ogilby there lay,
But loads of Sh____ almost choked the way.
Bilked stationers for yeomen stood prepared,
And Herringman was captain of the guard. *105*
The hoary prince in majesty appeared,
High on a throne of his own labors reared.
At his right hand our young Ascanius sate,
Rome's other hope, and pillar of the sate.
His brows thick fogs, instead of glories, grace, *110*
And lambent dullness played around his face.
As Hannibal did to the altars come,
Sworn by his sire a mortal foe to Rome,
So Sh____ swore, nor should his vow be vain,
That he till death true dullness would maintain; *115*
And, in his father's right, and realm's defense,
Ne'er to have peace with wit, nor truce with sense.
The king himself the sacred unction made,
As king by office, and as priest by trade.
In his sinister hand, instead of ball, *120*
He placed a mighty mug of potent ale;
Love's Kingdom to his right he did convey,
At once his scepter, and his rule of sway;
Whose righteous lore the prince had practiced young,
And from whose loins recorded *Psyche* sprung. *125*
His temples, last, with poppies were o'erspread,
That nodding seemed to consecrate his head.
Just at that point of time, if fame not lie,
On his left hand twelve reverend owls did fly.
So Romulus, 'tis sung, by Tiber's brook, *130*
Presage of sway from twice six vultures took.
The admiring throng loud acclamations make,
And omens of his future empire take.
The sire then shook the honors of his head,
And from his brows damps of oblivion shed *135*
Full on the filial dullness; long he stood,
Repelling from his breast the raging god;
At length burst out in this prophetic mood.
"Heavens bless my son, from Ireland let him reign
To far Barbadoes on the western main; *140*
Of his dominion may no end be known,

And greater than his father's be his throne;
Beyond *Love's Kingdom* let him stretch his pen!"
He paused, and all the people cried, "Amen."
Then thus continued he: "My son, advance 145
Still in new impudence, new ignorance.
Success let others teach, learn thou from me
Pangs without birth, and fruitless industry.
Let *Virtuosos* in five years be writ;
Yet not one thought accuse thy toil of wit. 150
Let gentle George in triumph tread the stage,
Make Dorimant betray, and Loveit rage;
Let Cully, Cockwood, Fopling, charm the pit,
And in their folly show the writer's wit.
Yet still thy fools shall stand in thy defense, 155
And justify their author's want of sense.
Let 'em be all by thy own model made
Of dullness, and desire no foreign aid;
That they to future ages may be known,
Not copies drawn, but issue of thy own. 160
Nay, let thy men of wit too be the same,
All full of thee, and differing but in name.
But let no alien S—dl—y interpose,
To lard with wit thy hungry *Epsom* prose.
And when false flowers of rhetoric thou wouldst cull, 165
Trust nature, do not labor to be dull;
But write thy best, and top; and, in each line,
Sir Formal's oratory will be thine;
Sir Formal, though unsought, attends thy quill,
And does thy northern dedications fill. 170
Nor let false friends seduce thy mind to fame,
By arrogating Jonson's hostile name.
Let father Flecknoe fire thy mind with praise,
And uncle Ogilby thy envy raise.
Thou art my blood, where Jonson has no part: 175
What share have we in nature, or in art?
Where did his wit on learning fix a brand,
And rail at arts he did not understand?
Where made he love in Prince Nicander's vein,
Or swept the dust in *Psyche's* humble strain? 180
Where sold he bargains, 'whip-stitch, kiss my arse,'

Promised a play and dwindled to a farce?
When did his Muse from Fletcher scenes purloin,
As thou whole Eth'rege dost transfuse to thine?
But so transfused as oils on waters flow, *185*
His always floats above, thine sinks below.
This is thy province, this thy wondrous way,
New humors to invent for each new play;
This is that boasted bias of thy mind,
By which one way, to dullness, 'tis inclined; *190*
Which makes thy writings lean on one side still,
And, in all changes, that way bends thy will.
Nor let thy mountain-belly make pretense
Of likeness; thine's a tympany of sense.
A tun of man in thy large bulk is writ, *195*
But sure thou'rt but a kilderkin of wit.
Like mine, thy gentle numbers feebly creep;
Thy tragic Muse gives smiles, thy comic sleep.
With whate'er gall thou sett'st thyself to write,
Thy inoffensive satires never bite. *200*
In thy felonious heart though venom lies,
It does but touch thy Irish pen, and dies.
Thy genius calls thee not to purchase fame
In keen iambics, but mild anagram.
Leave writing plays, and choose for thy command *205*
Some peaceful province in acrostic land.
There thou may'st wings display and altars raise,
And torture one poor word ten thousand ways.
Or, if thou wouldst thy different talents suit,
Set thy own songs, and sing them to thy lute." *210*
He said: but his last words were scarcely heard
For Bruce and Longville had a trap prepared,
And down they sent the yet declaiming bard.
Sinking he left his drugget robe behind,
Borne upwards by a subterranean wind. *215*
The mantle fell to the young prophet's part,
With double portion of his father's art.

[1682]

To the Memory of Mr. Oldham*

Farewell, too little, and too lately known,
Whom I began to think and call my own;
For sure our souls were near allied, and thine
Cast in the same poetic mould with mine.
One common note on either lyre did strike, *5*
And knaves and fools we both abhorred alike.
To the same goal did both our studies drive;
The last set out the soonest did arrive.
Thus Nissus fell upon the slippery place,
While his young friend° performed and won the race. *10*
O early ripe! to thy abundant store
What could advancing age have added more?
It might (what nature never gives the young)
Have taught the numbers° of thy native tongue.
But satire needs not those, and wit will shine *15*
Through the harsh cadence of a rugged line;
A noble error, and but seldom made,
When poets are by too much force betrayed.
Thy generous fruits, though gathered ere their prime,
Still showed a quickness, and maturing time *20*
But mellows what we write to the dull sweets of rhyme.
Once more, hail and farewell; farewell, thou young,
But ah too short, Marcellus° of our tongue;
Thy brows with ivy and with laurels bound;
But fate and gloomy night encompass thee around. *25*

[1684]

*Refers to the poet John Oldham, who died at age 30, and was best remembered for his *Satires upon the Jesuits*.

9–10 *Nissus*; *his young friend*: Virgil describes in the *Aeneid* these two friends who ran a race for the prize of an olive crown. **14** *numbers*: meters. **23** *Marcellus*: would have succeeded the Roman emperor Augustus, but died at age 20.

Song
from Marriage à-la-Mode

1

Why should a foolish Marriage Vow
  Which long ago was made,
Oblige us to each other now
  When Passion is decay'd?
We lov'd, and we lov'd, as long as we cou'd, *5*
  Till our Love was lov'd out in us both;
But our Marriage is dead, when the Pleasure is fled;
  'Twas Pleasure first made it an Oath.

2

If I have Pleasures for a Friend,
  And farther Love in store, *10*
What Wrong has he whose Joys did end,
  And who cou'd give no more?
'Tis a madness that he shou'd be jealous of me,
  Or that I shou'd bar him of another; *15*
For all we can gain is to give our selves pain,
  When neither can hinder the other.

***Aphra Behn** (1640–1689)—a poet, playwright, and novelist—was the first Englishwoman to make a living as a writer. Little is known for certain about her early life, but it is generally believed that she was born Eaffry Johnson near Canterbury, England. When she was a girl she sailed to the British colony of Surinam in the West Indies. Her father probably died en route, and Behn stayed there with her mother and sister for some time before returning to England to marry a Dutch merchant, who provided her surname. He died of bubonic plague within two years. Financially strapped, Behn worked for Charles II as a spy in Antwerp during the Dutch war, though the king refused to acknowledge the arrangement nor to compensate her upon her return. She was thrown in debtor's prison for a time. Behn moved to London, arriving just as the theaters were re-*

opened. She began writing plays for the Duke's Company at Dorset Gardens, and had much success. Her first play was a successfully produced in 1670; her comedy The Rover *(1677; 1681) was a smash hit. Following a carriage accident and a probable bout with syphilis, Behn died and was buried at Westminster Abbey.*

Aphra Behn

Love Armed*

Love in fantastic triumph sat,
Whilst bleeding hearts a round him flowed,
For whom fresh pains he did create,
And strange tyrannic power he showed;
From thy bright eyes he took his fire, *5*
Which round about, in sport he hurled;
But 'twas from mine he took desire,
Enough to undo the amorous world.

From me he took his sighs and tears,
From thee his pride and cruelty; *10*
From me his languishments and fears,
And every killing dart from thee;
Thus thou and I, the God have armed,
And set him up a deity;
But my poor heart alone is harmed, *15*
Whilst thine the victor is, and free.

[1677]

*song from *Abadelzer;* Love is portrayed in this poem as a cruel god, a merciless Cupid with his darts.

Epitaph on the Tombstone of a Child

The Last of Seven That Died Before

This Little, Silent, Gloomy Monument,
Contains all that was sweet and innocent;
The softest pratler that e'er found a Tongue,
His Voice was Musick and his Words a Song;
Which now each List'ning Angel smiling hears, *5*
Such pretty Harmonies compose the Spheres;
Wanton as unfledg'd Cupids, ere their Charms
Had learn'd the little arts of doing harms;
Fair as young Cherubins, as soft and kind,
And tho translated could not be refin'd; *10*
The Seventh dear pledge the Nuptial Joys had given,
Toil'd here on Earth, retir'd to rest in Heaven;
Where they the shining Host of Angels fill,
Spread their gay wings before the Throne, and smile.

[1685]

A Thousand Martyrs

A thousand martyrs I have made,
    All sacrificed to my desire;
A thousand beauties have betrayed,
    That languish in resistless fire.
The untamed heart to hand I brought, *5*
And fixed the wild and wandering thought.

I never vowed nor sighed in vain
    But both, though false, were well received.
The fair are pleased to give us pain,
    And what they wish is soon believed. *10*
And though I talked of wounds and smart,
Love's pleasures only touched my heart.

Alone the glory and the spoil
    I always laughing bore away;
The triumphs, without pain or toil, 15
    Without the hell, the heav'n of joy.
And while I thus at random rove
Despise the fools that whine for love.

[1688]

***Anne Finch** (1661–1720) was the daughter of Sir William Kingsmill, who died when the girl was five months old, and Anne Haselwood, who remarried and then soon died as well. Her mother's widower raised her; little else is known about her childhood. At 21 she was appointed a maid of honor to Mary of Modena, duchess of York, and lived in the court of Charles II, enjoying the company of her fellow maids and privately writing poetry. During these years she met and in 1684 married Colonel Heneage Finch, a gentleman to the Duke of York. Her husband held various public posts until William and Mary came into power in 1689. The Finches settled on the family property in Eastwell, Kent, inherited from the Earl of Winchilsea; they remained there, surrounded by friends of like intellect, for more than 25 years. Her collection* Miscellany Poems on Several Occasions *appeared in 1713. Finch died after a long illness. Some of her works were published only in the twentieth century.*

Anne Finch, Countess of Winchilsea

Adam Posed

Could our first father, at his toilsome plow,
Thorns in his path, and labor on his brow,
Clothed only in a rude, unpolished skin,
Could he a vain fantastic nymph have seen,
In all her airs, in all her antic graces, 5

Her various fashions, and more various faces;
How had it posed that skill, which late assigned
Just appellations to each several kind!
A right idea of the sight to frame;
T'have guessed from what new element she came; *10*
T'have hit the wav'ring form, or giv'n this thing a name.

[1713]

To Death

O King of terrors, whose unbounded sway
All that have life must certainly obey;
The King, the Priest, the Prophet, all are thine,
Nor would ev'n God (in flesh) thy stroke decline.
My name is on thy roll, and sure I must *5*
Increase thy gloomy kingdom in the dust.
My soul at this no apprehension feels,
But trembles at thy swords, thy racks, thy wheels;
Thy scorching fevers, which distract the sense,
And snatch us raving, unprepared, from hence; *10*
At thy contagious darts, that wound the heads
Of weeping friends, who wait at dying beds.
Spare these, and let thy time be when it will;
My bus'ness is to die, and thine to kill.
Gently thy fatal scepter on me lay, *15*
And take to thy cold arms, insensibly, thy prey.

[1713]

A Nocturnal Reverie

In such a night, when every louder wind
Is to its distant cavern safe confined;
And only gentle Zephyr° fans his wings,
And lonely Philomel,° still waking, sings;

4 *Philomel*: the nightingale. **3** *Zephyr:* the west wind.

Or from some tree, famed for the owl's delight, *5*
She, hollowing clear, directs the wanderer right;
In such a night, when passing clouds give place,
Or thinly veil the heavens' mysterious face;
When in some river, overhung with green,
The waving moon and trembling leaves are seen; *10*
When freshened grass now bears itself upright,
And makes cool banks to pleasing rest invite,
Whence springs the woodbind, and the bramble-rose,
And where the sleepy cowslip sheltered grows;
Whilst now a paler hue the foxglove takes, *15*
Yet checkers still with red the dusky brakes.
When scattered glow-worms, but in twilight fine,
Show trivial beauties watch their hour to shine;
Whilst Salisbury stands the test of every light,
In perfect charms, and perfect virtue bright; *20*
When odors, which declined repelling day,
Through temperate air uninterrupted stray;
When darkened groves their softest shadows wear,
And falling waters we distinctly hear;
When through the gloom more venerable shows *25*
Some ancient fabric, awful in repose,
While sunburnt hills their swarthy looks conceal,
And swelling haycocks thicken up the vale;
When the loosed horse now, as his pasture leads,
Comes slowly grazing through the adjoining meads, *30*
Whose stealing pace, and lengthened shade we fear,
Till torn-up forage in his teeth we hear;
When nibbling sheep at large pursue their food,
And unmolested kine rechew the cud;
When curlews° cry beneath the village walls, *35*
And to her straggling brood the partridge calls;
Their shortlived jubilee the creatures keep,
Which but endures, whilst tyrant man does sleep;
When a sedate content the spirit feels,
And no fierce light disturbs, whilst it reveals; *40*
But silent musings urge the mind to seek
Something, too high for syllables to speak;

35 *curlews*: a type of shore bird.

Till the free soul to a composedness charmed,
Finding the elements of rage disarmed,
O'er all below a solemn quiet grown, *45*
Joys in the inferior world, and thinks it like her own;
In such a night let me abroad remain,
Till morning breaks, and all's confused again;
Our cares, our toils, our clamors are renewed,
Or pleasures, seldom reached, again pursued. *50*

[1713]

On Myself

Good Heav'n, I thank thee, since it was designed
I should be framed, but of the weaker kind,
That yet, my Soul, is rescued from the love
Of all those trifles which their passions move.
Pleasures and praise and plenty have with me *5*
But their just value. If allowed they be,
Freely, and thankfully as much I taste,
As will not reason or religion waste.
If they're denied, I on my self can live,
And slight those aids unequal chance does give. *10*
When in the sun, my wings can be displayed,
And, in retirement, I can bless the shade.

[1902]

***Alexander Pope** (1688–1744) was born into a Roman Catholic family in London, where his father was a successful linen merchant. Because of his Catholicism, higher education was closed to Pope, and he was tutored by his father and a local priest. Childhood disease stunted his growth and weakened his spine. It was rumored that he wore padded clothes to hide his misshapen body. Precociously talented, Pope found early and immediate success as a poet. His* Pastorals *(1709) were allegedly composed when he was only 16 years old. Pope was associated for a short time with the Scriblerus Club, a group of writers including Jonathan Swift, John Gay,* *and others, who would meet to criticize "all the false tastes in learning." Other early books include his* Essay on Criticism *(1711) and* The Rape of the Lock *(1714), a mock epic. His later works, which included a translation of Homer's* Iliad *(1715) and* Odyssey *(1725–1726), eventually brought Pope financial security, allowing him to buy an estate at Twickenham, near Richmond, where he settled in 1719 with his mother. In his last year he worked with Rev. William Warburton on a collected edition, including* Essay on Man, *begun over ten years earlier.*

Alexander Pope

from An Essay on Criticism

II

Of all the causes which conspire to blind
Man's erring judgment, and misguide the mind,
What the weak head with strongest bias rules,
Is PRIDE, the never-failing vice of fools.
Whatever Nature has in worth denied, *5*
She gives in large recruits of needless pride;
For as in bodies, thus in souls we find
What wants in blood and spirits, swell'd with wind;
Pride, where wit fails, steps in to our defence,
And fills up all the mighty void of sense. *10*
If once right reason drives that cloud away,
Truth breaks upon us with resistless day.
Trust not yourself; but your defects to know,
Make use of every friend—and every foe.
A little learning is a dangerous thing; *15*
Drink deep, or taste not the Pierian spring;°
There shallow draughts intoxicate the brain,
And drinking largely sobers us again.
Fired at first sight with what the Muse imparts,
In fearless youth we tempt the height of arts, *20*
While from the bounded level of our mind,
Short views we take, nor see the lengths behind;
But more advanced, behold with strange surprise
New distant scenes of endless science rise!

16 *Pierian spring:* the spring of the Muses.

So pleased at first the towering Alps we try, *25*
Mount o'er the vales, and seem to tread the sky,
The eternal snows appear already passed,
And the first clouds and mountains seem the last;
But, those attain'd, we tremble to survey
The growing labours of the lengthen'd way, *30*
The increasing prospect tires our wandering eyes,
Hills peep o'er hills, and Alps on Alps arise!
A perfect judge will read each work of wit
With the same spirit that its author writ;
Survey the WHOLE, nor seeks slight faults to find *35*
Where Nature moves, and rapture warms the mind,
Nor lose, for that malignant dull delight,
The generous pleasure to be charm'd with wit.
But in such lays as neither ebb nor flow,
Correctly cold, and regularly low, *40*
That shunning faults, one quiet tenor keep;
We cannot blame indeed — but we may sleep.
In wit, as Nature, what affects our hearts
Is not th' exactness of peculiar parts;
'Tis not a lip, or eye, we beauty call, *45*
But the joint force and full result of all.
Thus when we view some well-proportion'd dome,
(The world's just wonder, and ev'n thine, O Rome!)
No single parts unequally surprise,
All comes united to th' admiring eyes; *50*
No monstrous height, or breadth or length appear;
The whole at once is bold and regular.
Whoever thinks a faultless piece to see,
Thinks what ne'er was, nor is, nor e'er shall be,
In every work regard the writer's end, *55*
Since none can compass more than they intend;
And if the means be just, the conduct true,
Applause, in spite of trivial faults, is due.
As men of breeding, sometimes men of wit,
To avoid great errors, must the less commit; *60*
Neglect the rules each verbal critic lays,
For not to know some trifles, is a praise.
Most critics, fond of some subservient art,
Still make the whole depend upon a part;
They talk of principles, but notions prize, *65*
And all to one loved folly sacrifice.

. . .

Avoid extremes; and shun the fault of such,
Who still are pleased too little or too much.
At every trifle scorn to take offence,
That always shows great pride, or little sense; *70*
Those heads, as stomachs, are not sure the best,
Which nauseate all, and nothing can digest.
Yet let not each gay turn thy rapture move;
For fools admire, but men of sense approve;
As things seem large which we through mists descry, *75*
Dulness is ever apt to magnify.
Some foreign writers, some our own despise;
The ancients only, or the moderns prize.
Thus wit, like faith, by each man is applied
To one small sect, and all are damn'd beside. *80*
Meanly they seek the blessing to confine,
And force that sun but on a part to shine,
Which not alone the southern wit sublimes,
But ripens spirits in cold northern climes;
Which from the first has shone on ages past, *85*
Enlights the present, and shall warm the last;
Though each may feel increases and decays,
And see now clearer and now darker days.
Regard not then if wit be old or new,
But blame the false, and value still the true. *90*

. . .

[1711]

from An Essay on Man

Epistle II

Know then thyself, presume not God to scan,
The proper study of mankind is man.
Placed on this isthmus of a middle state,
A being darkly wise, and rudely great.
With too much knowledge for the sceptic side, *5*
With too much weakness for the stoic's pride,
He hangs between; in doubt to act, or rest;

In doubt to deem himself a god, or beast;
In doubt his mind or body to prefer;
Born but to die, and reasoning but to err; *10*
Alike in ignorance, his reason such,
Whether he thinks too little, or too much;
Chaos of Thought and Passion, all confused;
Still by himself abused or disabused;
Created half to rise, and half to fall; *15*
Great lord of all things, yet a prey to all;
Sole judge of truth, in endless error hurl'd;
The glory, jest, and riddle of the world!
    Go, wondrous creature! mount where Science guides,
Go, measure earth, weigh air, and state the tides; *20*
Instruct the planets in what orbs to run,
Correct old Time, and regulate the sun;
Go, soar with Plato to th' empyreal sphere,
To the first good, first perfect, and first fair;
Or tread the mazy round his followers trod, *25*
And quitting sense call imitating God;
As Eastern priests in giddy circles run,
And turn their heads to imitate the sun.
Go, teach Eternal Wisdom how to rule —
Then drop into thyself, and be a fool! *30*
    Superior beings, when of late they saw
A mortal man unfold all Nature's law,
Admired such wisdom in an earthly shape,
And show'd a Newton as we show an ape.
    Could he, whose rules the rapid comet bind, *35*
Describe or fix one movement of his mind?
Who saw its fires here rise, and there descend,
Explain his own beginning, or his end?
Alas what wonder! Man's superior part
Uncheck'd may rise, and climb from art to art; *40*
But when his own great work is but begun,
What reason weaves, by passion is undone.
    Trace Science then, with modesty thy guide;
First strip off all her equipage of pride;
Deduct but what is vanity or dress, *45*
Or learning's luxury, or idleness;

Or tricks to show the stretch of human brain,
Mere curious pleasure, or ingenious pain;
Expunge the whole, or lop the excrescent parts
Of all our vices have created arts; *50*
Then see how little the remaining sum,
Which served the past, and must the times to come!

. . .

[1733]

Epigram

Engraved on the Collar of a Dog Which I Gave to His Royal Highness

I am his Highness' dog at Kew;
Pray tell me, sir, whose dog are you?

[1738]

Thomas Gray *(1716–1771) was born in London to a father who worked as a scribe and a mother who ran a hat shop. All 11 of his brothers and sisters died in infancy. Gray first attended Eton University, where he was a classmate and friend of Gothic novelist Horace Walpole. He then transferred to Cambridge, but left without taking a degree. After traveling with Walpole through Europe for two years, Gray returned to Cambridge in 1742 to live the remainder of his life as a writer and scholar. He studied subjects as varied as botany, architecture, Greek, and Old Norse, becoming such an institution at Cambridge that the university made him Regius Professor of History in 1768. He preferred isolation and privacy, however, leading him to publish some of his early work anonymously and to turn down the poet laureateship in 1757. By then he was extremely popular, largely due to his* Elegy Written in a Country Churchyard *(1751). He was buried in the same churchyard he memorialized in verse.*

Thomas Gray

Ode on the Death of a Favorite Cat, Drowned in a Tub of Goldfishes

'Twas on a lofty vase's side,
Where China's gayest art had dyed
    The azure flowers that blow;
Demurest of the tabby kind,
The pensive Selima, reclined, *5*
    Gazed on the lake below.

Her conscious tail her joy declared;
The fair round face, the snowy beard,
    The velvet of her paws,
Her coat, that with the tortoise vies, *10*
Her ears of jet, and emerald eyes,
    She saw; and purred applause.

Still had she gazed; but 'midst the tide
Two angel forms were seen to glide,
    The genii of the stream; *15*
Their scaly armor's Tyrian hue°
Through richest purple to the view
    Betrayed a golden gleam.

The hapless nymph with wonder saw;
A whisker first and then a claw, *20*
    With many an ardent wish,
She stretched in vain to reach the prize.
What female heart can gold despise?
    What cat's averse to fish?

Presumptuous maid! with looks intent *25*
Again she stretched, again she bent,
    Nor knew the gulf between.
(Malignant Fate sat by and smiled)
The slippery verge her feet beguiled,
    She tumbled headlong in. *30*

16 *Tyrian hue:* purple (The ancient world Tyre was famous for its purple dye).

Eight times emerging from the flood
She mewed to every watery god,
    Some speedy aid to send.
No dolphin came, no Nereid stirred;
Nor cruel Tom, nor Susan heard; *35*
    A favorite has no friend!

From hence, ye beauties, undeceived,
Know, one false step is ne'er retrieved,
    And be with caution bold.
Not all that tempts your wandering eyes *40*
And heedless hearts, is lawful prize;
    Nor all that glisters, gold.

[1748]

Elegy Written in a Country Churchyard

The curfew tolls the knell of parting day,
    The lowing herd wind slowly o'er the lea,
The plowman homeward plods his weary way,
    And leaves the world to darkness and to me.

Now fades the glimmering landscape on the sight, *5*
    And all the air a solemn stillness holds,
Save where the beetle wheels his droning flight,
    And drowsy tinklings lull the distant folds;

Save that from yonder ivy-mantled tower
    The moping owl does to the moon complain *10*
Of such, as wand'ring near her secret bower,
    Molest her ancient solitary reign.

Beneath those rugged elms, that yew tree's shade,
    Where heaves the turf in many a mold'ring heap,
Each in his narrow cell forever laid, *15*
    The rude° forefathers of the hamlet sleep.

16 *rude*: simple, ignorant.

The breezy call of incense-breathing morn,
    The swallow twitt'ring from the straw-built shed,
The cock's shrill clarion, or the echoing horn,°
    No more shall rouse them from their lowly bed. *20*

For them no more the blazing hearth shall burn,
    Or busy housewife ply her evening care;
No children run to lisp their sire's return,
    Or climb his knees the envied kiss to share.

Oft did the harvest to their sickle yield, *25*
    Their furrow oft the stubborn glebe° has broke;
How jocund did they drive their team afield!
    How bowed the woods beneath their sturdy stroke!

Let not Ambition mock their useful toil,
    Their homely joys, and destiny obscure; *30*
Nor Grandeur hear with a disdainful smile
    The short and simple annals of the poor.

The boast of heraldry,° the pomp of pow'r,
    And all that beauty, all that wealth e'er gave,
Awaits alike th' inevitable hour. *35*
    The paths of glory lead but to the grave.

Nor you, ye proud, impute to these the fault,
    If Mem'ry o'er their tomb no trophies raise,
Where through the long-drawn aisle and fretted° vault
    The pealing anthem swells the note of praise. *40*

Can storied urn° or animated bust
    Back to its mansion call the fleeting breath?
Can Honor's voice provoke the silent dust,
    Or Flatt'ry soothe the dull cold ear of Death?

Perhaps in this neglected spot is laid *45*
    Some heart once pregnant with celestial fire;
Hands that the rod of empire might have swayed,
    Or waked to ecstasy the living lyre.

19 *echoing horn*: fox-hunter's horn. **26** *glebe*: turf. **33** *heraldry*: noble birth. **39** *fretted*: inlaid with designs. **41** *storied urn*: vessel holding the ashes of the dead after cremation. *Storied* can mean (1) decorated with scenes; (2) inscribed with a life's story; or (3) celebrated in story or history. The *animated bust* is a lifelike sculpture of the dead, placed on a tomb.

But knowledge to their eyes her ample page
  Rich with the spoils of time did ne'er unroll; 50
Chill Penury° repressed their noble rage,
  And froze the genial current of the soul.

Full many a gem of purest ray serene,
  The dark unfathomed caves of ocean bear;
Full many a flower is born to blush unseen, 55
  And waste its sweetness on the desert air.

Some village Hampden,° that with dauntless breast
  The little tyrant of his field withstood;
Some mute inglorious Milton here may rest,
  Some Cromwell, guiltless of his country's blood.° 60

Th' applause of list'ning senates to command,
  The threats of pain and ruin to despise,
To scatter plenty o'er a smiling land,
  And read their hist'ry in a nation's eyes,

Their lot forbade; nor circumscribed alone 65
  Their growing virtues, but their crimes confined;
Forbade to wade through slaughter to a throne,
  And shut the gates of mercy on mankind,

The struggling pangs of conscious truth to hide,
  To quench the blushes of ingenuous° shame, 70
Or heap the shrine of Luxury and Pride
  With incense kindled at the Muse's flame.°

Far from the madding° crowd's ignoble strife,
  Their sober wishes never learned to stray;
Along the cool sequestered vale of life 75
  They kept the noiseless tenor° of their way.

51 *Penury*: Poverty. 57 *Hampden*: John Hampden (1594–1643), member of Parliament, had resisted illegal taxes on his lands imposed by Charles I. 60 *Cromwell . . . his country's blood*: Gray blames Oliver Cromwell (1599–1658) for strife and tyranny. As general of the armies of Parliament, Cromwell had won the Civil War against Charles I and had signed the king's death warrant. As Lord Protector of England (1653–1658), he had ruled with an iron hand. 70 *ingenuous*: innocent. 71–72 *heap the shrine . . . Muse's flame*: Gray chides mercenary poets who write poems to please their rich, high-living patrons. 73 *madding*: frenzied. 76 *tenor*: ongoing motion.

Yet ev'n these bones from insult to protect
  Some frail memorial still erected nigh,
With uncouth rhymes and shapeless sculpture decked,
  Implores the passing tribute of a sigh. *80*

Their name, their years, spelt by th' unlettered Muse,
  The place of fame and elegy supply;
And many a holy text around she strews,
  That teach the rustic moralist to die.

For who to dumb Forgetfulness a prey, *85*
  This pleasing anxious being e'er resigned,
Left the warm precincts of the cheerful day,
  Nor cast one longing ling'ring look behind?

On some fond breast the parting soul relies,
  Some pious drops the closing eye requires; *90*
Ev'n from the tomb the voice of Nature cries,
  Ev'n in our ashes live their wonted° fires.

For thee, who mindful of th' unhonored dead
  Dost in these lines their artless tale relate;
If chance,° by lonely contemplation led, *95*
  Some kindred spirit shall inquire thy fate,

Haply° some hoary-headed swain° may say,
  "Oft have we seen him at the peep of dawn
Brushing with hasty steps the dews away
  To meet the sun upon the upland lawn. *100*

"There at the foot of yonder nodding beech
  That wreathes its old fantastic roots so high,
His listless length at noontide would he stretch,
  And pore upon the brook that babbles by.

"Hard by yon wood, now smiling as in scorn, *105*
  Mutt'ring his wayward fancies he would rove,
Now drooping, woeful wan, like one forlorn,
  Or crazed with care, or crossed in hopeless love.

"One morn I missed him, on the customed hill,
  Along the heath and near his fav'rite tree; *110*

92 *wonted*: customary. 95 *If chance*: If by chance. 97 *Haply*: perhaps; *hoary-headed swain*: gray-haired shepherd.

Another came; nor yet beside the rill,°
Nor up the lawn, nor at the wood was he;

"The next with dirges due in sad array
Slow through the churchway path we saw him borne.
Approach and read (for thou canst read) the lay,° *115*
Graved on the stone beneath yon aged thorn."

The Epitaph

Here rests his head upon the lap of Earth
A youth to Fortune and to Fame unknown.
Fair Science° frowned not on his humble birth,
And Melancholy marked him for her own. *120*

Large was his bounty, and his soul sincere,
Heav'n did a recompense as largely send;
He gave to Mis'ry all he had, a tear,
He gained from Heav'n ('twas all he wished) a friend.

No farther seek his merits to disclose, *125*
Or draw his frailties from their dread abode
(There they alike in trembling hope repose),
The bosom of His Father and his God.

[1753]

111 *rill*: brook. **115** *lay*: song or poem. **119** *Science*: Knowledge.

The son of a clergyman, **Oliver Goldsmith** *(1730–1774) spent most of his childhood in the Irish countryside in Lissoy. He attended Trinity College, Dublin, graduating in 1750. After being rejected for ordination, Goldsmith studied medicine in Edinburgh and Leiden. He traveled for a year in Western Europe, then arrived in London to work as a physician and an usher. Goldsmith also launched his literary career at this time, reviewing books and writing essays and poetry. He formed many literary acquaintances, among them Samuel Johnson, who invited the young poet to join his famous "Club" and helped him publish his work, including* The Traveller *(1764) and* The Deserted Village *(1770). Dr. Johnson's generosity and attention saved the poor writer from debtor's prison, though Goldsmith is* *rumored to have remained in debt all his life. He wrote his famous novel* The Vicar of Wakefield *(1766) while held captive in his rooms by his debtors. He made his early career in letters as an editor and essayist, but soon turned to poetry, fiction, and plays. His untimely death at 44 was caused by kidney infection.*

Oliver Goldsmith

When Lovely Woman Stoops to Folly*

When lovely woman stoops to folly,
    And finds too late that men betray,
What charm can soothe her melancholy,
    What art can wash her guilt away?

The only art her guilt to cover, *5*
    To hide her shame from every eye,
To give repentance to her lover,
    And wring his bosom—is to die.

[1766]

*Song from Gray's novel *The Vicar of Wakefield.*

The Deserted Village

Sweet Auburn!° loveliest village of the plain,
Where health and plenty cheered the laboring swain,
Where smiling spring its earliest visit paid,
And parting summer's lingering blooms delayed;
Dear lovely bowers of innocence and ease, *5*
Seats of my youth, when every sport could please,
How often have I loitered o'er thy green,
Where humble happiness endeared each scene!
How often have I paused on every charm,
The sheltered cot, the cultivated farm, *10*

1 *Auburn*: the name of the fictional village Goldsmith describes.

The never-failing brook, the busy mill,
The decent church that topped the neighboring hill,
The hawthorn bush, with seats beneath the shade,
For talking age and whispering lovers made!
How often have I blessed the coming day, *15*
When toil remitting lent its turn to play,
And all the village train, from labor free,
Led up their sports beneath the spreading tree;
While many a pastime circled in the shade,
The young contending as the old surveyed; *20*
And many a gambol frolicked o'er the ground,
And sleights of art and feats of strength went round;
And still, as each repeated pleasure tired,
Succeeding sports the mirthful band inspired;
The dancing pair that simply sought renown, *25*
By holding out to tire each other down;
The swain mistrustless of his smutted face,
While secret laughter tittered round the place;
The bashful virgin's sidelong looks of love,
The matron's glance that would those looks reprove— *30*
These were thy charms, sweet village! sports like these,
With sweet succession taught even toil to please;
These round thy bowers their cheerful influence shed;
These were thy charms—but all these charms are fled.

Sweet smiling village, loveliest of the lawn, *35*
Thy sports are fled and all thy charms withdrawn;
Amidst thy bowers the tyrant's hand is seen,
And desolation saddens all thy green;
One only master grasps the whole domain,
And half a tillage stints thy smiling plain; *40*
No more thy glassy brook reflects the day,
But choked with sedges works its weedy way;
Along thy glades, a solitary guest,
The hollow-sounding bittern guards its nest;
Amidst thy desert walks the lapwing flies, *45*
And tires their echoes with unvaried cries.
Sunk are thy bowers in shapeless ruin all,
And the long grass o'ertops the moldering wall;
And, trembling, shrinking from the spoiler's hand,
Far, far away, thy children leave the land. *50*

Ill fares the land, to hastening ills a prey,
Where wealth accumulates and men decay;
Princes and lords may flourish or may fade;
A breath can make them as a breath has made;
But a bold peasantry, their country's pride, *55*
When once destroyed, can never be supplied.
A time there was, ere England's griefs began,
When every rood of ground° maintained its man;
For him light labor spread her wholesome store,
Just gave what life required, but gave no more; *60*
His best companions, innocence and health;
And his best riches, ignorance of wealth.

But times are altered; trade's unfeeling train
Usurp the land, and dispossess the swain;
Along the lawn, where scattered hamlets rose, *65*
Unwieldy wealth and cumbrous pomp repose;
And every want to opulence allied,
And every pang that folly pays to pride.
Those gentle hours that plenty bade to bloom,
Those calm desires that asked but little room, *70*
Those healthful sports that graced the peaceful scene,
Lived in each look, and brightened all the green—
These, far departing, seek a kinder shore,
And rural mirth and manners are no more.

Sweet Auburn! parent of the blissful hour, *75*
Thy glades forlorn confess the tyrant's power.
Here, as I take my solitary rounds
Amidst thy tangling walks and ruined grounds,
And, many a year elapsed, return to view
Where once the cottage stood, the hawthorn grew, *80*
Remembrance wakes with all her busy train,
Swells at my breast, and turns the past to pain.

In all my wanderings round this world of care,
In all my griefs—and God has given my share—
I still had hopes, my latest hours to crown, *85*
Amidst these humble bowers to lay me down;
To husband out life's taper at the close,
And keep the flame from wasting by repose.

58 *rood of ground*: measurement of land; a rod was approximately 16.5 feet, though the measure often differed from location to location.

I still had hopes, for pride attends us still,
Amidst the swains to show my book-learned skill, *90*
Around my fire an evening group to draw,
And tell of all I felt, and all I saw;
And, as a hare whom hounds and horns pursue,
Pants to the place from whence at first she flew,
I still had hopes, my long vexations past, *95*
Here to return—and die at home at last.

O blessed retirement, friend to life's decline,
Retreats from care, that never must be mine,
How happy he who crowns in shades like these
A youth of labor with an age of ease; *100*
Who quits a world where strong temptations try,
And, since 'tis hard to combat, learns to fly!
For him no wretches, born to work and weep,
Explore the mine, or tempt the dangerous deep;
No surly porter stands in guilty state, *105*
To spurn imploring famine from the gate;
But on he moves to meet his latter end,
Angels around befriending virtue's friend;
Bends to the grave with unperceived decay,
While resignation gently slopes the way; *110*
And, all his prospects brightening to the last,
His heaven commences ere the world be past.

Sweet was the sound, when oft at evening's close
Up yonder hill the village murmur rose;
There, as I passed with careless steps and slow, *115*
The mingling notes came softened from below;
The swain responsive as the milkmaid sung,
The sober herd that lowed to meet their young,
The noisy geese that gabbled o'er the pool,
The playful children just let loose from school, *120*
The watch-dog's voice that bayed the whispering wind,
And the loud laugh that spoke the vacant° mind—
These all in sweet confusion sought the shade,
And filled each pause the nightingale had made.
But now the sounds of population fail, *125*
No cheerful murmurs fluctuate in the gale,

122 *vacant*: empty of care.

No busy steps the grass-grown footway tread,
For all the bloomy flush of life is fled;
All but yon widowed, solitary thing,
That feebly bends beside the plashy spring; *130*
She, wretched matron, forced in age, for bread,
To strip the brook with mantling cresses spread,
To pick her wintry faggot° from the thorn,
To seek her nightly shed, and weep till morn—
She only left of all the harmless train, *135*
The sad historian of the pensive plain.

Near yonder copse, where once the garden smiled,
And still where many a garden flower grows wild,
There, where a few torn shrubs the place disclose,
The village preacher's modest mansion rose. *140*
A man he was to all the country dear,
And passing rich with forty pounds a year;
Remote from towns he ran his godly race,
Nor e'er had changed, nor wished to change his place;
Unpractised he to fawn, or seek for power, *145*
By doctrines fashioned to the varying hour;
Far other aims his heart had learned to prize,
More skilled to raise the wretched than to rise.
His house was known to all the vagrant train;
He chid their wanderings, but relieved their pain; *150*
The long-remembered beggar was his guest,
Whose beard descending swept his aged breast;
The ruined spendthrift, now no longer proud,
Claimed kindred there, and has his claims allowed;
The broken soldier, kindly bade to stay, *155*
Sat by his fire and talked the night away;
Wept o'er his wounds, or, tales of sorrow done,
Shouldered his crutch and showed how fields were won.
Pleased with his guests, the good man learned to glow,
And quite forgot their vices in their woe; *160*
Careless their merits or their faults to scan,
His pity gave ere charity began.

Thus to relieve the wretched was his pride,
And e'en his failings leaned to virtue's side;

133 *faggot*: firewood.

But in his duty prompt at every call, *165*
He watched and wept, he prayed and felt for all;
And, as a bird each fond endearment tries
To tempt its new-fledged offspring to the skies,
He tried each art, reproved each dull delay,
Allured to brighter worlds, and led the way. *170*

Beside the bed where parting life was laid,
And sorrow, guilt, and pain by turns dismayed,
The reverend champion stood. At his control
Despair and anguish fled the struggling soul;
Comfort came down the trembling wretch to raise, *175*
And his last faltering accents whispered praise.

At church, with meek and unaffected grace,
His looks adorned the venerable place;
Truth from his lips prevailed with double sway,
And fools who came to scoff remained to pray. *180*
The service past, around the pious man,
With steady zeal, each honest rustic ran;
Even children followed, with endearing wile,
And plucked his gown, to share the good man's smile.
His ready smile a parent's warmth expressed, *185*
Their welfare pleased him and their cares distressed;
To them his heart, his love, his griefs were given,
But all his serious thoughts had rest in Heaven.
As some tall cliff, that lifts its awful form,
Swells from the vale, and midway leaves the storm, *190*
Though round its breast the rolling clouds are spread,
Eternal sunshine settles on its head.

Beside yon straggling fence that skirts the way,
With blossomed furze unprofitably gay,
There, in his noisy mansion, skilled to rule, *195*
The village master taught his little school.
A man severe he was, and stern to view;
I knew him well, and every truant knew;
Well had the boding tremblers learned to trace
The day's disasters in his morning face; *200*
Full well they laughed with counterfeited glee
At all his jokes, for many a joke had he;
Full well the busy whisper, circling round,
Conveyed the dismal tidings when he frowned;

Yet he was kind, or, if severe in aught, *205*
The love he bore to learning was in fault;
The village all declared how much he knew;
'Twas certain he could write, and cipher too;
Lands he could measure, terms and tides presage,
And even the story ran that he could gauge; *210*
In arguing, too, the parson owned his skill,
For even though vanquished, he could argue still;
While words of learned length and thundering sound
Amazed the gazing rustics ranged around;
And still they gazed, and still the wonder grew *215*
That one small head could carry all he knew.

But past is all his fame. The very spot
Where many a time he triumphed is forgot.
Near yonder thorn that lifts its head on high,
Where once the sign-post caught the passing eye, *220*
Low lies that house° where nut-brown draughts inspired,
Where graybeard mirth and smiling toil retired,
Where village statesmen talked with looks profound,
And news much older than their ale went round.
Imagination fondly stoops to trace *225*
The parlor splendors of that festive place;
The whitewashed wall, the nicely sanded floor,
The varnished clock that clicked behind the door;
The chest contrived a double debt to pay,
A bed by night, a chest of drawers by day; *230*
The pictures placed for ornament and use,
The twelve good rules, the royal game of goose;°
The hearth, except when winter chilled the day,
With aspen boughs and flowers and fennel gay;
While broken teacups, wisely kept for show, *235*
Ranged o'er the chimney, glistened in a row.

Vain transitory splendors! Could not all
Reprieve the tottering mansion from its fall?
Obscure it sinks, nor shall it more impart
An hour's importance to the poor man's heart; *240*
Thither no more the peasant shall repair
To sweet oblivion of his daily care;

221 *that house*: a public house or pub. **232** *goose*: a board game.

No more the farmer's news, the barber's tale,
No more the woodman's ballad shall prevail;
No more the smith his dusky brow shall clear, 245
Relax his ponderous strength, and lean to hear;
The host himself no longer shall be found
Careful to see the mantling bliss go round;
Nor the coy maid, half willing to be pressed,
Shall kiss the cup to pass it to the rest. 250

Yes! let the rich deride, the proud disdain,
These simple blessings of the lowly train;
To me more dear, congenial to my heart,
One native charm, than all the gloss of art;
Spontaneous joys, where nature has its play, 255
The soul adopts, and owns their first-born sway;
Lightly they frolic o'er the vacant mind,
Unenvied, unmolested, unconfined.
But the long pomp, the midnight masquerade,
With all the freaks of wanton wealth arrayed,— 260
In these, ere triflers half their wish obtain,
The toiling pleasure sickens into pain;
And e'en while fashion's brightest arts decoy,
The heart distrusting asks if this be joy.

Ye friends to truth, ye statesmen, who survey 265
The rich man's joys increase, the poor's decay,
'Tis yours to judge how wide the limits stand
Between a splendid and an happy land.
Proud swells the tide with loads of freighted ore,
And shouting Folly hails them from her shore; 270
Hoards even beyond the miser's wish abound,
And rich men flock from all the world around.
Yet count our gains: this wealth is but a name
That leaves our useful products still the same.
Not so the loss: the man of wealth and pride 275
Takes up a space that many poor supplied;
Space for his lake, his park's extended bounds,
Space for his horses, equipage, and hounds;
The robe that wraps his limbs in silken sloth
Has robbed the neighboring fields of half their growth; 280
His seat, where solitary sports are seen,

Indignant spurns the cottage from the green;
Around the world each needful product flies,
For all the luxuries the world supplies;
While thus the land, adorned for pleasure all, *285*
In barren splendor feebly waits the fall.

As some fair female, unadorned and plain,
Secure to please while youth confirms her reign,
Slights every borrowed charm that dress supplies,
Nor shares with art the triumph of her eyes; *290*
But when those charms are past, for charms are frail,
When time advances and when lovers fail,
She then shines forth, solicitous to bless,
In all the glaring impotence of dress;
Thus fares the land, by luxury betrayed, *295*
In nature's simplest charms at first arrayed;
But verging to decline, its splendors rise,
Its vistas strike, its palaces surprise;
While, scourged by famine from the smiling land,
The mournful peasant leads his humble band; *300*
And while he sinks, without one arm to save,
The country blooms—a garden and a grave.

Where then, ah! where shall poverty reside,
To 'scape the pressure of contiguous pride?
If to some common's fenceless limits strayed, *305*
He drives his flock to pick the scanty blade,
Those fenceless fields the sons of wealth divide,
And even the bare-worn common is denied.°

If to the city sped—what waits him there?
To see profusion that he must not share; *310*
To see ten thousand baneful arts combined
To pamper luxury, and thin mankind;
To see those joys the sons of pleasure know
Extorted from his fellow-creature's woe.
Here while the courtier glitters in brocade, *315*
There the pale artist plies the sickly trade;
Here while the proud their long-drawn pomps display,
There the black gibbet glooms beside the way;

308 *common is denied*: refers to the private enclosure of what once were common public lands—a movement that impoverished many farmers and shepherds.

The dome where Pleasure holds her midnight reign,
Here, richly decked, admits the gorgeous train; *320*
Tumultuous grandeur crowds the blazing square,
The rattling chariots clash, the torches glare.
Sure scenes like these no troubles e'er annoy!
Sure these denote one universal joy!
Are these thy serious thoughts?—Ah, turn thine eyes *325*
Where the poor houseless shivering female lies.
She once, perhaps, in village plenty blessed,
Has wept at tales of innocence distressed;
Her modest looks the cottage might adorn,
Sweet as the primrose peeps beneath the thorn; *330*
Now lost to all—her friends, her virtue fled—
Near her betrayer's door she lays her head,
And, pinched with cold, and shrinking from the shower,
With heavy heart deplores that luckless hour,
When idly first, ambitious of the town, *335*
She left her wheel and robes of country brown.

Do thine, sweet Auburn, thine, the loveliest train—
Do thy fair tribes participate her pain?
E'en now, perhaps, by cold and hunger led,
At proud men's doors they ask a little bread. *340*

Ah, no! To distant climes, a dreary scene,
Where half the convex world intrudes between,
Through torrid tracts with fainting steps they go,
Where wild Altama° murmurs to their woe.
Far different there from all that charmed before, *345*
The various terrors of that horrid shore;
Those blazing suns that dart a downward ray,
And fiercely shed intolerable day;
Those matted woods where birds forget to sing,
But silent bats in drowsy clusters cling; *350*
Those poisonous fields with rank luxuriance crowned,
Where the dark scorpion gathers death around;
Where at each step the stranger fears to wake
The rattling terrors of the vengeful snake;
Where crouching tigers wait their hapless prey, *355*

344 *Altama*: or Altamaha, a river in Georgia.

And savage men more murderous still than they;
While oft in whirls the mad tornado flies,
Mingling the ravaged landscape with the skies.
Far different these from every former scene,
The cooling brook, the grassy-vested green, *360*
The breezy covert of the warbling grove,
That only sheltered thefts of harmless love.

Good Heaven! what sorrows gloomed that parting day
That called them from their native walks away;
When the poor exiles, every pleasure past, *365*
Hung round their bowers, and fondly looked their last,
And took a long farewell, and wished in vain
For seats like these beyond the western main;
And, shuddering still to face the distant deep,
Returned and wept, and still returned to weep. *370*
The good old sire the first prepared to go
To new-found worlds, and wept for others' woe;
But for himself, in conscious virtue brave,
He only wished for worlds beyond the grave.
His lovely daughter, lovelier in her tears, *375*
The fond companion of his helpless years,
Silent went next, neglected of her charms,
And left a lover's for a father's arms.
With louder plaints the mother spoke her woes,
And blessed the cot where every pleasure rose, *380*
And kissed her thoughtless babes with many a tear,
And clasped them close, in sorrow doubly dear;
Whilst her fond husband strove to lend relief
In all the silent manliness of grief.

O Luxury! thou cursed by Heaven's decree, *385*
How ill exchanged are things like these for thee!
How do thy potions, with insidious joy,
Diffuse their pleasures only to destroy!
Kingdoms by thee, to sickly greatness grown,
Boast of a florid vigor not their own; *390*
At every draught more large and large they grow,
A bloated mass of rank, unwieldly woe;
Till, sapped their strength, and every part unsound,
Down, down they sink, and spread a ruin round.

E'en now the devastation is begun, 395
And half the business of destruction done;
E'en now, methinks, as pondering here I stand,
I see the rural virtues leave the land;
Down where yon anchoring vessel spreads the sail,
That idly waiting flaps with every gale, 400
Downward they move, a melancholy band,
Pass from the shore, and darken all the strand.
Contented Toil, and hospitable Care,
And kind connubial Tenderness are there;
And Piety with wishes placed above, 405
And steady Loyalty, and faithful Love.
And thou, sweet Poetry, thou loveliest maid,
Still first to fly where sensual joys invade,
Unfit, in these degenerate times of shame,
To catch the heart, or strike for honest fame; 410
Dear charming nymph, neglected and decried,
My shame in crowds, my solitary pride;
Thou source of all my bliss and all my woe,
That found'st me poor at first, and keep'st me so;
Thou guide by which the nobler arts excel, 415
Thou nurse of every virtue, fare thee well!
Farewell! and oh! where'er thy voice be tried,
On Torno's cliffs, or Pambamarca's side,
Whether where equinoctial fervors glow,
Or winter wraps the polar world in snow, 420
Still let thy voice, prevailing over time,
Redress the rigors of the inclement clime;
Aid slighted truth with thy persuasive train;
Teach erring man to spurn the rage of gain;
Teach him, that states of native strength possessed, 425
Though very poor, may still be very blessed;
That trade's proud empire hastes to swift decay,
As ocean sweeps the labored mole° away;
While self-dependent power can time defy,
As rocks resist the billows and the sky.° 430

[1770]

428 *mole*: breakwater or storm pier. **426–430** The last four lines are by Dr. Johnson.

__William Blake__ (1757–1827)—a poet, painter, and printer—did not attend school. Born in London, he was apprenticed to an engraver early in life, and earned his living by illustrating books. He attended the Royal Academy for a very short time, then returned to engraving. Blake married Catherine Boucher in 1782, whom he taught to read and write. Although the couple never had a child, their marriage was long and happy. Blake published and illustrated his own poems, working as an engraver and book printer for most of his life. Blake experienced visions from childhood on, and he developed an interest in mysticism through studying Emanuel Swedenborg. Slowly Blake formed the personal mythology that became the foundation for most of his poetry. Blake's Songs of Innocence *(1789),* Songs of Experience *(1794), and* The Marriage of Heaven and Hell *(1790) are his best-known works. He had few admirers in his day. Late in life, however, a number of younger poets, such as Wordsworth and Coleridge, lauded his work.*

William Blake

The Chimney Sweeper*

When my mother died I was very young,
And my father sold me while yet my tongue
Could scarcely cry "'weep! 'weep! 'weep! 'weep!"
So your chimneys I sweep, & in soot I sleep.

There's little Tom Dacre, who cried when his head, *5*
That curl'd like a lamb's back, was shav'd; so I said
"Hush, Tom! never mind it, for when your head's bare
You know that the soot cannot spoil your white hair."

And so he was quiet, & that very night,
As Tom was a-sleeping, he had such a sight! *10*
That thousands of sweepers, Dick, Joe, Ned, & Jack,
Were all of them lock'd up in coffins of black.

And by came an Angel who had a bright key,
And he open'd the coffins & set them all free;
Then down a green plain leaping, laughing, they run, *15*
And wash in a river, and shine in the Sun.

*From *Songs of Innocence*

Then naked & white, all their bags left behind,
They rise upon clouds and sport in the wind;
And the Angel told Tom, if he'd be a good boy,
He'd have God for his father, & never want joy. 20

And so Tom awoke; and we rose in the dark,
And got with our bags & our brushes to work.
Tho' the morning was cold, Tom was happy & warm;
So if all do their duty they need not fear harm.

[1789]

Holy Thursday (I)*

'Twas on a Holy Thursday, their innocent faces clean,
The children walking two & two, in red & blue & green,
Grey-headed beadles walk'd before, with wands as white as snow,
Till into the high dome of Paul's they like Thames' waters flow.

O what a multitude they seem'd, these flowers of London town! 5
Seated in companies they sit with radiance all their own.
The hum of multitudes was there, but multitudes of lambs,
Thousands of little boys & girls raising their innocent hands.

Now like a mighty wind they raise to heaven the voice of song,
Or like harmonious thunderings the seats of Heaven among. 10
Beneath them sit the aged men, wise guardians of the poor;
Then cherish pity, lest you drive an angel from your door.

[1789]

*From *Songs of Innocence*

The Garden of Love

I went to the Garden of Love,
And saw what I never had seen:
A Chapel was built in the midst,
Where I used to play on the green.

And the gates of this Chapel were shut, 5
And "Thou shalt not" writ over the door;

So I turn'd to the Garden of Love
That so many sweet flowers bore;

And I saw it was filled with graves,
And tomb-stones where flowers should be; 10
And Priests in black gowns were walking their rounds,
And binding with briars my joys & desires.

[1794]

London

I wander thro' each charter'd street,
Near where the charter'd Thames does flow,
And mark in every face I meet
Marks of weakness, marks of woe.

In every cry of every Man, 5
In every Infant's cry of fear,
In every voice, in every ban,
The mind-forg'd manacles I hear.

How the Chimney-sweeper's cry
Every black'ning Church appalls; 10
And the hapless Soldier's sigh
Runs in blood down Palace walls.

But most thro' midnight streets I hear
How the youthful Harlot's curse
Blasts the new born Infant's tear, 15
And blights with plagues the Marriage hearse.

[1794]

A Poison Tree

I was angry with my friend;
I told my wrath, my wrath did end.
I was angry with my foe;
I told it not, my wrath did grow.

And I water'd it in fears, 5
Night & morning with my tears;
And I sunned it with smiles,
And with soft deceitful wiles.

And it grew both day and night,
Till it bore an apple bright; 10
And my foe beheld it shine,
And he knew that it was mine,

And into my garden stole
When the night had veil'd the pole;
In the morning glad I see 15
My foe outstretch'd beneath the tree.

[1794]

The Sick Rose

O Rose, thou art sick!
The invisible worm
That flies in the night,
In the howling storm,

Has found out thy bed 5
Of crimson joy,
And his dark secret love
Does thy life destroy.

[1794]

The Tyger

Tyger! Tyger! burning bright
In the forests of the night,
What immortal hand or eye
Could frame thy fearful symmetry?

In what distant deeps or skies   *5*
Burnt the fire of thine eyes?
On what wings dare he aspire?
What the hand dare seize the fire?

And what shoulder, and what art,
Could twist the sinews of thy heart?   *10*
And when thy heart began to beat,
What dread hand? and what dread feet?

What the hammer? what the chain?
In what furnace was thy brain?
What the anvil? what dread grasp   *15*
Dare its deadly terrors clasp?

When the stars threw down their spears,
And watered heaven with their tears,
Did he smile his work to see?
Did he who made the Lamb make thee?   *20*

Tyger! Tyger! burning bright
In the forests of the night,
What immortal hand or eye
Dare frame thy fearful symmetry?

[1794]

Auguries of Innocence

To see a World in a Grain of Sand
And a Heaven in a Wild Flower,
Hold Infinity in the palm of your hand
And Eternity in an hour.

A Robin Red breast in a Cage   *5*
Puts all Heaven in a Rage.
A dove house fill'd with doves & Pigeons
Shudders Hell thro' all its regions.
A dog starv'd at his Master's Gate
Predicts the ruin of the State.   *10*
A Horse misus'd upon the Road
Calls to Heaven for Human blood.
Each outcry of the hunted Hare

A fibre from the Brain does tear.
A Skylark wounded in the wing, 15
A Cherubim does cease to sing.
The Game Cock clip'd & arm'd for fight
Does the Rising Sun affright.
Every Wolf's & Lion's howl
Raises from Hell a Human Soul. 20
The wild deer, wand'ring here & there,
Keeps the Human Soul from Care.
The Lamb misus'd breeds Public strife
And yet forgives the Butcher's Knife.
The Bat that flits at close of Eve 25
Has left the Brain that won't Believe.
The Owl that calls upon the Night
Speaks the Unbeliever's fright.
He who shall hurt the little Wren
Shall never be belov'd by Men. 30
He who the Ox to wrath has mov'd
Shall never be by Woman lov'd.
The wanton Boy that kills the Fly
Shall feel the Spider's enmity.
He who torments the Chafer's sprite 35
Weaves a Bower in endless Night.
The Catterpiller on the Leaf
Repeats to thee thy Mother's grief.
Kill not the Moth nor Butterfly,
For the Last Judgment draweth nigh. 40
He who shall train the Horse to War
Shall never pass the Polar Bar.
The Begger's Dog & Widow's Cat,
Feed them & thou wilt grow fat.
The Gnat that sings his Summer's song 45
Poison gets from Slander's tongue.
The poison gets from Slander's tongue.
The poison of the Snake & Newt
Is the sweat of Envy's Foot.
The Poison of the Honey Bee 50
Is the Artist's Jealousy.
The Prince's Robes & Beggar's Rags
Are Toadstools on the Miser's Bags.
A truth that's told with bad intent

Beats all the Lies you can invent. 55
It is right it should be so;
Man was made for Joy & Woe;
And when this we rightly know
Thro' the World we safely go.
Joy & Woe are woven fine, 60
A Clothing for the Soul divine
Under every grief & pine
Runs a joy with silken twine.
The Babe is more than swadling Bands;
Throughout all these Human Lands 65
Tools were made, & Born were hands,
Every Farmer Understands.
Every Tear from Every Eye
Becomes a Babe in Eternity;
This is caught by Females bright 70
And return'd to its own delight.
The Bleat, the Bark, Bellow & Roar
Are Waves that Beat on Heaven's Shore.
The Babe that weeps the Rod beneath
Writes Revenge in realms of death. 75
The Beggar's Rags, fluttering in Air,
Does to Rags the Heavens tear.
The Soldier, arm'd with Sword & Gun,
Palsied strikes the Summer's Sun.
The poor Man's Farthing is worth more 80
Than all the Gold on Afric's Shore.
One Mite wrung from the Labrer's hands
Shall buy & sell the Miser's Lands;
Or, if protected from on high,
Does that whole Nation sell & buy. 85
He who mocks the Infant's Faith
Shall be mock'd in Age & Death.
He who shall teach the Child to Doubt
The rotting Grave shall ne'er get out.
He who respects the Infant's faith 90
Triumphs over Hell & Death.
The Child's Toys & the Old Man's Reasons
Are the Fruits of the Two seasons.
The Questioner, who sits so sly,
Shall never know how to Reply. 95

He who replies to words of Doubt
Doth put the Light of Knowledge out.
The Strongest Poison ever known
Came from Caesar's Laurel Crown.
Nought can deform the Human Race *100*
Like to the Armour's iron brace.
When Gold & Gems adorn the Plow
To peaceful Arts shall Envy Bow.
A Riddle or the Cricket's Cry
Is to Doubt a fit Reply. *105*
The Emmet's Inch & Eagle's Mile
Make Lame Philosophy to smile.
He who Doubts from what he sees
Will ne'er Believe, do what you Please.
If the Sun & Moon should doubt, *110*
They'd immediately Go out.
To be in a Passion you Good may do,
But no Good if a Passion is in you.
The Whore & Gambler, by the State
Licenc'd, build that Nation's Fate. *115*
The Harlot's cry from Street to Street
Shall weave Old England's winding Sheet.
The Winner's Shout, the Loser's Curse,
Dance before dead England's Hearse.
Every Night & every Morn *120*
Some to Misery are Born.
Every Morn & every Night
Some are Born to sweet delight.
Some are Born to sweet delight,
Some are Born to Endless Night. *125*
We are led to Believe a Lie
When we see not Thro' the Eye
Which was Born in a Night to perish in a Night
When the Soul Slept in Beams of Light.
God Appears & God is Light *130*
To those poor Souls who dwell in Night,
But does a Human Form Display
To those who Dwell in Realms of day.

[1800–1810]

Jerusalem*

And did those feet in ancient time
Walk upon England's mountains green?
And was the holy Lamb of God
On England's pleasant pastures seen?

And did the Countenance Divine 5
Shine forth upon our clouded hills?
And was Jerusalem builded here
Among these dark Satanic Mills?

Bring me my Bow of burning gold;
Bring me my Arrows of desire; 10
Bring me my Spear; O clouds unfold!
Bring me my Chariot of fire.

I will not cease from Mental Fight,
Nor shall my Sword sleep in my hand
Till we have built Jerusalem 15
In England's green & pleasant Land.

[1804–1810]

*From *Milton*

***Robert Burns** (1759–1796) was born in Alloway, Scotland, on a farm along the River Doon. He had only three years of traditional schooling, though as a boy he tirelessly studied the work of Shakespeare and Pope. His father, who could never pull the family out of poverty, died in 1784. Seeking enough money to emigrate to Jamaica, Burns published* Poems, Chiefly in the Scottish Dialect *(1786). The book was such a success that he chose to remain in Scotland. On the strength of his first collection, Burns was asked to help collect traditional songs for* The Scots Musical Museum. *He contributed about 200 songs, some of which he found and some of which he wrote himself. In 1788 he married Jean Armour, with whom he had already had two sets of twins. Burns returned to farming for a few years, but later finding work as a tax official allowed him to enjoy a less exhausting lifestyle. Even so, he died at 37 of rheumatic heart disease.*

Robert Burns

To a Mouse

On turning her up in her nest with the plough,
November, 1785

Wee, sleekit, cow'rin, tim'rous beastie,
O, what a panic's in thy breastie!
Thou need na start awa sae hasty,
Wi' bickering brattle!
I wad be laith to rin an' chase thee, 5
Wi' murd'ring pattle!

I'm truly sorry man's dominion
Has broken Nature's social union,
An' justifies that ill opinion
Which makes thee startle 10
At me, thy poor earth-born companion,
An' fellow-mortal!

I doubt na, whiles, but thou may thieve;
What then? poor beastie, thou maun live!
A daimen icker in a thrave 15
'S a sma' request:
I'll get a blessin wi' the lave,
And never miss't!

Thy wee bit housie, too, in ruin!
Its silly wa's the win's are strewin! 20
An' naething, now, to big a new ane,
O' foggage green!
An' bleak December's winds ensuin,
Baith snell an' keen!

Thou saw the fields laid bare and waste, 25
An' weary winter comin fast,
An' cozie here, beneath the blast,
Thou thought to dwell,
Till crash! the cruel coulter past
Out thro' thy cell. 30

That wee bit heap o' leaves an' stibble
Has cost thee mony a weary nibble!
Now thou's turned out, for a' thy trouble,
    But house or hald,
To thole the winter's sleety dribble, 35
    An' cranreuch cauld!

But, Mousie, thou art no thy lane,
In proving foresight may be vain:
The best laid schemes o' mice an' men
    Gang aft a-gley, 40
An' lea'e us nought but grief an' pain,
    For promised joy.

Still thou art blest, compared wi' me!
The present only toucheth thee:
But och! I backward cast my e'e 45
    On prospects drear!
An' forward, tho' I canna see,
    I guess an' fear!

[1785]

A Red, Red Rose

Oh, my love is like a red, red rose
  That's newly sprung in June;
My love is like the melody
  That's sweetly played in tune.

So fair art thou, my bonny lass, 5
  So deep in love am I;
And I will love thee still, my dear,
  Till a' the seas gang° dry.

Till a' the seas gang dry, my dear,
  And the rocks melt wi' the sun; 10
And I will love thee still, my dear,
  While the sands o' life shall run.

And fare thee weel, my only love!
  And fare thee weel awhile!

8 *gang*: go.

And I will come again, my love *15*
Though it were ten thousand mile.

[c. 1788]

For A' That and A' That

Is there for honest poverty
That hings his head, and a' that?
The coward slave, we pass him by;
We dare be poor for a' that!
For a' that, and a' that, *5*
Our toils obscure, and a' that;
The rank is but the guinea stamp—
The man's the gowd for a' that!

What tho' on hamely fare we dine,
Wear hodden gray, and a' that? *10*
Gie fools their silks, and knaves their wine—
A man's a man for a' that!
For a' that, and a' that,
Their tinsel show, and a' that;
The honest man, though e'er sae poor, *15*
Is king o' men, for a' that!

Ye see yon birkie, ca'd a lord,
Wha struts, an' stares, an' a' that—
Tho' hundreds worship at his word,
He's but a coof for a' that; *20*
For a' that, and a' that,
His riband, star, and a' that;
The man of independent mind,
He looks an' laughs at a' that.

A prince can mak a belted knight, *25*
A marquis, duke, and a' that;
But an honest man's aboon his might—
Gude faith, he mauna fa' that!
For a' that, and a' that,
Their dignities, an' a' that; *30*
The pith o' sense, and pride o' worth,
Are higher rank than a' that.

Then let us pray that come it may—
  As come it will for a' that—
That sense and worth, o'er a' the earth, 35
  May bear the gree, an' a' that.
    For a' that, and a' that,
      It's comin' yet, for a' that—
    That man to man, the warld o'er,
      Shall brithers be for a' that. 40

[1794]

Bonie Doon

Ye flowery banks o' bonie Doon,
  How can ye blume sae fair?
How can ye chant, ye little birds,
  And I sae fu' o' care?

Thou'll break my heart, thou bonie bird, 5
  That sings upon the bough;
Thou minds me o' the happy days,
  When my fause° luve was true.

Thou'll break my heart, thou bonie bird,
  That sings beside thy mate; 10
For sae I sat, and sae I sang,
  And wist° na o' my fate.

Aft hae I roved by bonie Doon
  To see the wood-bine twine,
And ilka° bird sang o' its luve, 15
  And sae did I o' mine.

Wi' lightsome heart I pu'd a rose
  Frae aff its thorny tree;
And my fause luver staw° my rose
  But left the thorn wi' me. 20

8 *fause*: false. 12 *wist*: knew: 15 *ilka*: every. 19 *staw*: stole.

Wi' lightsome heart I pu'd a rose,
Upon a morn in June;
And sae I fourish'd on the morn,
And sae was pu'd or noon!

[1792]

Generally considered the pioneer of the English Romantic tradition, ***William Wordsworth*** *(1770–1850) was born in Cumbria in England's Lake District, the son of an attorney. Both his parents had died by the time he was 13. Wordsworth went on to St. John's College, Cambridge. Passionate about the revolution, he traveled to France, where he fell in love and had a child with Annette Vallon, the daughter of a surgeon. The Reign of Terror prevented their marriage. Returning to England, Wordsworth settled first in Dorset with his sister Dorothy, herself a poet and writer of invaluable journals, and later in Somerset. There Wordsworth collaborated with Samuel Taylor Coleridge on* Lyrical Ballads *(1798). In their memorable descriptions of landscape, Wordsorth's poems cultivated the romantic notion of nature as a spiritual force that shapes human consciousness. In 1799, he and Dorothy moved together to Dove Cottage in Grasmere. They remained companions for the rest of his life. In 1802 Wordsworth married Mary Hutchinson, with whom he had five children. His politics became more conservative as he aged, which earned him criticism from younger poets such as Robert Browning and Percy Bysshe Shelley. Wordsworth was appointed Poet Laureate in 1843. His long autobiographical poem on "the growth of the poet's mind,"* The Prelude, *which was first drafted in 1799, was finally published, after many revisions, posthumously in 1850.*

William Wordsworth

Lines

Composed a few miles above Tintern Abbey, on revisiting the banks of the Wye during a tour. July 13, 1798

Five years have passed; five summers, with the length
Of five long winters! and again I hear
These waters, rolling from their mountain-springs
With a soft inland murmur. Once again
Do I behold these steep and lofty cliffs, *5*
That on a wild secluded scene impress
Thoughts of more deep seclusion; and connect
The landscape with the quiet of the sky.
The day is come when I again repose
Here, under this dark sycamore, and view *10*
These plots of cottage ground, these orchard tufts,
Which at this season, with their unripe fruits,
Are clad in one green hue, and lose themselves
'Mid groves and copses. Once again I see
These hedgerows, hardly hedgerows, little lines *15*
Of sportive wood run wild; these pastoral farms,
Green to the very door; and wreaths of smoke
Sent up, in silence, from among the trees!
With some uncertain notice, as might seem
Of vagrant dwellers in the houseless woods, *20*
Or of some Hermit's cave, where by his fire
The Hermit sits alone.

These beauteous forms,
Through a long absence, have not been to me
As is a landscape to a blind man's eye;
But oft, in lonely rooms, and 'mid the din *25*
Of towns and cities, I have owed to them,
In hours of weariness, sensations sweet,
Felt in the blood, and felt along the heart;
And passing even into my purer mind,
With tranquil restoration—feelings too *30*
Of unremembered pleasure; such, perhaps,
As have no slight or trivial influence
On that best portion of a good man's life,

His little, nameless, unremembered acts
Of kindness and of love. Nor less, I trust, *35*
To them I may have owed another gift,
Of aspect more sublime; that blessed mood,
In which the burthen of the mystery,
In which the heavy and the weary weight
Of all this unintelligible world, *40*
Is lightened—that serene and blessed mood,
In which the affections gently lead us on—
Until, the breath of this corporeal frame
And even the motion of our human blood
Almost suspended, we are laid asleep *45*
In body, and become a living soul;
While with an eye made quiet by the power
Of harmony, and the deep power of joy,
We see into the life of things.

If this
Be but a vain belief, yet, oh! how oft— *50*
In darkness and amid the many shapes
Of joyless daylight; when the fretful stir
Unprofitable, and the fever of the world,
Have hung upon the beatings of my heart—
How oft, in spirit, have I turned to thee, *55*
O sylvan Wye! thou wanderer through the woods,
How often has my spirit turned to thee!

And now, with gleams of half-extinguished thought,
With many recognitions dim and faint,
And somewhat of a sad perplexity, *60*
The picture of the mind revives again;
While here I stand, not only with the sense
Of present pleasure, but with pleasing thoughts
That in this moment there is life and food
For future years. And so I dare to hope, *65*
Though changed, no doubt, from what I was when first
I came among these hills; when like a roe
I bounded o'er the mountains, by the sides
Of the deep rivers, and the lonely streams,
Wherever nature led—more like a man *70*
Flying from something that he dreads than one
Who sought the thing he loved. For nature then
(The coarser pleasures of my boyish days,

And their glad animal movements all gone by)
To me was all in all.—I cannot paint *75*
What then I was. The sounding cataract
Haunted me like a passion; the tall rock,
The mountain, and the deep and gloomy wood,
Their colors and their forms, were then to me
An appetite; a feeling and a love, *80*
That had no need of a remoter charm,
By thought supplied, nor any interest
Unborrowed from the eye.—That time is past,
And all its aching joys are now no more,
And all its dizzy raptures. Not for this *85*
Faint I, nor mourn nor murmur; other gifts
Have followed; for such loss, I would believe,
Abundant recompense. For I have learned
To look on nature, not as in the hour
Of thoughtless youth; but hearing oftentimes *90*
The still, sad music of humanity,
Nor harsh nor grating, though of ample power
To chasten and subdue. And I have felt
A presence that disturbs me with the joy
Of elevated thoughts; a sense sublime *95*
Of something far more deeply interfused,
Whose dwelling is the light of setting suns,
And the round ocean and the living air,
And the blue sky, and in the mind of man;
A motion and a spirit, that impels *100*
All thinking things, all objects of all thought,
And rolls through all things. Therefore am I still
A lover of the meadows and the woods,
And mountains; and of all that we behold
From this green earth; of all the mighty world *105*
Of eye, and ear—both what they half create,
And what perceive; well pleased to recognize
In nature and the language of the sense
The anchor of my purest thoughts, the nurse,
The guide, the guardian of my heart, and soul *110*
Of all my moral being.

Nor perchance,
If I were not thus taught, should I the more
Suffer my genial spirits to decay;

For thou art with me here upon the banks
Of this fair river; thou my dearest Friend,° 115
My dear, dear Friend; and in thy voice I catch
The language of my former heart, and read
My former pleasures in the shooting lights
Of thy wild eyes. Oh! yet a little while
May I behold in thee what I was once, 120
My dear, dear Sister! and this prayer I make,
Knowing that Nature never did betray
The heart that loved her; 'tis her privilege,
Through all the years of this our life, to lead
From joy to joy; for she can so inform 125
The mind that is within us, so impress
With quietness and beauty, and so feed
With lofty thoughts, that neither evil tongues,
Rash judgments, nor the sneers of selfish men,
Nor greetings where no kindness is, nor all 130
The dreary intercourse of daily life,
Shall e'er prevail against us, or disturb
Our cheerful faith, that all which we behold
Is full of blessings. Therefore let the moon
Shine on thee in thy solitary walk; 135
And let the misty mountain winds be free
To blow against thee; and, in after years,
When these wild ecstasies shall be matured
Into a sober pleasure; when thy mind
Shall be a mansion for all lovely forms, 140
Thy memory be as a dwelling place
For all sweet sounds and harmonies; oh! then,
If solitude, or fear, or pain, or grief
Should be thy portion, with what healing thoughts
Of tender joy wilt thou remember me, 145
And these my exhortations! Nor, perchance—
If I should be where I no more can hear
Thy voice, nor catch from thy wild eyes these gleams
Of past existence—wilt thou then forget
That on the banks of this delightful stream 150
We stood together; and that I, so long
A worshiper of Nature, hither came
Unwearied in that service; rather say

115 *dearest Friend*: Dorothy Wordsworth (1771–1855), the poet's sister.

With warmer love—oh! with far deeper zeal
Of holier love. Nor wilt thou then forget *155*
That after many wanderings, many years
Of absence, these steep woods and lofty cliffs,
And this green pastoral landscape, were to me
More dear, both for themselves and for thy sake!

[1798]

She Dwelt Among the Untrodden Ways*

She dwelt among the untrodden ways
 Beside the springs of Dove,
A Maid whom there were none to praise
 And very few to love.

A violet by a mossy stone *5*
 Half hidden from the eye!
—Fair as a star, when only one
 Is shining in the sky.

She lived unknown, and few could know
 When Lucy ceased to be; *10*
But she is in her grave, and, oh,
 The difference to me!

[1800]

*From *The Lucy Poems*

Composed upon Westminster Bridge

September 3, 1802

Earth has not anything to show more fair;
Dull would he be of soul who could pass by
A sight so touching in its majesty;
This City now doth, like a garment, wear

The beauty of the morning; silent, bare, 5
Ships, towers, domes, theatres, and temples lie
Open unto the fields, and to the sky;
All bright and glittering in the smokeless air.
Never did sun more beautifully steep
In his first splendor, valley, rock, or hill; 10
Ne'er saw I, never felt, a calm so deep!
The river glideth at his own sweet will;
Dear God! the very houses seem asleep;
And all that mighty heart is lying still!

[1807]

Ode

Intimations of Immortality from Recollections of Early Childhood

The Child is father of the Man;
And I could wish my days to be
Bound each to each by natural piety.*

I

There was a time when meadow, grove, and stream,
The earth, and every common sight,
To me did seem
Appareled in celestial light,
The glory and the freshness of a dream. 5
It is not now as it hath been of yore—
Turn whereso'er I may,
By night or day,
The things which I have seen I now can see no more.

II

The Rainbow comes and goes, 10
And lovely is the Rose,
The Moon doth with delight
Look round her when the heavens are bare,
Waters on a starry night

***The child . . . by natural piety*: last three lines of Wordsworth's "My Heart Leaps Up" (1807).

Are beautiful and fair; *15*
The sunshine is a glorious birth;
But yet I know, where'er I go,
That there hath passed away a glory from the earth.

III

Now, while the birds thus sing a joyous song,
And while the young lambs bound *20*
As to the tabor's sound,
To me alone there came a thought of grief;
A timely utterance gave that thought relief,
And I again am strong;
The cataracts blow their trumpets from the steep; *25*
No more shall grief of mine the season wrong;
I hear the Echoes through the mountains throng,
The Winds come to me from the fields of sleep,
And all the earth is gay;
Land and sea *30*
Give themselves up to jollity,
And with the heart of May
Doth every Beast keep holiday—
Thou Child of Joy,
Shout round me, let me hear thy shouts, thou happy Shepherd-boy! *35*

IV

Ye blessèd Creatures, I have heard the call
Ye to each other make; I see
The heavens laugh with you in your jubilee;
My heart is at your festival,
My head hath its coronal,° *40*
The fullness of your bliss, I feel—I feel it all.
Oh, evil day! if I were sullen
While Earth herself is adorning,
This sweet May morning,
And the Children are culling *45*
On every side,
In a thousand valleys far and wide,
Fresh flowers; while the sun shines warm,
And the Babe leaps up on his Mother's arm—

40 *coronal*: floral crown.

I hear, I hear, with joy I hear! 50
—But there's a Tree, of many, one,
A single Field which I have looked upon,
Both of them speak of something that is gone;
The Pansy at my feet
Doth the same tale repeat; 55
Whither is fled the visionary gleam?
Where is it now, the glory and the dream?

V

Our birth is but a sleep and a forgetting;
The Soul that rises with us, our life's Star,
Hath had elsewhere its setting, 60
And cometh from afar;
Not in entire forgetfulness,
And not in utter nakedness,
But trailing clouds of glory do we come
From God, who is our home; 65
Heaven lies about us in our infancy!
Shades of the prison-house begin to close
Upon the growing Boy
But he
Beholds the light, and whence it flows, 70
He sees it in his joy;
The Youth, who daily farther from the east
Must travel, still is Nature's Priest,
And by the vision splendid
Is on his way attended; 75
At length the Man perceives it die away,
And fade into the light of common day.

VI

Earth fills her lap with pleasures of her own;
Yearnings she hath in her own natural kind,
And, even with something of a Mother's mind, 80
And no unworthy aim,
The homely Nurse doth all she can
To make her foster child, her Inmate Man,
Forget the glories he hath known,
And that imperial palace whence he came. 85

VII

Behold the Child among his newborn blisses,
A six-years' Darling of a pygmy size!
See, where 'mid work of his own hand he lies,
Fretted by sallies of his mother's kisses,
With light upon him from his father's eyes! 90
See, at his feet, some little plan or chart,
Some fragment from his dream of human life,
Shaped by himself with newly-learnèd art;
A wedding or a festival,
A mourning or a funeral; 95
And this hath now his heart,
And unto this he frames his song;
Then will he fit his tongue
To dialogues of business, love, or strife;
But it will not be long 100
Ere this be thrown aside,
And with new joy and pride
The little Actor cons another part;
Filling from time to time his "humorous stage"°
With all the Persons, down to palsied Age, 105
That Life brings with her in her equipage;
As if his whole vocation
Were endless imitation.

VIII

Thou, whose exterior semblance doth belie
Thy Soul's immensity; 110
Thou best Philosopher, who yet dost keep
Thy heritage, thou Eye among the blind,
That, deaf and silent, read'st the eternal deep,
Haunted forever by the eternal mind—
Mighty Prophet! Seer blest! 115
On whom those truths do rest,
Which we are toiling all our lives to find,
In darkness lost, the darkness of the grave;
Thou, over whom thy Immortality
Broods like the Day, a Master o'er a Slave, 120

104 *"humorous stage"*: phrase by Samuel Daniel (1563–1619) in a sonnet to Fulke Greville.

A Presence which is not to be put by;
Thou little Child, yet glorious in the might
Of heaven-born freedom on thy being's height,
Why with such earnest pains dost thou provoke
The years to bring the inevitable yoke, *125*
Thus blindly with thy blessedness at strife?
Full soon thy Soul shall have her earthly freight,
And custom lie upon thee with a weight,
Heavy as frost, and deep almost as life!

IX

O joy! that in our embers *130*
Is something that doth live,
That nature yet remembers
What was so fugitive!
The thought of our past years in me doth breed
Perpetual benediction; not indeed *135*
For that which is most worthy to be blest;
Delight and liberty, the simple creed
Of Childhood, whether busy or at rest,
With new-fledged hope still fluttering in his breast—
Not for these I raise *140*
The song of thanks and praise;
But for those obstinate questionings
Of sense and outward things,
Fallings from us, vanishings;
Blank misgivings of a Creature *145*
Moving about in worlds not realized,
High instincts before which our mortal Nature
Did tremble like a guilty Thing surprised;
But for those first affections,
Those shadowy recollections, *150*
Which, be they what they may,
Are yet the fountain light of all our day,
Are yet a master light of all our seeing;
Uphold us, cherish, and have power to make
Our noisy years seem moments in the being *155*
Of the eternal Silence: truths that wake,
To perish never;
Which neither listlessness, nor mad endeavor,
Nor Man nor Boy,

Nor all that is at enmity with joy, 160
Can utterly abolish or destroy!
Hence in a season of calm weather
Though inland far we be,
Our Souls have sight of that immortal sea
Which brought us hither, 165
Can in a moment travel thither,
And see the Children sport upon the shore,
And hear the mighty waters rolling evermore.

X

Then sing, ye Birds, sing, sing a joyous song!
And let the young Lambs bound 170
As to the tabor's sound!
We in thought will join your throng,
Ye that pipe and ye that play,
Ye that through your hearts today
Feel the gladness of the May! 175
What though the radiance which was once so bright
Be now forever taken from my sight,
Though nothing can bring back the hour
Of splendor in the grass, of glory in the flower;
We will grieve not, rather find 180
Strength in what remains behind;
In the primal sympathy
Which having been must ever be;
In the soothing thoughts that spring
Out of human suffering; 185
In the faith that looks through death,
In years that bring the philosophic mind.

XI

And O, ye Fountains, Meadows, Hills, and Groves,
Forebode not any severing of our loves!
Yet in my heart of hearts I feel your might; 190
I only have relinquished one delight
To live beneath your more habitual sway.
I love the Brooks which down their channels fret,
Even more than when I tripped lightly as they;
The innocent brightness of a newborn Day 195
Is lovely yet;

The clouds that gather round the setting sun
Do take a sober coloring from an eye
That hath kept watch o'er man's mortality;
Another race hath been, and other palms are won. *200*
Thanks to the human heart by which we live,
Thanks to its tenderness, its joys, and fears,
To me the meanest flower that blows can give
Thoughts that do often lie too deep for tears.

[1807]

The Solitary Reaper

Behold her, single in the field,
Yon solitary Highland Lass!
Reaping and singing by herself;
Stop here, or gently pass!
Alone she cuts and binds the grain, *5*
And sings a melancholy strain;
O listen! for the Vale profound
Is overflowing with the sound.

No Nightingale did ever chaunt
More welcome notes to weary bands *10*
Of travellers in some shady haunt,
Among Arabian sands;
A voice so thrilling ne'er was heard
In spring-time from the Cuckoo-bird,
Breaking the silence of the seas *15*
Among the farthest Hebrides.

Will no one tell me what she sings?—
Perhaps the plaintive numbers flow
For old, unhappy, far-off things,
And battles long ago; *20*
Or is it some more humble lay,
Familiar matter of to-day?
Some natural sorrow, loss, or pain,
That has been, and may be again?

Whate'er the theme, the Maiden sang *25*
As if her song could have no ending;
I saw her singing at her work,
And o'er the sickle bending—
I listened, motionless and still;
And, as I mounted up the hill, *30*
The music in my heart I bore,
Long after it was heard no more.

[1807]

I Wandered Lonely as a Cloud

I wandered lonely as a cloud
That floats on high o'er vales and hills,
When all at once I saw a crowd,
A host, of golden daffodils,
Beside the lake, beneath the trees, *5*
Fluttering and dancing in the breeze.

Continuous as the stars that shine
And twinkle on the milky way,
They stretched in never-ending line
Along the margin of a bay; *10*
Ten thousand saw I at a glance,
Tossing their heads in sprightly dance.

The waves beside them danced; but they
Out-did the sparkling waves in glee;
A poet could not but be gay, *15*
In such a jocund company;
I gazed—and gazed—but little thought
What wealth the show to me had brought;

For oft, when on my couch I lie
In vacant or in pensive mood, *20*
They flash upon that inward eye
Which is the bliss of solitude;

And then my heart with pleasure fills,
And dances with the daffodils.

[1807]

The World Is Too Much with Us

The world is too much with us; late and soon,
Getting and spending, we lay waste our powers;
Little we see in Nature that is ours;
We have given our hearts away, a sordid boon!
This Sea that bares her bosom to the moon; *5*
The winds that will be howling at all hours,
And are up-gathered now like sleeping flowers;
For this, for everything, we are out of tune;
It moves us not. Great God! I'd rather be
A Pagan suckled in a creed outworn; *10*
So might I, standing on this pleasant lea,
Have glimpses that would make me less forlorn;
Have sight of Proteus rising from the sea;
Or hear old Triton blow his wreathèd horn.

[1807]

Surprised by Joy—Impatient as the Wind

Surprised by joy—impatient as the Wind
I turned to share the transport—Oh! with whom
But Thee, deep buried in the silent tomb,
That spot which no vicissitude can find?
Love, faithful love, recalled thee to my mind— *5*
But how could I forget thee? Through what power,
Even for the least division of an hour,

Have I been so beguiled as to be blind
To my most grievous loss!—That thought's return
Was the worst pang that sorrow ever bore, *10*
Save one, one only, when I stood forlorn,
Knowing my heart's best treasure was no more;
That neither present time, or years unborn
Could to my sight that heavenly face restore.

[1815]

***Samuel Taylor Coleridge** (1772–1834) was born the thirteenth child of a clergyman in Devonshire, England. He studied classics at Jesus College, Cambridge. His taste for radical French politics and heavy drinking led him to drop out. He joined the army, yet his brother soon bought him out under an "insanity" clause. Coleridge had befriended Robert Southey while at Cambridge and with him planned a utopian settlement in the United States, which never materialized. The two young men courted and married a pair of sisters, Sara and Edith Fricker. Coleridge later collaborated with William Wordsworth on* Lyrical Ballads *(1798), which included his visionary narrative, "Rime of the Ancient Mariner." Coleridge also wrote enormous amounts of critical prose, including discourses on philosophy, politics, religion, and literature. Coleridge's marriage began to fall apart, as did his health. He fell in love with Sara Hutchinson, Wordsworth's future sister-in-law, and finally separated from his wife in 1807. He became addicted to opium ("Kubla Khan" was the result of an opium-induced dream), and spent his last 18 years under the care of Dr. James Gilman. Books such as* Christabel and Other Poems *(1816) earned him an immense following late in life.*

Samuel Taylor Coleridge

Frost at Midnight

The frost performs its secret ministry,
Unhelped by any wind. The owlet's cry
Came loud—and hark, again! loud as before.
The inmates of my cottage, all at rest,
Have left me to that solitude, which suits *5*

Abstruser musings, save that at my side
My cradled infant slumbers peacefully.
'Tis calm indeed! so calm, that it disturbs
And vexes meditation with its strange
And extreme silentness. Sea, hill, and wood, 10
This populous village! Sea, and hill, and wood,
With all the numberless goings-on of life,
Inaudible as dreams! the thin blue flame
Lies on my low-burnt fire, and quivers not;
Only that film,° which fluttered on the grate, 15
Still flutters there, the sole unquiet thing.
Methinks, its motion in this hush of nature
Gives it dim sympathies with me who live,
Making it a companionable form,
Whose puny flaps and freaks the idling Spirit 20
By its own moods interprets, every where
Echo or mirror seeking of itself,
And makes a toy of Thought.

But O! how oft,
How oft, at school, with most believing mind, 25
Presageful, have I gazed upon the bars,
To watch that fluttering *stranger!* and as oft
With unclosed lids, already had I dreamt
Of my sweet birth-place, and the old church-tower,
Whose bells, the poor man's only music, rang 30
From morn to evening, all the hot Fair-day,
So sweetly, that they stirred and haunted me
With a wild pleasure, falling on mine ear
Most like articulate sounds of things to come!
So gazed I, till the soothing things, I dreamt, 35
Lulled me to sleep, and sleep prolonged my dreams!
And so I brooded all the following morn,
Awed by the stern preceptor's° face, mine eye
Fixed with mock study on my swimming book;
Save if the door half opened, and I snatched 40
A hasty glance, and still my heart leaped up,
For still I hoped to see the *stranger's* face,
Townsman, or aunt, or sister more beloved,
My play-mate when we both were clothed alike!

15 *film*: a piece or ash; "In all parts of the kingdom these films are called 'strangers,' and supposed to portend the arrival of some absent friend" (Coleridge's note). **38** *preceptor*: teacher.

Dear Babe, that sleepest cradled by my side, 45
Whose gentle breathings, heard in this deep calm,
Fill up the interspersèd vacancies
And momentary pauses of the thought!
My babe so beautiful! it thrills my heart
With tender gladness, thus to look at thee, 50
And think that thou shalt learn far other lore,
And in far other scenes! For I was reared
In the great city, pent 'mid cloisters dim,
And saw nought lovely but the sky and stars.
But *thou*, my babe! shalt wander like a breeze 55
By lakes and sandy shores, beneath the crags
Of ancient mountain, and beneath the clouds,
Which image in their bulk both lakes and shores
And mountain crags; so shalt thou see and hear
The lovely shapes and sounds intelligible 60
Of that eternal language, which thy God
Utters, who from eternity doth teach
Himself in all, and all things in himself.
Great universal Teacher! he shall mould
Thy spirit, and by giving make it ask. 65

Therefore all seasons shall be sweet to thee,
Whether the summer clothe the general earth
With greenness, or the redbreast sit and sing
Betwixt the tufts of snow on the bare branch
Of mossy apple-tree, while the nigh thatch 70
Smokes in the sun-thaw; whether the eave-drops fall
Heard only in the trances of the blast,
Or if the secret ministry of frost
Shall hang them up in silent icicles,
Quietly shining to the quiet Moon. 75

[1798]

Kubla Khan

Or, a Vision in a Dream. A Fragment.

In Xanadu did Kubla Khan
A stately pleasure-dome decree;
Where Alph, the sacred river, ran

Through caverns measureless to man
    Down to a sunless sea. 5
So twice five miles of fertile ground
With walls and towers were girdled round;
And there were gardens bright with sinuous rills,
Where blossomed many an incense-bearing tree;
And here were forests ancient as the hills, 10
Enfolding sunny spots of greenery.

But oh! that deep romantic chasm which slanted
Down the green hill athwart a cedarn cover!
A savage place! as holy and enchanted
As e'er beneath a waning moon was haunted 15
By woman wailing for her demon-lover!
And from this chasm, with ceaseless turmoil seething,
As if this earth in fast thick pants were breathing,
A mighty fountain momently was forced;
Amid whose swift half-intermitted burst 20
Huge fragments vaulted like rebounding hail,
Or chaffy grain beneath the thresher's flail;
And 'mid these dancing rocks at once and ever
It flung up momently the sacred river.
Five miles meandering with a mazy motion 25
Through wood and dale the sacred river ran,
Then reached the caverns measureless to man,
And sank in tumult to a lifeless ocean;
And 'mid this tumult Kubla heard from far
Ancestral voices prophesying war! 30
    The shadow of the dome of pleasure
    Floated midway on the waves;
    Where was heard the mingled measure
    From the fountain and the caves.
It was a miracle of rare device, 35
A sunny pleasure-dome with caves of ice!

    A damsel with a dulcimer
    In a vision once I saw;
    It was an Abyssinian maid,
    And on her dulcimer she played, 40
    Singing of Mount Abora.
    Could I revive within me
    Her symphony and song,
    To such a deep delight 'twould win me,

That with music loud and long, 45
I would build that dome in air,
That sunny dome! those caves of ice!
And all who heard should see them there,
And all should cry, Beware! Beware!
His flashing eyes, his floating hair! 50
Weave a circle° round him thrice,
And close your eyes with holy dread,
For he on honey-dew hath fed,
And drunk the milk of Paradise.

[1797–98]

51 *circle*: magic spell intended to ward off evil spirits.

Captain John Byron, father of **George Gordon** *(1788–1824), married the rich Catherine Gordon, bankrupted her, and disappeared to France. Born in London, the poet spent the first decade of his life with his mother in poverty and uncertainty, which dramatically changed when at 10 he inherited a valuable estate and the title of baron. Born lame with a clubfoot, Byron compensated for his disability by displaying reckless courage, physical stamina, and sexual bravado. He attended Harrow and Trinity College, Cambridge, and traveled through southern Europe during his early twenties, returning to England to publish a thinly disguised autobiographical and quite melancholic work,* Childe Harold's Pilgrimage *(1812–1818), which made him famous at 24. Byron's father had a daughter from a previous marriage, Augusta. He and his half-sister reportedly had a sexual relationship that resulted in a child. Attempting to dodge the public outrage at rumors of incest, Byron hastily married Annabella Milbanke, though the turbulent relationship didn't last long. He fled England, lived for a time with Percy Shelley, and engaged in numerous heated love affairs. Byron produced his greatest work, the epic satire* Don Juan *(1819–1824), during these years of wandering. Increasingly interested in the conflict between the Greeks and the Turks, Byron sailed for Greece in 1823. Before he saw any action, however, he died of fever at age 36. At the time of his death, he was probably the most famous poet in Europe.*

George Gordon, Lord Byron

When We Two Parted

When we two parted
    In silence and tears,
Half broken-hearted
    To sever for years,
Pale grew thy cheek and cold, *5*
    Colder thy kiss;
Truly that hour foretold
    Sorrow to this.

The dew of the morning
    Sunk chill on my brow— *10*
It felt like the warning
    Of what I feel now.
Thy vows are all broken,
    And light is thy fame;
I hear thy name spoken, *15*
    And share in its shame.

They name thee before me,
    A knell to mine ear;
A shudder comes o'er me—
    Why wert thou so dear? *20*
They know not I knew thee,
    Who knew thee too well—
Long, long shall I rue thee,
    Too deeply to tell.

In secret we met— *25*
    In silence I grieve,
That thy heart could forget,
    Thy spirit deceive.
If I should meet thee
    After long years, *30*
How should I greet thee?
    With silence and tears.

[1807?]

The Ocean*

There is a pleasure in the pathless woods,
There is a rapture on the lonely shore,
There is society where none intrudes
By the deep sea, and music in its roar;
I love not man the less, but nature more, 5
From these our interviews, in which I steal
From all I may be, or have been before,
To mingle with the universe, and feel
What I can ne'er express, yet cannot all conceal.

Roll on, thou deep and dark blue Ocean—roll! 10
Ten thousand fleets sweep over thee in vain;
Man marks the earthwith ruin—his control
Stops with the shore—upon the watery plain
The wrecks are all thy deed, nor doth remain
A shadow of man's ravage, save his own, 15
When, for a moment, like a drop of rain,
He sinks into thy depths with bubbling groan,
Without a grave, unknelled, uncoffined, and unknown.

His steps are not upon thy paths—thy fields
Are not a spoil for him—thou dost arise 20
And shake him from thee; the vile strength he wields
For earth's destruction thou dost all despise,
Spurning him from thy bosom to the skies,
And send'st him, shivering in thy playful spray
And howling, to his gods, where haply lies 25
His petty hope in some near port or bay,
And dashest him again to earth—there let him lay.

The armaments which thunderstrike the walls
Of rock-built cities, bidding nations quake
And monarchs tremble in their capitals, 30
The oak leviathans, whose huge ribs make
Their clay creator the vain title take
Of lord of thee and arbiter of war—
These are thy toys, and, as the snowy flake,
They melt into thy yeast of waves, which mar 35
Alike the Armada's pride or spoils of Trafalgar.

*From *Childe Harold's Pilgrimage*, Canto IV.

Thy shores are empires, changed in all save thee;
Assyria, Greece, Rome, Carthage, what are they?
Thy waters wasted them while they were free,
And many a tyrant since; their shores obey 40
The stranger, slave, or savage; their decay
Has dried up realms to deserts; not so thou;
Unchangeable save to thy wild waves' play,
Time writes no wrinkles on thine azure brow;
Such as creation's dawn beheld, thou rollest now. 45

Thou glorious mirror, where the Almighty's form
Glasses itself in tempests; in all time,
Calm or convulsed—in breeze, or gale, or storm,
Icing the pole, or in the torrid clime
Dark-heaving; boundless, endless, and sublime, 50
The image of Eternity—the throne
Of the Invisible! even from out thy slime
The monsters of the deep are made; each zone
Obeys thee; thou goest forth, dread, fathomless, alone.

And I have loved thee, Ocean! and my joy 55
Of youthful sports was on thy breast to be
Borne, like thy bubbles, onward; from a boy
I wantoned with thy breakers—they to me
Were a delight; and if the freshening sea
Made them a terror, 't was a pleasing fear; 60
For I was as it were a child of thee,
And trusted to thy billows far and near,
And laid my land upon thy mane—as I do here.

[1809–1817]

The Destruction of Sennacherib*

The Assyrian came down like the wolf on the fold,
And his cohorts were gleaming in purple and gold;
And the sheen of their spears was like stars on the sea,
When the blue wave rolls nightly on deep Galilee.

*Sennecherib was an Assyrian king who conquered Babylon and was murdered by two of his jealous sons.

Like the leaves of the forest when summer is green, *5*
That host with their banners at sunset were seen;
Like the leaves of the forest when autumn hath blown,
That host on the morrow lay wither'd and strown.

For the Angel of Death spread his wings on the blast,
And breathed in the face of the foe as he pass'd; *10*
And the eyes of the sleepers wax'd deadly and chill,
And their hearts but once heaved, and forever grew still!

And there lay the steed with his nostril all wide,
But through it there roll'd not the breath of his pride;
And the foam of his gasping lay white on the turf, *15*
And cold as the spray of the rock-beating surf.

And there lay the rider distorted and pale,
With the dew on his brow, and the rust on his mail;
And the tents were all silent, the banners alone,
The lances unlifted, the trumpet unblown. *20*

And the widows of Ashur are loud in their wail,
And the idols are broke in the temple of Baal;
And the might of the Gentile, unsmote by the sword,
Hath melted like snow in the glance of the Lord!

[1815]

She Walks in Beauty

I

She walks in beauty, like the night
    Of cloudless climes and starry skies;
And all that's best of dark and bright
    Meet in her aspect and her eyes;
Thus mellowed to that tender light *5*
    Which heaven to gaudy day denies.

II

One shade the more, one ray the less,
    Had half impaired the nameless grace
Which waves in every raven tress,
    Or softly lightens o'er her face; *10*

Where thoughts serenely sweet express,
How pure, how dear their dwelling-place.

III

And on that cheek, and o'er that brow,
So soft, so calm, yet eloquent,
The smiles that win, the tints that glow, *15*
But tell of days in goodness spent,
A mind at peace with all below,
A heart whose love is innocent!

[1815]

So, We'll Go No More A-Roving

I

So, we'll go no more a-roving
So late into the night,
Though the heart be still as loving,
And the moon be still as bright.

II

For the sword outwears its sheath, *5*
And the soul wears out the breast,
And the heart must pause to breathe,
And love itself have rest.

III

Though the night was made for loving,
And the day returns too soon, *10*
Yet we'll go no more a-roving
By the light of the moon.

[1836]

***Percy Bysshe Shelley** (1792–1822) was born in Sussex, England, the eldest child to a wealthy family that expected him to pursue a parliamentary career. Instead, Shelley's strict and conventional upbringing caused him to rebel. He was expelled from Oxford in 1811 for coauthoring a pamphlet in defense of atheism. That same year, Shelley eloped to Scotland with the 16-year-old Harriet Westbrook. The marriage soon fell apart, and he disappeared to France with Mary Wollstonecraft (later famous as the author of* Frankenstein*) and her 15-year-old stepsister. When Shelley's estranged wife Harriet drowned herself in the Serpentine, he quickly married Wollstonecraft. His domestic life was never easy, as he endured the deaths of many of his children, a nervous breakdown by his wife Mary, and frequent financial troubles. At the news of his friend John Keats's death, Shelley wrote* Adonais *(1821). Shelley drowned in the Gulf of Spezia during a summer storm whille sailing back from visiting his friend Lord Byron. He was not quite 30 years old.*

Percy Bysshe Shelley
Ozymandias*

I met a traveler from an antique land
Who said: Two vast and trunkless legs of stone
Stand in the desert. Near them, on the sand,
Half sunk, a shattered visage lies, whose frown,
And wrinkled lip, and sneer of cold command, 5
Tell that its sculptor well those passions read
Which yet survive, stamped on these lifeless things,
The hand that mocked them and the heart that fed;
And on the pedestal these words appear:
"My name is Ozymandias, king of kings: 10
Look on my works, ye Mighty, and despair!"
Nothing beside remains. Round the decay
Of that colossal wreck, boundless and bare
The lone and level sands stretch far away.

[1818]

**Ozymandias*: Ramses II of Egypt (c. 1250 B.C.).

Ode to the West Wind

I

O Wild West Wind, thou breath of Autumn's being,
Thou, from whose unseen presence the leaves dead
Are driven, like ghosts from an enchanter fleeing,

Yellow, and black, and pale, and hectic red,
Pestilence-stricken multitudes; O thou, 5
Who chariotest to their dark wintry bed

The wingèd seeds, where they lie cold and low,
Each like a corpse within its grave, until
Thine azure sister of the Spring° shall blow

Her clarion o'er the dreaming earth, and fill 10
(Driving sweet buds like flocks to feed in air)
With living hues and odours plain and hill;

Wild Spirit, which art moving everywhere;
Destroyer and preserver; hear, oh, hear!

II

Thou on whose stream, 'mid the steep sky's commotion, 15
Loose clouds like earth's decaying leaves are shed,
Shook from the tangled boughs of Heaven and Ocean,

Angels of rain and lightning; there are spread
On the blue surface of thine aery surge,
Like the bright hair uplifted from the head 20

Of some fierce Mænad,° even from the dim verge
Of the horizon to the zenith's height,
The locks of the approaching storm. Thou dirge

Of the dying year, to which this closing night
Will be the dome of a vast sepulchre, 25
Vaulted with all thy congregated might

Of vapours, from whose solid atmosphere
Black rain, and fire, and hail will burst; oh, hear!

9 *azure sister of the Spring*: the South Wind. **21** *Mænad*: female worshipper of Dionysus, the god of wine and vegetation.

III

Thou who didst waken from his summer dreams
The blue Mediterranean, where he lay, *30*
Lulled by the coil of his crystalline streams,

Beside a pumice isle is Baiae's bay,°
And saw in sleep old palaces and towers
Quivering within the wave's intenser day,

All overgrown with azure moss and flowers *35*
So sweet, the sense faints picturing them! Thou
For whose path the Atlantic's level powers

Cleave themselves into chasms, while far below
The sea-blooms and the oozy woods which wear
The sapless foliage of the ocean, know *40*

Thy voice, and suddenly grow gray with fear,
And tremble and despoil themselves; oh, hear!

IV

If I were a dead leaf thou mightest bear;
If I were a swift cloud to fly with thee;
A wave to pant beneath thy power, and share *45*

The impulse of thy strength, only less free
Than thou, O uncontrollable! If even
I were as in my boyhood, and could be

The comrade of thy wanderings over Heaven,
As then, when to outstrip thy skiey speed *50*
Scarce seemed a vision; I would ne'er have striven

As thus with thee in prayer in my sore need.
Oh, lift me as a wave, a leaf, a cloud!
I fall upon the thorns of life! I bleed!

A heavy weight of hours has chained and bowed *55*
One too like thee: tameless, and swift, and proud.

V

Make me thy lyre, even as the forest is;
What if my leaves are falling like its own!
The tumult of thy mighty harmonies

32 *Baiae's bay*: a bay west of Naples surrounded by villas of Roman emperors.

Will take from both a deep, autumnal tone, *60*
Sweet though in sadness. Be thou, Spirit fierce,
My spirit! Be thou me, impetuous one!

Drive my dead thoughts over the universe
Like withered leaves to quicken a new birth!
And, by the incantation of this verse, *65*

Scatter, as from an unextinguished hearth
Ashes and sparks, my words among mankind!
Be through my lips to unawakened earth

The trumpet of a prophecy! O, Wind,
If Winter comes, can Spring be far behind? *70*

[1820]

To—

Music, when soft voices die,
Vibrates in the memory—
Odours, when sweet violets sicken,
Live within the sense they quicken.

Rose leaves, when the rose is dead, *5*
Are heaped for the beloved's bed;
And so thy thoughts, when thou art gone,
Love itself shall slumber on.

[1824]

England in 1819

An old, mad, blind, despised, and dying king°—
Princes, the dregs of their dull race, who flow
Through public scorn—mud from a muddy spring—
Rulers who neither see, nor feel, nor know,
But leech-like to their fainting country cling, *5*
Till they drop, blind in blood, without a blow—

1 *king*: George III, who was declared insane in 1811.

A peopled starve and stabbed in the untilled field—
An army, which liberticide and prey
Makes as a two-edged sword to all who wield—
Golden and sanguine laws which tempt and slay; *10*
Religion Christless, Godless—a book sealed;
A Senate—Time's worst statute unrepealed—
Are graves, from which a glorious Phantom may
Burst, to illumine our tempestuous day.

[1839]

John Keats *(1795–1821) was born in London, the son of a stable keeper. His father died when Keats was eight years old, and his mother when he was 14. The oldest in his family, Keats remained close to his two brothers and sister while studying medicine and working as a surgeon's apprentice. After earning his apothecary's license, however, Keats decided to quit medicine for literature. He published his first collection,* Poems, *in 1817. In 1818 Keats fell in love with 16-year-old Fanny Brawne, but his battle with tuberculosis prevented their marriage. He traveled to Italy in 1820, hoping to improve his health, but died a year later in Rome at age 25. Despite his short life and only three volumes of poetry, Keats produced enduring verse, including the narrative* Endymion *(1818), "Ode on a Grecian Urn," "Ode to a Nightingale," and his unfinished epic* Hyperion.

John Keats

On First Looking into Chapman's Homer*

Much have I traveled in the realms of gold,
    And many goodly states and kingdoms seen;
    Round many western islands have I been
Which bards in fealty° to Apollo° hold.

**Chapman's Homer* is the translation of the *Iliad* and the *Odyssey* by George Chapman (1599–1634).

4 *fealty*: the loyalty of a vassal to his lord; *Apollo*: god of Greek poetic inspiration.

Oft of one wide expanse had I been told   5
  That deep-browed Homer ruled as his demesne,°
  Yet did I never breathe its pure serene
Till I heard Chapman speak out loud and bold.
Then felt I like some watcher of the skies
  When a new planet swims into his ken;   10
Or like stout Cortez° when with eagle eyes
  He stared at the Pacific—and all his men
Looked at each other with a wild surmise—
  Silent, upon a peak in Darien.°

[1816]

6 *demesne*: domain. **11** *stout Cortez*: a famous mistake. **14** *Darien*: former name for the Isthmus of Panama.

When I Have Fears That I May Cease to Be

When I have fears that I may cease to be
  Before my pen has gleaned my teeming brain,
Before high-pilèd books, in charact'ry,°
  Hold like rich garners° the full-ripened grain;
When I behold, upon the night's starred face,   5
  Huge cloudy symbols of a high romance,
And think that I may never live to trace
  Their shadows with the magic hand of chance;
And when I feel, fair creature of an hour,
  That I shall never look upon thee more,   10
Never have relish in the fairy° power
  Of unreflecting° love—then on the shore
Of the wide world I stand alone, and think
  Till love and fame to nothingness do sink.

[1818; 1848]

3 *charac'try*: written language. **4** *garners*: storehouses. **11** *fairy*: supernatural. **12** *unreflecting*: thoughtless and spontaneous.

Bright Star! Would I Were Steadfast as Thou Art

Bright star! would I were steadfast as thou art—
Not in lone splendor hung aloft the night,
And watching, with eternal lids apart,
Like nature's patient, sleepless Eremite°
The moving waters at their priest-like task *5*
Of pure ablution round earth's human shores,
Or gazing on the new soft-fallen mask
Of snow upon the mountains and the moors—
No—yet still steadfast, still unchangeable,
Pillowed upon my fair love's ripening breast, *10*
To feel for ever its soft fall and swell,
Awake for ever in a sweet unrest,
Still, still to hear her tender-taken breath,
And so live ever—or else swoon to death.

[1819]

4 *Eremite*: hermit.

La Belle Dame sans Merci: A Ballad*

I

O what can ail thee, knight at arms,
Alone and palely loitering?
The sedge has wither'd from the lake,
And no birds sing.

II

O what can ail thee, knight at arms, *5*
So haggard and so woe-begone?

**La Belle Dame sans Merci* is French for "the beautiful woman without mercy." Keats borrowed the title from a fifteenth-century French poem.

The squirrel's granary is full,
        And the harvest's done.

III

I see a lily on thy brow
    With anguish moist and fever dew, 10
And on thy cheeks a fading rose
        Fast withereth too.

IV

I met a lady in the meads,
    Full beautiful, a fairy's child;
Her hair was long, her foot was light, 15
        And her eyes were wild.

V

I made a garland for her head,
    And bracelets too, and fragrant zone;
She look'd at me as she did love,
        And made sweet moan. 20

VI

I set her on my pacing steed,
    And nothing else saw all day long,
For sidelong would she bend, and sing
        A fairy's song.

VII

She found me roots of relish sweet, 25
    And honey wild, and manna dew,
And sure in language strange she said—
        I love thee true.

VIII

She took me to her elfin grot,
    And there she wept, and sigh'd full sore, 30
And there I shut her wild wild eyes
        With kisses four.

IX

And there she lulled me asleep,
  And there I dream'd—Ah! woe betide!
The latest dream I ever dream'd *35*
    On the cold hill's side.

X

I saw pale kings, and princes too,
  Pale warriors, death pale were they all;
They cried—"La belle dame sans merci
    Hath thee in thrall!" *40*

XI

I saw their starv'd lips in the gloam
  With horrid warning gaped wide,
And I awoke and found me here
    On the cold hill's side.

XII

And this is why I sojourn here, *45*
  Alone and palely loitering,
Though the sedge is wither'd from the lake,
    And no birds sing.

[1819; 1848]

Ode on a Grecian Urn

Thou still unravished bride of quietness,
  Thou foster-child of silence and slow time,
Sylvan historian, who canst thus express
  A flowery tale more sweetly than our rhyme:
What leaf-fringed legend haunts about thy shape *5*
  Of deities or mortals, or of both,
    In Tempe or the dales of Arcady?°
  What men or gods are these? What maidens loth?

7 *Tempe . . . Arcady*: pastoral valleys in Greece.

What mad pursuit? What struggle to escape?
What pipes and timbrels? What wild ecstasy? 10

Heard melodies are sweet, but those unheard
Are sweeter; therefore, ye soft pipes, play on;
Not to the sensual ear, but, more endeared,
Pipe to the spirit ditties of no tone;
Fair youth, beneath the trees, thou canst not leave 15
Thy song, nor ever can those trees be bare;
Bold Lover, never, never canst thou kiss,
Though winning near the goal—yet, do not grieve;
She cannot fade, though thou hast not thy bliss,
For ever wilt thou love, and she be fair! 20

Ah, happy, happy boughs! that cannot shed
Your leaves, nor ever bid the Spring adieu;
And, happy melodist, unwearièd,
For ever piping songs for ever new;
More happy love! more happy, happy love! 25
For ever warm and still to be enjoyed,
For ever panting, and for ever young;
All breathing human passion far above,
That leaves a heart high-sorrowful and cloyed,
A burning forehead, and a parching tongue. 30

Who are these coming to the sacrifice?
To what green altar, O mysterious priest,
Lead'st thou that heifer lowing at the skies,
And all her silken flanks with garlands drest?
What little town by river or sea shore, 35
Or mountain-built with peaceful citadel,
Is emptied of this folk, this pious morn?
And, little town, the streets for evermore
Will silent be; and not a soul to tell
Why thou art desolate, can e'er return. 40

O Attic° shape! Fair attitude! with brede°
Of marble men and maidens overwrought,
With forest branches and the trodden weed;
Thou, silent form, dost tease us out of thought
As doth Eternity: Cold Pastoral! 45

41 *Attic*: Athenian, referring to classical ideals of simplicity, purity, and grace; *brede*: design.

When old age shall this generation waste,
Thou shalt remain, in midst of other woe
Than ours, a friend to man, to whom thou say'st,
Beauty is truth, truth beauty—that is all
Ye know on earth, and all ye need to know. 50

[1820]

Ode on Melancholy

I

No, no, go not to Lethe,° neither twist
Wolfsbane,° tight-rooted, for its poisonous wine;
Nor suffer thy pale forehead to be kissed
By nightshade, ruby grape of Proserpine;°
Make not your rosary of yew berries, 5
Nor let the beetle, nor the death moth be
Your mournful Psyche, nor the downy owl
A partner in your sorrow's mysteries;
For shade to shade will come too drowsily,
And drown the wakeful anguish of the soul. 10

II

But when the melancholy fit shall fall
Sudden from heaven like a weeping cloud,
That fosters the droop-headed flowers all,
And hides the green hill in an April shroud;
Then glut thy sorrow on a morning rose, 15
Or on the rainbow of the salt sand-wave,
Or on the wealth of globèd peonies;
Or if thy mistress some rich anger shows,
Emprison her soft hand, and let her rave,
And feed deep, deep upon her peerless eyes. 20

1 *Lethe*: the river of oblivion in Hades, the classical Underworld; dead souls drank the waters of Lethe to forget their past lives. 2 *Wolfsbane*: a poisonous herb from which sedatives and painkillers were derived. 4 *Prosperpine*: Queen of the Underworld and wife of Pluto.

III

She dwells with Beauty—Beauty that must die;
And Joy, whose hand is ever at his lips
Bidding adieu; and aching Pleasure nigh,
Turning to poison while the bee-mouth sips;
Ay, in the very temple of Delight *25*
Veiled Melancholy has her sovran shrine,
Though seen of none save him whose strenuous tongue
Can burst Joy's grape against his palate fine;
His soul shall taste the sadness of her might,
And be among her cloudy trophies hung. *30*

[1820]

Ode to a Nightingale

I

My heart aches, and a drowsy numbness pains
My sense, as though of hemlock I had drunk,
Or emptied some dull opiate to the drains
One minute past, and Lethe-wards° had sunk;
'Tis not through envy of thy happy lot, *5*
But being too happy in thine happiness—
That thou, light-winged Dryad° of the trees,
In some melodious plot
Of beechen green, and shadows numberless,
Singest of summer in full-throated ease. *10*

II

O, for a draught of vintage! that hath been
Cooled a long age in the deep-delved earth,
Tasting of Flora° and the country green,
Dance, and Provençal song, and sunburned mirth!
O for a beaker full of the warm South, *15*

4 *Lethe-wards*: towards Lethe, the river described in the previous poem. **7** *Dryad*: wood nymph
13 *Flora*: the classical goddess of flowers and Spring.

Full of the true, the blushful Hippocrene,°
With beaded bubbles winking at the brim,
And purple-stained mouth;
That I might drink, and leave the world unseen,
And with thee fade away into the forest dim: *20*

III

Fade far away, dissolve, and quite forget
What thou among the leaves hast never known,
The weariness, the fever, and the fret
Here, where men sit and hear each other groan;
Where palsy shakes a few, sad, last gray hairs, *25*
Where youth grows pale, and specter-thin, and dies;
Where but to think is to be full of sorrow
And leaden-eyed despairs,
Where Beauty cannot keep her lustrous eyes,
Or new Love pine at them beyond tomorrow. *30*

IV

Away! away! for I will fly to thee,
Not charioted by Bacchus and his pards,°
But on the viewless wings of Poesy,
Though the dull brain perplexes and retards;
Already with thee! tender is the night, *35*
And haply the Queen Moon is on her throne,
Clustered around by all her starry Fays;
But here there is no light,
Save what from heaven is with the breezes blown
Through verdurous glooms and winding mossy ways. *40*

V

I cannot see what flowers are at my feet,
Nor what soft incense hangs upon the boughs,
But, in embalmed darkness, guess each sweet
Wherewith the seasonable month endows
The grass, the thicket, and the fruit-tree wild; *45*
White hawthorn, and the pastoral eglantine;
Fast fading violets covered up in leaves;
And mid-May's eldest child,

16 *Hippocrene*: the sacred fountain of the Muses, whose waters have the power to inspire poetry.
32 *pards*: leopards, the animals who pull the god Bacchus's chariot.

The coming musk rose, full of dewy wine,
    The murmurous haunt of flies on summer eves. *50*

VI

Darkling I listen; and, for many a time
  I have been half in love with easeful Death,
Called him soft names in many a mused rhyme,
  To take into the air my quiet breath;
Now more than ever seems it rich to die, *55*
  To cease upon the midnight with no pain,
    While thou art pouring forth thy soul abroad
        In such an ecstasy!
  Still wouldst thou sing, and I have ears in vain—
    To thy high requiem become a sod. *60*

VII

Thou wast not born for death, immortal bird!
  No hungry generations tread thee down;
The voice I hear this passing night was heard
  In ancient days by emperor and clown:
Perhaps the self-same song that found a path *65*
  Through the sad heart of Ruth, when, sick for home,
    She stood in tears amid the alien corn;°
        The same that oft-times hath
  Charmed magic casements, opening on the foam
    Of perilous seas, in fairy lands forlorn. *70*

VIII

Forlorn! the very word is like a bell
  To toll me back from thee to my sole self!
Adieu! the fancy cannot cheat so well
  As she is famed to do, deceiving elf.
Adieu! adieu! thy plaintive anthem fades *75*
  Past the near meadows, over the still stream,
    Up the hillside; and now 'tis buried deep
        In the next valley glades:
  Was it a vision, or a waking dream?
    Fled is that music—Do I wake or sleep? *80*

[1820]

66–67 *Ruth . . . alien corn*: In the Old Testament, Ruth is a widow who works Judah's fields.

To Autumn

I

Season of mists and mellow fruitfulness,
    Close bosom-friend of the maturing sun;
Conspiring with him how to load and bless
    With fruit the vines that round the thatch-eaves run;
To bend with apples the mossed cottage-trees,   *5*
    And fill all fruit with ripeness to the core;
        To swell the gourd, and plump the hazel shells
With a sweet kernel; to set budding more,
    And still more, later flowers for the bees,
    Until they think warm days will never cease,   *10*
        For Summer has o'er-brimmed their clammy cells.

II

Who hath not seen thee oft amid thy store?
    Sometimes whoever seeks abroad may find
Thee sitting careless on a granary floor,
    Thy hair soft-lifted by the winnowing wind;   *15*
Or on a half-reaped furrow sound asleep,
    Drowsed with the fume of poppies, while thy hook°
        Spares the next swath and all its twinèd flowers;
And sometimes like a gleaner thou dost keep
    Steady thy laden head across a brook;   *20*
    Or by a cider-press, with patient look,
        Thou watchest the last oozings hours by hours.

III

Where are the songs of Spring? Ay, where are they?
    Think not of them, thou hast thy music too—
While barrèd clouds bloom the soft-dying day,   *25*
    And touch the stubble-plains with rosy hue;
Then in a wailful choir the small gnats mourn
    Among the river sallows,° borne aloft
        Or sinking as the light wind lives or dies;
And full-grown lambs loud bleat from hilly bourn;°   *30*

17 *hook*: sickle. 28 *sallows*: willows. 30 *bourn*: perhaps a brook. In current English, the word is related to "burn," but in archaic English, a *bourn* can also be a boundary.

Hedge-crickets sing; and now with treble soft
The red-breast whistles from a garden-croft°
And gathering swallows twitter in the skies.

[1820]

32 *garden-croft*: garden plot.

Ralph Waldo Emerson *(1803–1882) was born in Boston to a well-educated family. His father, a Unitarian minister and a founding member of the Anthology Society, died when Emerson was 7, leaving the family in poverty. At the age of 14 he entered Harvard University, where he graduated as Class Poet in 1821, even though he had been an average student. After working as a teacher, he entered Harvard's Divinity School in 1825. He was ordained four years later and became junior pastor of Boston's Second Church. Emerson married Ellen Tucker, who soon died of tuberculosis. He quit his position with the church the following year and set out for Europe. After nine months of travel and intellectual growth, Emerson returned to the States, settled in Concord, and remarried. Emerson also founded the Transcendental Club, a discussion group of disaffected Unitarian ministers, and he cofounded the literary journal* Dial *in 1841. By the time Emerson published* Poems *in 1846, he had developed an international reputation as a lecturer and essayist. Failing health and severe memory loss marked his final years. He died of pneumonia.*

Ralph Waldo Emerson

Concord Hymn*

Sung at the Completion of the Battle Monument, July 4, 1837

By the rude bridge that arched the flood,
Their flag to April's breeze unfurled,
Here once the embattled farmers stood
And fired the shot heard round the world.

*This poem was written for the dedication of the Concord Battle monument, erected to commemorate the efforts of American minutemen against the British troops on April 19, 1775.

The foe long since in silence slept; *5*
  Alike the conqueror silent sleeps;
And Time the ruined bridge has swept
  Down the dark stream which seaward creeps.

On this green bank, by this soft stream,
  We set to-day a votive stone; *10*
That memory may their deed redeem,
  When, like our sires, our sons are gone.

Spirit, that made those heroes dare
  To die, and leave their children free,
Bid Time and Nature gently spare *15*
  The shaft we raise to them and thee.

[1847]

The Rhodora

On Being Asked, Whence Is the Flower?

In May, when sea-winds pierced our solitudes,
I found the fresh Rhodora in the woods,
Spreading its leafless blooms in a damp nook,
To please the desert and the sluggish brook.
The purple petals, fallen in the pool, *5*
Made the black water with their beauty gay;
Here might the red-bird come his plumes to cool,
And court the flower that cheapens his array.
Rhodora! if the sages ask thee why
This charm is wasted on the earth and sky, *10*
Tell them, dear, that if eyes were made for seeing,
Then Beauty is its own excuse for being;
Why thou wert there, O rival of the rose!
I never thought to ask, I never knew;
But, in my simple ignorance, suppose *15*
The self-same Power that brought me there brought you.

[1847]

Brahma*

If the red slayer think he slays,
Or if the slain think he is slain,
They know not well the subtle ways
I keep, and pass, and turn again.

Far or forgot to me is near; *5*
Shadow and sunlight are the same;
The vanished gods to me appear;
And one to me are shame and fame.

They reckon ill who leave me out;
When me they fly, I am the wings; *10*
I am the doubter and the doubt,
And I the hymn the Brahmin sings.

The strong gods pine for my abode,
And pine in vain the sacred Seven,
But thou, meek lover of the good! *15*
Find me, and turn thy back on heaven.

[1867]

**Brahma*: in the Hindu religion, the holy power that is the source of the universe; also refers to India's highest-ranking social caste.

Days

Daughters of Time, the hypocritic Days,
Muffled and dumb like barefoot dervishes,
And marching single in an endless file,
Bring diadems° and fagots° in their hands.
To each they offer gifts after his will, *5*
Bread, kingdom, stars, and sky that holds them all.
I, in my pleached° garden, watched the pomp,
Forgot my morning wishes, hastily
Took a few herbs and apples, and the Day
Turned and departed silent. I, too late, *10*
Under her solemn fillet saw the scorn.

[1867]

4 *diadems*: royal crowns. *fagots*: bundles of sticks. 7 *pleached*: shaded by interweaved vines or branches.

Born near Durham, England, ***Elizabeth Barrett Browning*** *(1806–1861) was the eldest of 12 children in a wealthy family. Her intensely protective father kept strict watch over his children, which—along with Browning's chronic health problems—kept her confined to the family home for much of her early life. When she began a correspondence with the poet Robert Browning in 1841 and met him four years later, she was already an invalid. Forced to keep their romantic relationship a secret—due to her father's order that none of his children were ever to wed—the couple eloped to Italy the following year. There they gave birth to a son, and resided mostly in Florence until her death 15 years later. Browning's work was much admired during her lifetime, even more so than her husband's. The popularity of* Poems *(1844) made her a favorite to succeed Wordsworth as Poet Laureate in 1850, though the post was ultimately given to Tennyson. Browning's* Sonnets from the Portuguese *(1850) is still widely read.*

Elizabeth Barrett Browning

Grief

I tell you, hopeless grief is passionless;
  That only men incredulous of despair,
  Half-taught in anguish, through the midnight air
Beat upward to God's throne in loud access
Of shrieking and reproach. Full desertness *5*
  In souls, as countries, lieth silent-bare
  Under the blanching, vertical eye-glare
Of the absolute Heavens. Deep-hearted man, express
Grief for the Dead in silence like to death:
  Most like a monumental statue set *10*
In everlasting watch and moveless woe
Till itself crumble to the dust beneath.
  Touch it: the marble eyelids are not wet—
If it could weep, it could arise and go.

[1844]

How Do I Love Thee? Let Me Count the Ways*

How do I love thee? Let me count the ways.
I love thee to the depth and breadth and height
My soul can reach, when feeling out of sight
For the ends of being and ideal grace.
I love thee to the level of every day's *5*
Most quiet need, by sun and candle-light.
I love thee freely, as men strive for right.
I love thee purely, as they turn from praise.
I love thee with the passion put to use
In my old griefs, and with my childhood's faith. *10*
I love thee with a love I seemed to lose
With my lost saints. I love thee with the breath,
Smiles, tears, of all my life; and, if God choose,
I shall but love thee better after death.

[1850]

*This poem and the next one are from *Sonnets from the Portuguese.*

I Thought Once How Theocritus* Had Sung

I thought once how Theocritus had sung
Of the sweet years, the dear and wished-for years,
Who each one in a gracious hand appears
To bear a gift for mortals, old or young;
And, as I mused it in his antique tongue, *5*
I saw, in gradual vision through my tears,
The sweet, sad years, the melancholy years,
Those of my own life, who by turns had flung
A shadow across me. Straightway I was 'ware,
So weeping, how a mystic Shape did move *10*
Behind me, and drew me backward by the hair,

**Theocritus*: in Ancient Greece, the first pastoral poet.

And a voice said in mastery, while I strove—
"Guess now who holds thee?"—"Death," I said. But, there,
The silver answer rang—"Not Death, but Love."

[1850]

***Henry Wadsworth Longfellow** (1807–1882), the most popular American poet of the nineteenth century, was born in Portland, Massachusetts (now Maine), into a wealthy family descended from the Pilgrims. His lawyer father enrolled him in Bowdoin College when he was 15, to prepare him for a career in law, medicine, or ministry. (Nathaniel Hawthorne was a classmate and became a lifelong friend.) By the time of his 1825 graduation, Longfellow had already decided to dedicate his life to literature. He lived on and off in Europe to prepare for teaching positions at Bowdoin and Harvard. His wife, who traveled with him, died in the Netherlands from complications following a miscarriage. Longfellow was married in 1843 to the heiress Frances Appleton, with whom he had six children. His 1847 narrative poem* Evangeline *was an immense success, as were* Hiawatha *(1855) and "Paul Revere's Ride" (1863). (During one nine-week period* Evangeline *went through six printings.) Longfellow retired from teaching in 1854, and devoted the remainder of his life to writing poetry. Fanny was killed in an accident in 1861 when her dress caught fire. Longfellow, who tried to save her, was also badly burned. He was an international celebrity by the time of his death in Cambridge.*

Henry Wadsworth Longfellow

Proem to Evangeline

A Tale of Acadie

This is the forest primeval. The murmuring pines and the
hemlocks,
Bearded with moss, and in garments green, indistinct in the
twilight,
Stand like Druids° of eld, with voices sad and prophetic,
Stand like harpers hoar, with beards that rest on their bosoms.

3 *Druids*: ancient Celtic priests known as prophets and sorcerers.

Loud from its rocky caverns, the deep-voiced neighboring ocean *5*
Speaks, and in accents disconsolate answers the wail of the
forest.

This is the forest primeval; but where are the hearts that
beneath it
Leaped like the roe, when he hears in the woodland the voice
of the huntsman?
Where is the thatch-roofed village, the home of Acadian°
farmers—
Men whose lives glided on like rivers that water the woodlands, *10*
Darkened by shadows of earth, but reflecting an image of
heaven?
Waste are those pleasant farms, and the farmers forever
departed!
Scattered like dust and leaves, when the mighty blasts of
October
Seize them, and whirl them aloft, and sprinkle them far o'er the
ocean.
Naught but tradition remains of the beautiful village of *15*
Grand-Pré.°

Ye who believe in affection that hopes, and endures, and is
patient,
Ye who believe in the beauty and strength of woman's devotion,
List to the mournful tradition, still sung by the pines of the forest;
List to a Tale of Love in Acadie, home of the happy.

[1847]

9 *Acadian*: Acadia is the eastern region of Canada, which includes the coast. 15 *Grand-Pré*: Canadian village, home to many farmers and artisans.

The Jewish Cemetery at Newport*

How strange it seems! These Hebrews in their graves,
Close by the street of this fair seaport town,
Silent beside the never-silent waves,
At rest in all this moving up and down!

*This poem was written after the poet visited a cemetery in Newport, Rhode Island.

The trees are white with dust, that o'er their sleep *5*
    Wave their broad curtains in the south-wind's breath,
While underneath these leafy tents they keep
    The long, mysterious Exodus of Death.

And these sepulchral stones, so old and brown,
    That pave with level flags their burial-place, *10*
Seem like the tablets of the Law, thrown down
    And broken by Moses at the mountain's base.

The very names recorded here are strange,
    Of foreign accent, and of different climes;
Alvares and Rivera interchange *15*
    With Abraham and Jacob of old times.

"Blessed be God! for he created Death!"
    The mourners said, "and Death is rest and peace;"
Then added, in the certainty of faith,
    "And giveth Life that nevermore shall cease." *20*

Closed are the portals of their Synagogue,
    No Psalms of David now the silence break,
No Rabbi reads the ancient Decalogue
    In the grand dialect the Prophets spake.

Gone are the living, but the dead remain, *25*
    And not neglected; for a hand unseen,
Scattering its bounty, like a summer rain,
    Still keeps their graves and their remembrance green.

How came they here? What burst of Christian hate,
    What persecution, merciless and blind, *30*
Drove o'er the sea—that desert desolate—
    These Ishmaels and Hagars° of mankind?

They lived in narrow streets and lanes obscure,
    Ghetto and Judenstrass,° in mirk and mire;
Taught in the school of patience to endure *35*
    The life of anguish and the death of fire.

All their lives long, with the unleavened bread
    And bitter herbs of exile and its fears,
The wasting famine of the heart they fed,
    And slaked its thirst with marah° of their tears. *40*

32 *Ishmaels and Hagars*: a servant to Sarah, Abraham's wife, Hagar bore a son, Ishmael, with Abraham. Due to Sarah's jealousy, Ishmael and Hagar were exiled. 34 *Ghetto and Judenstrass*: sections of the city in which Jews were forced to live. 40 *marah*: Hebrew word for bitterness.

Anathema marantha!° Was the cry
  That rang from town to town, from street to street;
At every gate the accursed Mordecai°
  Was mocked and jeered, and spurned by Christian feet.

Pride and humiliation hand in hand *45*
  Walked with them through the world where'er they went;
Trampled and beaten were they as the sand,
  And yet unshaken as the continent.

For in the background figures vague and vast
  Of patriarchs and of prophets rose sublime, *50*
And all the great traditions of the Past
  They saw reflected in the coming time.

And thus for ever with reverted look
  The mystic volume of the world they read,
Spelling it backward, like a Hebrew book. *55*
  Till life became a Legend of the Dead.

But ah! what once has been shall be no more!
  The groaning earth in travail and in pain
Brings forth its races, but does not restore,
  And the dead nations never rise again. *60*

[1858]

41 *Anathema marantha*: a Greek Aramaic curse to Jews, it applies to "those who love not the Lord."
43 *Mordecai*: elder Hebrew man persecuted by the ruler Haman.

Snow-Flakes

Out of the bosom of the Air,
  Out of the cloud-folds of her garments shaken,
Over the woodlands brown and bare,
  Over the harvest-fields forsaken,
    Silent, and soft, and slow *5*
    Descends the snow.

Even as our cloudy fancies take
  Suddenly shape in some divine expression,
Even as the troubled heart doth make

In the white countenance confession, 10
The troubled sky reveals
The grief it feels.

This is the poem of the air,
Slowly in silent syllables recorded;
This is the secret of despair, 15
Long in its cloudy bosom hoarded,
Now whispered and revealed
To wood and field.

[1863]

The Tide Rises, the Tide Falls

The tide rises, the tide falls,
The twilight darkens, the curlew calls;
Along the sea-sands damp and brown
The traveller hastens toward the town,
And the tide rises, the tide falls. 5

Darkness settles on roofs and walls,
But the sea, the sea in the darkness calls;
The little waves, with their soft, white hands,
Efface the footprints in the sands,
And the tide rises, the tide falls. 10

The morning breaks; the steeds in their stalls
Stamp and neigh, as the hostler calls;
The day returns, but nevermore
Returns the traveller to the shore,
And the tide rises, the tide falls. 15

[1880]

The Cross of Snow*

In the long, sleepless watches of the night,
  A gentle face—the face of one long dead—
  Looks at me from the wall, where round its head
  The night-lamp casts a halo of pale light.
Here in this room she died; and soul more white *5*
  Never through martyrdom of fire was led
  To its repose; nor can in books be read
  The legend of a life more benedight.°
There is a mountain in the distant West
  That, sun-defying, in its deep ravines *10*
  Displays a cross of snow upon its side.
Such is the cross I wear upon my breast
  These eighteen years, through all the changing scenes
  And seasons, changeless since the day she died.

[1886]

*This poem refers to Longfellow's second wife who was burnt to death.
8 *benedight*: blessed.

***Edward FitzGerald** (1809–1883) was born into a wealthy family of eight children, and spent most of his life in Suffolk, England. He attended Trinity College, Cambridge, graduating in 1830 without distinction. FitzGerald, who never had a profession, spent his adult life in quiet solitude at his parents' estate in Suffolk, where he tended his garden, sailed, and entertained such guests as Tennyson and Carlyle. He married Lucy Barton in 1856. The couple was so mismatched and unhappy that they separated after only eight months. Through his friendship to Edward Byles Cowell, FitzGerald began studying languages, especially Persian, Spanish, and Greek. He translated loosely from these tongues, often adapting the work for a modern English audience.* The Rubaiyat of Omar Khayyam, *which appeared in 1859, was largely ignored until Dante Gabriel Rossetti found a remaindered copy and encouraged FitzGerald to publish a revised and expanded edition.* The Rubaiyat *eventually went through several editions and became internationally known. FitzGerald's eyesight had deteriorated significantly by the time of his death at 74.*

Edward FitzGerald

Excerpts from The Rubáiyát of Omar Khayyám of Naishápúr*

1

Wake! For the Sun, who scattered into flight
The Stars before him from the Field of Night,
  Drives Night along with them from Heav'n, and strikes
The Sultán's Turret with a Shaft of Light.

3

And, as the Cock crew, those who stood before *5*
The Tavern shouted—"Open then the Door!
  "You know how little while we have to stay,
"And, once departed, may return no more."

7

Come, fill the Cup, and in the fire of Spring
Your Winter-garment of Repentance fling; *10*
  The Bird of Time has but a little way
To flutter—and the Bird is on the Wing.

9

Each Morn a thousand Roses brings, you say;
Yes, but where leaves the Rose of Yesterday?
  And this first Summer month that brings the Rose *15*
Shall take Jamshýd and Kaikobád° away.

11

A Book of Verses underneath the Bough,
A Jug of Wine, a Loaf of Bread—and Thou
  Beside me singing in the Wilderness—
Oh, Wilderness were Paradise enow! *20*

*Omar Khayyám (1048–1131) was a Persian poet, mathematician, and astronomer. Rubáiyáts are quatrains.

16 *Jamshy'd and Kaikobád:* Persian kings.

13

Some for the Glories of This World; and some
Sigh for the Prophet's Paradise to come;
    Ah, take the Cash, and let the Credit go,
Nor heed the rumble of a distant Drum!

18

They say the Lion and the Lizard keep *25*
The Courts where Jamshýd gloried and drank deep;
    And Bahrám, that great Hunter—the Wild Ass
Stamps o'er his Head, but cannot break his Sleep.

19

I sometimes think that never blows so red
The Rose as where some buried Caesar bled; *30*
    That every Hyacinth the Garden wears
Dropt in her Lap from some once lovely Head.

22

For some we loved, the loveliest and the best
That from his Vintage rolling Time hath prest,
    Have drunk their Cup a Round or two before, *35*
And one by one crept silently to rest.

24

Ah, make the most of what we yet may spend,
Before we too into the Dust descend;
    Dust into Dust, and under Dust to lie,
Sans Wine, sans Song, sans Singer, and sans End! *40*

26

Why, all the Saints and Sages who discussed
Of the Two Worlds so wisely—they are thrust
    Like foolish Prophets forth; their Words to Scorn
Are scattered, and their Mouths are stopt with Dust.

27

Myself when young did eagerly frequent *45*
Doctor and Saint, and heard great argument

About it and about; but evermore
Came out by the same door where in I went.

32

There was the Door to which I found no Key;
There was the Veil through which I might not see; *50*
Some little talk awhile of ME and THEE
There was—and then no more of THEE and ME.

47

When You and I behind the Veil are past,
Oh, but the long, long while the World shall last,
Which of our Coming and Departure heeds *55*
As the Sea's self should heed a pebble-cast.

55

You know, my Friends, with what a brave Carouse
I made a Second Marriage in my house;
Divorced old barren Reason from my Bed,
And took the Daughter of the Vine to Spouse. *60*

64

Strange, is it not? that of the myriads who
Before us passed the door of Darkness through,
Not one returns to tell us of the Road,
Which to discover we must travel too.

68

We are no other than a moving row *65*
Of Magic Shadow-shapes that come and go
Round with the Sun-illumined Lantern held
In Midnight by the Master of the Show;

69

But helpless Pieces of the Game He plays
Upon his Checkerboard of Nights and Days; *70*
Hither and thither moves, and checks, and slays,
And one by one back in the Closet lays.

71

The Moving Finger writes; and, having writ,
Moves on; nor all your Piety nor Wit
    Shall lure it back to cancel half a Line, *75*
Nor all your Tears wash out a Word of it.

93

Indeed the Idols I have loved so long
Have done my credit in this World much wrong;
    Have drowned my Glory in a shallow Cup,
And sold my Reputation for a Song. *80*

96

Yet Ah, that Spring should vanish with the Rose!
That Youth's sweet-scented manuscript should close!
    The Nightingale that in the branches sang,
Ah whence, and whither flown again, who knows!

99

Ah Love! could you and I with Him conspire *85*
To grasp this sorry Scheme of Things entire,
    Would not we shatter it to bits—and then
Remold it nearer to the Heart's Desire!

[1859; revised 1879]

***Edgar Allan Poe** (1809–1849) was born in Boston, Massachusetts, the son of traveling actors who died when he was very young. A wealthy Virginia tobacco exporter raised Poe and provided him with a solid education. Poe dropped out of the University of Virginia, having tried to gamble his way out of debt. He joined the Army, but was soon discharged. His stint at West Point proved short as well; Poe was dishonorably discharged for neglecting his duties. In 1836 he married his cousin, Virginia Clemm. Poe began working as a journalist and edited a number of prominent magazines and journals, where he frequently published his own stories, poems, and essays. His first collection of stories,* Tales of the Grotesque and

Arabesque *(1839), and his book of verse,* The Raven and other Poems *(1845), earned Poe immense fame. Still he struggled financially and drank heavily. His wife died in 1847, and he followed her to the grave two years later. Despite his untimely (and somewhat mysterious) death in Baltimore at age 40, Poe left behind a body of startlingly original fiction and poetry.*

Edgar Allan Poe
"Alone"

From childhood's hour I have not been
As others were—I have not seen
As others saw—I could not bring
My passions from a common spring—
From the same source I have not taken *5*
My sorrow—I could not awaken
My heart to joy at the same tone—
And all I lov'd—I lov'd alone—
Then—in my childhood—in the dawn
Of a most stormy life—was drawn *10*
From ev'ry depth of good and ill
The mystery which binds me still—
From the torrent, or the fountain—
From the red cliff of the mountain—
From the sun that 'round me roll'd *15*
In its autumn tint of gold—
From the lightning in the sky
As it pass'd me flying by—
From the thunder, and the storm—
And the cloud that took the form *20*
(When the rest of Heaven was blue)
Of a demon in my view—

[c. 1829]

To Helen

Helen, thy beauty is to me
Like those Nicean° barks of yore,
That gently, o'er a perfumed sea
The weary, way-worn wanderer bore
To his own native shore. 5

On desperate seas long wont to roam,
Thy hyacinth hair, thy classic face
Thy Naiad° airs have brought me home
To the glory that was Greece
And the grandeur that was Rome. 10

Lo! in yon brilliant window-niche
How statue-like I see thee stand!
The agate lamp within thy hand,
Ah! Psyche,° from the regions which
Are Holy Land! 15

[1831; revised 1845]

2 *Nicean*: may refer to Nice, a city in Southern France. 8 *Naiad*: water nymph. 14 *Psyche*: the soul.

The Haunted Palace*

In the greenest of our valleys
By good angels tenanted,
Once a fair and stately palace—
Radiant palace—reared its head.
In the monarch Thought's dominion— 5
It stood there!
Never seraph spread a pinion
Over fabric half so fair!

Banners yellow, glorious, golden,
On its roof did float and flow— 10
(This—all this—was in the olden
Time long ago)

*This poem appears in Poe's tale "The Fall of the House of Usher."

And every gentle air that dallied,
    In that sweet day,
Along the ramparts plumed and pallid, *15*
    A wingéd odor went away.

Wanderers in that happy valley,
    Through two luminous windows, saw
Spirits moving musically,
    To a lute's well-tunéd law, *20*
Round about a throne where, sitting,
    Porphyrogene,°
In state his glory well befitting
    The ruler of the realm was seen.

And all with pearl and ruby glowing *25*
    Was the fair palace door,
Through which came flowing, flowing, flowing,
    And sparkling evermore,
A troop of Echoes whose sweet duty
    Was but to sing, *30*
In voices of surpassing beauty,
    The wit and wisdom of their king.

But evil things, in robes of sorrow,
    Assailed the monarch's high estate.
(Ah, let us mourn!—for never morrow *35*
    Shall dawn upon him, desolate!)
And round about his home the glory
    That blushed and bloomed,
Is but a dim-remembered story
    Of the old-time entombed. *40*

And travellers, now, within that valley,
    Through the encrimsoned windows see
Vast forms that move fantastically
    To a discordant melody,
While, like a ghastly rapid river, *45*
    Through the pale door
A hideous throng rush out forever
    And laugh—but smile no more.

[1839]

22 *Porphyrogene*: born into nobility or high-rank.

The Raven

Once upon a midnight dreary, while I pondered, weak and weary,
Over many a quaint and curious volume of forgotten lore—
While I nodded, nearly napping, suddenly there came a tapping,
As of some one gently rapping, rapping at my chamber door.
"'Tis some visitor," I muttered, "tapping at my chamber door— *5*
Only this and nothing more."

Ah, distinctly I remember it was in the bleak December;
And each separate dying ember wrought its ghost upon the floor.
Eagerly I wished the morrow;—vainly I had sought to borrow
From my books surcease of sorrow—sorrow for the lost Lenore— *10*
For the rare and radiant maiden whom the angels name Lenore—
Nameless *here* for evermore.

And the silken, sad, uncertain rustling of each purple curtain
Thrilled me—filled me with fantastic terrors never felt before;
So that now, to still the beating of my heart, I stood repeating *15*
"'Tis some visitor entreating entrance at my chamber door;—
Some late visitor entreating entrance at my chamber door;—
This it is and nothing more."

Presently my soul grew stronger; hesitating then no longer,
"Sir," said I, "or Madam, truly your forgiveness I implore; *20*
But the fact is I was napping, and so gently you came rapping,
And so faintly you came tapping, tapping at my chamber door,
That I scarce was sure I heard you"—here I opened wide the
door;—
Darkness there and nothing more.

Deep into that darkness peering, long I stood there wondering, *25*
fearing,
Doubting, dreaming dreams no mortal ever dared to dream before;
But the silence was unbroken, and the stillness gave no token,
And the only word there spoken was the whispered word, "Lenore?"
This I whispered, and an echo murmured back the word, "Lenore!"
Merely this and nothing more. *30*

Back into the chamber turning, all my soul within me burning,
Soon again I heard a tapping somewhat louder than before.
"Surely," said I, "surely that is something at my window lattice;
Let me see, then, what thereat is, and this mystery explore—

Let my heart be still a moment and this mystery explore;— 35
'Tis the wind and nothing more!"

Open here I flung the shutter, when, with many a flirt and flutter,
In there stepped a stately Raven of the saintly days of yore;
Not the least obeisance made he; not a minute stopped or stayed he;
But, with mien of lord or lady, perched above my chamber door— 40
Perched upon a bust of Pallas° just above my chamber door—
Perched, and sat, and nothing more.

Then this ebony bird beguiling my sad fancy into smiling,
By the grave and stern decorum of the countenance it wore,
"Though thy crest be shorn and shaven, thou," I said, "art sure no craven, 45
Ghastly grim and ancient Raven wandering from the Nightly shore—
Tell me what thy lordly name is on the Night's Plutonian shore!"
Quoth the Raven, "Nevermore."

Much I marvelled this ungainly fowl to hear discourse so plainly,
Though its answer little meaning—little relevancy bore; 50
For we cannot help agreeing that no living human being
Ever yet was blessed with seeing bird above his chamber door—
Bird or beast upon the sculptured bust above his chamber door,
With such name as "Nevermore."

But the Raven, sitting lonely on the placid bust, spoke only 55
That one word, as if his soul in that one word he did outpour.
Nothing farther then he uttered—not a feather then he fluttered—
Till I scarcely more than muttered, "Other friends have flown before—
On the morrow *he* will leave me, as my Hopes have flown before."
Then the bird said, "Nevermore." 60

Startled at the stillness broken by reply so aptly spoken,
"Doubtless," said I, "what it utters is its only stock and store
Caught from some unhappy master whom unmerciful Disaster
Followed fast and followed faster till his songs one burden bore—
Till the dirges of his Hope that melancholy burden bore 65
Of 'Never—nevermore.' "

41 *Pallas*: Athena, goddess of wisdom.

But the Raven still beguiling all my sad fancy into smiling,
Straight I wheeled a cushioned seat in front of bird and bust
        and door;
Then, upon the velvet sinking, I betook myself to linking
Fancy unto fancy, thinking what this ominous bird of yore— *70*
What this grim, ungainly, ghastly, gaunt, and ominous bird
        of yore
                                Meant in croaking "Nevermore."

This I sat engaged in guessing, but no syllable expressing
To the fowl whose fiery eyes now burned into my bosom's core;
This and more I sat divining, with my head at ease reclining *75*
On the cushion's velvet lining that the lamp-light gloated o'er,
But whose velvet-violet lining with the lamp-light gloating o'er,
                                She shall press, ah, nevermore!

Then, methought, the air grew denser, perfumed from an unseen
        censer
Swung by seraphim whose foot-falls tinkled on the tufted floor. *80*
"Wretch," I cried, "thy God hath lent thee—by these angels
        he hath sent thee.
Respite—respite and nepenthe° from thy memories of Lenore;
Quaff, oh quaff this kind nepenthe and forget this lost Lenore!"
                                Quoth the Raven, "Nevermore."

"Prophet!" said I, "thing of evil!—prophet still, if bird or devil!— *85*
Whether Tempter sent, or whether tempest tossed thee here
        ashore,
Desolate yet all undaunted, on this desert land enchanted—
On this home by Horror haunted—tell me truly, I implore—
Is there—*is* there balm in Gilead?—tell me—tell me, I implore!"
                                Quoth the Raven, "Nevermore." *90*

"Prophet!" said I, "thing of evil!—prophet still, if bird or devil!
By that Heaven that bends above us—by that God we both
        adore—
Tell this soul with sorrow laden if, within the distant Aidenn,°
It shall clasp a sainted maiden whom the angels name Lenore—
Clasp a rare and radiant maiden whom the angels name Lenore." *95*
                                Quoth the Raven, "Nevermore."

83 *nepenthe*: a drug that causes forgetfulness. 93 *Aidenn*: Eden.

"Be that word our sign of parting, bird or fiend!" I shrieked,
upstarting—
"Get thee back into the tempest and the Night's Plutonian shore!
Leave no black plume as a token of that lie thy soul hath spoken!
Leave my loneliness unbroken!—quit the bust above my door! *100*
Take thy beak from out my heart, and take thy form from
off my door!"
Quoth the Raven, "Nevermore."

And the Raven, never flitting, still is sitting, *still* is sitting
On the pallid bust of Pallas just above my chamber door;
And his eyes have all the seeming of a demon's that is dreaming, *105*
And the lamp-light o'er him streaming throws his shadow on
the floor;
And my soul from out that shadow that lies floating on the floor
Shall be lifted—nevermore!

[1845]

Annabel Lee

It was many and many a year ago,
In a kingdom by the sea,
That a maiden there lived whom you may know
By the name of Annabel Lee;
And this maiden she lived with no other thought *5*
Than to love and be loved by me.

I was a child and *she* was a child,
In this kingdom by the sea,
But we loved with a love that was more than love—
I and my Annabel Lee— *10*
With a love that the wingéd seraphs of Heaven
Coveted her and me.

And this was the reason that, long ago,
In this kingdom by the sea,
A wind blew out of a cloud, chilling *15*
My beautiful Annabel Lee;

So that her highborn kinsmen came
    And bore her away from me,
To shut her up in a sepulchre
    In this kingdom by the sea. *20*

The angels, not half so happy in Heaven,
    Went envying her and me—
Yes!—that was the reason (as all men know,
    In this kingdom by the sea)
That the wind came out of the cloud by night, *25*
    Chilling and killing my Annabel Lee.

But our love it was stronger by far than the love
    Of those who were older than we—
    Of many far wiser than we—
And neither the angels in Heaven above, *30*
    Nor the demons down under the sea,
Can ever dissever my soul from the soul
    Of the beautiful Annabel Lee;—

For the moon never beams, without bringing me dreams
    Of the beautiful Annabel Lee; *35*
And the stars never rise, but I feel the bright eyes
    Of the beautiful Annabel Lee—
And so, all the night-tide, I lie down by the side
    Of my darling—my darling—my life and my bride,
    In the sepulchre there by the sea— *40*
    In her tomb by the sounding sea.

[1849]

***Alfred Tennyson** (1809–1892) was born in Lincolnshire, England, one of 12 children of a hard-drinking country priest. Tennyson attended Trinity College, Cambridge, but left before taking a degree. His 14-year engagement to Emily Sellwood—its length due to Tennyson's financial struggles—finally resulted in marriage in 1850. That same year he published his acclaimed* In Memoriam *(1850), and Queen Victoria named him Poet Laureate, a post he held for four decades. Tennyson gained widespread fame in his lifetime, especially for such books as* Idylls of the King *(1859; 1889, a 12-part narrative of Arthur and his Round Table). Late in life* *he wrote a number of plays. Queen Victoria made Tennyson a baron in 1883, at which point he added "Lord" to his name. He is buried near Browning and Chaucer in the Poets' Corner of Westminster Abbey.*

Alfred, Lord Tennyson

Ulysses

It little profits that an idle king,
By this still hearth, among these barren crags,
Matched with an agèd wife, I mete and dole
Unequal laws unto a savage race
That hoard, and sleep, and feed, and know not me. *5*
I cannot rest from travel; I will drink
Life to the lees. All times I have enjoyed
Greatly, have suffered greatly, both with those
That loved me, and alone; on shore, and when
Through scudding drifts the rainy Hyades *10*
Vexed the dim sea. I am become a name;
For always roaming with a hungry heart
Much have I seen and known—cities of men
And manners, climates, councils, governments,
Myself not least, but honored of them all— *15*
And drunk delight of battle with my peers,
Far on the ringing plains of windy Troy.
I am a part of all that I have met;
Yet all experience is an arch wherethrough
Gleams that untraveled world whose margin fades *20*
Forever and forever when I move.
How dull it is to pause, to make an end,
To rust unburnished, not to shine in use!
As though to breathe were life! Life piled on life
Were all too little, and of one to me *25*
Little remains; but every hour is saved
From that eternal silence, something more,
A bringer of new things; and vile it were
For some three suns to store and hoard myself,
And this grey spirit yearning in desire *30*
To follow knowledge like a sinking star,

Beyond the utmost bound of human thought.
    This is my son, mine own Telemachus,
To whom I leave the scepter and the isle—
Well-loved of me, discerning to fulfill *35*
This labor, by slow prudence to make mild
A rugged people, and through soft degrees
Subdue them to the useful and the good.
Most blameless is he, centered in the sphere
Of common duties, decent not to fail *40*
In offices of tenderness, and pay
Meet adoration to my household gods,
When I am gone. He works his work, I mine.
    There lies the port; the vessel puffs her sail;
There gloom the dark, broad seas. My mariners, *45*
Souls that have toiled, and wrought, and thought with me—
That ever with a frolic welcome took
The thunder and the sunshine, and opposed
Free hearts, free foreheads—you and I are old;
Old age hath yet his honor and his toil. *50*
Death closes all; but something ere the end,
Some work of noble note, may yet be done,
Not unbecoming men that strove with Gods.
The lights begin to twinkle from the rocks;
The long day wanes; the low moon climbs; the deep *55*
Moans round with many voices. Come, my friends,
'Tis not too late to seek a newer world.
Push off, and sitting well in order smite
The sounding furrows; for my purpose holds
To sail beyond the sunset, and the baths *60*
Of all the western stars, until I die.
It may be that the gulfs will wash us down;
It may be we shall touch the Happy Isles,
And see the great Achilles, whom we knew.
Though much is taken, much abides; and though *65*
We are not now that strength which in old days
Moved earth and heaven, that which we are, we are—
One equal temper of heroic hearts,
Made weak by time and fate, but strong in will
To strive, to seek, to find, and not to yield. *70*

[1833; 1842]

Break, Break, Break

Break, break, break,
  On thy cold gray stones, O Sea!
And I would that my tongue could utter
  The thoughts that arise in me.

O well for the fisherman's boy, *5*
  That he shouts with his sister at play!
O well for the sailor lad,
  That he sings in his boat on the bay!

And the stately ships go on
  To their haven under the hill; *10*
But O for the touch of a vanish'd hand,
  And the sound of a voice that is still!

Break, break, break,
  At the foot of thy crags, O Sea!
But the tender grace of a day that is dead *15*
  Will never come back to me.

[1834; 1842]

Now Sleeps the Crimson Petal*

  Now sleeps the crimson petal, now the white;
Nor waves the cypress in the palace walk;
Nor winks the gold fin in the porphyry font.
The fire-fly wakens; waken thou with me.

  Now droops the milk-white peacock like a ghost, *5*
And like a ghost she glimmers on to me.

  Now lies the Earth all Danaë° to the stars,
And all thy heart lies open unto me.

*This poem and the next are songs from *The Princess*.

7 *Danaë*: a Greek princess imprisoned by her father in a tower to keep her from suitors. Zeus visited her as a shower of gold, which resulted in the birth of their son Perseus.

Now slides the silent meteor on, and leaves
A shining furrow, as thy thoughts in me. *10*

Now folds the lily all her sweetness up,
And slips into the bosom of the lake.
So fold thyself, my dearest, thou, and slip
Into my bosom and be lost in me.

[1847]

Tears, Idle Tears

Tears, idle tears, I know not what they mean,
Tears from the depth of some divine despair
Rise in the heart, and gather to the eyes,
In looking on the happy autumn-fields,
And thinking of the days that are no more. *5*

Fresh as the first beam glittering on a sail,
That brings our friends up from the underworld,
Sad as the last which reddens over one
That sinks with all we love below the verge;
So sad, so fresh, the days that are no more. *10*

Ah, sad and strange as in dark summer dawns
The earliest pipe of half-awakened birds
To dying ears, when unto dying eyes
The casement slowly grows a glimmering square;
So sad, so strange, the days that are no more. *15*

Dear as remembered kisses after death,
And sweet as those by hopeless fancy feigned
On lips that are for others; deep as love,
Deep as first love, and wild with all regret;
O Death in Life, the days that are no more! *20*

[1847]

from In Memoriam A.H.H.*

II

Old yew, which graspest at the stones
    That name the underlying dead,
    Thy fibres net the dreamless head,
Thy roots are wrapt about the bones.

The seasons bring the flower again, *5*
    And bring the firstling to the flock;
    And in the dusk of thee the clock
Beats out the little lives of men.

O, not for thee the glow, the bloom,
    Who changest not in any gale, *10*
    Nor branding summer suns avail
To touch thy thousand years of gloom;

And gazing on thee, sullen tree,
    Sick for thy stubborn hardihood,
    I seem to fail from out my blood *15*
And grow incorporate into thee.

VII

Dark house, by which once more I stand
    Here in the long unlovely street,
    Doors, where my heart was used to beat
So quickly, waiting for a hand,

A hand that can be clasped no more— *5*
    Behold me, for I cannot sleep,
    And like a guilty thing I creep
At earliest morning to the door.

He is not here; but far away
    The noise of life begins again, *10*
    And ghastly through the drizzling rain
On the bald street breaks the blank day.

**A.H.H.*: Arthur Henry Hallam (1811–1833), the poet's friend from college.

L

Be near me when my light is low,
    When the blood creeps, and the nerves prick
    And tingle; and the heart is sick,
And all the wheels of being slow.

Be near me when the sensuous frame   5
    Is rack'd with pangs that conquer trust;
    And Time, a maniac scattering dust,
And Life, a Fury slinging flame.

Be near me when my faith is dry,
    And men the flies of latter spring,   10
    That lay their eggs, and sting and sing
And weave their petty cells and die.

Be near me when I fade away,
    To point the term of human strife,
    And on the low dark verge of life   15
The twilight of eternal day.

[1850]

The Eagle

A Fragment

He clasps the crag with crooked hands;
Close to the sun in lonely lands,
Ringed with the azure world, he stands.

The wrinkled sea beneath him crawls;
He watches from his mountain walls,   5
And like a thunderbolt he falls.

[1851]

Tithonus*

The woods decay, the woods decay and fall,
The vapors weep their burthen to the ground,
Man comes and tills the field and lies beneath,
And after many a summer dies the swan.
Me only cruel immortality *5*
Consumes; I wither slowly in thine arms,
Here at the quiet limit of the world,
A white-hair'd shadow roaming like a dream
The ever-silent spaces of the East,
Far-folded mists, and gleaming halls of morn. *10*

Alas! for this gray shadow, once a man—
So glorious in his beauty and thy choice,
Who madest him thy chosen, that he seem'd
To his great heart none other than a God!
I ask'd thee, "Give me immortality." *15*
Then didst thou grant mine asking with a smile,
Like wealthy men who care not how they give.
But thy strong Hours indignant work'd their wills,
And beat me down and marr'd and wasted me,
And tho' they could not end me, left me maim'd *20*
To dwell in presence of immortal youth,
Immortal age beside immortal youth,
And all I was in ashes. Can thy love,
Thy beauty, make amends, tho' even now,
Close over us, the silver star, thy guide, *25*
Shines in those tremulous eyes that fill with tears
To hear me? Let me go; take back thy gift.
Why should a man desire in any way
To vary from the kindly race of men,
Or pass beyond the goal of ordinance *30*
Where all should pause, as is most meet for all?

A soft air fans the cloud apart; there comes
A glimpse of that dark world where I was born.
Once more the old mysterious glimmer steals
From thy pure brows, and from thy shoulders pure, *35*
And bosom beating with a heart renew'd.
Thy cheek begins to redden thro' the gloom,

*A Trojan prince who was granted by Aurora—goddess of the dawn—everlasting life. He forgot, however, to request everlasting youth.

Thy sweet eyes brighten slowly close to mine,
Ere yet they blind the stars, and the wild team
Which love thee, yearning for thy yoke, arise, 40
And shake the darkness from their loosen'd manes,
And beat the twilight into flakes of fire.

Lo! ever thus thou growest beautiful
In silence, then before thine answer given
Departest, and thy tears are on my cheek. 45

Why wilt thou ever scare me with thy tears,
And make me tremble lest a saying learnt,
In days far-off, on that dark earth, be true?
"The Gods themselves cannot recall their gifts."

Ay me! ay me! with what another heart 50
In days far-off, and with what other eyes
I used to watch—if I be he that watch'd—
The lucid outline forming round thee; saw
The dim curls kindle into sunny rings;
Changed with thy mystic change, and felt my blood 55
Glow with the glow that slowly crimson'd all
Thy presence and thy portals, while I lay,
Mouth, forehead, eyelids, growing dewy-warm
With kisses balmier than half-opening buds
Of April, and could hear the lips that kiss'd 60
Whispering I knew not what of wild and sweet,
Like that strange song I heard Apollo sing,
While Ilion like a mist rose into towers.

Yet hold me not for ever in thine East;
How can my nature longer mix with thine? 65
Coldly thy rosy shadows bathe me, cold
Are all thy lights, and cold my wrinkled feet
Upon thy glimmering thresholds, when the steam
Floats up from those dim fields about the homes
Of happy men that have the power to die, 70
And grassy barrows of the happier dead.
Release me, and restore me to the ground.
Thou seest all things, thou wilt see my grave;
Thou wilt renew thy beauty morn by morn,
I earth in earth forget these empty courts, 75
And thee returning on thy silver wheels.

[1860]

Born outside of London, **Robert Browning** *(1812–1889) began his education largely at home in his father's six-thousand-volume library. Browning matriculated at London University when he was 16 years old, but completed only one term before dropping out to travel through Russia and Italy. He corresponded with the poet Elizabeth Barrett while in Italy, eventually receiving her permission to visit; the couple eloped in 1846, despite the disapproval of her father. After his wife's death in 1861, Browning returned to London to focus on his literary career. His popularity soared. Some of his most important works were* Men and Women *(1855) and* The Ring and the Book *(1868–1869), a long narrative about a seventeenth-century murder trial in Rome. Greatly admired by later poets such as Ezra Pound and T. S. Eliot for his mastery of dramatic monologue, Browning's influence on English-language poetry has been profound. He died in Venice at 77 and is buried in Westminster Abbey.*

Robert Browning

My Last Duchess

*Ferrara**

That's my last Duchess painted on the wall,
Looking as if she were alive. I call
That piece a wonder, now; Frà Pandolf's° hands
Worked busily a day, and there she stands.
Will't please you sit and look at her? I said 5
"Frà Pandolf" by design, for never read
Strangers like you that pictured countenance,
The depth and passion of its earnest glance,
But to myself they turned (since none puts by
The curtain I have drawn for you, but I) 10
And seemed as they would ask me, if they durst,
How such a glance came there; so, not the first
Are you to turn and ask thus. Sir, 'twas not
Her husband's presence only, called that spot
Of joy into the Duchess' cheek; perhaps 15
Frà Pandolf chanced to say, "Her mantle laps
Over my lady's wrist too much," or "Paint

*Ferrara is a city in Northern Italy. The speaker is probably modeled after the city's Duke, Alfonso II d'Este (1533–1598).

3 *Frà Pandolf*: name of a fictitious artist.

Must never hope to reproduce the faint
Half-flush that dies along her throat." Such stuff
Was courtesy, she thought, and cause enough *20*
For calling up that spot of joy. She had
A heart—how shall I say?—too soon made glad,
Too easily impressed; she liked whate'er
She looked on, and her looks went everywhere.
Sir, 'twas all one! My favor at her breast, *25*
The dropping of the daylight in the West,
The bough of cherries some officious fool
Broke in the orchard for her, the white mule
She rode with round the terrace—all and each
Would draw from her alike the approving speech, *30*
Or blush, at least. She thanked men—good! but thanked
Somehow—I know not how—as if she ranked
My gift of a nine-hundred-years-old name
With anybody's gift. Who'd stoop to blame
This sort of trifling? Even had you skill *35*
In speech—which I have not—to make your will
Quite clear to such an one, and say "Just this
Or that in you disgusts me; here you miss,
Or there exceed the mark"—and if she let
Herself be lessoned so, nor plainly set *40*
Her wits to yours, forsooth, and made excuse—
E'en then would be some stooping; and I choose
Never to stoop. Oh, sir, she smiled, no doubt,
Whene'er I passed her; but who passed without
Much the same smile? This grew; I gave commands; *45*
Then all smiles stopped together. There she stands
As if alive. Will't please you rise? We'll meet
The company below, then. I repeat,
The Count your master's known munificence
Is ample warrant that no just pretense *50*
Of mine for dowry will be disallowed;
Though his fair daughter's self, as I avowed
At starting, is my object. Nay, we'll go
Together down, sir. Notice Neptune, though,
Taming a sea-horse, thought a rarity, *55*
Which Claus of Innsbruck° cast in bronze for me!

[1842]

56 *Claus of Innsbruck*: name of a fictitious artist.

Porphyria's* Lover

The rain set early in tonight,
    The sullen wind was soon awake,
It tore the elm-tops down for spite,
    And did its worst to vex the lake;
    I listened with heart fit to break. *5*
When glided in Porphyria; straight
    She shut the cold out and the storm,
And kneeled and made the cheerless grate
    Blaze up, and all the cottage warm;
    Which done, she rose, and from her form *10*
Withdrew the dripping cloak and shawl,
    And laid her soiled gloves by, untied
Her hat and let the damp hair fall,
    And, last, she sat down by my side
    And called me. When no voice replied, *15*
She put my arm about her waist,
    And made her smooth white shoulder bare,
And all her yellow hair displaced,
    And, stooping, made my cheek lie there,
    And spread, o'er all, her yellow hair, *20*
Murmuring how she loved me—she
    Too weak, for all her heart's endeavor,
To set its struggling passion free
    From pride, and vainer ties dissever,
    And give herself to me forever. *25*
But passion sometimes would prevail,
    Nor could tonight's gay feast restrain
A sudden thought of one so pale
    For love of her, and all in vain;
    So, she was come through wind and rain. *30*
Be sure I looked up at her eyes
    Happy and proud; at last I knew
Porphyria worshipped me; surprise
    Made my heart swell, and still it grew
    While I debated what to do. *35*
That moment she was mine, mine, fair,
    Perfectly pure and good; I found

*Porphyria suggests the color purple, that of nobility and royalty.

A thing to do, and all her hair
    In one long yellow string I wound
    Three times her little throat around, *40*
And strangled her. No pain felt she;
    I am quite sure she felt no pain.
As a shut bud that holds a bee,
    I warily oped her lids; again
    Laughed the blue eyes without a stain. *45*
And I untightened next the tress
    About her neck; her cheek once more
Blushed bright beneath my burning kiss;
    I propped her head up as before,
    Only, this time my shoulder bore *50*
Her head, which droops upon it still;
    The smiling rosy little head
So glad it has its utmost will,
    That all it scorned at once is fled,
    And I, its love, am gained instead! *55*
Porphyria's love; she guessed not how
    Her darling one wish would be heard.
And thus we sit together now,
    And all night long we have not stirred,
    And yet God has not said a word! *60*

[1842]

Soliloquy of the Spanish Cloister

I

Gr-r-r—there go, my heart's abhorrence!
    Water your damned flower-pots, do!
If hate killed men, Brother Lawrence,
    God's blood, would not mine kill you!
What? your myrtle-bush wants trimming? *5*
    Oh, that rose has prior claims—
Needs its leaden vase filled brimming?
    Hell dry you up with its flames!

II

At the meal we sit together;
  Salve tibi!° I must hear   10
Wise talk of the kind of weather,
  Sort of season, time of year;
Not a plenteous cork-crop; scarcely
  Dare we hope oak-galls, I doubt;
What's the Latin name for "parsley"?   15
  What's the Greek name for "swine's snout"°?

III

Whew! We'll have our platter burnished,
  Laid with care on our own shelf!
With a fire-new spoon we're furnished,
  And a goblet for ourself,   20
Rinsed like something sacrificial
  Ere 'tis fit to touch our chaps—
Marked with L. for our initial!
  (He-he! There his lily snaps!)

IV

Saint, forsooth! While Brown Dolores   25
  Squats outside the Convent bank
With Sanchicha, telling stories,
  Steeping tresses in the tank,
Blue-black, lustrous, thick like horsehairs,
  —Can't I see his dead eye glow,   30
Bright as 'twere a Barbary corsair's?°
  (That is, if he'd let it show!)

V

When he finishes refection,
  Knife and fork he never lays
Cross-wise, to my recollection,   35
  As I do, in Jesu's praise.
I the Trinity illustrate,
  Drinking watered orange-pulp—
In three sips the Arian° frustrate;
  While he drains his at one gulp!   40

10 *Salve tibi!*: Hail to thee! **16** *swine's snout*: archaic name for dandelion. **31** *Barbary corsair*: a pirate of north Africa's Barbary Coast. **39** *Arian*: a follower of Arius (256–336), a heretic who denied the doctrine of the Trinity.

VI

Oh, those melons! if he's able
  We're to have a feast; so nice!
One goes to the Abbot's table,
  All of us get each a slice.
How go on your flowers? None double? *45*
  Not one fruit-sort can you spy?
Strange!—And I, too, at such trouble,
  Keep them close-nipped on the sly!

VII

There's a great text in Galatians,°
  Once you trip on it, entails *50*
Twenty-nine distinct damnations,
  One sure, if another fails;
If I trip him just a-dying,
  Sure of heaven as sure can be,
Spin him round and send him flying *55*
  Off to hell, a Manichee?°

VIII

Or, my scrofulous French novel
  On grey paper with blunt type!
Simply glance at it, you grovel
  Hand and foot in Belial's° gripe; *60*
If I double down its pages
  At the woeful sixteenth print,
When he gathers his greengages,
  Ope a sieve and slip it in't?

IX

Or, there's Satan!—one might venture *65*
  Pledge one's soul to him, yet leave
Such a flaw in the indenture
  As he'd miss till, past retrieve,
Blasted lay that rose-acacia
  We're so proud of! *Hy, Zy, Hine. . . .* *70*
'St, there's Vespers! *Plena gratia*
  Ave, Virgo!° Gr-r-r—you swine!

[1842]

49 *a great text in Galatians*: Biblical text difficult to interpret. 56 *Manichee*: heretical follower of the Persian philosopher Mani. 60 *Belial*: Satan, or wickedness. 71-72 *Plena...Virgo!*: Hail, Virgin, full of grace!

Meeting at Night

The gray sea and the long black land;
And the yellow half-moon large and low;
And the startled little waves that leap
In fiery ringlets from their sleep,
As I gain the cove with pushing prow, *5*
And quench its speed i' the slushy sand.

Then a mile of warm sea-scented beach;
Three fields to cross till a farm appears;
A tap at the pane, the quick sharp scratch
And blue spurt of a lighted match, *10*
And a voice less loud, through its joys and fears,
Than the two hearts beating each to each!

[1845]

Parting at Morning

Round the cape of a sudden came the sea,
And the sun looked over the mountain's rim;
And straight was a path of gold for him,
And the need of a world of men for me.

[1845]

After the early death of their mother, **Emily Brontë** *(1818–1848) and her sisters Anne and Charlotte were raised by their aunt in Haworth, England. They enrolled for short, unhappy periods in school, but were mostly educated at home. The three girls, who would later become influential writers, created complex imaginary worlds in their youth. (Emily and Anne conjured Gondal, the setting for many of Emily's poems.) Emily worked as a governess near Halifax in 1837, and traveled with Charlotte to Brussels five years later to study language, but she was* *called home after the death of her aunt. She remained in Haworth for the rest of her short life. Charlotte claims to have "discovered" Emily's poems in 1845. She compiled a collection of verse by all three sisters,* Poems by Currer, Ellis, and Acton Bell*—these were the pseudonyms of Charlotte, Emily, and Anne, respectively. The book attracted no special notice when it appeared in 1846, but Emily's novel* Wuthering Heights *(1847) became acknowledged as a masterpiece shortly after her death. She died of tuberculosis at the age of 30.*

Emily Brontë

Remembrance

Cold in the earth, and the deep snow piled above thee!
Far, far removed, cold in the dreary grave!
Have I forgot, my Only Love, to love thee,
Severed at last by Time's all-wearing wave?

Now, when alone, do my thoughts no longer hover   *5*
Over the mountains on Angora's shore;
Resting their wings where heath and fern-leaves cover
That noble heart for ever, ever more?

Cold in the earth, and fifteen wild Decembers
From those brown hills have melted into spring—   *10*
Faithful indeed is the spirit that remembers
After such years of change and suffering!

Sweet Love of youth, forgive if I forget thee
While the World's tide is bearing me along;
Sterner desires and darker hopes beset me,   *15*
Hopes which obscure but cannot do thee wrong.

No other Sun has lightened up my heaven;
No other Star has ever shone for me;
All my life's bliss from thy dear life was given—
All my life's bliss is in the grave with thee.   *20*

But when the days of golden dreams had perished
And even Despair was powerless to destroy,
Then did I learn how existence could be cherished,
Strengthened and fed without the aid of joy;

Then did I check the tears of useless passion, *25*
Weaned my young soul from yearning after thine;
Sternly denied its burning wish to hasten
Down to that tomb already more than mine!

And even yet, I dare not let it languish,
Dare not indulge in Memory's rapturous pain; *30*
Once drinking deep of that divinest anguish,
How could I seek the empty world again?

[1846]

Love and Friendship

Love is like the wild rose-brier;
  Friendship like the holly-tree.
The holly is dark when the rose-brier blooms,
  But which will bloom most constantly?

The wild rose-brier is sweet in spring, *5*
  Its summer blossoms scent the air;
Yet wait till winter comes again,
  And who will call the wild-brier fair?

Then, scorn the silly rose-wreath now,
  And deck thee with the holly's sheen, *10*
That, when December blights thy brow,
  He still may leave thy garland green.

[1850]

No Coward Soul Is Mine

No coward soul is mine
No trembler in the world's storm-troubled sphere;
I see Heaven's glories shine,
And Faith shines equal arming me from Fear.

O God within my breast, 5
Almighty ever-present Deity!
Life, that in me hast rest,
As I Undying Life, have power in Thee!

Vain are the thousand creeds
That move men's hearts, unutterably vain, 10
Worthless as withered weeds,
Or idlest froth amid the boundless main,

To waken doubt in one
Holding so fast by thy infinity,
So surely anchored on 15
The steadfast rock of Immortality.

With wide-embracing love
Thy spirit animates eternal years,
Pervades and broods above,
Changes, sustains, dissolves, creates and rears. 20

Though Earth and man were gone,
And suns and universes ceased to be,
And thou wert left alone,
Every Existence would exist in thee.

There is not room for Death 25
Nor atom that his might could render void;
Since thou art Being and Breath,
And what thou art may never be destroyed.

[1850]

One of eight children, **Walt Whitman** *(1819–1892) was born in the farming community of West Hills, Long Island, where his father was a carpenter and farmer. The family moved to Brooklyn, New York, when Whitman was four, and he attended public school there until the age of 11, when he began to work full-time as a messenger and for newspapers and printers. He was employed as a reporter, editor, typesetter, and, beginning at 17, as a schoolteacher.* Leaves of Grass *(1855), his most significant work, was constantly revised, going through nine separate editions before his death in 1892. When the Civil War broke out, Whitman volunteered in the New York hospitals as a nurse, also working as a government clerk during the day for the Interior Department. (He was fired from the job after the Secretary of the Interior read* Leaves of Grass *and was offended.) Other writers publicly supported Whitman during this scandal, and finally his reputation was restored. After Whitman had a stroke in 1873, he moved to Camden, New Jersey, to be near his dying mother, and remained in that town until his death almost two decades later.*

Walt Whitman

When I Heard the Learn'd Astronomer

When I heard the learn'd astronomer,
When the proofs, the figures, were ranged in columns before me,
When I was shown the charts and diagrams, to add, divide, and
measure them,
When I sitting heard the astronomer where he lectured with much
applause in the lecture-room,
How soon unaccountable I became tired and sick, 5
Till rising and gliding out I wander'd off by myself,
In the mystical moist night-air, and from time to time,
Look'd up in perfect silence at the stars.

[1865]

I Hear America Singing

I hear America singing, the varied carols I hear,
Those of mechanics, each one singing his as it should be blithe
and strong,
The carpenter singing his as he measures his plank or beam,
The mason singing his as he makes ready for work, or leaves
off work,
The boatman singing what belongs to him in his boat, the 5
deckhand singing on the steamboat deck,
The shoemaker singing as he sits on his bench, the hatter
singing as he stands,
The wood-cutter's song, the ploughboy's on his way in the
morning, or at noon intermission or at sundown,
The delicious singing of the mother, or of the young wife at
work, or of the girl sewing or washing,
Each singing what belongs to him or her and to none else,
The day what belongs to the day—at night the party of 10
young fellows, robust, friendly,
Singing with open mouths their strong melodious songs.

[1867]

I Saw in Louisiana a Live-Oak Growing

I saw in Louisiana a live-oak growing,
All alone stood it and the moss hung down from the branches,
Without any companion it grew there uttering joyous leaves
of dark green,
And its look, rude, unbending, lusty, made me think of myself,
But I wonder'd how it could utter joyous leaves standing alone 5
there without its friend near, for I knew I could not,
And I broke off a twig with a certain number of leaves upon it,
and twined around it a little moss,

And brought it away, and I have placed it in sight in my room,
It is not needed to remind me as of my own dear friends,
(For I believe lately I think of little else than of them,)
Yet it remains to me a curious token, it makes me think of manly love; *10*
For all that, and though the live-oak glistens there in Louisiana solitary in a wide flat space,
Uttering joyous leaves all its life without a friend a lover near,
I know very well I could not.

[1867]

Out of the Cradle Endlessly Rocking

Out of the cradle endlessly rocking,
Out of the mocking-bird's throat, the musical shuttle,
Out of the Ninth-month° midnight,
Over the sterile sands and the fields beyond, where the child leaving his bed wander'd alone, bareheaded, barefoot,
Down from the shower'd halo, *5*
Up from the mystic play of shadows twining and twisting as if they were alive,
Out from the patches of briers and blackberries,
From the memories of the bird that chanted to me,
From your memories sad brother, from the fitful risings and fallings I heard,
From under that yellow half-moon late-risen and swollen as if with tears, *10*
From those beginning notes of yearning and love there in the mist,
From the thousand responses of my heart never to cease,
From the myriad thence-arous'd words,
From the word stronger and more delicious than any,
From such as now they start the scene revisiting, *15*
As a flock, twittering, rising, or overhead passing,
Borne hither, ere all eludes me, hurriedly,
A man, yet by these tears a little boy again,
Throwing myself on the sand, confronting the waves,
I, chanter of pains and joys, uniter of here and hereafter, *20*

3 *Ninth-month*: Quaker term for September.

Taking all hints to use them, but swiftly leaping beyond them,
A reminiscence sing.

Once Paumanok,°
When the lilac-scent was in the air and Fifth-month grass
was growing,
Up this seashore in some briers, 25
Two feather'd guests from Alabama, two together,
And their nest, and four light-green eggs spotted with brown,
And every day the he-bird to and fro near at hand,
And every day the she-bird crouch'd on her nest, silent,
with bright eyes,
And every day I, a curious boy, never too close, never 30
disturbing them,
Cautiously peering, absorbing, translating.

Shine! shine! shine!
Pour down your warmth, great sun!
While we bask, we two together.

Two together! 35
Winds blow south, or winds blow north,
Day come white, or night come black,
Home, or rivers and mountains from home,
Singing all time, minding no time,
While we two keep together. 40

Till of a sudden,
May-be kill'd, unknown to her mate,
One forenoon the she-bird crouch'd not on the nest,
Nor return'd that afternoon, nor the next,
Nor ever appear'd again. 45

And thenceforward all summer in the sound of the sea,
And at night under the full of the moon in calmer weather,
Over the hoarse surging of the sea,
Or flitting from brier to brier by day,
I saw, I heard at intervals the remaining one, the he-bird, 50
The solitary guest from Alabama.

Blow! blow! blow!
Blow up sea-winds along Paumanok's shore;
I wait and I wait till you blow my mate to me.

23 *Paumanok*: Native American name for Long Island, NY.

Yes, when the stars glisten'd, 55
All night long on the prong of a moss-scallop'd stake,
Down almost amid the slapping waves,
Sat the lone singer wonderful causing tears.

He call'd on his mate,
He pour'd forth the meanings which I of all men know. 60

Yes my brother I know,
The rest might not, but I have treasur'd every note,
For more than once dimly down to the beach gliding,
Silent, avoiding the moonbeams, blending myself with the shadows,
Recalling now the obscure shapes, the echoes, the sounds and 65
sights after their sorts,
The white arms out in the breakers tirelessly tossing,
I, with bare feet, a child, the wind wafting my hair,
Listen'd long and long.

Listen'd to keep, to sing, now translating the notes,
Following you my brother. 70

Soothe! soothe! soothe!
Close on its wave soothes the wave behind,
And again another behind embracing and lapping, every one close,
But my love soothes not me, not me.

Low hangs the moon, it rose late, 75
It is lagging—O I think it is heavy with love, with love.

O madly the sea pushes upon the land,
With love, with love.

O night! do I not see my love fluttering out among the breakers?
What is that little black thing I see there in the white? 80

Loud! loud! loud!
Loud I call to you, my love!

High and clear I shoot my voice over the waves,
Surely you must know who is here, is here,
You must know who I am, my love. 85

Low-hanging moon!
What is that dusky spot in your brown yellow?
O it is the shape, the shape of my mate!
O moon do not keep her from me any longer.

Land! land! O land! 90
Whichever way I turn, O I think you could give me my mate back again if you only would,
For I am almost sure I see her dimly whichever way I look.

O rising stars!
Perhaps the one I want so much will rise, will rise with some of you.

O throat! O trembling throat! 95
Sound clearer through the atmosphere!
Pierce the woods, the earth,
Somewhere listening to catch you must be the one I want.

Shake out carols!
Solitary here, the night's carols! 100
Carols of lonesome love! death's carols!
Carols under that lagging, yellow, waning moon!
O under that moon where she droops almost down into the sea!
O reckless despairing carols.

But soft! sink low! 105
Soft! let me just murmur,
And do you wait a moment you husky-nois'd sea,
For somewhere I believe I heard my mate responding to me,
So faint, I must be still, be still to listen,
But not altogether still, for then she might not come immediately to me. 110

Hither my love!
Here I am! here!
With this just-sustain'd note I announce myself to you,
This gentle call is for you my love, for you.

Do not be decoy'd elsewhere, 115
That is the whistle of the wind, it is not my voice,
That is the fluttering, the fluttering of the spray,
Those are the shadows of leaves.

O darkness! O in vain!
O I am very sick and sorrowful. 120
O brown halo in the sky near the moon, drooping upon the sea!
O troubled reflection in the sea!

O throat! O throbbing heart!
And I singing uselessly, uselessly all the night.

O past! O happy life! O songs of joy! 125
In the air, in the woods, over fields,
Loved! loved! loved! loved! loved!
But my mate no more, no more with me!
We two together no more.

The aria sinking, 130
All else continuing, the stars shining,
The winds blowing, the notes of the bird continuous echoing,
With angry moans the fierce old mother incessantly moaning,
On the sands of Paumanok's shore gray and rustling,
The yellow half-moon enlarged, sagging down, drooping, 135
the face of the sea almost touching,
The boy ecstatic, with his bare feet the waves, with his hair
the atmosphere dallying,
The love in the heart long pent, now loose, now at last
tumultuously bursting,
The aria's meaning, the ears, the soul, swiftly depositing,
The strange tears down the cheeks coursing,
The colloquy there, the trio, each uttering, 140
The undertone, the savage old mother incessantly crying,
To the boy's soul's questions sullenly timing, some drown'd
secret hissing,
To the outsetting bard.

Demon or bird! (said the boy's soul,)
Is it indeed toward your mate you sing? or is it really to me? 145
For I, that was a child, my tongue's use sleeping, now I have
heard you,
Now in a moment I know what I am for, I awake,
And already a thousand singers, a thousand songs, clearer,
louder and more sorrowful than yours,
A thousand warbling echoes have started to life within me,
never to die.

O you singer solitary, singing by yourself, projecting me, 150
O solitary me listening, never more shall I cease perpetuating you,
Never more shall I escape, never more the reverberations,
Never more the cries of unsatisfied love be absent from me,

Never again leave me to be the peaceful child I was before
what there in the night,
By the sea under the yellow and sagging moon, *155*
The messenger there arous'd, the fire, the sweet hell within,
The unknown want, the destiny of me.

O give me the clew!° (it lurks in the night here somewhere,)
O if I am to have so much, let me have more!

A word then, (for I will conquer it,) *160*
The word final, superior to all,
Subtle, sent up—what is it?—I listen;
Are you whispering it, and have been all the time, you sea-waves?
Is that it from your liquid rims and wet sands?

Whereto answering, the sea, *165*
Delaying not, hurrying not,
Whisper'd me through the night, and very plainly before daybreak,
Lisp'd to me the low and delicious word death,
And again death, death, death, death,
Hissing melodious, neither like the bird nor like my arous'd *170*
child's heart,
But edging near as privately for me rustling at my feet,
Creeping thence steadily up to my ears and laving me softly
all over,
Death, death, death, death, death.

Which I do not forget,
But fuse the song of my dusky demon and brother, *175*
That he sang to me in the moonlight on Paumanok's gray beach,
With the thousand responsive songs at random,
My own songs awaked from that hour,
And with them the key, the word up from the waves,
The word of the sweetest song and all songs, *180*
That strong and delicious word which, creeping to my feet,
(Or like some old crone rocking the cradle, swathed in sweet
garments, bending aside,)
The sea whisper'd me.

[1881]

158 *clew*: clue.

A Noiseless Patient Spider

A noiseless patient spider,
I mark'd where on a little promontory it stood isolated,
Mark'd how to explore the vacant vast surrounding,
It launch'd forth filament, filament, filament, out of itself,
Ever unreeling them, ever tirelessly speeding them. *5*

And you O my soul where you stand,
Surrounded, detached, in measureless oceans of space,
Ceaselessly musing, venturing, throwing, seeking the spheres
to connect them,
Till the bridge you will need be form'd, till the ductile anchor hold,
Till the gossamer thread you fling catch somewhere, O my soul. *10*

[1881]

from Song of Myself

I

I celebrate myself, and sing myself,
And what I assume you shall assume,
For every atom belonging to me as good belongs to you.

I loafe and invite my soul,
I lean and loafe at my ease observing a spear of summer grass. *5*

My tongue, every atom of my blood, form'd from this soil, this air,
Born here of parents born here from parents the same, and
their parents the same,
I, now thirty-seven years old in perfect health begin,
Hoping to cease not till death.

Creeds and schools in abeyance, *10*
Retiring back a while sufficed at what they are, but never forgotten,
I harbor for good or bad, I permit to speak at every hazard,
Nature without check with original energy.

6

A child said *What is the grass?* fetching it to me with full hands;
How could I answer the child? I do not know what it is any
more than he.

I guess it must be the flag of my disposition, out of hopeful
green stuff woven.

Or I guess it is the handkerchief of the Lord,
A scented gift and remembrancer designedly dropt, *5*
Bearing the owner's name someway in the corners, that we
may see and remark, and say *Whose?*

Or I guess the grass is itself a child, the produced babe of the
vegetation.

Or I guess it is a uniform hieroglyphic,
And it means, Sprouting alike in broad zones and narrow zones,
Growing among black folks as among white, *10*
Kanuck,° Tuckahoe,° Congressman, Cuff,° I give them the same,
I receive them the same.

And now it seems to me the beautiful uncut hair of graves.

Tenderly will I use you curling grass,
It may be you transpire from the breasts of young men,
It may be if I had known them I would have loved them, *15*
It may be you are from old people, or from offspring taken
soon out of their mothers' laps,
And here you are the mothers' laps.

This grass is very dark to be from the white heads of old
mothers,
Darker than the colorless beards of old men,
Dark to come from under the faint red roofs of mouths. *20*

O I perceive after all so many uttering tongues,
And I perceive they do not come from the roofs of mouths
for nothing.

I wish I could translate the hints about the dead young men
and women,

11 *Kanuck*: French-Canadian. *Tuckahoe*: coastal Virginian. *Cuff*: black slave.

And the hints about old men and mothers, and the offspring
taken soon out of their laps.

What do you think has become of the young and old men? 25
And what do you think has become of the women and children?

They are alive and well somewhere,
The smallest sprout shows there is really no death,
And if ever there was it led forward life, and does not wait
at the end to arrest it,
And ceas'd the moment life appear'd. 30

All goes onward and outward, nothing collapses,
And to die is different from what any one supposed, and luckier.

21

I am the poet of the Body and I am the poet of the Soul,
The pleasures of heaven are with me and the pains of hell
are with me,
The first I graft and increase upon myself, the latter I translate
into a new tongue.

I am the poet of the woman the same as the man,
And I say it is as great to be a woman as to be a man, 5
And I say there is nothing greater than the mother of men.

I chant the chant of dilation or pride,
We have had ducking and deprecating about enough,
I show that size is only development.

Have you outstript the rest? are you the President? 10
It is a trifle, they will more than arrive there every one,
and still pass on.

I am he that walks with the tender and growing night,
I call to the earth and sea half-held by the night.

Press close bare-bosom'd night—press close magnetic
nourishing night!
Night of south winds—night of the large few stars! 15
Still nodding night—mad naked summer night.

Smile O voluptuous cool-breath'd earth!
Earth of the slumbering and liquid trees!
Earth of departed sunset—earth of the mountains misty-topt!
Earth of the vitreous pour of the full moon just tinged with blue! *20*
Earth of shine and dark mottling the tide of the river!
Earth of the limpid gray of clouds brighter and clearer for my sake!
Far-swooping elbow'd earth—rich apple-blossom'd earth!
Smile, for your lover comes.

Prodigal, you have given me love—therefore I to you give love! *25*
O unspeakable passionate love.

52

The spotted hawk swoops by and accuses me, he complains
of my gab and my loitering.

I too am not a bit tamed, I too am untranslatable,
I sound my barbaric yawp over the roofs of the world.

The last scud of day holds back for me,
It flings my likeness after the rest and true as any on the *5*
shadow'd wilds,
It coaxes me to the vapor and the dusk.

I depart as air, I shake my white locks at the runaway sun,
I effuse my flesh in eddies, and drift it in lacy jags.

I bequeath myself to the dirt to grow from the grass I love,
If you want me again look for me under your boot-soles. *10*

You will hardly know who I am or what I mean,
But I shall be good health to you nevertheless,
And filter and fibre your blood.

Failing to fetch me at first keep encouraged,
Missing me one place search another, *15*
I stop somewhere waiting for you.

[1891–1892]

***Matthew Arnold** (1822–1888) was born in Middlesex, England, on Christmas Eve. In 1828 Arnold's father was appointed headmaster of Rugby School, where the young boy was enrolled. Although he was a poor student, he won a fellowship to attend Oriel College, Oxford, and also educated himself in literature and classical and German philosophy. Arnold gave up his fellowship at the age of 24 and accepted a position as assistant master at the Rugby School. After only one term, he set out for London to work as the private secretary to Lord Lansdowne, the lord president of the Privy Council. Arnold was appointed as an inspector of schools in 1851, which allowed him to travel widely and provided the financial security he needed to marry Frances Lucy Wightman. The couple had six children. For 35 years Arnold worked as a school inspector, publishing widely on social and educational issues, as well as literary criticism. At the age of 34, he was elected to a five-year appointment as Oxford University's poetry chair. Arnold died of a heart attack in Liverpool.*

Matthew Arnold

Shakespeare

Others abide our question. Thou art free.
We ask and ask—thou smilest and art still,
Out-topping knowledge. For the loftiest hill,
Who to the stars uncrowns his majesty,

Planting his stedfast footsteps in the sea, *5*
Making the heaven of heavens his dwelling-place,
Spares but the cloudy border of his base
To the foiled searching of mortality;

And thou, who didst the stars and sunbeams know,
Self-schooled, self-scanned, self-honored, self-secure, *10*
Didst tread on earth unguessed at—better so!

All pains the immortal spirit must endure,
All weakness which impairs, all griefs which bow,
Find their sole speech in that victorious brow.

[1849]

Dover Beach

The sea is calm tonight.
The tide is full, the moon lies fair
Upon the straits; on the French coast the light
Gleams and is gone; the cliffs of England stand,
Glimmering and vast, out in the tranquil bay. *5*
Come to the window, sweet is the night-air!
Only, from the long line of spray
Where the sea meets the moon-blanched land,
Listen! you hear the grating roar
Of pebbles which the waves draw back, and fling, *10*
At their return, up the high strand,
Begin, and cease, and then again begin,
With tremulous cadence slow, and bring
The eternal note of sadness in.

Sophocles long ago *15*
Heard it on the Aegean, and it brought
Into his mind the turbid ebb and flow
Of human misery; we
Find also in the sound a thought,
Hearing it by this distant northern sea. *20*

The Sea of Faith
Was once, too, at the full, and round earth's shore
Lay like the folds of a bright girdle furled.
But now I only hear
Its melancholy, long, withdrawing roar, *25*
Retreating, to the breath
Of the night-wind, down the vast edges drear
And naked shingles° of the world.

Ah, love, let us be true
To one another! for the world, which seems *30*
To lie before us like a land of dreams,
So various, so beautiful, so new,
Hath really neither joy, nor love, nor light,

28 *naked shingles*: pebbled beaches.

Nor certitude, nor peace, nor help for pain;
And we are here as on a darkling° plain *35*
Swept with confused alarms of struggle and flight,
Where ignorant armies clash by night.

[1867]

35 *darkling*: becoming dark.

Coventry Patmore *(1823–1896), son of the journalist and editor P. G. Patmore, was born in Essex, England. Patmore's literary curiosities were fueled at an early age by his father. He published his first collection,* Poems, *at age 21. When his father went bankrupt buying railroad shares, Patmore's parents left England and the young man was forced to live by his wits. He first wrote translations and articles for various periodicals, and later became an assistant librarian at the British Museum, a position he held for 20 years. In 1847 he married Emily Augusta Andrews, with whom he had six children. She died after 15 years of happy marriage. Suffering two years of deep depression and declining health, Patmore traveled to Rome where he met his second wife, the heiress Marianne Caroline Byles. A Roman Catholic, she influenced Patmore to convert and provided him the means to quit his job at the museum. She died in 1880, and the following year he married his third wife, Harriet Robson, who had been the governess of his children. They remained together until his death. His most enduring verse is from* The Unknown Eros and Other Odes *(1877).*

Coventry Patmore

A Farewell

With all my will, but much against my heart,
We two now part.
My Very Dear,
Our solace is, the sad road lies so clear.
It needs no art, *5*
With faint, averted feet

And many a tear,
In our opposéd paths to persevere.
Go thou to East, I West.
We will not say *10*
There's any hope, it is so far away.
But, O my Best!
When the one darling of our widowhead,
The nursling Grief,
Is dead, *15*
And no dews blur our eyes
To see the peach-bloom come in evening skies,
Perchance we may,
Where now this night is day,
And even through faith of still averted feet, *20*
Making full circle of our banishment,
Amazéd meet;
The bitter journey to the bourne so sweet
Seasoning the termless feast of our content
With tears of recognition never dry. *25*

[1877]

Magna Est Veritas*

Here, in this little Bay,
Full of tumultuous life and great repose,
Where, twice a day,
The purposeless, glad ocean comes and goes,
Under high cliffs, and far from the huge town, *5*
I sit me down.
For want of me the world's course will not fail;
When all its work is done, the lie shall rot;
The truth is great, and shall prevail,
When none cares whether it prevail or not. *10*

[1877]

Magna Est Veritas: the truth is great (Latin).

The Toys

My little Son, who look'd from thoughtful eyes
And moved and spoke in quiet grown-up wise,
Having my law the seventh time disobey'd,
I struck him, and dismiss'd
With hard words and unkiss'd, *5*
His Mother, who was patient, being dead.
Then, fearing lest his grief should hinder sleep,
I visited his bed,
But found him slumbering deep,
With darken'd eyelids, and their lashes yet *10*
From his late sobbing wet.
And I, with moan,
Kissing away his tears, left others of my own;
For, on a table drawn beside his head,
He had put, within his reach, *15*
A box of counters and a red-vein'd stone,
A piece of glass abraded by the beach
And six or seven shells,
A bottle with bluebells
And two French copper coins, ranged there with careful art, *20*
To comfort his sad heart.
So when that night I pray'd
To God, I wept, and said;
Ah, when at last we lie with tranced breath,
Not vexing Thee in death, *25*
And Thou rememberest of what toys
We made our joys,
How weakly understood,
Thy great commanded good,
Then, fatherly not less *30*
Than I whom Thou hast moulded from the clay,
Thou'lt leave Thy wrath, and say,
'I will be sorry for their childishness.'

[1877]

Gabriel Charles Dante Rossetti—who changed his name to **Dante Gabriel Rossetti** *(1828–1882)—was the son of an Italian political refugee who settled in London and the brother of Christina Rossetti. In his youth, he focused his creative energies largely on painting, and continued to be an influential visual artist throughout his life. After two years in the Royal Academy schools, he trained with Ford Madox Brown. Rossetti then linked up with William Holman Hunt and Sir John Everett Millais, and they founded the Pre-Raphaelite Brotherhood with four other painters in 1848. Rossetti met Elizabeth Siddal in 1850 and married her a decade later. By that time she was in ill health, and died in two years of an overdose of pills, maybe intentionally. Rossetti buried a manuscript of his poems in her grave. (The poems were recovered and published in 1870 as* Poems.*) He later became intimate with Jane Morris, the wife of his friend William Morris. Their relationship grew increasingly intimate—reportedly with William's approval—as she often posed for his paintings. Suffering from insomnia, Rossetti began adding the drug chloral to his whiskey. His eventual addiction contributed to his death.*

Dante Gabriel Rossetti

Sudden Light

I have been here before,
But when or how I cannot tell;
I know the grass beyond the door,
The sweet keen smell,
The sighing sound, the lights around the shore. *5*

You have been mine before,
How long ago I may not know;
But just when at that swallow's soar
Your neck turned so,
Some veil did fall — I knew it all of yore. *10*

Has this been thus before?
And shall not thus time's eddying flight
Still with our lives our love restore
In death's despite,
And day and night yield one delight once more? *15*

[1854; 1863]

The Woodspurge

The wind flapped loose, the wind was still,
Shaken out dead from tree and hill;
I had walked on at the wind's will —
I sat now, for the wind was still.

Between my knees my forehead was — *5*
My lips, drawn in, said not Alas!
My hair was over in the grass,
My naked ears heard the day pass.

My eyes, wide open, had the run
Of some ten weeds to fix upon; *10*
Among those few, out of the sun,
The woodspurge flowered, three cups in one.

From perfect grief there need not be
Wisdom or even memory;
One thing then learnt remains to me — *15*
The woodspurge has a cup of three.

[1856; 1870]

Silent Noon

Your hands lie open in the long fresh grass—
The finger-points look through like rosy blooms;
Your eyes smile peace. The pasture gleams and glooms
'Neath billowing skies that scatter and amass.
All round our nest, far as the eye can pass, *5*
Are golden kingcup-fields with silver edge
Where the cow-parsley skirts the hawthorn-hedge.
'Tis visible silence, still as the hour-glass.

Deep in the sun-searched growths the dragon-fly
Hangs like a blue-thread loosened from the sky— *10*
So this wing'd hour is dropt to us from above.
Oh! clasp we to our hearts, for deathless dower,

This close-companioned inarticulate hour
When two-fold silence was the song of love.

[1870–1881]

***Emily Dickinson** (1830–1886) spent virtually all of her life in her family home in Amherst, Massachusetts. Her father was a prominent lawyer who served a term in the U.S. Congress. Dickinson attended one year of college at Mount Holyoke Female Seminary in nearby South Hadley. She proved a good student, but suffered from homesickness and poor health. This brief period of study and a few trips to Boston, Philadelphia, and Washington were the only occasions for which Dickinson left home during her 55-year life. Although she composed 1775 known poems, she published only seven in her lifetime. She often sent copies of poems to friends in letters, but only after her death would the full extent of her production become known when a cache of manuscripts was discovered in a trunk in the homestead attic—handwritten booklets of poems sewn together with needle and thread. By the end of her life, she had become a locally famous recluse. She was buried, according to her own instructions, within sight of the family home.*

Emily Dickinson

I Felt a Funeral, in My Brain

I felt a Funeral, in my Brain,
And Mourners to and fro
Kept treading—treading—till it seemed
That Sense was breaking through—

And when they all were seated, 5
A Service, like a Drum—
Kept beating—beating—till I thought
My Mind was going numb—

And then I heard them lift a Box
And creak across my Soul *10*
With those same Boots of Lead, again,
Then Space—began to toll,

As all the Heavens were a Bell,
And Being, but an Ear,
And I, and Silence, some strange Race *15*
Wrecked, solitary, here—

And then a Plank in Reason, broke,
And I dropped down, and down—
And hit a World, at every plunge,
And Finished knowing—then— *20*

[c. 1861]

I'm Nobody! Who Are You?

I'm Nobody! Who are you?
Are you—Nobody—too?
Then there's a pair of us!
Dont tell! they'd banish us—you know!

How dreary—to be—Somebody! *5*
How public—like a Frog—
To tell your name—the livelong June—
To an admiring Bog!

[c. 1861]

I Taste a Liquor Never Brewed

I taste a liquor never brewed—
From Tankards scooped in Pearl—

Not all the Vats upon the Rhine
Yield such an Alcohol!

Inebriate of Air—am I— *5*
And Debauchee of Dew—
Reeling—thro endless summer days—
From inns of Molten Blue—

When "Landlords" turn the drunken Bee
Out of the Foxglove's door— *10*
When Buttlerflies—renounce their "drams"—
I shall but drink the more!

Till Seraphs swing their snowy Hats
And Saints—to windows run—
To see the little Tippler *15*
Leaning against the—Sun—

[1861]

Wild Nights—Wild Nights!

Wild Nights—Wild Nights!
Were I with thee
Wild Nights should be
Our luxury!

Futile—the Winds— *5*
To a Heart in port—
Done with the Compass—
Done with the Chart!

Rowing in Eden—
Ah, the Sea! *10*
Might I but moor—Tonight—
In Thee!

[c. 1861]

The Soul Selects Her Own Society

The Soul selects her own Society—
Then—shuts the Door—
To her divine Majority—
Present no more—

Unmoved—she notes the Chariots—pausing— *5*
At her low Gate—
Unmoved—an Emperor be kneeling
Upon her Mat—

I've known her—from an ample nation—
Choose One— *10*
Then—close the Valves of her attention—
Like Stone—

[c. 1862]

This Is My Letter to the World

This is my letter to the World
That never wrote to Me—
The simple News that Nature told—
With tender Majesty

Her Message is committed *5*
To Hands I cannot see—
For love of Her—Sweet—countrymen—
Judge tenderly—of Me

[1862]

Because I Could Not Stop for Death

Because I could not stop for Death—
He kindly stopped for me—
The Carriage held but just Ourselves—
And Immortality.

We slowly drove—He knew no haste *5*
And I had put away
My labor and my leisure too,
For His Civility—

We passed the School, where Children strove
At Recess—in the Ring— *10*
We passed the Fields of Gazing Grain—
We passed the Setting Sun—

Or rather—He passed Us—
The Dews drew quivering and chill—
For only Gossamer, my Gown— *15*
My Tippet°—only Tulle°—

We paused before a House that seemed
A Swelling of the Ground—
The Roof was scarcely visible—
The Cornice—in the Ground— *20*

Since then—'tis Centuries—and yet
Feels shorter than the Day
I first surmised the Horses Heads
Were toward Eternity—

[c. 1863]

16 *Tippet*: cape. *Tulle*: net-like fabric.

Tell All the Truth but Tell It Slant

Tell all the Truth but tell it slant—
Success in Circuit lies
Too bright for our infirm Delight
The Truth's superb surprise
As Lightning to the Children eased *5*
With explanation kind
The Truth must dazzle gradually
Or every man be blind—

[c. 1868]

Success Is Counted Sweetest

Success is counted sweetest
By those who ne'er succeed.
To comprehend a nectar
Requires sorest need.

Not one of all the purple Host° *5*
Who took the Flag today
Can tell the definition
So clear of Victory

As he defeated—dying—
On whose forbidden ear *10*
The distant strains of triumph
Burst agonized and clear!

[1859; publ. 1878]

5 *purple Host*: an army.

Christina *[Georgina]* ***Rossetti*** *(1830–1894), sister of Dante Gabriel Rossetti, was born in London and educated at home by her mother. Her father, a political refugee from Italy, lost his job due to illness, requiring the children to find employment. Poor health prevented Christina from working as a governess, so she stayed at home and wrote poetry, prose, and encyclopedia entries. She was engaged for a time to the painter James Collinson—a founding member of the Pre-Raphaelite Brotherhood with Dante—but the engagement was called off when Collinson converted to Roman Catholicism. Like Dante, Christina contributed poems to* The Germ *(1850), edited by their other brother William Michael Rossetti. She had two marriage proposals during her lifetime, both of which she declined due to her strong religious conviction and her frail health. Leading a quiet life at home, she helped her mother as a schoolteacher in the 1850s. Through the next decade Rossetti worked at the House of Charity at Highgate, offering assistance to homeless and downtrodden women. Her brother published* New Poems *(1896) after her death from cancer.*

Christina Rossetti

Song

When I am dead, my dearest,
    Sing no sad songs for me;
Plant thou no roses at my head,
    Nor shady cypress tree;
Be the green grass above me *5*
    With showers and dewdrops wet;
And if thou wilt, remember,
    And if thou wilt, forget.

I shall not see the shadows,
    I shall not feel the rain; *10*
I shall not hear the nightingale
    Sing on, as if in pain;
And dreaming through the twilight
    That doth not rise nor set,
Haply I may remember, *15*
    And haply may forget.

[1848; 1862]

Up-Hill

Does the road wind up-hill all the way?
    Yes, to the very end.
Will the day's journey take the whole long day?
    From morn to night, my friend.

But is there for the night a resting-place? *5*
    A roof for when the slow dark hours begin.
May not the darkness hide it from my face?
    You cannot miss that inn.

Shall I meet other wayfarers at night?
    Those who have gone before. *10*
Then must I knock, or call when just in sight?
    They will not keep you standing at that door.

Shall I find comfort, travel-sore and weak?
    Of labor you shall find the sum.
Will there be beds for me and all who seek? *15*
    Yea, beds for all who come.

[1862]

Amor Mundi*

"Oh where are you going with your love-locks flowing
    On the west wind blowing along this valley track?"
"The downhill path is easy, come with me an it please ye,
    We shall escape the uphill by never turning back."

So they two went together in glowing August weather, *5*
    The honey-breathing heather lay to their left and right;
And dear she was to dote on, her swift feet seemed to float on
    The air like soft twin pigeons too sportive to alight.

"Oh what is that in heaven where gray cloud-flakes are seven,
    Where blackest clouds hang riven just at the rainy skirt?" *10*
"Oh that's a meteor sent us, a message dumb, portentous,
    An undeciphered solemn signal of help or hurt."

**Amor Mundi*: love of the world.

"Oh what is that glides quickly where velvet flowers grow thickly,
Their scent comes rich and sickly?"—"A scaled and hooded worm."
"Oh what's that in the hollow, so pale I quake to follow?" 15
"Oh that's a thin dead body which waits the eternal term."

"Turn again, O my sweetest,—turn again, false and fleetest;
This beaten way thou beatest I fear is hell's own track."
"Nay, too steep for hill-mounting; nay, too late for cost-counting;
This downhill path is easy, but there's no turning back." 20

[1865; 1875]

Charles Lutwidge Dodgson, who wrote under the pseudonym **Lewis Carroll** *(1832–1898), was born the eldest of 11 children in a family that prized art and literature. Among other creative endeavors, they produced a family magazine. He was born in Daresbury, a small village where his father served as rector of the church. Carroll attended Rugby and later Christ Church College, Oxford. His stutter prevented him from becoming a clergyman, so he turned to teaching. He began as a lecturer at Oxford in mathematics when only 23. In 1862 Carroll took a riverboat ride with the three young daughters of the college dean, and began concocting a story for them that eventually grew into his highly imaginative novel,* Alice's Adventures in Wonderland *(1865). The children's book, which was loved by readers of all ages, was a smash success internationally; an equally popular sequel followed,* Through the Looking Glass *(1872). Both books contained some of the poems Carroll is now celebrated for. A fine photographer as well, he produced portraits of his friend Tennyson's sons, and often photographed children. Carroll also published books on mathematics and logic. His poetry was collected in* Phantasmagoria and Other Poems *(1869). He died of influenza in Surrey.*

Lewis Carroll

Father William*

"You are old, Father William," the young man said,
"And your hair has become very white;

*From Carroll's *Alice's Adventures in Wonderland.*

And yet you incessantly stand on your head—
Do you think, at your age, it is right?"

"In my youth," Father William replied to his son, *5*
"I feared it might injure the brain;
But now that I'm perfectly sure I have none,
Why, I do it again and again."

"You are old," said the youth, "as I mentioned before,
And have grown most uncommonly fat; *10*
Yet you turned a back somersault in at the door—
Pray, what is the reason of that?"

"In my youth," said the sage, as he shook his gray locks,
"I kept all my limbs very supple
By the use of this ointment—one shilling the box— *15*
Allow me to sell you a couple."

"You are old," said the youth, "and your jaws are too weak
For anything tougher than suet;
Yet you finished the goose, with the bones and the beak—
Pray, how did you manage to do it?" *20*

"In my youth," said his father, "I took to the law,
And argued each case with my wife;
And the muscular strength, which it gave to my jaw,
Has lasted the rest of my life."

"You are old," said the youth, "one would hardly suppose *25*
That your eye was as steady as ever;
Yet you balanced an eel on the end of your nose—
What made you so awfully clever?"

"I have answered three questions, and that is enough,"
Said his father; "don't give yourself airs! *30*
Do you think I can listen all day to such stuff?
Be off, or I'll kick you downstairs!"

[1865]

Jabberwocky*

'Twas brillig, and the slithy toves
  Did gyre and gimble in the wabe;
All mimsy were the borogoves,
  And the mome raths outgrabe.

"Beware the Jabberwock, my son! *5*
  The jaws that bite, the claws that catch!
Beware the Jubjub bird, and shun
  The frumious Bandersnatch!"

He took his vorpal sword in hand;
  Long time the manxome foe he sought— *10*
So rested he by the Tumtum tree
  And stood awhile in thought.

And, as in uffish thought he stood,
  The Jabberwock, with eyes of flame,
Came whiffling through the tulgey wood, *15*
  And burbled as it came!

One, two! One, two! And through and through
  The vorpal blade went snicker-snack!
He left it dead, and with its head
  He went galumphing back. *20*

"And hast thou slain the Jabberwock?
  Come to my arms, my beamish boy!
O frabjous day! Callooh, Callay!"
  He chortled in his joy.

'Twas brillig, and the slithy toves *25*
  Did gyre and gimble in the wabe;
All mimsy were the borogoves,
  And the mome raths outgrabe.

[1871]

*From Carroll's *Through the Looking Glass.* Explained by Humpty Dumpty, the poem contains several invented and portmanteau words.

The Walrus and the Carpenter*

The sun was shining on the sea,
  Shining with all his might;
He did his very best to make
  The billows smooth and bright—
And this was odd, because it was *5*
  The middle of the night.

The moon was shining sulkily,
  Because she thought the sun
Had got no business to be there
  After the day was done— *10*
"It's very rude of him," she said,
  "To come and spoil the fun!"

The sea was wet as wet could be,
  The sands were dry as dry.
You could not see a cloud, because *15*
  No cloud was in the sky;
No birds were flying overhead—
  There were no birds to fly.

The Walrus and the Carpenter
  Were walking close at hand; *20*
They wept like anything to see
  Such quantities of sand;
"If this were only cleared away,"
  They said, "it would be grand!"

"If seven maids with seven mops *25*
  Swept it for half a year,
Do you suppose," the Walrus said,
  "That they could get it clear?"
"I doubt it," said the Carpenter,
  And shed a bitter tear. *30*

"O Oysters, come and walk with us!"
  The Walrus did beseech.
"A pleasant walk, a pleasant talk,
  Along the briny beach;

*from *Through the Looking Glass*

We cannot do with more than four, *35*
  To give a hand to each."

The eldest Oyster looked at him,
  But never a word he said;
The eldest Oyster winked his eye,
  And shook his heavy head— *40*
Meaning to say he did not choose
  To leave the oyster-bed.

But four young Oysters hurried up,
  All eager for the treat;
Their coats were brushed, their faces washed, *45*
  Their shoes were clean and neat—
And this was odd, because, you know,
  They hadn't any feet.

Four other Oysters followed them,
  And yet another four; *50*
And thick and fast they came at last,
  And more, and more, and more—
All hopping through the frothy waves,
  And scrambling to the shore.

The Walrus and the Carpenter *55*
  Walked on a mile or so,
And then they rested on a rock
  Conveniently low;
And all the little Oysters stood
  And waited in a row. *60*

"The time has come," the Walrus said,
  "To talk of many things;
Of shoes—and ships—and sealing wax—
  Of cabbages—and kings—
And why the sea is boiling hot— *65*
  And whether pigs have wings."

"But wait a bit," the Oysters cried,
  "Before we have our chat;
For some of us are out of breath,
  And all of us are fat!" *70*
"No hurry!" said the Carpenter.
  They thanked him much for that.

"A loaf of bread," the Walrus said,
    "Is what we chiefly need;
Pepper and vinegar besides *75*
    Are very good indeed—
Now, if you're ready, Oysters dear,
    We can begin to feed."

"But not on us!" the Oysters cried,
    Turning a little blue. *80*
"After such kindness, that would be
    A dismal thing to do!"
"The night is fine," the Walrus said.
    "Do you admire the view?

"It was so kind of you to come! *85*
    And you are very nice!"
The Carpenter said nothing but
    "Cut us another slice.
I wish you were not quite so deaf—
    I've had to ask you twice!" *90*

"It seems a shame," the Walrus said,
    "To play them such a trick,
After we've brought them out so far,
    And made them trot so quick!"
The Carpenter said nothing but *95*
    "The butter's spread too thick!"

"I weep for you," the Walrus said;
    "I deeply sympathize."
With sobs and tears he sorted out
    Those of the largest size, *100*
Holding his pocket-handkerchief
    Before his streaming eyes.

"O Oysters," said the Carpenter,
    "You've had a pleasant run!
Shall we be trotting home again?" *105*
    But answer came there none—
And this was scarcely odd, because
    They'd eaten every one.

[1871]

***Algernon Charles Swinburne** (1837–1909), born in London, spent most of his childhood on the Isle of Wight. He went to school at Eton, where his experience of corporal punishment instilled in him a lifelong obsession with flagellation. At Balliol College, Oxford, he came to know Dante Gabriel Rossetti and the Pre-Raphaelites. Swinburne had been raised Catholic, but he left Oxford in 1860 an atheist, and without taking a degree. That year he published his first book, two verse plays, to no acclaim. Swinburne's physical, temperamental, and sexual oddities have attracted much attention. He was a very small man with a large head, frequented by nervous ticks and collapses. His heavy drinking so damaged his health that a friend, Theodore Watts-Dunton, had to intervene and regulate the poet's life. Swinburne lived with Watts-Dutton and his wife for the next 30 years. Swinburne's decadent lifestyle was clearly expressed in his controversial collection* Poems as well as Ballads *(1866). The book caused a sensation, calling forth both enthusiastic responses to his unconventional themes as well as disgust at his "indecency." He wrote poetry, prose, and drama until the end of his life, which came at 72 from pneumonia.*

Algernon Charles Swinburne

When the Hounds of Spring Are on Winter's Traces*

When the hounds of spring are on winter's traces,
    The mother of months in meadow or plain
Fills the shadows and windy places
    With lisp of leaves and ripple of rain;
And the brown bright nightingale amorous 5
Is half assuaged for Itylus,°
For the Thracian° ships and the foreign faces,
    The tongueless vigil, and all the pain.

*from *Atalanta in Calydon*

6 *Itylus*: in Greek mythology, the daughter of King Zethus of Thebes and Aedon, who accidentally killed her. Out of pity, the gods transformed her into a nightingale. 7 *Thracian*: of Thrace, an ancient Greek region now located in Greece, Turkey, and Bulgaria.

Come with bows bent and with emptying of quivers,
    Maiden most perfect, lady of light, *10*
With a noise of winds and many rivers,
    With a clamor of waters, and with might;
Bind on thy sandals, O thou most fleet,
Over the splendor and speed of thy feet;
For the faint east quickens, the wan west shivers, *15*
    Round the feet of the day and the feet of the night.

Where shall we find her, how shall we sing to her,
    Fold our hands round her knees, and cling?
O that man's heart were as fire and could spring to her,
    Fire, or the strength of the streams that spring! *20*
For the stars and the winds are unto her
As raiment, as songs of the harp-player;
For the risen stars and the fallen cling to her,
    And the southwest wind and the west wind sing.

For winter's rains and ruins are over, *25*
    And all the season of snows and sins;
The days dividing lover and lover,
    The light that loses, the night that wins;
And time remembered is grief forgotten,
And frosts are slain and flowers begotten, *30*
And in green underwood and cover
    Blossom by blossom the spring begins.

The full streams feed on flower of rushes,
    Ripe grasses trammel a traveling foot,
The faint fresh flame of the young year flushes *35*
    From leaf to flower and flower to fruit;
And fruit and leaf are as gold and fire,
And the oat is heard above the lyre,
And the hoofèd heel of a satyr crushes
    The chestnut-husk at the chestnut-root. *40*

And Pan° by noon and Bacchus° by night,
    Fleeter of foot than the fleet-foot kid,
Follows with dancing and fills with delight
    The Mænad° and the Bassarid;°
And soft as lips that laugh and hide *45*
The laughing leaves of the trees divide,

41 *Pan*: Greek god of forests, fields, and flocks. *Bacchus*: god of wine. **44** *Mænad, Bassarid,* and **49** *Bacchanal*: frenzied female worshippers of Bacchus.

And screen from seeing and leave in sight
    The god pursuing, the maiden hid.

The ivy falls with the Bacchanal's° hair
    Over her eyebrows hiding her eyes; *50*
The wild vine slipping down leaves bare
    Her bright breast shortening into sighs;
The wild vine slips with the weight of its leaves,
But the berried ivy catches and cleaves
To the limbs that glitter, the feet that scare *55*
    The wolf that follows, the fawn that flies.

[1865]

The Garden of Proserpine*

Here, where the world is quiet;
    Here, where all trouble seems
Dead winds' and spent waves' riot
    In doubtful dreams of dreams;
I watch the green field growing *5*
For reaping folk and sowing,
For harvest-time and mowing,
    A sleepy world of streams.

I am tired of tears and laughter,
    And men that laugh and weep; *10*
Of what may come hereafter
    For men that sow to reap;
I am weary of days and hours,
Blown buds of barren flowers,
Desires and dreams and powers *15*
    And everything but sleep.

Here life has death for neighbour,
    And far from eye or ear
Wan waves and wet winds labour,
    Weak ships and spirits steer; *20*
They drive adrift, and whither

*Prosperpine was queen of the classical Underworld.

They wot not who make thither;
But no such winds blow hither,
    And no such things grow here.

No growth of moor or coppice, *25*
    No heather-flower or vine,
But bloomless buds of poppies,
    Green grapes of Proserpine,
Pale beds of blowing rushes
Where no leaf blooms or blushes *30*
Save this whereout she crushes
    For dead men deadly wine.

Pale, without name or number,
    In fruitless fields of corn,
They bow themselves and slumber *35*
    All night till light is born;
And like a soul belated,
In hell and heaven unmated,
By cloud and mist abated
    Comes out of darkness morn. *40*

Though one were strong as seven,
    He too with death shall dwell,
Nor wake with wings in heaven,
    Nor weep for pains in hell;
Though one were fair as roses, *45*
His beauty clouds and closes;
And well though love reposes,
    In the end it is not well.

Pale, beyond porch and portal,
    Crowned with calm leaves, she stands *50*
Who gathers all things mortal
    With cold immortal hands;
Her languid lips are sweeter
Than love's who fears to greet her
To men that mix and meet her *55*
    From many times and lands.

She waits for each and other,
    She waits for all men born;
Forgets the earth her mother,
    The life of fruits and corn; *60*

And spring and seed and swallow
Take wing for her and follow
Where summer song rings hollow
    And flowers are put to scorn.

There go the loves that wither, *65*
    The old loves with wearier wings;
And all dead years draw thither,
    And all disastrous things;
Dead dreams of days forsaken,
Blind buds that snows have shaken, *70*
Wild leaves that winds have taken,
    Red strays of ruined springs.

We are not sure of sorrow,
    And joy was never sure;
To-day will die to-morrow; *75*
    Time stoops to no man's lure;
And love, grown faint and fretful,
With lips but half regretful
Sighs, and with eyes forgetful
    Weeps that no loves endure. *80*

From too much love of living,
    From hope and fear set free,
We thank with brief thanksgiving
    Whatever gods may be
That no life lives for ever; *85*
That dead men rise up never;
That even the weariest river
    Winds somewhere safe to sea.

Then star nor sun shall waken,
    Nor any change of light; *90*
Nor sound of waters shaken,
    Nor any sound or sight;
Nor wintry leaves nor vernal,
Nor days nor things diurnal;
Only the sleep eternal *95*
    In an eternal night.

[1866]

Sapphics*

All the night sleep came not upon my eyelids,
Shed not dew, nor shook nor unclosed a feather,
Yet with lips shut close and with eyes of iron
    Stood and beheld me.

Then to me so lying awake a vision *5*
Came without sleep over the seas and touched me,
Softly touched mine eyelids and lips; and I too,
    Full of the vision,

Saw the white implacable Aphrodite,
Saw the hair unbound and the feet unsandalled *10*
Shine as fire of sunset on western waters;
    Saw the reluctant

Feet, the straining plumes of the doves that drew her,
Looking always, looking with necks reverted,
Back to Lesbos,° back to the hills whereunder *15*
    Shone Mitylene;°

Heard the flying feet of the Loves behind her
Make a sudden thunder upon the waters,
As the thunder flung from the strong unclosing
    Wings of a great wind. *20*

So the goddess fled from her place, with awful
Sound of feet and thunder of wings around her;
While behind a clamour of singing women
    Severed the twilight.

Ah the singing, ah the delight, the passion! *25*
All the Loves wept, listening; sick with anguish,
Stood the crowned nine Muses about Apollo;
    Fear was upon them,

While the tenth sang wonderful things they knew not,
Ah the tenth, the Lesbian! the nine were silent, *30*
None endured the sound of her song for weeping;
    Laurel by laurel,

Faded all their crowns; but about her forehead,
Round her woven tresses and ashen temples

*The title describes the Greek meter in which the poem is written. This meter, named for the Greek poet Sappho who invented it, is very difficult to write in English.

15 *Lesbos:* Greek island where Sappho lived. **16** *Mitylene:* the town of Sappho's birth.

White as dead snow, paler than grass in summer, *35*
    Ravaged with kisses,

Shone a light of fire as a crown for ever.
Yea, almost the implacable Aphrodite
Paused, and almost wept; such a song was that song.
    Yea, by her name too *40*

Called her, saying, "Turn to me, O my Sappho";
Yet she turned her face from the Loves, she saw not
Tears for laughter darken immortal eyelids,
    Heard not about her

Fearful fitful wings of the doves departing, *45*
Saw not how the bosom of Aphrodite
Shook with weeping, saw not her shaken raiment,
    Saw not her hands wrung;

Saw the Lesbians kissing across their smitten
Lutes with lips more sweet than the sound of lutestrings, *50*
Mouth to mouth and hand upon hand, her chosen,
    Fairer than all men;

Only saw the beautiful lips and fingers,
Full of songs and kisses and little whispers,
Full of music; only beheld among them *55*
    Soar, as a bird soars

Newly fledged, her visible song, a marvel,
Made of perfect sound and exceeding passion,
Sweetly shapen, terrible, full of thunders,
    Clothed with the wind's wings. *60*

Then rejoiced she, laughing with love, and scattered
Roses, awful roses of holy blossom;
Then the Loves thronged sadly with hidden faces
    Round Aphrodite,

Then the Muses, stricken at heart, were silent; *65*
Yea, the gods waxed pale; such a song was that song.
All reluctant, all with a fresh repulsion,
    Fled from before her.

All withdrew long since, and the land was barren,
Full of fruitless women and music only. *70*
Now perchance, when winds are assuaged at sunset,
    Lulled at the dewfall,

By the grey sea-side, unassuaged, unheard of,
Unbeloved, unseen in the ebb of twilight,
Ghosts of outcast women return lamenting, *75*
    Purged not in Lethe,

Clothed about with flame and with tears, and singing
Songs that move the heart of the shaken heaven,
Songs that break the heart of the earth with pity,
    Hearing, to hear them. *80*

[1866]

***Thomas Hardy** (1840–1928) spent most of his life in the county of Dorset in southern England. Although he had an early interest in poetry, he was quickly discouraged by rejections from editors, so he turned to fiction, a more financially secure option. He spent 16 years studying architecture, mostly as an apprentice in London, and read avidly in his spare time. Hardy enjoyed some success from his fiction, though it was uneven. The same year* Far from the Madding Crowd, *the novel most celebrated in his lifetime, was published (1874), he finally had the means to marry Emma Lavinia Gifford. A number of his books were serialized in magazines, which often requested that Hardy edit out material that could be offensive to readers. The critical dissent following the publication of the sexually progressive* Jude the Obscure *(1895) finally moved him to abandon fiction for poetry. Hardy's wife died in 1912 and two years later he married his former secretary. His ashes were buried in Westminster Abbey. His heart, at his request, was buried in the Stinsford churchyard in the grave of his first wife and beside his father.*

Thomas Hardy

Hap

If but some vengeful god would call to me
From up the sky, and laugh; "Thou suffering thing,
Know that thy sorrow is my ecstasy,
That thy love's loss is my hate's profiting!"

Then would I bear it, clench myself, and die, *5*
Steeled by the sense of ire unmerited;

Half-eased in that a Powerfuller than I
Had willed and meted me the tears I shed.

But not so. How arrives it joy lies slain,
And why unblooms the best hope ever sown? *10*
—Crass Casualty obstructs the sun and rain,
And dicing Time for gladness casts a moan . . .
These purblind Doomsters had as readily strown
Blisses about my pilgrimage as pain.

[1866; 1898]

"I Look into My Glass"

I look into my glass,
And view my wasting skin,
And say, "Would God it came to pass
My heart had shrunk as thin!"

For then, I, undistrest *5*
By hearts grown cold to me,
Could lonely wait my endless rest
With equanimity.

But Time, to make me grieve,
Part steals, lets part abide; *10*
And shakes this fragile frame at eve
With throbbings of noontide.

[1898]

Neutral Tones

We stood by a pond that winter day,
And the sun was white, as though chidden of God,
And a few leaves lay on the starving sod;
    —They had fallen from an ash, and were gray.

Your eyes on me were as eyes that rove *5*
Over tedious riddles of years ago;
And some words played between us to and fro
    On which lost the more by our love.

The smile on your mouth was the deadest thing
Alive enough to have strength to die; *10*
And a grin of bitterness swept thereby
  Like an ominous bird a-wing. . . .

Since then, keen lessons that love deceives,
And wrings with wrong, have shaped to me
Your face, and the God-curst sun, and a tree, *15*
  And a pond edged with grayish leaves.

[1867; 1898]

The Darkling Thrush

I leant upon a coppice gate
  When Frost was spectre-gray,
And Winter's dregs made desolate
  The weakening eye of day.
The tangled bine-stems scored the sky *5*
  Like strings of broken lyres,
And all mankind that haunted nigh
  Had sought their household fires.

The land's sharp features seemed to be
  The Century's corpse outleant, *10*
His crypt the cloudy canopy,
  The wind his death-lament.
The ancient pulse of germ and birth
  Was shrunken hard and dry,
And every spirit upon earth *15*
  Seemed fervourless as I.

At once a voice arose among
  The bleak twigs overhead
In a full-hearted evensong
  Of joy illimited; *20*
An aged thrush, frail, gaunt, and small,
  In blast-beruffled plume,
Had chosen thus to fling his soul
  Upon the growing gloom.

So little cause for carolings *25*
  Of such ecstatic sound

Was written on terrestrial things
        Afar or nigh around,
That I could think there trembled through
        His happy good-night air   *30*
Some blessed Hope, whereof he knew
        And I was unaware.

[1901]

The Ruined Maid

"O 'Melia, my dear, this does everything crown!
Who could have supposed I should meet you in Town?
And whence such fair garments, such prosperi-ty?"—
"O didn't you know I'd been ruined?" said she.

—"You left us in tatters, without shoes or socks,   *5*
Tired of digging potatoes, and spudding up docks;°
And now you've gay bracelets and bright feathers three!"—
"Yes; that's how we dress when we're ruined," said she.

—"At home in the barton° you said 'thee' and 'thou,'
And 'thik oon,' and 'theäs oon,' and 't'other'; but now   *10*
Your talking quite fits 'ee for high compa-ny!"—
"Some polish is gained with one's ruin," said she.

—"Your hands were like paws then, your face blue and bleak
But now I'm bewitched by your delicate cheek,
And your little gloves fit as on any la-dy!"—   *15*
"We never do work when we're ruined," said she.

—"You used to call home-life a hag-ridden dream,
And you'd sigh, and you'd sock;° but at present you seem
To know not of megrims° or melancho-ly!"—
"True. One's pretty lively when ruined," said she.   *20*

—"I wish I had feathers, a fine sweeping gown,
And a delicate face, and could strut about Town!"—
"My dear—a raw country girl, such as you be,
Cannot quite expect that. You ain't ruined," said she.

[1866; 1901]

6 *spudding up docks*: digging up dockweed. 9 *barton*: barnyard. 18 *sock*: groan. 19 *megrims*: blues.

The Convergence of the Twain

Lines on the Loss of the Titanic

I

In a solitude of the sea
Deep from human vanity,
And the Pride of Life that planned her, stilly couches she.

II

Steel chambers, late the pyres
Of her salamandrine° fires, 5
Cold currents thrid,° and turn to rhythmic tidal lyres.

III

Over the mirrors meant
To glass the opulent
The sea-worm crawls—grotesque, slimed, dumb, indifferent.

IV

Jewels in joy designed 10
To ravish the sensuous mind
Lie lightless, all their sparkles bleared and black and blind.

V

Dim moon-eyed fishes near
Gaze at the gilded gear
And query; "What does this vaingloriousness down here?" . . . 15

VI

Well; while was fashioning
This creature of cleaving wing,
The Immanent Will that stirs and urges everything

5 *salamandrine*: like a salamander, a lizard said to thrive in fires, or like a spirit of the same name that inhabits fire, according to alchemists. 6 *thrid*: thread.

VII

Prepared a sinister mate
For her—so gaily great— *20*
A Shape of Ice, for the time far and dissociate.

VIII

And as the smart ship grew
In stature, grace, and hue,
In shadowy silent distance grew the Iceberg too.

IX

Alien they seemed to be; *25*
No mortal eye could see
The intimate welding of their later history,

X

Or sign that they were bent
By paths coincident
On being anon twin halves of one august event, *30*

XI

Till the Spinner of the Years
Said "Now!" And each one hears,
And consummation comes, and jars two hemispheres.

[1914]

Channel Firing

That night your great guns, unawares,
Shook all our coffins as we lay,
And broke the chancel window-squares,
We thought it was the Judgment-day

And sat upright. While drearisome *5*
Arose the howl of wakened hounds;
The mouse let fall the altar-crumb,
The worms drew back into the mounds,

The glebe cow drooled. Till God called, "No;
It's gunnery practice out at sea *10*

Just as before you went below;
The world is as it used to be;

"All nations striving strong to make
Red war yet redder. Mad as hatters
They do no more for Christés sake *15*
Than you who are helpless in such matters.

"That this is not the judgment-hour
For some of them's a blessed thing,
For if it were they'd have to scour
Hell's floor for so much threatening. . . . *20*

"Ha, ha. It will be warmer when
I blow the trumpet (if indeed
I ever do; for you are men,
And rest eternal sorely need)."

So down we lay again. "I wonder, *25*
Will the world ever saner be,"
Said one, "than when He sent us under
In our indifferent century!"

And many a skeleton shook his head.
"Instead of preaching forty year," *30*
My neighbour Parson Thirdly said,
"I wish I had stuck to pipes and beer."

Again the guns disturbed the hour,
Roaring their readiness to avenge,
As far inland as Stourton Tower, *35*
And Camelot, and starlit Stonehenge.

[1914]

Gerard Manley Hopkins *(1844–1889) was born in Stratford, England, the eldest of eight children. He won a prize for his poetry in high school, which was to be the most recognition he received for his work until long after his death. Hopkins studied classics at Balliol College, Oxford, and converted to the Roman Catholic Church, which greatly estranged him from his Protestant family. He became a Jesuit two years later and symbolically burned his poems, though fortunately he had sent some copies to his Oxford friend Robert Bridges. For years he did not write. Hopkins was appointed to the* *chair of Greek and Latin at University College in Dublin in 1884. Weak and exhausted from his academic and administrative duties, he wrote a series of "Dark Sonnets" (or "sonnets of desolation"). He died from typhoid fever, reportedly due to Dublin's polluted water supply. Apart from a couple of appearances in anthologies, none of Hopkins's work was published until Bridges edited his* Poems *in 1918, nearly 30 years after his death.*

Gerard Manley Hopkins

God's Grandeur

The world is charged with the grandeur of God.
　It will flame out, like shining from shook foil;
　It gathers to a greatness, like the ooze of oil
Crushed.° Why do men then now not reck his rod?°
Generations have trod, have trod, have trod; *5*
　And all is seared with trade; bleared, smeared with toil;
　And wears man's smudge and shares man's smell; the soil
Is bare now, nor can foot feel, being shod.

And for all this, nature is never spent;
　There lives the dearest freshness deep down things;° *10*
And though the last lights off the black West went°
　Oh, morning, at the brown brink eastward, springs—
Because the Holy Ghost over the bent
　World broods with warm breast and with ah! bright wings.

[1877; 1918]

3–4 *It gathers . . . Crushed*: The grandeur of God will rise and be manifest, as oil rises and collects from crushed olives or grain. 4 *reck his rod*: heed His law. 10 *deep down things*: the poet omits the preposition *in* or *within* before *things*. 11 *last lights . . . went*: when King Henry VIII broke from the Catholic Church in 1534 and established the Church of England.

Pied Beauty

Glory be to God for dappled things—
　For skies of couple-color as a brinded° cow;
　　For rose-moles all in stipple upon trout that swim;
Fresh-firecoal chestnut-falls; finches' wings;

2 *brinded*: streaked.

Landscape plotted and pieced—fold, fallow, and plow; *5*
And áll trádes, their gear and tackle and trim.°

All things counter, original, spare, strange;
Whatever is fickle, freckled (who know how?)
With swift, slow; sweet, sour; adazzle, dim;
He fathers-forth whose beauty is past change; *10*
Praise him.

[1877; 1918]

6 *trim*: equipment.

The Windhover*

To Christ Our Lord

I caught this morning morning's minion, king-
dom of daylight's dauphin, dapple-dawn-drawn Falcon, in his riding
Of the rolling level underneath him steady air, and striding
High there, how he rung upon the rein of a wimpling wing°
In his ecstasy! then off, off forth on swing, *5*
As a skate's heel sweeps smooth on a bow-bend; the hurl and
gliding
Rebuffed the big wind. My heart in hiding
Stirred for a bird,—the achieve of, the mastery of the thing!

Brute beauty and valor and act, oh, air, pride, plume, here
Buckle! AND the fire that breaks from thee then, a billion *10*
Times told lovelier, more dangerous, O my chevalier!

No wonder of it; shéer plód makes plow down sillion°
Shine, and blue-bleak embers, ah my dear,
Fall, gall themselves, and gash gold-vermilion.

[1877; 1918]

*A windhover is a small falcon; its name stems from its ability to hover on the wind.

4 *rung . . . wing*: A horse is "rung upon the rein" when its trainer holds the end of a long rein and has the horse circle; *wimpling* possibly means curving or pleated or rippling. 12 *sillion*: furrow.

Spring and Fall

To a young child

Márgarét, áre you ǵrieving
Over Goldengrove unleaving°
Leáves, líke the things of man, you
With your fresh thoughts care for, can you?
Áh! ás the heart grows older 5
It will come to such sights colder
By and by, nor spare a sigh
Though worlds of wanwood leafmeal lie;
And yet you *will* weep and know why.
Now no matter, child, the name; 10
Sórrow's spríngs áre the same.
Nor mouth had, no nor mind, expressed
What heart heard of, ghost° guessed;
It ís the blight man was born for,
It is Margaret you mourn for. 15

[1880; 1918]

2 *unleaving*: shedding its leaves. 13 *ghost*: sprit.

No Worst, There Is None

No worst, there is none. Pitched past pitch of grief,
More pangs will, schooled at forepangs, wilder wring.
Comforter, where, where is your comforting?
Mary, mother of us, where is your relief?

My cries heave, herds-long; huddle in a main, a chief 5
Woe, world-sorrow; on an age-old anvil wince and sing—
Then lull, then leave off. Fury had shrieked "No ling-
ering! Let me be fell;° force° I must be brief."

O the mind, mind has mountains; cliffs of fall
Frightful, sheer, no-man-fathomed. Hold them cheap 10

8 *fell*: fierce; *force*: perforce.

May who ne'er hung there. Nor does long our small
Durance° deal with that steep or deep. Here! creep,
Wretch, under a comfort serves in a whirlwind; all
Life death does end and each day dies with sleep.

[1885; 1918]

12 *Durance*: endurance.

The childhood of **A.**[*lfred*] **E.**[*dward*] **Housman** *(1859–1936) was an unhappy one. Born in Worcestershire, near Shropshire, England, he was the eldest of seven children; his father was a failed attorney and his mother died when he was 12. Housman won a scholarship to St. John's College, Oxford, to study classics. There he befriended Moses Jackson, an athletic, handsome, and outgoing young man—everything that Housman was not. It is believed that the poet was in love with Jackson, though his feelings were unrequited. Housman was a brilliant student, yet he somehow failed his final examinations and left Oxford without honors or a degree. He lived mostly in self-imposed exile for the next 11 years, taking a job at the patent office in London. Even though he was widely known and respected as a Latin scholar in his day, Housman is now remembered more for his poetry, which is remarkable considering that he produced only two slim collections during his lifetime (published 26 years apart); the first was* A Shropshire Lad *(1896). Housman held the chair of Latin at University College, London, for 19 years, and in 1911 was elected to the Kennedy Chair of Latin at Cambridge, where he remained until his death.*

A. E. Housman

Into My Heart an Air That Kills

Into my heart an air that kills
    From yon far country blows;
What are those blue remembered hills,
    What spires, what farms are those?

That is the land of lost content, 5
I see it shining plain,
The happy highways where I went
And cannot come again.

[1896]

Loveliest of Trees, the Cherry Now

Loveliest of trees, the cherry now
Is hung with bloom along the bough,
And stands about the woodland ride°
Wearing white for Eastertide.

Now, of my threescore years and ten, 5
Twenty will not come again,
And take from seventy springs a score,
It only leaves me fifty more.

And since to look at things in bloom
Fifty springs are little room, 10
About the woodlands I will go
To see the cherry hung with snow.

[1896]

3 *ride*: path.

To an Athlete Dying Young

The time you won your town the race
We chaired you through the market-place;
Man and boy stood cheering by,
And home we brought you shoulder-high.

Today, the road all runners come, *5*
Shoulder-high we bring you home,
And set you at your threshold down,
Townsman of a stiller town.

Smart lad, to slip betimes away
From fields where glory does not stay, *10*
And early though the laurel grows
It withers quicker than the rose.

Eyes the shady night has shut
Cannot see the record cut,
And silence sounds no worse than cheers *15*
After earth has stopped the ears.

Now you will not swell the rout
Of lads that wore their honors out,
Runners whom renown outran
And the name died before the man. *20*

So set, before its echoes fade,
The fleet foot on the sill of shade,
And hold to the low lintel up
The still-defended challenge-cup.

And round that early-laureled head *25*
Will flock to gaze the strengthless dead,
And find unwithered on its curls
The garland briefer than a girl's.

[1896]

With Rue My Heart Is Laden

With rue my heart is laden
  For golden friends I had,
For many a rose-lipt maiden
  And many a lightfoot lad.

By brooks too broad for leaping *5*
  The lightfoot boys are laid;

The rose-lipt girls are sleeping
    In fields where roses fade.

[1896]

Epitaph on an Army of Mercenaries

These, in the day when heaven was falling,
    The hour when earth's foundations fled,
Followed their mercenary calling
    And took their wages and are dead.

Their shoulders held the sky suspended;   5
    They stood, and earth's foundations stay;
What God abandoned, these defended,
    And saved the sum of things for pay.

[1922]

Joseph ***Rudyard Kipling*** *(1865–1936) was born in Bombay, India. His father was an artist and professor. Kipling's early childhood in India was happy, but after the death of his infant brother in 1870, he and his sister were abruptly sent to England for schooling. The children were placed with a cruel and abusive foster family and did not see their parents for five years. The suffering he endured during this time haunted Kipling's writing throughout his life. He returned to India at 17 to work as a journalist. Publishing both poetry and fiction, Kipling's fame spread rapidly from India to England and then to the rest of the world. His most famous works include* The Jungle Book *(1894),* Kim *(1901), and his stories, such as "The Man Who Would Be King." For the next 30 years Kipling was the most popular writer in the English-speaking world. He married an American and lived for a time in Vermont, where the couple had three children. Kipling turned down many honors. One award he did accept, however, was the Nobel Prize for literature in 1907, becoming the first English-language author to receive that honor. His comfortable success was shattered when his only son was killed in World War I. Kipling's own health declined as he approached his seventies, and he died following an intestinal hemorrhage.*

Rudyard Kipling
Recessional

God of our fathers, known of old,
    Lord of our far-flung battle-line,
Beneath whose awful Hand we hold
    Dominion over palm and pine—
Lord God of Hosts, be with us yet, *5*
Lest we forget—lest we forget!

The tumult and the shouting dies;
    The Captains and the Kings depart;
Still stands Thine ancient sacrifice,
    An humble and a contrite heart, *10*
Lord God of Hosts, be with us yet,
Lest we forget—lest we forget!

Far-called, our navies melt away;
    On dune and headland sinks the fire;
Lo, all our pomp of yesterday *15*
    Is one with Nineveh and Tyre!°
Judge of the Nations, spare us yet,
Lest we forget—lest we forget!

If, drunk with sight of power, we loose
    Wild tongues that have not Thee in awe, *20*
Such boastings as the Gentiles use,
    Or lesser breeds without the Law—
Lord God of Hosts, be with us yet,
Lest we forget—lest we forget!

For heathen heart that puts her trust *25*
    In reeking tube and iron shard,
All valiant dust that builds on dust,
    And guarding, calls not Thee to guard.
For frantic boast and foolish word—
Thy mercy on Thy People, Lord! *30*

[1899]

16 *Nineveh and Tyre*: Capital cities of Assyria and Phoenicia respectively, great ancient empires.

Danny Deever

"What are the bugles blowin' for?" said Files-on-Parade.
"To turn you out, to turn you out," the Colour-Sergeant said.
"What makes you look so white, so white?" said Files-on-Parade.
"I'm dreadin' what I've got to watch," the Colour-Sergeant said.
For they're hangin' Danny Deever, you can hear the Dead March play, 5
The Regiment's in 'ollow square—they're hangin' him to-day;
They've taken of his buttons off an' cut his stripes away,
An' they're hangin' Danny Deever in the mornin'.

"What makes the rear-rank breathe so 'ard?" said Files-on-Parade.
"It's bitter cold, it's bitter cold," the Colour-Sergeant said. 10
"What makes that front-rank man fall down?" said Files-on-Parade.
"A touch o' sun, a touch o' sun," the Colour-Sergeant said.
They are hangin' Danny Deever, they are marchin' of 'im round,
They 'ave 'alted Danny Deever by 'is coffin on the ground;
An' 'e'll swing in 'arf a minute for a sneakin' shootin' hound— 15
O they're hangin' Danny Deever in the mornin'!

"'Is cot was right-'and cot to mine," said Files-on-Parade.
"'E's sleepin' out an' far to-night," the Colour-Sergeant said.
"I've drunk 'is beer a score o' times," said Files-on-Parade.
"'E's drinkin' bitter beer alone," the Colour-Sergeant said. 20
They are hangin' Danny Deever, you must mark 'im to 'is place,
For 'e shot a comrade sleepin'—you must look 'im in the face;
Nine 'undred of 'is county an' the Regiment's disgrace,
While they're hangin' Danny Deever in the mornin'.

"What's that so black agin the sun?" said Files-on-Parade. 25
"It's Danny fightin' 'ard for life," the Colour-Sergeant said.
"What's that that whimpers over'ead?" said Files-on-Parade.
"It's Danny's soul that's passin' now," the Colour-Sergeant said.
For they're done with Danny Deever, you can 'ear the quickstep play,
The Regiment's in column, an' they're marchin' us away; 30
Ho! the young recruits are shakin', an' they'll want their beer to-day,
After hangin' Danny Deever in the mornin'!

[1890]

Cities and Thrones and Powers

Cities and Thrones and Powers
    Stand in Time's eye,
Almost as long as flowers,
    Which daily die;
But, as new buds put forth *5*
    To glad new men,
Out of the spent and unconsidered Earth
    The Cities rise again.

This season's Daffodil,
    She never hears *10*
What change, what chance, what chill,
    Cut down last year's;
But with bold countenance,
    And knowledge small,
Esteems her seven days' continuance *15*
    To be perpetual.

So Time that is o'er-kind
    To all that be,
Ordains us e'en as blind,
    As bold as she; *20*
That in our very death,
    And burial sure,
Shadow to shadow, well persuaded, saith,
    "See how our works endure!"

[1905]

Harp Song of the Dane Women

What is a woman that you forsake her,
And the hearth-fire and the home-acre,
To go with the old grey Widow-maker?

She has no house to lay a guest in—
But one chill bed for all to rest in, 5
That the pale suns and the stray bergs nest in.

She has no strong white arms to fold you,
But the ten-times-fingering weed to hold you—
Out on the rocks where the tide has rolled you.

Yet, when the signs of summer thicken, 10
And the ice breaks, and the birch-buds quicken,
Yearly you turn from our side, and sicken—

Sicken again for the shouts and the slaughters.
You steal away to the lapping waters,
And look at your ship in her winter-quarters. 15

You forget our mirth, and talk at the tables,
The kine in the shed and the horse in the stables—
To pitch her sides and go over her cables.

Then you drive out where the storm-clouds swallow,
And the sound of your oar-blades, falling hollow, 20
Is all we have left through the months to follow.

Ah, what is Woman that you forsake her,
And the hearth-fire and the home-acre,
To go with the old grey Widow-maker?

[t/k]

from Epitaphs of the War*

1914–18

"Equality of Sacrifice"

A. "I was a Have." *B.* "I was a 'have-not.' "
(*Together.*) "What hast thou given which I gave not?"

A Servant

We were together since the War began.
He was my servant—and the better man.

*World War I

A Son

My son was killed while laughing at some jest. I would I knew 5
What it was, and it might serve me in a time when jests are few.

An Only Son

I have slain none except my Mother.
She (Blessing her slayer) died of grief for me.

Ex-Clerk

Pity not! The Army gave
Freedom to a timid slave; 10
In which Freedom did he find
Strength of body, will, and mind;
By which strength he came to prove
Mirth, Companionship, and Love;
For which Love to Death he went; 15
In which Death he lies content.

Hindu Sepoy in France

This man in his own country prayed we know not to what Powers.
We pray Them to reward him for his bravery in ours.

The Coward

I could not look on Death, which being known,
Men led me to him, blindfold and alone. 20

Shock

My name, my speech, my self I had forgot.
My wife and children came—I knew them not.
I died. My Mother followed. At her call
And on her bosom I remembered all.

A Grave Near Cairo

Gods of the Nile, should this stout fellow here 25
Get out—get out! He knows not shame nor fear.

Pelicans in the Wilderness

A Grave near Halfa

The blown sand heaps on me, that none may learn
    Where I am laid for whom my children grieve. . . .

O wings that beat at dawning, ye return
    Out of the desert to your young at eve! *30*

Two Canadian Memorials

I

We giving all gained all.
    Neither lament us nor praise.
Only in all things recall,
    It is Fear, not Death, that slays.

II

From little towns in a far land we came, *35*
    To save our honour and a world aflame.
By little towns in a far land we sleep;
    And trust that world we won for you to keep!

The Beginner

On the first hour of my first day
    In the front trench I fell. *40*
(Children in boxes at a play
    Stand up to watch it well.)

R. A. F. (Aged Eighteen)

Laughing through clouds, his milk-teeth still unshed,
Cities and men he smote from overhead.
His deaths delivered, he returned to play *45*
Childlike, with childish things now put away.

The Refined Man

I was of delicate mind. I stepped aside for my needs,
    Disdaining the common office. I was seen from afar and killed. . . .
How is this matter for mirth? Let each man be judged by his deeds.
    I have paid my price to live with myself on the terms that I *50*
        willed.

Native Water-Carrier (M. E. F.)

Prometheus brought down fire to men.
    This brought up water.
The Gods are jealous—now, as then,
    Giving no quarter.

Batteries Out of Ammunition

If any mourn us in the workshop, say *55*
We died because the shift kept holiday.

Common Form

If any question why we died,
Tell them, because our fathers lied.

A Dead Statesman

I could not dig; I dared not rob;
Therefore I lied to please the mob. *60*
Now all my lies are proved untrue
And I must face the men I slew.
What tale shall serve me here among
Mine angry and defrauded young?

A Drifter Off Tarentum

He from the wind-bitten North with ship and companions descended, *65*
Searching for eggs of death spawned by invisible hulls.
Many he found and drew forth. Of a sudden the fishery ended
In flame and a clamorous breath known to the eye-pecking gulls.

Destroyers in Collision

For Fog and Fate no charm is found
To lighten or amend. *70*
I, hurrying to my bride, was drowned—
Cut down by my best friend.

Unknown Female Corpse

Headless, lacking foot and hand,
Horrible I come to land.
I beseech all women's sons *75*
Know I was a mother once.

Salonikan Grave

I have watched a thousand days
Push out and crawl into night
Slowly as tortoises.

Now I, too, follow these. *80*
It is fever, and not the fight—
Time, not battle—that slays.

The Bridegroom

Call me not false, beloved,
  If, from thy scarce-known breast
So little time removed, *85*
  In other arms I rest.

For this more ancient bride,
  Whom coldly I embrace,
Was constant at my side
  Before I saw thy face. *90*

Our marriage, often set—
  By miracle delayed—
At last is consummate,
  And cannot be unmade.

Live, then, whom Life shall cure, *95*
  Almost, of Memory,
And leave us to endure
  Its immortality.

Actors

On a Memorial Tablet in Holy Trinity Church, Stratford-on-Avon

We counterfeited once for your disport
  Men's joy and sorrow; but our day has passed. *100*
We pray you pardon all where we fell short—
  Seeing we were your servants to this last.

Journalists

On a Panel in the Hall of the Institute of Journalists

We have served our day.

[1919; 1940]

***William Butler Yeats** (1865–1939) was born in Dublin into an Irish Protestant family that moved to London when he was still young. William and his younger brother Jack practiced art (Jack B. Yeats became an important Irish painter), but William's interests soon turned to literature. Fascinated with the supernatural, he joined the Golden Dawn—a secret society that practiced ritual magic—and remained involved with them for over 30 years. Yeats moved back to London to pursue a literary career, and fell in love with Maud Gonne, a beautiful revolutionary who instilled in him a strong sense of Irish nationalism. He began writing nationalist-themed plays, which he staged in Ireland. The Irish National Theatre Company was founded, and Yeats served as their first president. His literary fame rose to great heights during his lifetime. He accepted a post as a senator of the Irish Free State soon after the civil war of 1922, and served for six years. In 1923 Yeats was awarded the Nobel Prize for literature. Among his most accomplished works are* The Wild Swans at Coole *(1917),* The Tower *(1928), and* The Winding Stair *(1929). He died in the south of France.*

William Butler Yeats

The Lake Isle of Innisfree

I will arise and go now, and go to Innisfree,
And a small cabin build there, of clay and wattles made;
Nine bean-rows will I have there, a hive for the honey-bee,
And live alone in the bee-loud glade.

And I shall have some peace there, for peace comes dropping slow, *5*
Dropping from the veils of the morning to where the cricket sings;
There midnight's all a glimmer, and noon a purple glow,
And evening full of the linnet's wings.

I will arise and go now, for always night and day
I hear lake water lapping with low sounds by the shore; *10*
While I stand on the roadway, or on the pavements gray,
I hear it in the deep heart's core.

[1892]

When You Are Old

When you are old and grey and full of sleep,
And nodding by the fire, take down this book,
And slowly read, and dream of the soft look
Your eyes had once, and of their shadows deep;

How many loved your moments of glad grace, *5*
And loved your beauty with love false or true,
But one man loved the pilgrim soul in you,
And loved the sorrows of your changing face;

And bending down beside the glowing bars,
Murmur, a little sadly, how Love fled *10*
And paced upon the mountains overhead
And hid his face amid a crowd of stars.

[1893]

No Second Troy

Why should I blame her that she filled my days
With misery, or that she would of late
Have taught to ignorant men most violent ways,
Or hurled the little streets upon the great,
Had they but courage equal to desire? *5*
What could have made her peaceful with a mind
That nobleness made simple as a fire,
With beauty like a tightened bow, a kind
That is not natural in an age like this,
Being high and solitary and most stern? *10*
Why, what could she have done, being what she is?
Was there another Troy for her to burn?

[1910]

An Irish Airman Foresees His Death

I know that I shall meet my fate
Somewhere among the clouds above;
Those that I fight I do not hate,
Those that I guard I do not love;
My country is Kiltartan Cross, *5*
My countrymen Kiltartan's poor,
No likely end could bring them loss
Or leave them happier than before.
Nor law, nor duty bade me fight,
Nor public men, nor cheering crowds, *10*
A lonely impulse of delight
Drove to this tumult in the clouds;
I balanced all, brought all to mind,
The years to come seemed waste to breath,
A waste of breath the years behind *15*
In balance with this life, this death.

[1919]

The Second Coming

Turning and turning in the widening gyre°
The falcon cannot hear the falconer;
Things fall apart; the center cannot hold;
Mere anarchy is loosed upon the world,
The blood-dimmed tide is loosed, and everywhere *5*
The ceremony of innocence is drowned;
The best lack all conviction, while the worst
Are full of passionate intensity.

Surely some revelation is at hand;
Surely the Second Coming is at hand; *10*
The Second Coming! Hardly are those words out

1 *gyre*: spiral.

When a vast image out of *Spiritus Mundi*°
Troubles my sight: somewhere in sands of the desert
A shape with lion body and the head of a man,
A gaze blank and pitiless as the sun, 15
Is moving its slow thighs, while all about it
Reel shadows of the indignant desert birds.
The darkness drops again; but now I know
That twenty centuries of stony sleep
Were vexed to nightmare by a rocking cradle, 20
And what rough beast, its hour come round at last,
Slouches towards Bethlehem to be born?

[1921]

12 *Spiritus Mundi*: the spirit world (Latin).

Leda and the Swan*

A sudden blow: the great wings beating still
Above the staggering girl, her thighs caressed
By the dark webs, her nape caught in his bill,
He holds her helpless breast upon his breast.

How can those terrified vague fingers push 5
The feathered glory from her loosening thighs?
And how can body, laid in that white rush,
But feel the strange heart beating where it lies?

A shudder in the loins engenders there
The broken wall, the burning roof and tower 10
And Agamemnon dead.
Being so caught up,
So mastered by the brute blood of the air,
Did she put on his knowledge with his power
Before the indifferent beak could let her drop?

[1924]

*Leda was the mother of Helen of Troy. Zeus, in the form of a swan, raped Leda.

Sailing to Byzantium*

That is no country for old men. The young
In one another's arms, birds in the trees
—Those dying generations—at their song,
The salmon-falls, the mackerel-crowded seas,
Fish, flesh, or fowl, commend all summer long *5*
Whatever is begotten, born, and dies.
Caught in that sensual music all neglect
Monuments of unaging intellect.

An aged man is but a paltry thing,
A tattered coat upon a stick, unless *10*
Soul clap its hands and sing, and louder sing
For every tatter in its mortal dress,
Nor is there singing school but studying
Monuments of its own magnificence;
And therefore I have sailed the seas and come *15*
To the holy city of Byzantium.

O sages standing in God's holy fire
As in the gold mosaic of a wall,
Come from the holy fire, perne in a gyre,°
And be the singing-masters of my soul. *20*
Consume my heart away; sick with desire
And fastened to a dying animal
It knows not what it is; and gather me
Into the artifice of eternity.

Once out of nature I shall never take *25*
My bodily form from any natural thing,
But such a form as Grecian goldsmiths make
Of hammered gold and gold enameling
To keep a drowsy Emperor awake;
Or set upon a golden bough to sing *30*
To lords and ladies of Byzantium
Of what is past, or passing, or to come.

[1927]

*Byzantium was the capital of the Byzantine Empire, the city now called Istanbul.

19 *perne in a gyre*: spin down a spiral.

Crazy Jane Talks with the Bishop

I met the Bishop on the road
And much said he and I.
"Those breasts are flat and fallen now,
Those veins must soon be dry;
Live in a heavenly mansion, *5*
Not in some foul sty."

"Fair and foul are near of kin,
And fair needs foul," I cried.
"My friends are gone, but that's a truth
Nor° grave nor bed denied, *10*
Learned in bodily lowliness
And in the heart's pride.

"A woman can be proud and stiff
When on love intent;
But Love has pitched his mansion in *15*
The place of excrement;
For nothing can be sole or whole
That has not been rent."

[1933]

10 *Nor*: Neither.

Edwin Arlington Robinson *(1869–1935) was raised in Gardiner, Maine—the place he called "Tilbury Town" in many of his poems. He attended Harvard for two years before he was forced to leave due to the death of his father and his family's financial burden. Robinson lived at home and cared for his family—which included one morphine-addicted brother and one alcoholic—until the poet was almost 30 years old. His mother passed away and Robinson finally left for New York, picking up odd jobs where he could. He lived in extreme poverty, and published his first collection—revised into* The Children of the Night *in 1897. President Theodore Roosevelt, who had been given the collection by one of his sons, reviewed the almost unknown book and gave Robinson a comfortable job at the New*

York Customs House. The post ended with Taft's election, and Robinson again fell into poverty and began drinking heavily. In 1921 his Collected Poems *won the first of his three Pulitzer Prizes, and he finally enjoyed the financial security that had long eluded him. In 1935 Robinson was diagnosed with inoperable cancer, and soon died.*

Edwin Arlington Robinson

Richard Cory

Whenever Richard Cory went down town,
We people on the pavement looked at him:
He was a gentleman from sole to crown,
Clean favored, and imperially slim.

And he was always quietly arrayed, *5*
And he was always human when he talked;
But still he fluttered pulses when he said,
"Good-morning," and he glittered when he walked.

And he was rich—yes, richer than a king—
And admirably schooled in every grace: *10*
In fine, we thought that he was everything
To make us wish that we were in his place.

So on we worked, and waited for the light,
And went without the meat, and cursed the bread;
And Richard Cory, one calm summer night, *15*
Went home and put a bullet through his head.

[1897]

Miniver Cheevy

Miniver Cheevy, child of scorn,
    Grew lean while he assailed the seasons;
He wept that he was ever born,
    And he had reasons.

Miniver loved the days of old *5*
    When swords were bright and steeds were prancing;

The vision of a warrior bold
    Would set him dancing.

Miniver sighed for what was not,
    And dreamed, and rested from his labors; *10*
He dreamed of Thebes and Camelot,°
    And Priam's° neighbors.

Miniver mourned the ripe renown
    That made so many a name so fragrant;
He mourned Romance, now on the town, *15*
    And Art, a vagrant.

Miniver loved the Medici,°
    Albeit he had never seen one;
He would have sinned incessantly
    Could he have been one. *20*

Miniver cursed the commonplace
    And eyed a khaki suit with loathing;
He missed the medieval grace
    Of iron clothing.

Miniver scorned the gold he sought, *25*
    But sore annoyed was he without it;
Miniver thought, and thought, and thought,
    And thought about it.

Miniver Cheevy, born too late,
    Scratched his head and kept on thinking; *30*
Miniver coughed, and called it fate,
    And kept on drinking.

[1910]

11 *Thebes*: a city in ancient Greece and the setting of many famous Greek myths; *Camelot*: the legendary site of King Arthur's Court. 12 *Priam*: the last king of Troy, his "neighbors" would have included Helen of Troy, Aeneas, and other famous figures. 17 *the Medici*: the ruling family of Florence during the high Renaissance, the Medici were renowned patrons of the arts.

Eros Turannos*

She fears him, and will always ask
    What fated her to choose him;
She meets in his engaging mask
    All reasons to refuse him;
But what she meets and what she fears   5
Are less than are the downward years,
Drawn slowly to the foamless weirs
    Of age, were she to lose him.

Between a blurred sagacity
    That once had power to sound him,   10
And Love, that will not let him be
    The Judas that she found him,
Her pride assuages her almost,
As if it were alone the cost.—
He sees that he will not be lost,   15
    And waits and looks around him.

A sense of ocean and old trees
    Envelops and allures him;
Tradition, touching all he sees,
    Beguiles and reassures him;   20
And all her doubts of what he says
Are dimmed with what she knows of days—
Till even prejudice delays
    And fades, and she secures him.

The falling leaf inaugurates   25
    The reign of her confusion;
The pounding wave reverberates
    The dirge of her illusion;
And home, where passion lived and died,
Becomes a place where she can hide,   30
While all the town and harbor side
    Vibrate with her seclusion.

We tell you, tapping on our brows,
    The story as it should be,—
As if the story of a house   35

*The title is Greek for "Love the tyrant."

Were told, or ever could be;
We'll have no kindly veil between
Her visions and those we have seen,—
As if we guessed what hers have been,
Or what they are or would be. 40

Meanwhile we do no harm; for they
That with a god have striven,
Not hearing much of what we say,
Take what the god has given;
Though like waves breaking it may be, 45
Or like a changed familiar tree,
Or like a stairway to the sea
Where down the blind are driven.

[1916]

Mr. Flood's Party

Old Eben Flood, climbing alone one night
Over the hill between the town below
And the forsaken upland hermitage
That held as much as he should ever know
On earth again of home, paused warily. 5
The road was his with not a native near;
And Eben, having leisure, said aloud,
For no man else in Tilbury Town to hear:

"Well, Mr. Flood, we have the harvest moon
Again, and we may not have many more; 10
The bird is on the wing, the poet says,
And you and I have said it here before.
Drink to the bird." He raised up to the light
The jug that he had gone so far to fill,
And answered huskily: "Well, Mr. Flood, 15
Since you propose it, I believe I will."

Alone, as if enduring to the end
A valiant armor of scarred hopes outworn,
He stood there in the middle of the road

Like Roland's ghost° winding a silent horn. 20
Below him, in the town among the trees,
Where friends of other days had honored him,
A phantom salutation of the dead
Rang thinly till old Eben's eyes were dim.

Then, as a mother lays her sleeping child 25
Down tenderly, fearing it may awake,
He set the jug down slowly at his feet
With trembling care, knowing that most things break;
And only when assured that on firm earth
It stood, as the uncertain lives of men 30
Assuredly did not, he paced away,
And with his hand extended paused again:

"Well, Mr. Flood, we have not met like this
In a long time; and many a change has come
To both of us, I fear, since last it was 35
We had a drop together. Welcome home!"
Convivially returning with himself,
Again he raised the jug up to the light;
And with an acquiescent quaver said:
"Well, Mr. Flood, if you insist, I might. 40

"Only a very little, Mr. Flood—
For auld lang syne.° No more, sir; that will do."
So, for the time, apparently it did,
And Eben evidently thought so too;
For soon amid the silver loneliness 45
Of night he lifted up his voice and sang,
Secure, with only two moons listening,
Until the whole harmonious landscape rang—

"For auld lang syne." The weary throat gave out,
The last word wavered, and the song was done. 50
He raised again the jug regretfully
And shook his head, and was again alone.

20 *Like Roland's ghost*: In the medieval French romance, *The Song of Roland*, the title character was one of Charlemagne's paladins or knights-errant. Roland possessed an enchanted ivory horn that could be heard for hundreds of miles. In his last battle Roland refuses to blow the horn for help until the moment before his own death. **42** *auld lang syne*: traditional Scottish song, first penned by Robert Burns.

There was not much that was ahead of him,
And there was nothing in the town below—
Where strangers would have shut the many doors *55*
That many friends had opened long ago.

[1921]

New England

Here where the wind is always north-north-east
And children learn to walk on frozen toes,
Wonder begets an envy of all those
Who boil elsewhere with such a lyric yeast
Of love that you will hear them at a feast *5*
Where demons would appeal for some repose,
Still clamoring where the chalice overflows
And crying wildest who have drunk the least.

Passion is here a soilure of the wits,
We're told, and Love a cross for them to bear; *10*
Joy shivers in the corner where she knits
And Conscience always has the rocking-chair,
Cheerful as when she tortured into fits
The first cat that was ever killed by Care.

[1925]

***Paul Laurence Dunbar** (1872–1906) was born in Dayton, Ohio, the son of former slaves, and was educated in Dayton's public schools. The only African American in his class, he was elected class president and class poet, edited the school paper, and composed the graduation song. Despite this early success, he couldn't find suitable work after graduation because of his race. He worked as an elevator operator, continuing to write and publish poems in local newspapers, as he had in high school. Dunbar self-published his first collection,* Oak and Ivy, *in 1893. The young poet was soon hired by the famous abolitionist Frederick Douglass for clerical work at the World's Columbian Exposition in Chicago. This led to Dunbar meeting many other important writers and cultivating influential friendships.*

Dunbar set out on a popular reading tour of England, and obtained a year-long appointment as an assistant at the Library of Congress upon returning. A few months later he married the poet and teacher Alice Ruth Moore. Though his popularity soared, his heavy drinking led to pneumonia and tuberculosis. He died in Dayton at 33.

Paul Laurence Dunbar

We Wear the Mask

We wear the mask that grins and lies,
It hides our cheeks and shades our eyes,—
This debt we pay to human guile;
With torn and bleeding hearts we smile,
And mouth with myriad subtleties. *5*

Why should the world be overwise,
In counting all our tears and sighs?
Nay, let them only see us, while
    We wear the mask.

We smile, but, O great Christ, our cries *10*
To thee from tortured souls arise.
We sing, but oh the clay is vile
Beneath our feet, and long the mile;
But let the world dream otherwise,
    We wear the mask! *15*

[1895]

Sympathy

I know what the caged bird feels, alas!
    When the sun is bright on the upland slopes;
When the wind stirs soft through the springing grass,
And the river flows like a stream of glass;
    When the first bird sings and the first bud opes, *5*
And the faint perfume from its chalice° steals—
I know what the caged bird feels!

6 *chalice*: suggests that the flower is like a cup.

I know why the caged bird beats his wing
  Till its blood is red on the cruel bars;
For he must fly back to his perch and cling *10*
When he fain would be on the bough a-swing;
  And a pain still throbs in the old, old scars
And they pulse again with a keener sting—
I know why he beats his wing!

I know why the caged bird sings, ah me, *15*
  When his wing is bruised and his bosom sore,—
When he beats his bars and he would be free;
It is not a carol of joy or glee,
  But a prayer that he sends from his heart's deep core,
But a plea, that upward to Heaven he flings— *20*
I know why the caged bird sings!

[1899]

The Poet

He sang of life, serenely sweet,
  With, now and then, a deeper note.
  From some high peak, nigh yet remote,
He voiced the world's absorbing beat.

He sang of love when earth was young, *5*
  And Love, itself, was in his lays.°
  But ah, the world, it turned to praise
A jingle in a broken tongue.

[1903]

6 *lays*: songs.

To a Captious Critic

Dear critic, who my lightness so deplores,
Would I might study to be prince of bores,
Right wisely would I rule that dull estate—
But, sir, I may not; till you abdicate.

[1903]

***Robert** [Lee] **Frost** (1874–1963) was born in San Francisco. After the death of his father, the family moved to Lawrence, Massachusetts, where the young poet spent the next decade in poverty. He won a scholarship to Dartmouth College, though within a few weeks he dropped out—just as he would leave Harvard five years later. Instead he devoted himself to courting his high-school sweetheart, Elinor White. They were married for 43 years and had six children. Early on, Frost eked out a living as a chicken farmer with a few stints as a schoolteacher. In 1912 he moved the family to England and published his first book of poems,* A Boy's Will *(1913), before returning to America. Frost's domestic life was marked by enormous suffering. Only one of his six children lived out a natural and healthy life. After the death of his wife, Frost's later years were marked by increasing emotional isolation. He won every major poetry prize the nation had to offer, including four Pulitzers—a record no other writer has ever matched. Frost was known as a gifted narrative poet who worked in the formal tradition. The height of his celebrity came when the 86-year-old poet read at John F. Kennedy's 1961 presidential inauguration.*

Robert Frost

Mowing

There was never a sound beside the wood but one,
And that was my long scythe whispering to the ground.
What was it it whispered? I knew not well myself;
Perhaps it was something about the heat of the sun,
Something, perhaps, about the lack of sound— *5*
And that was why it whispered and did not speak.
It was no dream of the gift of idle hours,
Or easy gold at the hand of fay or elf:
Anything more than the truth would have seemed too weak
To the earnest love that laid the swale in rows, *10*
Not without feeble-pointed spikes of flowers
(Pale orchises), and scared a bright green snake.
The fact is the sweetest dream that labor knows.
My long scythe whispered and left the hay to make.

[1913]

After Apple-Picking

My long two-pointed ladder's sticking through a tree
Toward heaven still,
And there's a barrel that I didn't fill
Beside it, and there may be two or three
Apples I didn't pick upon some bough. *5*
But I am done with apple-picking now.
Essence of winter sleep is on the night,
The scent of apples: I am drowsing off.
I cannot rub the strangeness from my sight
I got from looking through a pane of glass *10*
I skimmed this morning from the drinking trough
And held against the world of hoary grass.
It melted, and I let it fall and break.
But I was well
Upon my way to sleep before it fell, *15*
And I could tell
What form my dreaming was about to take.
Magnified apples appear and disappear,
Stem end and blossom end,
And every fleck of russet showing clear. *20*
My instep arch not only keeps the ache,
It keeps the pressure of a ladder-round.
I feel the ladder sway as the boughs bend.
And I keep hearing from the cellar bin
The rumbling sound *25*
Of load on load of apples coming in.
For I have had too much
Of apple-picking: I am overtired
Of the great harvest I myself desired.
There were ten thousand thousand fruit to touch, *30*
Cherish in hand, lift down, and not let fall.
For all
That struck the earth,
No matter if not bruised or spiked with stubble,
Went surely to the cider-apple heap *35*
As of no worth.

One can see what will trouble
This sleep of mine, whatever sleep it is.
Were he not gone,
The woodchuck could say whether it's like his *40*
Long sleep, as I describe its coming on,
Or just some human sleep.

[1914]

Mending Wall

Something there is that doesn't love a wall,
That sends the frozen-ground-swell under it,
And spills the upper boulders in the sun;
And makes gaps even two can pass abreast.
The work of hunters is another thing: *5*
I have come after them and made repair
Where they have left not one stone on a stone,
But they would have the rabbit out of hiding,
To please the yelping dogs. The gaps I mean,
No one has seen them made or heard them made, *10*
But at spring mending-time we find them there.
I let my neighbor know beyond the hill;
And on a day we meet to walk the line
And set the wall between us once again.
We keep the wall between us as we go. *15*
To each the boulders that have fallen to each.
And some are loaves and some so nearly balls
We have to use a spell to make them balance:
"Stay where you are until our backs are turned!"
We wear our fingers rough with handling them. *20*
Oh, just another kind of out-door game,
One on a side. It comes to little more:
There where it is we do not need the wall:
He is all pine and I am apple orchard.
My apple trees will never get across *25*
And eat the cones under his pines, I tell him.
He only says, "Good fences make good neighbors."

Spring is the mischief in me, and I wonder
If I could put a notion in his head:
"*Why* do they make good neighbors? Isn't it *30*
Where there are cows? But here there are no cows.
Before I built a wall I'd ask to know
What I was walling in or walling out,
And to whom I was like to give offence.
Something there is that doesn't love a wall, *35*
That wants it down." I could say "Elves" to him,
But it's not elves exactly, and I'd rather
He said it for himself. I see him there
Bringing a stone grasped firmly by the top.
In each hand, like an old-stone savage armed. *40*
He moves in darkness as it seems to me,
Not of woods only and the shade of trees.
He will not go behind his father's saying,
And he likes having thought of it so well
He says again, "Good fences make good neighbors." *45*

[1914]

Birches

When I see birches bend to left and right
Across the lines of straighter darker trees,
I like to think some boy's been swinging them.
But swinging doesn't bend them down to stay.
Ice-storms do that. Often you must have seen them *5*
Loaded with ice a sunny winter morning
After a rain. They click upon themselves
As the breeze rises, and turn many-colored
As the stir cracks and crazes their enamel.
Soon the sun's warmth makes them shed crystal shells *10*
Shattering and avalanching on the snow-crust—
Such heaps of broken glass to sweep away
You'd think the inner dome of heaven had fallen.
They are dragged to the withered bracken by the load,
And they seem not to break; though once they are bowed *15*

So low for long, they never right themselves:
You may see their trunks arching in the woods
Years afterwards, trailing their leaves on the ground
Like girls on hands and knees that throw their hair
Before them over their heads to dry in the sun. *20*
But I was going to say when Truth broke in
With all her matter-of-fact about the ice-storm
I should prefer to have some boy bend them
As he went out and in to fetch the cows—
Some boy too far from town to learn baseball, *25*
Whose only play was what he found himself,
Summer or winter, and could play alone.
One by one he subdued his father's trees
By riding them down over and over again
Until he took the stiffness out of them, *30*
And not one but hung limp, not one was left
For him to conquer. He learned all there was
To learn about not launching out too soon
And so not carrying the tree away
Clear to the ground. He always kept his poise *35*
To the top branches, climbing carefully
With the same pains you use to fill a cup
Up to the brim, and even above the brim.
Then he flung outward, feet first, with a swish,
Kicking his way down through the air to the ground. *40*
So was I once myself a swinger of birches.
And so I dream of going back to be.
It's when I'm weary of considerations,
And life is too much like a pathless wood
Where your face burns and tickles with the cobwebs *45*
Broken across it, and one eye is weeping
From a twig's having lashed across it open.
I'd like to get away from earth awhile
And then come back to it and begin over.
May no fate willfully misunderstand me *50*
And half grant what I wish and snatch me away
Not to return. Earth's the right place for love:
I don't know where it's likely to go better.
I'd like to go by climbing a birch tree,

And climb black branches up a snow-white trunk 55
Toward heaven, till the tree could bear no more,
But dipped its top and set me down again.
That would be good both going and coming back.
One could do worse than be a swinger of birches.

[1916]

The Road Not Taken*

Two roads diverged in a yellow wood,
And sorry I could not travel both
And be one traveler, long I stood
And looked down one as far as I could
To where it bent in the undergrowth; 5

Then took the other, as just as fair,
And having perhaps the better claim,
Because it was grassy and wanted wear;
Though as for that the passing there
Had worn them really about the same, 10

And both that morning equally lay
In leaves no step had trodden black.
Oh, I kept the first for another day!
Yet knowing how way leads on to way,
I doubted if I should ever come back. 15

I shall be telling this with a sigh
Somewhere ages and ages hence:
Two roads diverged in a wood, and I—
I took the one less traveled by,
And that has made all the difference. 20

[1916]

*According to Frost biographer, Lawrance Thompson, this poem was inspired by walks Frost took with his friend, the English poet Edward Thomas: "After one of their best flower-gathering walks, he had said to Thomas, 'No matter which road you take, you'll always sigh and wish you'd taken another.' "

Fire and Ice

Some say the world will end in fire,
Some say in ice.
From what I've tasted of desire
I hold with those who favor fire.
But if it had to perish twice, *5*
I think I know enough of hate
To say that for destruction ice
Is also great
And would suffice.

[1923]

Nothing Gold Can Stay

Nature's first green is gold,
Her hardest hue to hold.
Her early leaf's a flower;
But only so an hour.
Then leaf subsides to leaf. *5*
So Eden sank to grief,
So dawn goes down to day.
Nothing gold can stay.

[1923]

Stopping by Woods on a Snowy Evening

Whose woods these are I think I know.
His house is in the village though;
He will not see me stopping here
To watch his woods fill up with snow.

My little horse must think it queer 5
To stop without a farmhouse near
Between the woods and frozen lake
The darkest evening of the year.

He gives his harness bells a shake
To ask if there is some mistake. 10
The only other sound's the sweep
Of easy wind and downy flake.

The woods are lovely, dark and deep.
But I have promises to keep,
And miles to go before I sleep, 15
And miles to go before I sleep.

[1923]

Acquainted with the Night

I have been one acquainted with the night.
I have walked out in rain—and back in rain.
I have outwalked the furthest city light.

I have looked down the saddest city lane.
I have passed by the watchman on his beat 5
And dropped my eyes, unwilling to explain.

I have stood still and stopped the sound of feet
When far away an interrupted cry
Came over houses from another street,

But not to call me back or say good-bye; 10
And further still at an unearthly height,
One luminary clock against the sky

Proclaimed the time was neither wrong nor right:
I have been one acquainted with the night.

[1928]

Provide, Provide

The witch that came (the withered hag)
To wash the steps with pail and rag,
Was once the beauty Abishag,°

The picture pride of Hollywood.
Too many fall from great and good 5
For you to doubt the likelihood.

Die early and avoid the fate.
Or if predestined to die late,
Make up your mind to die in state.

Make the whole stock exchange your own! 10
If need be occupy a throne,
Where nobody can call *you* crone.

Some have relied on what they knew;
Others on being simply true.
What worked for them might work for you. 15

No memory of having starred
Atones for later disregard,
Or keeps the end from being hard.

Better to go down dignified
With boughten friendship at your side 20
Than none at all. Provide, provide!

[1936]

3 *Abishag*: the beautiful young woman who nursed King David in his old age.

***Wallace Stevens** (1879–1955) was born in Reading, Pennsylvania. His father was a prosperous lawyer, his mother a former schoolteacher. In high school he played football, took the classical curriculum, which included Greek and Latin, and failed to pass one year. Stevens entered Harvard University as a special student, which allowed him to attend classes at a reduced tuition but not qualify for a degree. He moved to New York to work as a reporter and editor, though his father strongly disapproved of Stevens's literary aspirations and the young poet reluctantly agreed to study at New York Law School. Stevens worked at various legal jobs in Manhattan,* *though his business career was not successful. He married in 1909, but never enjoyed a happy relationship. In 1916 Stevens accepted a position at Hartford Accident and Indemnity. He would never leave the city nor the company. In 1923, at the age of 43, he published his brilliant first book,* Harmonium. *The debut was a commercial failure, but it announced him as a major poet. His* Collected Poems *(1953) won the Pulitzer.*

Wallace Stevens

The Snow Man*

One must have a mind of winter
To regard the frost and the boughs
Of the pine-trees crusted with snow;

And have been cold a long time
To behold the junipers shagged with ice, *5*
The spruces rough in the distant glitter

Of the January sun; and not to think
Of any misery in the sound of the wind,
In the sound of a few leaves,

Which is the sound of the land *10*
Full of the same wind
That is blowing in the same bare place

For the listener, who listens in the snow,
And, nothing himself, beholds
Nothing that is not there and the nothing that is. *15*

[1923]

*In a letter dated April 18, 1944, Stevens wrote, "I shall explain The Snow Man as an example of the necessity of identifying oneself with reality in order to understand and enjoy it."

The Emperor of Ice-Cream

Call the roller of big cigars,
The muscular one, and bid him whip
In kitchen cups concupiscent curds.
Let the wenches dawdle in such dress
As they are used to wear, and let the boys *5*

Bring flowers in last month's newspapers.
Let be be finale of seem.
The only emperor is the emperor of ice-cream.

Take from the dresser of deal,°
Lacking the three glass knobs, that sheet *10*
On which she embroidered fantails° once
And spread it so as to cover her face.
If her horny feet protrude, they come
To show how cold she is, and dumb.
Let the lamp affix its beam. *15*
The only emperor is the emperor of ice-cream.

[1923]

9 *deal*: cheap wood. **11** *fantails*: fantailed pigeons.

Disillusionment of Ten O'Clock

The houses are haunted
By white night-gowns.
None are green,
Or purple with green rings,
Or green with yellow rings, *5*
Or yellow with blue rings.
None of them are strange,
With socks of lace
And beaded ceintures.°
People are not going *10*
To dream of baboons and periwinkles.
Only, here and there, an old sailor,
Drunk and asleep in his boots,
Catches tigers
In red weather. *15*

[1923]

9 *ceintures*: belts.

Sunday Morning*

I

Complacencies of the peignoir,° and late
Coffee and oranges in a sunny chair,
And the green freedom of a cockatoo
Upon a rug mingle to dissipate
The holy hush of ancient sacrifice. *5*
She dreams a little, and she feels the dark
Encroachment of that old catastrophe,
As a calm darkens among water-lights.
The pungent oranges and bright, green wings
Seem things in some procession of the dead, *10*
Winding across wide water, without sound.
The day is like wide water, without sound,
Stilled for the passing of her dreaming feet
Over the seas, to silent Palestine,
Dominion of the blood and sepulchre.° *15*

II

Why should she give her bounty to the dead?
What is divinity if it can come
Only in silent shadows and in dreams?
Shall she not find in comforts of the sun,
In pungent fruit and bright, green wings, or else *20*
In any balm or beauty of the earth,
Things to be cherished like the thought of heaven?
Divinity must live within herself:
Passions of rain, or moods in falling snow;
Grievings in loneliness, or unsubdued *25*
Elations when the forest blooms; gusty
Emotions on wet roads on autumn nights;
All pleasures and all pains, remembering
The bough of summer and the winter branch.
These are the measures destined for her soul. *30*

*In a letter dated March 31, 1928, Stevens wrote, "The poem is simply an explanation of paganism, although, of course, I did not think that I was expressing paganism when I wrote it."

1 *peignoir:* negligée. **14–15** *silent Palestine . . . blood and sepulchre:* Christ's tomb was in Palestine, and the blood may refer both to his crucifixion and to the wine of the Last Supper.

III

Jove° in the clouds had his inhuman birth.
No mother suckled him, no sweet land gave
Large-mannered motions to his mythy mind.
He moved among us, as a muttering king,
Magnificent, would move among his hinds,° *35*
Until our blood, commingling, virginal,
With heaven, brought such requital to desire
The very hinds discerned it, in a star.
Shall our blood fail? Or shall it come to be
The blood of paradise? And shall the earth *40*
Seem all of paradise that we shall know?
The sky will be much friendlier then than now,
A part of labor and a part of pain,
And next in glory to enduring love,
Not this dividing and indifferent blue. *45*

IV

She says, "I am content when wakened birds,
Before they fly, test the reality
Of misty fields, by their sweet questionings;
But when the birds are gone, and their warm fields
Return no more, where, then, is paradise?" *50*
There is not any haunt of prophesy,
Nor any old chimera of the grave,
Neither the golden underground, nor isle
Melodious, where spirits gat them home,
Nor visionary south, nor cloudy palm *55*
Remote on heaven's hill, that has endured
As April's green endures; or will endure
Like her remembrance of awakened birds,
Or her desire for June and evening, tipped
By the consummation of the swallow's wings. *60*

V

She says, "But in contentment I still feel
The need of some imperishable bliss."

31 *Jove*: or Zeus, was the son of a Titan and was suckled by a goat. **35** *hinds*: servants or rustics.

Death is the mother of beauty; hence from her,
Alone, shall come fulfilment to our dreams
And our desires. Although she strews the leaves *65*
Of sure obliteration on our paths,
The path sick sorrow took, the many paths
Where triumph rang its brassy phrase, or love
Whispered a little out of tenderness,
She makes the willow shiver in the sun *70*
For maidens who were wont to sit and gaze
Upon the grass, relinquished to their feet.
She causes boys to pile new plums and pears
On disregarded plate.° The maidens taste
And stray impassioned in the littering leaves. *75*

VI

Is there no change of death in paradise?
Does ripe fruit never fall? Or do the boughs
Hang always heavy in that perfect sky,
Unchanging, yet so like our perishing earth,
With rivers like our own that seek for seas *80*
They never find, the same receding shores
That never touch with inarticulate pang?
Why set the pear upon those river-banks
Or spice the shores with odors of the plum?
Alas, that they should wear our colors there, *85*
The silken weavings of our afternoons,
And pick the strings of our insipid lutes!°
Death is the mother of beauty, mystical,
Within whose burning bosom we devise
Our earthly mothers waiting, sleeplessly. *90*

VII

Supple and turbulent, a ring of men
Shall chant in orgy on a summer morn
Their boisterous devotion to the sun,
Not as a god, but as a god might be,

74 *disregarded plate:* the common, household silver. 87 *lutes*: stringed instruments commonly used in the Renaissance.

Naked among them, like a savage source. *95*
Their chant shall be a chant of paradise,
Out of their blood, returning to the sky;
And in their chant shall enter, voice by voice,
The windy lake wherein their lord delights,
The trees, like serafin,° and echoing hills, *100*
That choir among themselves long afterward.
They shall know well the heavenly fellowship
Of men that perish and of summer morn.
And whence they came and whither they shall go
The dew upon their feet shall manifest. *105*

VIII

She hears, upon that water without sound,
A voice that cries, "The tomb in Palestine
Is not the porch of spirits lingering.
It is the grave of Jesus, where he lay."
We live in an old chaos of the sun, *110*
Or old dependency of day and night,
Or island solitude, unsponsored, free,
Of that wide water, inescapable.
Deer walk upon our mountains, and the quail
Whistle about us their spontaneous cries; *115*
Sweet berries ripen in the wilderness;
And, in the isolation of the sky,
At evening, casual flocks of pigeons make
Ambiguous undulations as they sink,
Downward to darkness, on extended wings. *120*

[1923]

100 *serafin*: seraphim, angels of the Lord.

Anecdote of the Jar

I placed a jar in Tennessee,
And round it was, upon a hill.
It made the slovenly wilderness
Surround that hill.

The wilderness rose up to it, *5*
And sprawled around, no longer wild.
The jar was round upon the ground
And tall and of a port in air.

It took dominion everywhere.
The jar was gray and bare. *10*
It did not give of bird or bush,
Like nothing else in Tennessee.

[1923]

Thirteen Ways of Looking at a Blackbird

I

Among twenty snowy mountains,
The only moving thing
Was the eye of the black bird.

II

I was of three minds,
Like a tree *5*
In which there are three blackbirds.

III

The blackbird whirled in the autumn winds.
It was a small part of the pantomime.

IV

A man and a woman
Are one. *10*
A man and a woman and a blackbird
Are one.

V

I do not know which to prefer,
The beauty of inflections

Or the beauty of innuendoes, *15*
The blackbird whistling
Or just after.

VI

Icicles filled the long window
With barbaric glass.
The shadow of the blackbird *20*
Crossed it, to and fro.
The mood
Traced in the shadow
An indecipherable cause.

VII

O thin men of Haddam,° *25*
Why do you imagine golden birds?
Do you not see how the blackbird
Walks around the feet
Of the women about you?

VIII

I know noble accents *30*
And lucid, inescapable rhythms;
But I know, too,
That the blackbird is involved
In what I know.

IX

When the blackbird flew out of sight, *35*
It marked the edge
Of one of many circles.

X

At the sight of blackbirds
Flying in a green light,
Even the bawds of euphony *40*
Would cry out sharply.

25 In a letter of July 1, 1953, Stevens explained, "The thin men of Haddam are entirely fictitious although some years ago one of the citizens of that place wrote to me to ask what I had in mind. I just liked the name."

XI

He rode over Connecticut
In a glass coach.
Once, a fear pierced him,
In that he mistook *45*
The shadow of his equipage°
For blackbirds.

XII

The river is moving.
The blackbird must be flying.

XIII

It was evening all afternoon. *50*
It was snowing
And it was going to snow.
The blackbird sat
In the cedar-limbs.

[1923]

46 *equipage*: coach.

Of Mere Being

The palm at the end of the mind,
Beyond the last thought, rises
In the bronze decor,

A gold-feathered bird
Sings in the palm, without human meaning, *5*
Without human feeling, a foreign song.

You know then that it is not the reason
That makes us happy or unhappy.
The bird sings. Its feathers shine.

The palm stands on the edge of space. *10*
The wind moves slowly in the branches.
The bird's fire-fangled feathers dangle down.

[1957]

***William Carlos Williams** (1883–1963) was born in Rutherford, New Jersey, into a highly cultured household. His father was an English-born businessman and his mother, a painter, was of Basque, Spanish, Dutch, and Jewish ancestry. From an early age, Williams listened to his relatives speak Spanish and French. He enrolled at the University of Pennsylvania to study medicine, and there he met his lifelong friend Ezra Pound. Williams studied pediatrics in Germany, then set up a private practice in his hometown of Rutherford and remained there until his death more than 50 years later. He married Florence Herman in 1912, and they had two sons. Although his medical career was demanding and exhausting, Williams slowly became an indispensable and influential American poet. He was particularly notable for introducing a natural American idiom and diction into his poetry. The post of Poetry Consultant to the Library of Congress (later renamed Poet Laureate) was offered to him in 1952, but the appointment was retracted due to protests about his alleged Communist sympathies and his public defense of Pound. Williams was eventually forced to quit his medical practice after a series of strokes.* Pictures from Brueghel *(1962) won the Pulitzer Prize shortly after his death.*

William Carlos Williams

Danse Russe*

If when my wife is sleeping
and the baby and Kathleen°
are sleeping
and the sun is a flame-white disc
in silken mists 5
above shining trees,—
if I in my north room
dance naked, grotesquely
before my mirror
waving my shirt round my head 10
and singing softly to myself:
"I am lonely, lonely.
I was born to be lonely,

*The title means "Russian Dance." The Ballets Russe had been in New York in 1916.

2 *Kathleen*: Kathleen was a nursemaid to the Williams children.

I am best so!"
If I admire my arms, my face, *15*
my shoulders, flanks, buttocks
against the yellow drawn shades, —

Who shall say I am not
the happy genius of my household?

[1917]

Queen-Anne's-Lace*

Her body is not so white as
anemone petals nor so smooth—nor
so remote a thing. It is a field
of the wild carrot taking
the field by force; the grass *5*
does not raise above it.
Here is no question of whiteness,
white as can be, with a purple mole
at the center of each flower.
Each flower is a hand's span *10*
of her whiteness. Wherever
his hand has lain there is
a tiny purple blemish. Each part
is a blossom under his touch
to which the fibres of her being *15*
stem one by one, each to its end,
until the whole field is a
white desire, empty, a single stem,
a cluster, flower by flower,
a pious wish to whiteness gone over— *20*
or nothing.

[1921]

*The title refers to a common white flower. Williams once said that the woman in the poem was his wife, Flossie.

To Waken an Old Lady

Old age is
a flight of small
cheeping birds
skimming
bare trees 5
above a snow glaze.
Gaining and failing
they are buffeted
by a dark wind—
But what? 10
On harsh weedstalks
the flock has rested,
the snow
is covered with broken
seedhusks 15
and the wind tempered
by a shrill
piping of plenty.

[1921]

The Widow's Lament in Springtime

Sorrow is my own yard
where the new grass
flames as it has flamed
often before but not
with the cold fire 5
that closes round me this year.
Thirtyfive years
I lived with my husband.
The plumtree is white today
with masses of flowers. 10
Masses of flowers
load the cherry branches

and color some bushes
yellow and some red
but the grief in my heart *15*
is stronger than they
for though they were my joy
formerly, today I notice them
and turn away forgetting.
Today my son told me *20*
that in the meadows,
at the edge of the heavy woods
in the distance, he saw
trees of white flowers.
I feel that I would like *25*
to go there
and fall into those flowers
and sink into the marsh near them.

[1921]

Spring and All

By the road to the contagious hospital°
under the surge of the blue
mottled clouds driven from the
northeast—a cold wind. Beyond, the
waste of broad, muddy fields *5*
brown with dried weeds, standing and fallen

patches of standing water
the scattering of tall trees

All along the road the reddish
purplish, forked, upstanding, twiggy *10*
stuff of bushes and small trees
with dead, brown leaves under them
leafless vines—

Lifeless in appearance, sluggish
dazed spring approaches— *15*

1 *contagious hospital*: a hospital for patients with infectious diseases.

They enter the new world naked,
cold, uncertain of all
save that they enter. All about them
the cold, familiar wind—

Now the grass, tomorrow *20*
the stiff curl of wildcarrot leaf

One by one objects are defined—
It quickens: clarity, outline of leaf

But now the stark dignity of
entrance—Still, the profound change *25*
has come upon them: rooted, they
grip down and begin to awaken

[1923]

The Red Wheelbarrow

so much depends
upon

a red wheel
barrow

glazed with rain *5*
water

beside the white
chickens

[1923]

The Yachts

contend in a sea which the land partly encloses
shielding them from the too-heavy blows
of an ungoverned ocean which when it chooses

tortures the biggest hulls, the best man knows
to pit against its beatings, and sinks them pitilessly. *5*
Mothlike in mists, scintillant in the minute

brilliance of cloudless days, with broad bellying sails
they glide to the wind tossing green water
from their sharp prows while over them the crew crawls

ant-like, solicitously grooming them, releasing, *10*
making fast as they turn, lean far over and having
caught the wind again, side by side, head for the mark.

In a well guarded arena of open water surrounded by
lesser and greater craft which, sycophant, lumbering
and flittering follow them, they appear youthful, rare *15*

as the light of a happy eye, live with the grace
of all that in the mind is fleckless, free and
naturally to be desired. Now the sea which holds them

is moody, lapping their glossy sides, as if feeling
for some slightest flaw but fails completely. *20*
Today no race. Then the wind comes again. The yachts

move, jockeying for a start, the signal is set and they
are off. Now the waves strike at them but they are too
well made, they slip through, though they take in canvas.

Arms with hands grasping seek to clutch at the prows. *25*
Bodies thrown recklessly in the way are cut aside.
It is a sea of faces about them in agony, in despair

until the horror of the race dawns staggering the mind,
the whole sea become an entanglement of watery bodies
lost to the world bearing what they cannot hold. Broken, *30*

beaten, desolate, reaching from the dead to be taken up
they cry out, failing, failing! their cries rising
in waves still as the skillful yachts pass over.

[1935]

***D.[avid] H.[erbert] Lawrence** (1885–1930) was born in Nottinghamshire, England, the fourth son of a coalminer and a former schoolteacher. Fearing he would end up working in the mines, Lawrence's mother fervently encouraged his studies. Lawrence attended University College, Nottingham. After graduation he worked as a teacher, and in 1912 eloped to Germany with Frieda Weekley, a noblewoman and the wife of a former professor. She was six years his senior and already the mother of three children. He had his first taste of controversy when his 1915 novel* The Rainbow *was banned upon publication, due to foul language and candid sexual situations. He and Frieda traveled widely after the war, though Lawrence was soon diagnosed with tuberculosis and given two years to live. The best known of his novels,* Lady Chatterley's Lover *(1928), was also banned but finally published in the United States and England over 30 years later. Though his poetry was much admired by critics such as Ezra Pound and Edward Thomas, his controversial work received only one minor award in his lifetime. He died in a sanatorium in France.*

D. H. Lawrence

Piano

Softly, in the dusk, a woman is singing to me;
Taking me back down the vista of years, till I see
A child sitting under the piano, in the boom of the tingling strings
And pressing the small, poised feet of a mother who smiles as she
    sings.

In spite of myself, the insidious mastery of song   *5*
Betrays me back, till the heart of me weeps to belong
To the old Sunday evenings at home, with winter outside
And hymns in the cozy parlour, the tinkling piano our guide.

So now it is vain for the singer to burst into clamour
With the great black piano appassionato. The glamour   *10*
Of childish days is upon me, my manhood is cast
Down in the flood of remembrance, I weep like a child for the past.

[1918]

Snake

A snake came to my water-trough
On a hot, hot day, and I in pyjamas for the heat,
To drink there.

In the deep, strange-scented shade of the great dark carob tree
I came down the steps with my pitcher *5*
And must wait, must stand and wait, for there he was at the trough
before me.

He reached down from a fissure in the earth-wall in the gloom
And trailed his yellow-brown slackness soft-bellied down, over the
edge of the stone trough
And rested his throat upon the stone bottom,
And where the water had dripped from the tap, in a small *10*
clearness,
He sipped with his straight mouth,
Softly drank through his straight gums, into his slack long body,
Silently.

Someone was before me at my water-trough,
And I, like a second comer, waiting. *15*

He lifted his head from his drinking, as cattle do,
And looked at me vaguely, as drinking cattle do,
And flickered his two-forked tongue from his lips, and mused a
moment,
And stooped and drank a little more,
Being earth-brown, earth-golden from the burning bowels of the *20*
earth
On the day of Sicilian July, with Etna° smoking.

The voice of my education said to me
He must be killed,
For in Sicily the black, black snakes are innocent, the gold are
venomous.

And voices in me said, If you were a man *25*
You would take a stick and break him now, and finish him off.

21 *Etna*: Mount Etna is an active volcano in eastern Sicily.

But must I confess how I liked him,
How glad I was he had come like a guest in quiet, to drink at my
water-trough
And depart peaceful, pacified, and thankless,
Into the burning bowels of this earth? 30

Was it cowardice, that I dared not kill him?
Was it perversity, that I longed to talk to him?
Was it humility, to feel so honoured?
I felt so honoured.

And yet those voices: 35
If you were not afraid, you would kill him!

And truly I was afraid, I was most afraid,
But even so, honoured still more
That he should seek my hospitality
From out the dark door of the secret earth. 40

He drank enough
And lifted his head, dreamily, as one who has drunken,
And flickered his tongue like a forked night on the air, so black,
Seeming to lick his lips,
And looked around like a god, unseeing, into the air, 45
And slowly turned his head,
And slowly, very slowly, as if thrice adream,
Proceeded to draw his slow length curving round
And climb again the broken bank of my wall-face.

And as he put his head into that dreadful hole, 50
And as he slowly drew up, snake-easing his shoulders, and entered
farther,
A sort of horror, a sort of protest against his withdrawing into that
horrid black hole,
Deliberately going into the blackness, and slowly drawing himself after,
Overcame me now his back was turned.

I looked around, I put down my pitcher. 55
I picked up a clumsy log
And threw it at the water-trough with a clatter.

I think I did not hit him,
But suddenly that part of him that was left behind convulsed in
undignified haste,
Writhed like lightning, and was gone 60

Into the black hole, the earth-lipped fissure in the wall-front,
At which, in the intense still noon, I stared with fascination.

And immediately I regretted it.
I thought how paltry, how vulgar, what a mean act!
I despised myself and the voices of my accursed human education. *65*

And I thought of the albatross,
And I wished he would come back, my snake.

For he seemed to me again like a king,
Like a king in exile, uncrowned in the underworld,
Now due to be crowned again. *70*

And so, I missed my chance with one of the lords
Of life.
And I have something to expiate;
A pettiness.

[1923]

Bavarian Gentians*

Not every man has gentians in his house
in soft September, at slow, sad Michaelmas.°

Bavarian gentians, big and dark, only dark
darkening the daytime, torch-like with the smoking blueness of
Pluto's° gloom,
ribbed and torch-like, with their blaze of darkness spread blue *5*
down flattening into points, flattened under the sweep of white day
torch-flower of the blue-smoking darkness, Pluto's dark-blue daze,
black lamps from the halls of Dis,° burning dark blue,
giving off darkness, blue darkness, as Demeter's pale lamps give off
light,
lead me then, lead the way. *10*

Reach me a gentian, give me a torch!
let me guide myself with the blue, forked torch of this flower

*Bavaria is a region in southern Germany. Gentians are plants that bear blue or yellow flowers.

2 *Michaelmas*: The feast of St. Michael (September 29). 4 *Pluto*: Roman name for Hades, in Greek mythology the ruler of the Underworld, who abducted Persephone to be his bride. Each spring Persephone returns to earth and is welcomed by her mother Demeter, goddess of fruitfulness; each winter she departs again, to dwell with her husband below. 8 *Dis*: Pluto's realm.

down the darker and darker stairs, where blue is darkened on blueness
even where Persephone goes, just now, from the frosted September
to the sightless realm where darkness is awake upon the dark *15*
and Persephone herself is but a voice
or a darkness invisible enfolded in the deeper dark
of the arms Plutonic, and pierced with the passion of dense gloom,
among the splendor of torches of darkness, shedding darkness on the
lost bride and her groom.

[1932]

***Ezra** [Loomis] **Pound** (1885–1972), the great literary mentor of modernism, was born in Hailey, Idaho, but raised mostly in Philadelphia, where his father worked for the U.S. Mint. In 1901 the 16-year-old Pound enrolled at the University of Pennsylvania, but soon transferred to Hamilton College to study foreign languages. Throughout his career, he not only translated widely from eight languages, he also published in Italian and French. Settling in London, Pound began the major creative undertaking of his life, the* Cantos. *He also lived in Paris for four years, where he linked up with the American émigrés now known as "The Lost Generation." Settling in Italy in 1924, Pound became a devoted admirer of Benito Mussolini. He broadcasted anti-American sentiments for an Italian-government radio show during World War II, was indicted* in absentia *for treason, and arrested in 1945. Through the efforts of his literary friends, Pound was declared unfit for trial by reason of insanity and confined to a mental hospital, where he remained for 13 years. He was finally discharged in 1958 and soon returned to Italy. Pound died in Venice.*

Ezra Pound

Portrait d'une Femme*

Your mind and you are our Sargasso Sea,°
London has swept about you this score years
And bright ships left you this or that in fee:

*French, "Portrait of a Lady."

1 *Sargasso Sea*: part of the North Atlantic so choked with seaweed that it was said to have trapped ships.

Ideas, old gossip, oddments of all things,
Strange spars of knowledge and dimmed wares of price. 5
Great minds have sought you—lacking someone else.
You have been second always. Tragical?
No. You preferred it to the usual thing:
One dull man, dulling and uxorious,
One average mind—with one thought less, each year. 10
Oh, you are patient, I have seen you sit
Hours, where something might have floated up.
And now you pay one. Yes, you richly pay.
You are a person of some interest, one comes to you
And takes strange gain away: 15
Trophies fished up; some curious suggestion;
Fact that leads nowhere; and a tale or two,
Pregnant with mandrakes, or with something else
That might prove useful and yet never proves,
That never fits a corner or shows use, 20
Or finds its hour upon the loom of days:
The tarnished, gaudy, wonderful old work;
Idols and ambergris and rare inlays,
These are your riches, your great store; and yet
For all this sea-hoard of deciduous things, 25
Strange woods half sodden, and new brighter stuff:
In the slow float of differing light and deep,
No! there is nothing! In the whole and all,
Nothing that's quite your own.
Yet this is you. 30

[1912]

The Return

See, they° return; ah, see the tentative
Movements, and the slow feet,
The trouble in the pace and the uncertain
Wavering!

1 *they:* the pagan gods.

See, they return, one, and by one, 5
With fear, as half-awakened;
As if the snow should hesitate
And murmur in the wind,
                    and half-turn back;
These were the "Wing'd-with-Awe," 10
                    Inviolable.

Gods of the wingèd shoe!°
With them the silver hounds,
                    sniffing the trace of air!

Haie! Haie! 15
     These were the swift to harry;
These the keen-scented;
These were the souls of blood.

Slow on the leash,
                    pallid the leash-men! 20

[1912]

12 *Gods of the wingèd shoe*: a Homeric epithet indicating Hermes, messenger of the gods.

The Garden

En robe de parade.

—*Samain**

Like a skein of loose silk blown against a wall
She walks by the railing of a path in Kensington Gardens,
And she is dying piece-meal
                    of a sort of emotional anæmia.

And round about there is a rabble 5
Of the filthy, sturdy, unkillable infants of the very poor.
They shall inherit the earth.°

*Epigraph quoted from Albert Samain's *Au Jardin de l'Infante* (1893). The French words mean "dressed for show."

7 *inherit the earth*: cf. Matthew 5:5; "Blessed are the meek: for they shall inherit the earth."

In her is the end of breeding.
Her boredom is exquisite and excessive.
She would like some one to speak to her, *10*
And is almost afraid that I
            will commit that indiscretion.

[1915]

The Garret

Come, let us pity those who are better off than we are.
Come, my friend, and remember
    that the rich have butlers and no friends,
And we have friends and no butlers.
Come, let us pity the married and the unmarried. *5*

Dawn enters with little feet
    like a gilded Pavlova,°
And I am near my desire.
Nor has life in it aught better
Than this hour of clear coolness, *10*
    the hour of waking together.

[1915]

7 *Pavlova*: Anna Pavlova, Russian ballerina (1885–1931).

In a Station of the Metro

The apparition of these faces in the crowd;
Petals on a wet, black bough.

[1915]

The River-Merchant's Wife: a Letter*

While my hair was still cut straight across my forehead
I played about the front gate, pulling flowers.
You came by on bamboo stilts, playing horse,
You walked about my seat, playing with blue plums.
And we went on living in the village of Chokan:° *5*
Two small people, without dislike or suspicion.

At fourteen I married My Lord you.
I never laughed, being bashful.
Lowering my head, I looked at the wall.
Called to, a thousand times, I never looked back. *10*

At fifteen I stopped scowling,
I desired my dust to be mingled with yours
Forever and forever and forever.
Why should I climb the lookout?

At sixteen you departed, *15*
You went into far Ku-to-yen,° by the river of swirling eddies,
And you have been gone five months.
The monkeys make sorrowful noise overhead.

You dragged your feet when you went out.
By the gate now, the moss is grown, the different mosses, *20*
Too deep to clear them away!
The leaves fall early this autumn, in wind.
The paired butterflies are already yellow with August
Over the grass in the West garden;
They hurt me. I grow older. *25*
If you are coming down through the narrows of the river Kiang,
Please let me know before hand,
And I will come out to meet you
    As far as Cho-fu-sa.°

[1915]

*A free translation from the Chinese poet Li Po. Pound was fascinated by the dramatic monologues of Browning, and thought this poem might have fit among them "without causing any surprise save by its simplicity and its naïve beauty."

5 *Chokan*: a suburb of Nanking. **16** *Ku-to-yen*: an island in the river. **29** *Cho-fu-sa*: "the long Wind Beach," hundreds of miles up river from Nanking.

Salutation

O generation of the thoroughly smug
    and thoroughly uncomfortable,
I have seen fishermen picnicking in the sun,
I have seen them with untidy families,
I have seen their smiles full of teeth   *5*
    and heard ungainly laughter.
And I am happier than you are,
And they were happier than I am;
And the fish swim in the lake
    and do not even own clothing.   *10*

[1915]

***H. D.** [Hilda Doolittle] (1886–1961) was born in Bethlehem, Pennsylvania, the sixth child of an astronomer father and an artist mother. When she was 15 she met the year-older Ezra Pound at a Halloween party and fell in love with him. They were engaged for a time, but H. D.'s father refused to give his blessing for marriage, so the relationship ended. She attended Bryn Mawr College for less than two years, dropping out due to poor marks. She later moved to Europe with a woman lover, and there rekindled her friendship with Pound. He championed her work and cast her to the forefront of the imagist movement. In 1913 H. D. married the poet Richard Aldington, though the marriage soon dissolved. While suffering from exhaustion and influenza after the deaths of her brother and father, she fell in love with Bryher (Winnifred Ellerman)—the wealthy woman she would live with for most of her remaining life. H. D. had a nervous breakdown in 1946 and spent her final years in Switzerland.*

H. D.

Oread*

Whirl up, sea—
whirl your pointed pines,
splash your great pines

**Oread*: a nymph of the mountains.

on our rocks,
hurl your green over us, 5
cover us with your pools of fir.

[1915]

Garden

I

You are clear
O rose, cut in rock,
hard as the descent of hail.

I could scrape the colour
from the petals 5
like spilt dye from a rock.

If I could break you
I could break a tree.

If I could stir
I could break a tree— 10
I could break you.

II

O wind, rend open the heat,
cut apart the heat,
rend it to tatters.

Fruit cannot drop
through this thick air— 15
fruit cannot fall into heat
that presses up and blunts
the points of pears
and rounds the grapes.

Cut the heat— *20*
plough through it,
turning it on either side
of your path.

[1916]

Sea Rose

Rose, harsh rose,
marred and with stint of petals,
meagre flower, thin,
sparse of leaf,

more precious *5*
than a wet rose
single on a stem—
you are caught in the drift.

Stunted, with small leaf,
you are flung on the sand, *10*
you are lifted
in the crisp sand
that drives in the wind.

Can the spice-rose
drip such acrid fragrance *15*
hardened in a leaf?

[1916]

Sea Violet

The white violet
is scented on its stalk,
the sea-violet
fragile as agate,
lies fronting all the wind *5*
among the torn shells
on the sand-bank.

The greater blue violets
flutter on the hill,
but who would change for these *10*
who would change for these
one root of the white sort?

Violet
your grasp is frail
on the edge of the sand-hill, *15*
but you catch the light—
frost, a star edges with its fire.

[1916]

Storm

You crash over the trees,
you crack the live branch—
the branch is white,
the green crushed,
each leaf is rent like split wood. *5*

You burden the trees
with black drops,
you swirl and crash—
you have broken off a weighted leaf
in the wind, *10*
it is hurled out,
whirls up and sinks,
a green stone.

[1916]

Helen*

All Greece hates
the still eyes in the white face,
the lustre as of olives
where she stands,
and the white hands. *5*

All Greece reviles
the wan face when she smiles,
hating it deeper still
when it grows wan and white,
remembering past enchantments *10*
and past ills.

Greece sees unmoved,
God's daughter, born of love,
the beauty of cool feet
and slenderest knees, *15*
could love indeed the maid,
only if she were laid,
white ash amid funereal cypresses.

[1924]

*In Greek mythology, Helen, most beautiful of all women, was the daughter of a mortal, Leda, by the god Zeus. Her kidnapping set off the long and devastating Trojan War. While married to Menelaus, king of the Greek city-state of Sparta, Helen was carried off by Paris, prince of Troy. Menelaus and his brother Agamemnon raised an army, besieged Troy for ten years, and eventually recaptured her. One episode of the Trojan War is related in the *Iliad*, Homer's epic poem, composed before 700 BC.

***Robinson Jeffers** (1887–1962) was born in the suburbs of Pittsburgh, Pennsylvania. His father was a professor and Presbyterian minister. The young Jeffers was given a rigorous education, both at home and overseas. By the time he was 12, Jeffers was fluent in many tongues. He entered the University of Pittsburgh at 15 and was awarded sophomore standing, though he transferred to Occidental College, from which he graduated at 17. Jeffers then studied literature, medicine, and forestry, but realized that poetry was his calling. At USC, he fell in love with Una Call Kuster, a married woman.*

After seven years of guilt-ridden romance, Una obtained a divorce and married Jeffers the next day. They moved north to Carmel. Over the next ten years Jeffers wrote the most remarkable, ambitious, and odd series of narratives poems in American literature, including Roan Stallion *(1925) and* The Double Axe *(1948). Almost immediately his long narrative poems divided audiences. After Una's slow death from cancer in 1950, he sank into a prolonged depression aggravated by heavy drinking. His eyesight failed. Jeffers published only one book during the last 14 years of his life.*

Robinson Jeffers

To the Stone-Cutters

Stone-cutters fighting time with marble, you foredefeated
Challengers of oblivion
Eat cynical earnings, knowing rock splits, records fall down,
The square-limbed Roman letters
Scale in the thaws, wear in the rain. The poet as well 5
Builds his monument mockingly;
For man will be blotted out, the blithe earth die, the brave sun
Die blind and blacken to the heart:
Yet stones have stood for a thousand years, and pained thoughts
found
The honey of peace in old poems. 10

[1924]

Shine, Perishing Republic

While this America settles in the mould of its vulgarity, heavily thickening to empire,
And protest, only a bubble in the molten mass, pops and sighs out, and the mass hardens,

I sadly smiling remember that the flower fades to make fruit, the fruit rots to make earth.
Out of the mother; and through the spring exultances, ripeness and decadence; and home to the mother.

You making haste haste on decay: not blameworthy; life is good, be it stubbornly long or suddenly 5
A mortal splendor: meteors are not needed less than mountains: shine, perishing republic.

But for my children, I would have them keep their distance from the thickening center; corruption
Never has been compulsory, when the cities lie at the monster's feet there are left the mountains.

And boys, be in nothing so moderate as in love of man, a clever servant, insufferable master.
There is the trap that catches noblest spirits, that caught— they say—God, when he walked on earth. 10

[1925]

Hurt Hawks

I

The broken pillar of the wing jags from the clotted shoulder,
The wing trails like a banner in defeat,
No more to use the sky forever but live with famine
And pain a few days: cat nor coyote
Will shorten the week of waiting for death, there is game without talons. 5
He stands under the oak-bush and waits
The lame feet of salvation; at night he remembers freedom
And flies in a dream, the dawns ruin it.
He is strong and pain is worse to the strong, incapacity is worse.
The curs of the day come and torment him 10
At distance, no one but death the redeemer will humble that head,
The intrepid readiness, the terrible eyes.
The wild God of the world is sometimes merciful to those
That ask mercy, not often to the arrogant.
You do not know him, you communal people, or you have forgotten him; 15
Intemperate and savage, the hawk remembers him;
Beautiful and wild, the hawks, and men that are dying, remember him.

II

I'd sooner, except the penalties, kill a man than a hawk; but the great
redtail
Had nothing left but unable misery
From the bones too shattered for mending, the wing that trailed 20
under his talons when he moved.
We had fed him six weeks, I gave him freedom,
He wandered over the foreland hill and returned in the evening,
asking for death,
Not like a beggar, still eyed with the old
Implacable arrogance. I gave him the lead gift in the twilight. What
fell was relaxed,
Owl-downy, soft feminine feathers; but what 25
Soared: the fierce rush: the night-herons by the flooded river cried
fear at its rising
Before it was quite unsheathed from reality.

[1928]

Hands

Inside a cave in a narrow canyon near Tassajara°
The vault of rock is painted with hands,
A multitude of hands in the twilight, a cloud of men's palms, no more,
No other picture. There's no one to say
Whether the brown shy quiet people who are dead intended 5
Religion or magic, or made their tracings
In the idleness of art; but over the division of years these careful
Signs-manual are now like a sealed message
Saying: "Look: we also were human; we had hands, not paws. All hail
You people with the cleverer hands, our supplanters 10
In the beautiful country; enjoy her a season, her beauty, and come
down
And be supplanted; for you also are human."

[1929]

1 *Tassajara*: site of hot springs in the Santa Lucia Mountains. The cave Jeffers refers to is several miles from the springs. As in the Four Corners area of the American Southwest, Indians left ceremonial pictographs of their own hands in the shelter of caves.

Rock and Hawk

Here is a symbol in which
Many high tragic thoughts
Watch their own eyes.

This gray rock, standing tall
On the headland, where the sea-wind *5*
Lets no tree grow,

Earthquake-proved, and signatured
By ages of storms: on its peak
A falcon has perched.

I think, here is your emblem *10*
To hang in the future sky;
Not the cross, not the hive,

But this; bright power, dark peace;
Fierce consciousness joined with final
Disinterestedness; *15*

Life with calm death; the falcon's
Realist eyes and act
Married to the massive

Mysticism of stone,
Which failure cannot cast down *20*
Nor success make proud.

[1935]

Carmel Point

The extraordinary patience of things!
This beautiful place defaced with a crop of suburban houses—
How beautiful when we first beheld it,
Unbroken field of poppy and lupin walled with clean cliffs;
No intrusion but two or three horses pasturing, *5*
Or a few milch cows rubbing their flanks on the outcrop rock-heads—
Now the spoiler has come: does it care?
Not faintly. It has all time. It knows the people are a tide

That swells and in time will ebb, and all
Their works dissolve. Meanwhile the image of the pristine beauty *10*
Lives in the very grain of the granite,
Safe as the endless ocean that climbs our cliff.—As for us:
We must uncenter our minds from ourselves;
We must unhumanize our views a little, and become confident
As the rock and ocean that we were made from. *15*

[1954]

***Marianne Moore** (1887–1972) was born in Kirkwood, Missouri, outside St. Louis. She never knew her father, who was hospitalized for a nervous breakdown and did not return to the family. Moore's mother moved her children to Carlisle, Pennsylvania, and enrolled her daughter at the girls' prep school where she taught. Matriculating at Bryn Mawr College, Moore was rejected from the English department, so she studied law, history, politics, and biology. She and her mother were inseparable for most of their lives, moving together to New York City. Moore's literary career soon flourished—partly due to her correspondences with figures such as H. D., Ezra Pound, and T. S. Eliot. Her* Collected Poems *(1951) won the Pulitzer Prize, the National Book Award, and the Bollingen Prize—the three top awards in American poetry. Late in life she became a celebrity, featured in popular magazines and interviewed on late-night television talk shows. Moore died at age 85 from a stroke.*

Marianne Moore

The Fish

wade
through black jade.
    Of the crow-blue mussel shells, one keeps
        adjusting the ash heaps;
    opening and shutting itself like *5*

an
injured fan.
  The barnacles which encrust the side
    of the wave, cannot hide
  there for the submerged shafts of the *10*

sun,
split like spun
  glass, move themselves with spotlike swiftness
    into the crevices—
  in and out, illuminating *15*

the
turquoise sea
  of bodies. The water drives a wedge
    of iron through the iron edge
  of the cliff, whereupon the stars, *20*

pink
rice grains, ink-
  bespattered jelly-fish, crabs like green
    lilies and submarine
  toadstools, slide each on the other. *25*

All
external
  marks of abuse are present on this
    defiant edifice—
  all the physical features of *30*

ac-
cident—lack
  of cornice, dynamite grooves, burns, and
    hatchet strokes, these things stand
  out on it; the chasm side is *35*

dead.
Repeated
  evidence has proved that it can live
    on what cannot revive
  its youth. The sea grows old in it. *40*

[1921]

Poetry*

I too, dislike it: there are things that are important beyond all this
fiddle.
Reading it, however, with a perfect contempt for it, one discovers
that there is in
it after all, a place for the genuine.
Hands that can grasp, eyes
that can dilate, hair that can rise 5
if it must, these things are important not because a

high sounding interpretation can be put upon them but because they
are
useful; when they become so derivative as to become unintelligible,
the same thing may be said for all of us—that we
do not admire what 10
we cannot understand. The bat,
holding on upside down or in quest of something to

eat, elephants pushing, a wild horse taking a roll, a tireless wolf under
a tree, the immovable critic twinkling his skin like a horse that
feels a flea, the base-
ball fan, the statistician—case after case 15
could be cited did
one wish it; nor is it valid
to discriminate against "business documents and

school-books"; all these phenomena are important. One must make a
distinction
however: when dragged into prominence by half poets, 20
the result is not poetry,
nor till the autocrats among us can be
"literalists of
the imagination"°—above
insolence and triviality and can present

**Diary of Tolstoy;* Dutton, p. 84: "Where the boundary between prose and poetry lies, shall never be able to understand. The question is raised in manuals of style, yet the answer to it lies beyond me. Poetry is verse: prose is not verse. Or else poetry is everything with the exception of business documents and school books." [Moore's note]

22–23 *"literalists of the imagination"*: Yeats; Ideas of Good and Evil, 1903; William Blake and his Illustrations to *The Divine Comedy*; p. 182; "The limitation of his view was from the very intensity of his vision; he was a too literal realist of imagination, as others are of nature; and because he believed that the figures seen by the mind's eye, when exalted by inspiration were 'eternal existences,' symbols of divine essences, he hated every grace of style that might obscure their lineaments." [Moore's notes, 1924]

for inspection, imaginary gardens with real toads in them, 25
shall we have
it. In the meantime, if you demand on one hand, in defiance of
their opinion—
the raw material of poetry in
all its rawness and
that which is, on the other hand,
genuine then you are interested in poetry. 30

[several versions; first 1921, final 1967]

To a Steam Roller

The illustration
is nothing to you without the application.
You lack half wit. You crush all the particles down
into close conformity, and then walk back and forth on them.

Sparkling chips of rock 5
are crushed down to the level of the parent block.
Were not "impersonal judgment in æsthetic
matters, a metaphysical impossibility," you

might fairly achieve
it. As for butterflies, I can hardly conceive 10
of one's attending upon you, but to question
the congruence of the complement is vain, if it exists.

[1921]

Silence

My father used to say,
"Superior people never make long visits,
have to be shown Longfellow's grave
or the glass flowers at Harvard.°

1–4 *My father used to say*: a remark in conversation; Miss A. M. Homans, Professor Emeritus of Hygiene, Wellesley College. "My father used to say, 'superior people never make long visits, then people are not so glad when you've gone.' When I am visiting, I like to go about by myself. I never had to be shown Longfellow's grave nor the glass flowers at Harvard." [Moore's note, 1924] "My father used to say, 'Superior people never make long visits. When I am visiting, I like to go about by myself. I never had to be shown Longfellow's grave or the glass flowers at Harvard.' " Miss A. M. Homans. [Moore's note, 1967]

Self-reliant like the cat— 5
that takes its prey to privacy,
the mouse's limp tail hanging like a shoelace from its mouth—
they sometimes enjoy solitude,
and can be robbed of speech
by speech which has delighted them. 10
The deepest feeling always shows itself in silence;
not in silence, but restraint."
Nor was he insincere in saying, "Make my house your inn."°
Inns are not residences.

[1924]

13 *"Make my house your inn"*: Edmund Burke to a stranger with whom he had fallen into conversation in a bookshop. Life of Burke: James Prior; " 'Throw yourself into a coach,' said he. 'Come down and make my house your inn.' " [Moore's note, 1924] Edmund Burke, in Burke's Life, by Sir James Prior (1872). " 'Throw yourself into a coach,' said he. 'Come down and make my house your inn.' " [Moore's note, 1967]

The Mind Is an Enchanting Thing

is an enchanted thing
  like the glaze on a
katydid-wing
    subdivided by sun
    till the nettings are legion. 5
Like Gieseking playing Scarlatti;

like the apteryx-awl
  as a beak, or the
kiwi's rain-shawl
    of haired feathers, the mind 10
    feeling its way as though blind,
walks along with its eyes on the ground.

It has memory's ear
  that can hear without
having to hear. 15
    Like the gyroscope's fall,
    truly unequivocal
because trued by regnant certainty,

it is a power of
    strong enchantment. It *20*
is like the dove-
        neck animated by
        sun; it is memory's eye;
it's conscientious inconsistency.

It tears off the veil; tears *25*
    the temptation, the
mist the heart wears,
        from its eyes—if the heart
        has a face; it takes apart
dejection. It's fire in the dove-neck's *30*

iridescence; in the
    inconsistencies
of Scarlatti.
        Unconfusion submits
        its confusion to proof; it's *35*
not a Herod's oath that cannot change.

[1944]

T.[homas] S.[tearns] ***Eliot*** *(1888–1965) was born in St. Louis, Missouri, where his father was a brick manufacturer and his mother a poet and biographer. Eliot entered Harvard in 1906, and began graduate studies in philosophy in 1909. He wrote his first major poem, "The Love Song of J. Alfred Prufrock," while still at Harvard. Eliot also studied modern poetry, comparative religions, French, and Sanskrit. Traveling to London on a fellowship, he met Ezra Pound, whose friendship was highly influential. He hastily married an Englishwoman, Vivien Haigh-Wood, who suffered from health problems and nervous disorders, which led to their separation in 1932. During those difficult years, Eliot worked extremely long hours as a bank clerk at Lloyd's of London. At night he dedicated himself to writing. He left banking in 1925 to join the publishing firm of Faber and Faber, where he worked for the rest of his life. During the 1920s Eliot experienced a growing religious faith, and in 1927 he received baptism in the Anglican Church—the same year that he became a British subject. In 1948 Eliot won the Nobel Prize, based upon such accomplishments as* The Waste Land *(1922),* The Four Quartets *(1943), and his critical work.*

T. S. Eliot

The Love Song of J. Alfred Prufrock

S'io credessi che mia risposta fosse
A persona che mai tornasse al mondo,
Questa fiamma staria senza più scosse.
Ma per ciò che giammai di questo fondo
Non tornò vivo alcun, s'i' odo il vero,
Senza tema d'infamia ti rispondo.*

Let us go then, you and I,
When the evening is spread out against the sky
Like a patient etherized upon a table;
Let us go, through certain half-deserted streets,
The muttering retreats *5*
Of restless nights in one-night cheap hotels
And sawdust restaurants with oyster-shells:
Streets that follow like a tedious argument
Of insidious intent
To lead you to an overwhelming question . . . *10*
Oh, do not ask, "What is it?"
Let us go and make our visit.

In the room the women come and go
Talking of Michelangelo.

The yellow fog that rubs its back upon the window-panes, *15*
The yellow smoke that rubs its muzzle on the window-panes,
Licked its tongue into the corners of the evening,
Lingered upon the pools that stand in drains,
Let fall upon its back the soot that falls from chimneys,
Slipped by the terrace, made a sudden leap, *20*
And seeing that it was a soft October night,
Curled once about the house, and fell asleep.

*The epigraph is from Dante's *Inferno* (XXVII, 61-6): "If I thought my response would be to one who would ever return to earth, this fire would remain unmoving. But no one has ever returned from this gulf alive. If what I hear is true, I can answer you without fear of infamy."

And indeed there will be time°
For the yellow smoke that slides along the street
Rubbing its back upon the window-panes; *25*
There will be time, there will be time
To prepare a face to meet the faces that you meet;
There will be time to murder and create,
And time for all the works and days of hands°
That lift and drop a question on your plate; *30*
Time for you and time for me,
And time yet for a hundred indecisions,
And for a hundred visions and revisions,
Before the taking of a toast and tea.

In the room the women come and go *35*
Talking of Michelangelo.

And indeed there will be time
To wonder, "Do I dare?" and, "Do I dare?"
Time to turn back and descend the stair,
With a bald spot in the middle of my hair— *40*
(They will say: "How his hair is growing thin!")
My morning coat, my collar mounting firmly to the chin,
My necktie rich and modest, but asserted by a simple pin—
(They will say: "But how his arms and legs are thin!")
Do I dare *45*
Disturb the universe?
In a minute there is time
For decisions and revisions which a minute will reverse.

For I have known them all already, known them all—
Have known the evenings, mornings, afternoons, *50*
I have measured out my life with coffee spoons;
I know the voices dying with a dying fall
Beneath the music from a farther room.
So how should I presume?

And I have known the eyes already, known them all— *55*
The eyes that fix you in a formulated phrase,

23 *there will be time*: from Ecclesiastes 3. See also Andrew Marvell (1621–1678), "To His Coy Mistress": "Had we but world enough and time, / This coyness, lady, were no crime." **29** *works and days*: "Works and Days" is the title of a poem by Hesiod (eighth century BC).

And when I am formulated, sprawling on a pin,
When I am pinned and wriggling on the wall,
Then how should I begin
To spit out all the butt-ends of my days and ways? *60*
    And how should I presume?

And I have known the arms already, known them all—
Arms that are braceleted and white and bare
(But in the lamplight, downed with light brown hair!)
Is it perfume from a dress *65*
That makes me so digress?
Arms that lie along a table, or wrap about a shawl.
    And should I then presume?
    And how should I begin?

. . . . .

Shall I say, I have gone at dusk through narrow streets *70*
And watched the smoke that rises from the pipes
Of lonely men in shirt-sleeves, leaning out of windows? . . .

I should have been a pair of ragged claws
Scuttling across the floors of silent seas.

. . . . .

And the afternoon, the evening, sleeps so peacefully! *75*
Smoothed by long fingers,
Asleep . . . tired . . . or it malingers,
Stretched on the floor, here beside you and me.
Should I, after tea and cakes and ices,
Have the strength to force the moment to its crisis? *80*
But though I have wept and fasted, wept and prayed,
Though I have seen my head (grown slightly bald) brought in
    upon a platter,°
I am no prophet—and here's no great matter;
I have seen the moment of my greatness flicker,
And I have seen the eternal Footman hold my coat, and snicker, *85*
And in short, I was afraid.

And would it have been worth it, after all,
After the cups, the marmalade, the tea,
Among the porcelain, among some talk of you and me,

82 *head . . . upon a platter*: At the command of King Herod, John the Baptist was beheaded. His head was brought on a silver dish to please Queen Herodias (Matthew 14:3–11).

Would it have been worth while, 90
To have bitten off the matter with a smile,
To have squeezed the universe into a ball°
To roll it towards some overwhelming question,
To say: "I am Lazarus,° come from the dead,
Come back to tell you all, I shall tell you all"— 95
If one, settling a pillow by her head,
Should say: "That is not what I meant at all.
That is not it, at all."

And would it have been worth it, after all,
Would it have been worth while, 100
After the sunsets and the dooryards and the sprinkled streets,
After the novels, after the teacups, after the skirts that trail along
the floor—
And this, and so much more?—
It is impossible to say just what I mean!
But as if a magic lantern threw the nerves in patterns on a 105
screen:
Would it have been worth while
If one, settling a pillow or throwing off a shawl,
And turning toward the window, should say:
"That is not it at all,
That is not what I meant, at all." 110

. . . . .

No! I am not Prince Hamlet, nor was meant to be;
Am an attendant lord, one that will do
To swell a progress, start a scene or two,
Advise the prince; no doubt, an easy tool,
Deferential, glad to be of use, 115
Politic, cautious, and meticulous;
Full of high sentence, but a bit obtuse;
At times, indeed, almost ridiculous—
Almost, at times, the Fool.°

92 *universe into a ball*: Marvell, "To His Coy Mistress": "Let us roll all our strength and all/Our sweetness up into a ball, / And tear our pleasures with rough strife / Through the iron gates of life." Another ironic echo of the *carpe diem* theme. **94** "*I am Lazarus*": In the Bible (John 11:1–44) Christ raises Lazarus from the dead. Yet another Lazarus comments on the experience of death in Luke 16:19–31. **112–119** Prufrock may be referring here to Polonius, advisor to the King in *Hamlet*. The fool was a stock figure in Shakespeare's plays. In *Hamlet* the fool is dead—Yorick, whom Hamlet remembers in a soliloquy.

I grow old . . . I grow old . . . 120
I shall wear the bottoms of my trousers rolled.

Shall I part my hair behind?° Do I dare to eat a peach?
I shall wear white flannel trousers, and walk upon the beach.
I have heard the mermaids singing,° each to each.

I do not think that they will sing to me. 125

I have seen them riding seaward on the waves
Combing the white hair of the waves blown back
When the wind blows the water white and black.

We have lingered in the chambers of the sea
By sea-girls wreathed with seaweed red and brown 130
Till human voices wake us, and we drown.

[1917]

122 *Shall I part my hair behind?*: Eliot's Harvard roommate, Conrad Aiken, wrote in his 1952 memoir, *Ushant*, that it was considered daring in their college days to part one's hair behind. Others have speculated that this refers to the effort to cover a bald spot. **124** *mermaids singing*: One of Donne's impossible challenges in the song "Go and catch a falling star" is "Teach me to hear mermaids singing."

Preludes*

I

The winter evening settles down
With smell of steaks in passageways.
Six o'clock.
The burnt-out ends of smoky days.
And now a gusty shower wraps 5
The grimy scraps
Of withered leaves about your feet
And newspapers from vacant lots;
The showers beat
On broken blinds and chimney-pots, 10
And at the corner of the street
A lonely cab-horse steams and stamps.

And then the lighting of the lamps.

*The title suggests brief musical variations, as in Chopin.

II

The morning comes to consciousness
Of faint stale smells of beer 15
From the sawdust-trampled street
With all its muddy feet that press
To early coffee-stands.

With the other masquerades
That time resumes, 20
One thinks of all the hands
That are raising dingy shades
In a thousand furnished rooms.

III

You tossed a blanket from the bed,
You lay upon your back, and waited; 25
You dozed, and watched the night revealing
The thousand sordid images
Of which your soul was constituted;
They flickered against the ceiling.
And when all the world came back 30
And the light crept up between the shutters
And you heard the sparrows in the gutters,
You had such a vision of the street
As the street hardly understands;
Sitting along the bed's edge, where 35
You curled the papers from your hair,
Or clasped the yellow soles of feet
In the palms of both soiled hands.

IV

His soul stretched tight across the skies
That fade behind a city block, 40
Or trampled by insistent feet
At four and five and six o'clock;
And short square fingers stuffing pipes,
And evening newspapers, and eyes
Assured of certain certainties, 45
The conscience of a blackened street
Impatient to assume the world.

I am moved by fancies that are curled
Around these images, and cling:
The notion of some infinitely gentle *50*
Infinitely suffering thing.

Wipe your hand across your mouth, and laugh;
The worlds revolve like ancient women
Gathering fuel in vacant lots.

[1917]

La Figlia che Piange

O quam te memorem virgo . . .*

Stand on the highest pavement of the stair—
Lean on a garden urn—
Weave, weave the sunlight in your hair—
Clasp your flowers to you with a pained surprise—
Fling them to the ground and turn *5*
With a fugitive resentment in your eyes:
But weave, weave the sunlight in your hair.

So I would have had him leave,
So I would have had her stand and grieve,
So he would have left *10*
As the soul leaves the body torn and bruised,
As the mind deserts the body it has used.
I should find
Some way incomparably light and deft,
Some way we both should understand, *15*
Simple and faithless as a smile and shake of the hand.

She turned away, but with the autumn weather
Compelled my imagination many days,
Many days and many hours:
Her hair over her arms and her arms full of flowers. *20*

*The title is Italian, "The Weeping Girl." The epigraph is from Virgil's *Aneneid*: "How may I name thee, maiden . . . "

And I wonder how they should have been together!
I should have lost a gesture and a pose.
Sometimes these cogitations still amaze
The troubled midnight and the noon's repose.

[1917]

The Waste Land

'Nam Sibyllam quidem Cumis ego ipse oculis meis vidi in ampulla pendere, et cum illi pueri dicerent: *Σlβυλλα τl θέλεις*; respondebat illa: *άποθανεîυ θέλω*.'

For Ezra Pound
*il miglior fabbro.**

I. The Burial of the Dead°

April is the cruellest month,° breeding
Lilacs out of the dead land, mixing
Memory and desire, stirring
Dull roots with spring rain.
Winter kept us warm, covering *5*
Earth in forgetful snow, feeding
A little life with dried tubers.
Summer surprised us, coming over the Starnbergersee°
With a shower of rain; we stopped in the colonnade,
And went on in sunlight, into the Hofgarten,° *10*
And drank coffee, and talked for an hour.
Bin gar keine Russin, stamm' aus Litauen, echt deutsch.°

*See Eliot's Notes on "The Waste Land," pages 365–370. As Eliot's notes attest, this is from Jessie L. Weston's study, though one may also find the phrase in Tennyson's *Idylls of the King*. *Epigraph*: Latin and Greek. Petronius, *Satyricon*, Chapter 48, tells that Apollo had granted eternal life to the Sibyl, but not eternal youth: "For once I saw with my own eyes the Sibyl at Cumae hanging in a cage, and when the young men asked, 'Sibyl, what do you want?' she replied, 'I want to die.' " *Dedication*: The dedication to Ezra Pound quotes from Dante's tribute to Arnaut Daniel, "the better maker."

I. *The Burial of the Dead*: The title is a phrase from the Anglican burial service.

1 Eliot's opening is a deliberate contrast to the Prologue of Chaucer's *The Canterbury Tales*. **8** *Starnbergersee*: lake near Munich. **10** *Hofgarten*: park in that city. Lines **8–18** are said to be based on a conversation Eliot had with Countess Marie Larisch of Austria. **12** *Bin . . . deutsch*: German, "I'm no Russian, I'm from Lithuania, true German." Some critics note that the German spoken here is not entirely correct.

And when we were children, staying at the arch-duke's,
My cousin's, he took me out on a sled,
And I was frightened. He said, Marie,
Marie, hold on tight. And down we went. *15*
In the mountains, there you feel free.
I read, much of the night, and go south in the winter.

What are the roots that clutch, what branches grow
Out of this stony rubbish? Son of man,° *20*
You cannot say, or guess, for you know only
A heap of broken images, where the sun beats,
And the dead tree gives no shelter, the cricket no relief,°
And the dry stone no sound of water. Only
There is shadow under this red rock, *25*
(Come in under the shadow of this red rock),
And I will show you something different from either
Your shadow at morning striding behind you
Or your shadow at evening rising to meet you;
I will show you fear in a handful of dust. *30*
Frisch weht der Wind
Der Heimat zu
Mein Irisch Kind,
Wo weilest du?°
"You gave me hyacinths° first a year ago; *35*
"They called me the hyacinth girl."
—Yet when we came back, late, from the hyacinth garden,
Your arms full, and your hair wet, I could not
Speak, and my eyes failed, I was neither
Living nor dead, and I knew nothing, *40*
Looking into the heart of light, the silence.
Oed' und leer das Meer.°

Madame Sosostris,° famous clairvoyante,
Had a bad cold, nevertheless

20, 23 See Eliot's notes at the end of the poem. **31–34** *Frisch . . . weilest du*: German, from Wagner's *Tristan und Isolde*. A sailor sings these lines on the ship bearing Isolde to Cornwall and her soon-to-be-husband, King Mark, whom she does not love: "The wind blows fresh / To the homeland; / My Irish lass, / Where are you lingering?" **35** Hyacinths were associated with ancient fertility rites. In Greek mythology, Hyacinthus was a prince beloved of Apollo. After accidentally killing the youth in a game, Apollo caused flowers to spring up from his blood. Hyacinths came to symbolize death and resurrection. **42** *Oed' und leer das Meer*: From *Tristan und Isolde*. Tristan has been wounded after being caught in adultery with Isolde. He hopes she will come to heal him, but a shepherd keeping watch sings, "Desolate and empty the sea." **43** *Madame Sosostris*: a name Eliot borrowed, in slightly altered form, from Aldous Huxley's comic novel *Chrome Yellow* (1921).

Is known to be the wisest woman in Europe, *45*
With a wicked pack of cards.° Here, said she,
Is your card, the drowned Phoenician Sailor,°
(Those are pearls that were his eyes. Look!)°
Here is Belladonna,° the Lady of the Rocks,
The lady of situations. *50*
Here is the man with three staves,° and here the Wheel,
And here is the one-eyed merchant,° and this card,
Which is blank, is something he carries on his back,
Which I am forbidden to see. I do not find
The Hanged Man. Fear death by water. *55*
I see crowds of people, walking round in a ring.
Thank you. If you see dear Mrs. Equitone,°
Tell her I bring the horoscope myself:
One must be so careful these days.

Unreal City,° *60*
Under the brown fog of a winter dawn,
A crowd flowed over London Bridge, so many,
I had not thought death had undone so many.°
Sighs, short and infrequent, were exhaled,
And each man fixed his eyes before his feet.° *65*
Flowed up the hill and down King William Street,
To where Saint Mary Woolnoth kept the hours
With a dead sound on the final stroke of nine.°
There I saw one I knew, and stopped him, crying: "Stetson!
"You who were with me in the ships at Mylae!° *70*

46 See Eliot's note. **47** The Phoenecian sailor returns as Phlebas in Part IV. This card does not exist in the Tarot deck. **48** In Act I of Shakespeare's *The Tempest* we meet Prince Ferdinand, who is convinced that his father has drowned by Ariel's deceiving song: "Full fathom five thy father lies, / Of his bones are coral made, / Those are pearls that were his eyes. / Nothing of him that doth fade, / But doth suffer a sea-change, / Into something rich and strange." Thus Eliot echoes his themes of death and resurrection. **49** *Belladonna*: Italian for "beautiful lady" (an appellation given by Dante to Beatrice). It is also the name of a poisonous plant. Leonardo da Vinci's painting of *La Giaconda* (or *Mona Lisa*) may be the Lady of the Rocks. Eliot may have had in mind Walter Pater's description of the painting in *The Renaissance*. **51** Eliot associates the man with three staves, a figure in the Tarot pack, with the Fisher King. The Wheel of Fortune is also alluded to here. **52** The merchant may return as Mr. Eugenides in Part III. This card does not exist in the Tarot deck. **57** The name Mrs. Equitone echoes that of Eleanor of Aquitaine, who was famous for her romances. The name recurs at the conclusion of Eliot's poem. **60** *Unreal City*: the *fourmillante cité* of Baudelaire's poem "The Seven Old Men" (*Les sept vieillards*). **63** In Dante's *Inferno* (III, 55–57) the souls in limbo are described: "So long a train of people / That I would never have believed / That death had undone so many." **65** In Canto IV of *Inferno* Dante describes the sighs of the virtuous pagans who lived before Christ. **68** See Eliot's note. **70** *ships at Mylae*: The Battle at Mylae took place during the first Punic War between Rome and Carthage. The poem also alludes here to World War I.

"That corpse you planted last year in your garden,
"Has it begun to sprout? Will it bloom this year?
"Or has the sudden frost disturbed its bed?
"O keep the Dog far hence, that's friend to men,
"Or with his nails he'll dig it up again! *75*
"You! hypocrite lecteur!—mon semblable,—mon frère!"°

II. A Game of Chess°

The Chair she sat in, like a burnished throne,°
Glowed on the marble, where the glass
Held up by standards wrought with fruited vines
From which a golden Cupidon peeped out *80*
(Another hid his eyes behind his wing)
Doubled the flames of sevenbranched candelabra
Reflecting light upon the table as
The glitter of her jewels rose to meet it,
From satin cases poured in rich profusion. *85*
In vials of ivory and coloured glass
Unstoppered, lurked her strange synthetic perfumes,
Unguent, powdered, or liquid—troubled, confused
And drowned the sense in odours; stirred by the air
That freshened from the window, these ascended *90*
In fattening the prolonged candle-flames,
Flung their smoke into the laquearia,°
Stirring the pattern on the coffered ceiling.
Huge sea-wood fed with copper
Burned green and orange, framed by the coloured stone, *95*
In which sad light a carvèd dolphin swam.
Above the antique mantel was displayed

74–75 See Eliot's note. **76** *hypocrite lecteur! . . . mon frère!*: Baudelaire's line from the Preface to *Les fleurs du mal* translates, "Hypocrite reader!—my double—my brother!"

II. *A Game of Chess*: In an earlier draft this section was titled "In the Cage." The new title was borrowed from Thomas Middleton's plays, *A Game of Chess* and *Women Beware Women*, where a chess game parallels erotic manipulations.

77 The opening of this section echoes the speech of Enobarbus in Shakespeare's *Antony and Cleopatra* (II, ii), describing Cleopatra's barge. This may be another example of the "Belladonna" theme in the poem. **91–92** These lines allude to the banquet given for Aeneas by Dido in Book I of Virgil's *Aeneid*.

As though a window gave upon the sylvan scene
The change of Philomel,° by the barbarous king
So rudely forced; yet there the nightingale *100*
Filled all the desert with inviolable voice
And still she cried, and still the world pursues,
"Jug Jug"° to dirty ears.
And other withered stumps of time
Were told upon the walls; staring forms *105*
Leaned out, leaning, hushing the room enclosed.
Footsteps shuffled on the stair.
Under the firelight, under the brush, her hair
Spread out in fiery points
Glowed into words, then would be savagely still. *110*

"My nerves are bad to-night. Yes, bad. Stay with me.
"Speak to me. Why do you never speak. Speak.
        "What are you thinking of? What thinking? What?
"I never know what you are thinking. Think."°

I think we are in rats' alley *115*
Where the dead men lost their bones.

"What is that noise?"
            The wind under the door.
"What is that noise now? What is the wind doing?"
            Nothing again nothing. *120*
                                    "Do
"You know nothing? Do you see nothing? Do you remember
"Nothing?"

        I remember
Those are pearls that were his eyes. *125*
"Are you alive, or not? Is there nothing in your head?"

                                    But
O O O O that Shakespeherian Rag°—

99 *Philomel*: In Greek mythology, King Tereus raped Philomela, sister of his wife, Procne. Tereus cut out Philomela's tongue to ensure her silence. In revenge, Procne killed her son, Itys, and fed his flesh to Tereus. Before Tereus could get his revenge, the gods took pity on the sisters, changing Philomela to the nightingale, Procne to the swallow. 103 *"Jug Jug"*: a degraded representation of the nightingale's song from Elizabethan times. 111–114 In *The Waste Land Manuscript* we can see that Vivien Eliot wrote "WONDERFUL" in the margin next to this passage. 128 *Shakespeherian Rag*: refers to an actual song performed in Ziegfeld's Follies of 1912.

It's so elegant
So intelligent 130
"What shall I do now? What shall I do?'
"I shall rush out as I am, and walk the street
"With my hair down, so. What shall we do tomorrow?
"What shall we ever do?"
The hot water at ten. 135
And if it rains, a closed car at four.
And we shall play a game of chess,
Pressing lidless eyes and waiting for a knock upon the door.

When Lil's husband got demobbed,° I said—
I didn't mince my words, I said to her myself, 140
HURRY UP PLEASE ITS TIME°
Now Albert's coming back, make yourself a bit smart.
He'll want to know what you done with that money he gave you
To get yourself some teeth. He did, I was there.
You have them all out, Lil, and get a nice set, 145
He said, I swear, I can't bear to look at you.
And no more can't I, I said, and think of poor Albert,
He's been in the army four years, he wants a good time,
And if you don't give it him, there's others will, I said.
Oh is there, she said. Something o' that, I said. 150
Then I'll know who to thank, she said, and give me a straight look.
HURRY UP PLEASE ITS TIME
If you don't like it you can get on with it, I said.
Others can pick and choose if you can't.
But if Albert makes off, it won't be for lack of telling. 155
You ought to be ashamed, I said, to look so antique.
(And her only thirty-one.)
I can't help it, she said, pulling a long face,
It's them pills I took, to bring it off, she said.
(She's had five already, and nearly died of young George.) 160
The chemist° said it would be all right, but I've never been the same.
You *are* a proper fool, I said.
Well, if Albert won't leave you alone, there it is, I said,
What you get married for if you don't want children?

139 *demobbed*: demobilized. This is one of Pound's stringent bits of editing. Eliot had written, "When Lil's husband was coming back out of the Transport Corps. . . ." **141** *HURRY UP PLEASE ITS TIME*: This is what a barkeep in an English pub would call out at closing time. **161** *chemist*: In England a chemist is a druggist.

HURRY UP PLEASE ITS TIME 165
Well, that Sunday Albert was home, they had a hot gammon,°
And they asked me in to dinner, to get the beauty of it hot—
HURRY UP PLEASE ITS TIME
HURRY UP PLEASE ITS TIME
Goonight Bill. Goonight Lou. Goonight May. Goonight. 170
Ta ta. Goonight. Goonight.
Good night, ladies, good night, sweet ladies, good night, good night.°

III. The Fire Sermon°

The river's tent is broken; the last fingers of leaf
Clutch and sink into the wet bank. The wind
Crosses the brown land, unheard. The nymphs are departed. 175
Sweet Thames, run softly, till I end my song.°
The river bears no empty bottles, sandwich papers,
Silk handkerchiefs, cardboard boxes, cigarette ends
Or other testimony of summer nights. The nymphs are departed.
And their friends, the loitering heirs of City directors; 180
Departed, have left no addresses.
By the waters of Leman I sat down and wept° . . .
Sweet Thames, run softly till I end my song,
Sweet Thames, run softly, for I speak not loud or long.
But at my back in a cold blast I hear° 185
The rattle of the bones, and chuckle spread from ear to ear.

A rat crept softly through the vegetation
Dragging its slimy belly on the bank
While I was fishing in the dull canal
On a winter evening round behind the gashouse 190

166 *gammon*: ham. **172** *Good night . . . good night*: from Ophelia's farewell speech (*Hamlet*, IV, v.) before she drowns herself.

III. *The Fire Sermon:* See Eliot's note about the title. He had studied Buddhism at Harvard. In this sermon, Buddha advised his followers to transcend the fires of passion and become detached from earthly sensations.

176 *Sweet Thames . . .*: Eliot quotes from Spenser's "Prothalamion," a wedding song in which nymphs figure as "lovely Daughters of the Flood." Eliot's poem contains both Thames-maidens and Wagner's Rhine-maidens from *Die Götterdämmerung*. **182** Echoes Psalm 137, "By the rivers of Babylon, there we sat down, yea, we wept, when we remembered Zion." Leman is Lake Geneva as it is known in Switzerland. Eliot was recovering near there when he finished *The Waste Land*. **185** Echoes Marvell's "To His Coy Mistress": "But at my back I always hear / Time's wingèd chariot hurrying near . . ."

Musing upon the king my brother's wreck°
And on the king my father's death before him.
White bodies naked on the low damp ground
And bones cast in a little low dry garret,
Rattled by the rat's foot only, year to year. *195*
But at my back from time to time I hear
The sound of horns and motors, which shall bring
Sweeney to Mrs. Porter in the spring.
O the moon shone bright on Mrs. Porter
And on her daughter *200*
They wash their feet in soda water°
Et O ces voix d'enfants, chantant dans la coupole!°

Twit twit twit
Jug jug jug jug jug jug
So rudely forc'd.° *205*
Tereu

Unreal City
Under the brown fog of a winter noon
Mr. Eugenides, the Smyrna merchant
Unshaven, with a pocket full of currants *210*
C.i.f. London: documents at sight,°
Asked me in demotic French
To luncheon at the Cannon Street Hotel°
Followed by a weekend at the Metropole.°

At the violet hour, when the eyes and back *215*
Turn upward from the desk, when the human engine waits
Like a taxi throbbing waiting,
I Tiresias, though blind, throbbing between two lives,°

191 See note above for line 48. This too echoes *The Tempest* (I, ii). **199–201** See Eliot's note. **202** *Et O . . . coupole!*: Verlaine, *Parsifal*: "And O those voices of children, singing in the dome!" The poem is about a quest for the Holy Grail, and the allusion echoes the quest motif throughout *The Waste Land*. In Wagner's opera based on the same story, an enchantress washes the knight's feet so he may enter the Grail Castle. There he heals the ailing Fisher King. The opera concludes with a chorus of children praising Christ's power. **203–205** *Twit twit twit . . . So rudely forc'ed*: Another allusion to Philomela and Tereus. **211** See Eliot's note for line 210. **213** *Cannon Street Hotel*: A London hotel used by businessmen traveling to and from the continent. Also a meeting place for homosexuals, since homosexuality was both scandalous and illegal at the time. **214** *Metropole*: seaside resort hotel in Brighton. **218** See Eliot's note. The Latin passage he quoted there from Ovid is a retelling of the story in which Tiresias separated two copulating snakes and was transformed into a woman. Years later he repeated the gesture and was changed back into a man. Since he had been both man and woman, Jupiter and Juno asked him to settle a dispute; they wanted to know whether men or women enjoyed sex more. Tiresias answered that women did, which made Juno furious. She blinded him, but Jupiter took pity on him and gave him the gift of prophecy.

Old man with wrinkled female breasts, can see
At the violet hour, the evening hour that strives *220*
Homeward, and brings the sailor home from sea,°
The typist home at teatime, clears her breakfast, lights
Her stove, and lays out food in tins.
Out of the window perilously spread
Her drying combinations touched by the sun's last rays, *225*
On the divan are piled (at night her bed)
Stockings, slippers, camisoles, and stays.
I Tiresias, old man with wrinkled dugs
Perceived the scene, and foretold the rest—
I too awaited the expected guest. *230*
He, the young man carbuncular,° arrives,
A small house agent's clerk, with one bold stare,
One of the low on whom assurance sits
As a silk hat on a Bradford millionaire.°
The time is now propitious, as he guesses, *235*
The meal is ended, she is bored and tired,
Endeavours to engage her in caresses
Which still are unreproved, if undesired.
Flushed and decided, he assaults at once;
Exploring hands encounter no defence; *240*
His vanity requires no response,
And makes a welcome of indifference.
(And I Tiresias have foresuffered all
Enacted on this same divan or bed;
I who have sat by Thebes below the wall° *245*
And walked among the lowest of the dead.)
Bestows one final patronising kiss,
And gropes his way, finding the stairs unlit . . .

She turns and looks a moment in the glass,
Hardly aware of her departed lover; *250*
Her brain allows one half-formed thought to pass:
"Well now that's done: and I'm glad it's over."
When lovely woman stoops to folly and
Paces about her room again, alone,

221 This alludes both to Sappho (see Eliot's note) and Robert Louis Stevenson. **231** *carbuncular*: may refer to acne in this case. **234** *Bradford millionaire*: refers to a war profiteer, thus *nouveau riche* and by implication low class. **245** This alludes to the Oedipus cycle of Sophocles.

She smoothes her hair with automatic hand, *255*
And puts a record on the gramophone.

'This music crept by me upon the waters'°
And along the Strand, up Queen Victoria Street.
O City city, I can sometimes hear
Beside a public bar in Lower Thames Street, *260*
The pleasant whining of a mandoline
And a clatter and a chatter from within
Where fishmen lounge at noon: where the walls
Of Magnus Martyr hold
Inexplicable splendour of Ionian white and gold. *265*

The river sweats
Oil and tar
The barges drift
With the turning tide
Red sails *270*
Wide
To leeward, swing on the heavy spar.
The barges wash
Drifting logs
Down Greenwich reach *275*
Past the Isle of Dogs.°
Weialala leia
Wallala leialala

Elizabeth and Leicester°
Beating oars *280*
The stern was formed
A gilded shell
Red and gold
The brisk swell
Rippled both shores *285*
Southwest wind
Carried down stream
The peal of bells
White towers
Weialala leia *290*
Wallala leialala

257 See note above for line 48. **276** *Isle of Dogs*: a peninsula on the left bank of the Thames, opposite Greenwich. **279** See Eliot's note. Elizabeth and Leicester are, of course, another example of failed connection between the sexes.

"Trams and dusty trees.
Highbury bore me. Richmond and Kew
Undid me.° By Richmond I raised my knees
Supine on the floor of a narrow canoe." *295*

"My feet are at Moorgate, and my heart
Under my feet. After the event
He wept. He promised 'a new start.'
I made no comment. What should I resent?"

"On Margate Sands.° *300*
I can connect
Nothing with nothing.
The broken fingernails of dirty hands.
My people humble people who expect
Nothing." *305*
la la

To Carthage then I came°

Burning burning burning burning°
O Lord Thou pluckest me out°
O Lord Thou pluckest *310*

burning

IV. Death by Water°

Phlebas the Phoenician, a fortnight dead,
Forgot the cry of gulls, and the deep sea swell
And the profit and loss.
A current under sea *315*
Picked his bones in whispers. As he rose and fell
He passed the stages of his age and youth

293–294 In *Purgatorio*, the ghost of Pia de Tolomei tells Dante, "Sienna made me, Maremma unmade me" because her husband murdered her in Maremma. **300** *Margate Sands*: Eliot convalesced in Margate in 1921 before undergoing therapy in Switzerland. **307** *To Carthage then I came*: quote from St. Augustine's *Confessions*, in which Carthage is described as "a cauldron of unholy loves." **308** See Eliot's note. **309** See Eliot's note.

IV. *Death by Water*: See Eliot's poem in French, "Dans le Restaurant." Also Milton's "Lycidas" for an example of death by drowning in the pastoral tradition, and death that leads to a resurrection. This theme is also echoed in the novels of Charles Dickens, particularly *Our Mutual Friend* (1865).

Entering the whirlpool.
                Gentile or Jew
O you who turn the wheel and look to windward, *320*
Consider Phlebas, who was once handsome and tall as you.

V. What the Thunder Said°

After the torchlight red on sweaty faces
After the frosty silence in the gardens
After the agony in stony places
The shouting and the crying *325*
Prison and palace and reverberation
Of thunder of spring over distant mountains
He who was living is now dead
We who were living are now dying
With a little patience *330*

Here is no water but only rock
Rock and no water and the sandy road
The road winding above among the mountains
Which are mountains of rock without water
If there were water we should stop and drink *335*
Amongst the rock one cannot stop or think
Sweat is dry and feet are in the sand
If there were only water amongst the rock
Dead mountain mouth of carious teeth that cannot spit
Here one can neither stand nor lie nor sit *340*
There is not even silence in the mountains
But dry sterile thunder without rain
There is not even solitude in the mountains
But red sullen faces sneer and snarl
From doors of mudcracked houses *345*
                                                  If there were water
    And no rock
    If there were rock
    And also water

V. *What the Thunder Said*: See Eliot's notes on page 365 about Jessie L. Weston's study *From Ritual to Romance*. With regard to the Chapel Perilous, readers might also refer to *Sir Gawain and the Green Knight*.

And water 350
A spring
A pool among the rock
If there were the sound of water only
Not the cicada
And dry grass singing 355
But sound of water over a rock
Where the hermit-thrush sings in the pine trees
Drip drop drip drop drop drop drop
But there is no water

Who is the third who walks always beside you?° 360
When I count, there are only you and I together
But when I look ahead up the white road
There is always another one walking beside you
Gliding wrapt in a brown mantle, hooded
I do not know whether a man or a woman 365
— But who is that on the other side of you?

What is that sound high in the air°
Murmur of maternal lamentation
Who are those hooded hordes swarming
Over endless plains, stumbling in cracked earth 370
Ringed by the flat horizon only
What is the city over the mountains
Cracks and reforms and bursts in the violet air
Falling towers
Jerusalem Athens Alexandria 375
Vienna London
Unreal

A woman drew her long black hair out tight
And fiddled whisper music on those strings
And bats with baby faces in the violet light 380
Whistled, and beat their wings
And crawled head downward down a blackened wall
And upside down in air were towers
Tolling reminiscent bells, that kept the hours
And voices singing out of empty cisterns and exhausted wells 385

360 See Eliot's note. Also Luke 24:13–16. **367–377** See Eliot's note.

In this decayed hole among the mountains
In the faint moonlight, the grass is singing
Over the tumbled graves, about the chapel°
There is the empty chapel, only the wind's home.
It has no windows, and the door swings, *390*
Dry bones can harm no one.
Only a cock stood on the rooftree
Co co rico co co rico
In a flash of lightning. Then a damp gust
Bringing rain *395*

Ganga° was sunken, and the limp leaves
Waited for rain, while the black clouds
Gathered far distant, over Himavant.°
The jungle crouched, humped in silence.
Then spoke the thunder *400*

DA°
Datta: what have we given?°
My friend, blood shaking my heart
The awful daring of a moment's surrender
Which an age of prudence can never retract *405*
By this, and this only, we have existed
Which is not to be found in our obituaries
Or in memories draped by the beneficent spider
Or under seals broken by the lean solicitor
In our empty rooms *410*

DA
Dayadhvam: I have heard the key
Turn in the door once and turn once only
We think of the key, each in his prison
Thinking of the key, each confirms a prison *415*
Only at nightfall, aethereal rumours
Revive for a moment a broken Coriolanus

DA
Damyata: The boat responded
Gaily, to the hand expert with sail and oar *420*

388 *chapel*: suggests the Perilous Chapel, a fearful place that the knight must enter on his quest for the Grail. Gawain must enter such a place before he battles the Green Knight. **396** *Ganga*: one of the sacred rivers of India, the Ganges. **398** *Himavant*: the Himalayan Mountain Range. **401** The thunder says this. The Russian word for "yes" is also intended. **402–420** See Eliot's notes for lines 402, 408 and 412.

The sea was calm, your heart would have responded
Gaily, when invited, beating obedient
To controlling hands

I sat upon the shore
Fishing,° with the arid plain behind me 425
Shall I at least set my lands in order?°
London Bridge is falling down falling down falling down
Poi s'ascose nel foco che gli affina°
Quando fiam uti chelidon°—O swallow swallow
Le Prince d' Aquitaine à la tour abolie° 430
These fragments I have shored against my ruins
Why then Ile fit you. Hieronymo's mad againe.°
Datta. Dayadhvam. Damyata.
Shantih shantih shantih°

[1922]

[Eliot's Notes on "The Waste Land," 1922]

Not only the title, but the plan and a good deal of the incidental symbolism of the poem were suggested by Miss Jessie L. Weston's book on the Grail legend: *From Ritual to Romance* (Cambridge). Indeed, so deeply am I indebted, Miss Weston's book will elucidate the difficulties of the poem much better than my notes can do; and I recommend it (apart from the great interest of the book itself) to any who think such elucidation of the poem worth the trouble. To another work of anthropology I am indebted in general, one which has influenced our generation profoundly; I mean *The Golden Bough;* I have used especially the two volumes *Adonis, Attis, Osiris.* Anyone who is acquainted with these works will immediately recognise in the poem certain references to vegetation ceremonies.

425 See Eliot's note. **426** In Isaiah 38:1 the Lord says, "Set thine house in order: for thou shalt die, and not live." **428** *Poi . . . affina*: quotes from Dante's *Purgatorio* (Canto XXVI) in which Arnaut Daniel speaks, and afterwards Dante reports that the spirit hid in a refining fire. **429** "When shall I be like the swallow?" Philomela asks in a Latin poem cited by Eliot in his note. In Swinburne's "Itylus" we find the lines "Swallow, my sister, O sister swallow, / How can thy heart be full of spring?" **430** *Le Prince . . . abolie*: from Gerard de Nerval's poem called "The Disinherited" (El Desdichado). Here the poet is compared to "The Prince of Aquitaine at the ruined tower." **432** See Eliot's note. **434** See Eliot's note.

I. The Burial of the Dead

Line 20. Cf. Ezekiel II, i.
23. Cf. Ecclesiastes XII, v.
31. V. *Tristan und Isolde*, I, verses 5–8.
42. Id. III, verse 24.
46. I am not familiar with the exact constitution of the Tarot pack of cards, from which I have obviously departed to suit my own convenience. The Hanged Man, a member of the traditional pack, fits my purpose in two ways: because he is associated in my mind with the Hanged God of Frazer, and because I associate him with the hooded figure in the passage of the disciples to Emmaus in Part V. The Phoenician Sailor and the Merchant appear later; also the "crowds of people," and Death by Water is executed in Part IV. The Man with Three Staves (an authentic member of the Tarot pack) I associate, quite arbitrarily, with the Fisher King himself.
60. Cf. Baudelaire:
"Fourmillante cité, cité pleine de rêves,
"Où le spectre en plein jour raccroche le passant!"
63. Cf. *Inferno*, III, 55–57:
"si lunga tratta
di gente, ch'io non avrei mai creduto
che morte tanta n'avesse disfatta."
64. Cf. *Inferno*, IV, 25–27:
"Quivi, secondo che per ascoltare,
"non avea pianto, ma' che di sospiri,
"che l'aura eterna facevan tremare."
68. A phenomenon which I have often noticed.
74. Cf. the Dirge in Webster's *White Devil.*
76. V. Baudelaire, Preface to *Fleurs du Mal.*

II. A Game of Chess

77. Cf. *Antony and Cleopatra,* II, ii, l. 190.
92. Laquearia. V. *Aeneid*, I, 726:
dependent lychni laquearibus aureis incensi, et noctem flammis funalia vincunt.
98. Sylvan scene. V. Milton, *Paradise Lost*, IV, 140.
99. V. Ovid, *Metamorphoses*, VI, Philomela.
100. Cf. Part III, l. 204.
115. Cf. Part III, l. 195.

118. Cf. Webster: "Is the wind in that door still?"
126. Cf. Part I, l. 37, 48.
138. Cf. the game of chess in Middleton's *Women beware Women.*

III. The Fire Sermon

176. V. Spenser, *Prothalamion.*
192. Cf. *The Tempest*, I, ii.
196. Cf. Marvell, *To His Coy Mistress.*
197. Cf. Day, *Parliament of Bees:*

"When of the sudden, listening, you shall hear,
"A noise of horns and hunting, which shall bring
"Actaeon to Diana in the spring,
"Where all shall see her naked skin . . ."

199. I do not know the origin of the ballad from which these lines are taken: it was reported to me from Sydney, Australia.
202. V. Verlaine, *Parsifal.*
210. The currants were quoted at a price "cost insurance and freight to London;" and the Bill of Lading, etc., were to be handed to the buyer upon payment of the sight draft.
218. Tiresias, although a mere spectator and not indeed a "character," is yet the most important personage in the poem, uniting all the rest. Just as the one-eyed merchant, seller of currants, melts into the Phoenician Sailor, and the latter is not wholly distinct from Ferdinand Prince of Naples, so all the women are one woman, and the two sexes meet in Tiresias. What Tiresias *sees*, in fact, is the substance of the poem. The whole passage from Ovid is of great anthropological interest:

". . . Cum Iunone iocos et maior vestra profecto est
Quam, quae contingit maribus," dixisse, "voluptas."
Illa negat; placuit quae sit sententia docti
Quaerere Tiresiae: venus huic erat utraque nota.
Nam duo magnorum viridi coeuntia silva
Corpora serpentum baculi violaverat ictu
Deque viro factus, mirabile, femina septem
Egerat autumnos; octavo rursus eosdem
Vidit et "est vestrae si tanta potentia plagae,"
Dixit "ut auctoris sortem in contraria mutet,
Nunc quoque vos feriam!" percussis anguibus isdem
Forma prior rediit genetivaque venit imago.
Arbiter hic igitur sumptus de lite iocosa
Dicta Iovis firmat; gravius Saturnia iusto

Nec pro materia fertur doluisse suique
Iudicis aeterna damnavit lumina nocte,
At pater omnipotens (neque enim licet inrita cuiquam
Facta dei fecisse deo) pro lumine adempto
Scire futura dedit poenamque levavit honore.

221. This may not appear as exact as Sappho's lines, but I had in mind the "longshore" or "dory" fisherman, who returns at nightfall.

253. V. Goldsmith, the song in *The Vicar of Wakefield.*

257. V. *The Tempest*, as above.

264. The interior of St. Magnus Martyr is to my mind one of the finest among Wren's interiors. See *The Proposed Demolition of Nineteen City Churches:* (P. S. King & Son, Ltd.).

266. The Song of the (three) Thames-daughters begins here. From line 292 to 306 inclusive they speak in turn. V. *Götterdämmerung*, III, i: the Rhine-daughters.

279. V. Froude, *Elizabeth*, Vol. I, ch. iv, letter of De Quadra to Philip of Spain:

"In the afternoon we were in a barge, watching the games on the river. (The queen) was alone with Lord Robert and myself on the poop, when they began to talk nonsense, and went so far that Lord Robert at last said, as I was on the spot there was no reason why they should not be married if the queen pleased."

293. Cf. *Purgatorio*, V. 133:

"Ricorditi di me, che son la Pia;
"Siena mi fe', disfecemi Maremma."

307. V. St. Augustine's *Confessions:* "to Carthage then I came, where a cauldron of unholy loves sang all about mine ears."

308. The complete text of the Buddha's Fire Sermon (which corresponds in importance to the Sermon on the Mount) from which these words are taken, will be found translated in the late Henry Clarke Warren's *Buddhism in Translation* (Harvard Oriental Series). Mr. Warren was one of the great pioneers of Buddhist studies in the Occident.

309. From St. Augustine's *Confessions* again. The collocation of these two representatives of eastern and western asceticism, as the culmination of this part of the poem, is not an accident.

V. What the Thunder Said

In the first part of Part V three themes are employed: the journey to Emmaus, the approach to the Chapel Perilous (see Miss Weston's book) and the present decay of eastern Europe.

357. This is *Turdus aonalaschkae pallasii*, the hermit-thrush which I have heard in Quebec Province. Chapman says (*Handbook of Birds of Eastern North America*) "it is most at home in secluded woodland and thickety retreats. Its notes are not remarkable for variety or volume, but in purity and sweetness of tone and exquisite modulation they are unequalled." Its "water-dripping song" is justly celebrated.
360. The following lines were stimulated by the account of one of the Antarctic expeditions (I forget which, but I think one of Shackleton's): it was related that the party of explorers, at the extremity of their strength, had the constant delusion that there was *one more member* than could actually be counted.
367–77. Cf. Hermann Hesse, *Blick ins Chaos:* "Schon ist halb Europa, schon ist zumindest der halbe Osten Europas auf dem Wege zum Chaos, fährt betrunken im heiligem Wahn am Abgrund entlang und singt dazu, singt betrunken und hymnisch wie Dmitri Karamasoff sang. Ueber diese Lieder lacht der Bürger beleidigt, der Heilige und Seher hört sie mit Tränen."
402. "Datta, dayadhvam, damyata" (Give, sympathise, control). The fable of the meaning of the Thunder is found in the *Brihadaranyaka—Upanishad*, 5, I. A translation is found in Deussen's *Sechzig Upanishads des Veda*, p. 489.
408. Cf. Webster, *The White Devil*, V, vi:

> ". . . they'll remarry
> Ere the worm pierce your winding-sheet, ere the spider
> Make a thin curtain for your epitaphs."

412. Cf. *Inferno*, XXXIII, 46:

> "ed io sentii chiavar l'uscio di sotto
> all'orrible torre."

Also F. H. Bradley, *Appearance and Reality*, p. 346.
"My external sensations are no less private to myself than are my thoughts or my feelings. In either case my experience falls within my own circle, a circle closed on the outside; and, with all its elements alike, every sphere is opaque to the others which surround it. . . .In brief, regarded as an existence which appears in a soul, the whole world for each is peculiar and private to that soul."
425. V. Weston: *From Ritual to Romance*; chapter on the Fisher King.
428. V. *Purgatorio*, XXVI, 148.

> " 'Ara vos prec per aquella valor
> 'que vos condus al som de l'escalina,

'sovegna vos a temps de ma dolor.'
Poi s'ascose nel foco che gli affina."

429. V. *Pervigilium Veneris*. Cf. Philomela in Parts II and III.
430. V. Gerard de Nerval, Sonnet *El Desdichado*.
432. V. Kyd's *Spanish Tragedy*.
434. Shantih. Repeated as here, a formal ending to an Upanishad. "The Peace which passeth understanding" is our equivalent to this word.

***John Crowe Ransom** (1888–1974) was born in Pulaski, Tennessee. His father was a Methodist minister who frequently moved the family throughout the state. A bright student, Ransom matriculated at Vanderbilt University when he was only 15 to study philosophy and classics. Graduating in 1909, Ransom won a Rhodes scholarship to attend Christ Church in Oxford. He returned to Vanderbilt to join the faculty, though after a short time he left to fight in World War I. After the war, Ransom completed his first book,* Poems about God *(1919), and returned to Vanderbilt. There, along with Allen Tate and others, he cofounded the* Fugitive *magazine. Kenyon College offered Ransom a chair in 1937, where he remained until his retirement 22 years later. He founded the* Kenyon Review *and turned his creative attentions largely towards criticism and teaching. Ransom's most important critical collection was* The New Criticism *(1941), which coined the term that would be applied to a generation of poet-critics. His ashes are buried behind the Kenyon College library.*

John Crowe Ransom

Winter Remembered

Two evils, monstrous either one apart,
Possessed me, and were long and loath at going:
A cry of Absence, Absence, in the heart,
And in the wood the furious winter blowing.

Think not, when fire was bright upon my bricks, 5
And past the tight boards hardly a wind could enter,
I glowed like them, the simple burning sticks,
Far from my cause, my proper heat and center.

Better to walk forth in the frozen air
And wash my wound in the snows; that would be healing; *10*
Because my heart would throb less painful there,
Being caked with cold, and past the smart of feeling.

And where I walked, the murderous winter blast
Would have this body bowed, these eyeballs streaming,
And though I think this heart's blood froze not fast *15*
It ran too small to spare one drop for dreaming.

Dear love, these fingers that had known your touch,
And tied our separate forces first together,
Were ten poor idiot fingers not worth much,
Ten frozen parsnips hanging in the weather. *20*

[1924]

Blue Girls

Twirling your blue skirts, travelling the sward
Under the towers of your seminary,
Go listen to your teachers old and contrary
Without believing a word.

Tie the white fillets° then about your hair *5*
And think no more of what will come to pass
Than bluebirds that go walking on the grass
And chattering on the air.

Practise your beauty, blue girls, before it fail;
And I will cry with my loud lips and publish *10*
Beauty which all our power shall never establish,
It is so frail.

For I could tell you a story which is true;
I know a woman with a terrible tongue,
Blear eyes fallen from blue, *15*
All her perfections tarnished—yet it is not long
Since she was lovelier than any of you.

[1927]

5 *fillets*: ribbons.

Dead Boy

The little cousin is dead, by foul subtraction,
A green bough from Virginia's aged tree,
And none of the country kin like the transaction,
Nor some of the world of outer dark, like me.

A boy not beautiful, nor good, nor clever, *5*
A black cloud full of storms too hot for keeping,
A sword beneath his mother's heart—yet never
Woman bewept her babe as this is weeping.

A pig with a pasty face, so I had said,
Squealing for cookies, kinned by poor pretense *10*
With a noble house. But the little man quite dead,
I see the forbears' antique lineaments.

The elder men have strode by the box of death
To the wide flag porch, and muttering low send round
The bruit of the day. O friendly waste of breath! *15*
Their hearts are hurt with a deep dynastic wound.

He was pale and little, the foolish neighbors say;
The first-fruits, saith the Preacher, the Lord hath taken;
But this was the old tree's late branch wrenched away,
Grieving the sapless limbs, the shorn and shaken. *20*

[1927]

Piazza Piece

—I am a gentleman in a dustcoat° trying
To make you hear. Your ears are soft and small
And listen to an old man not at all,
They want the young men's whispering and sighing.
But see the roses on your trellis dying *5*
And hear the spectral singing of the moon;
For I must have my lovely lady soon,
I am a gentleman in a dustcoat trying.

1 *dustcoat*: often worn in early automobiles to keep the road dust off one's clothing.

—I am a lady young in beauty waiting
Until my truelove comes, and then we kiss. *10*
But what grey man among the vines is this
Whose words are dry and faint as in a dream?
Back from my trellis, Sir, before I scream!
I am a lady young in beauty waiting.

[1927]

***Edna St. Vincent Millay** (1892–1950) was born in Rockland, Maine. The eldest of three daughters, Millay began writing poetry in childhood. She was already well known as a poet by the time she entered Barnard College, later transferring to Vassar. Millay then settled in Greenwich Village, in New York City, writing verse plays and acting for the newly established Provincetown Players. She wrote, under a pseudonym, satiric articles for popular magazines and embarked on numerous love affairs with both men and women. After her volume,* The Harp Weaver *(1923), made her the first woman to win the Pulitzer Prize in poetry, Millay became the most famous woman poet in the United States. She engaged in many heated affairs before meeting Eugen Jan Boissevain, an older Dutch-Irish businessman, whom she married in 1923. He remained devoted to her despite her overt infidelities. Millay's later career followed a slow downward trajectory as her health declined. She spent more of her time in isolation at Steepletop, a large farm in upstate New York, and suffered a nervous breakdown. In 1949 Boissevain died. A year later the 58-year-old poet died of a heart attack at Steepletop.*

Edna St. Vincent Millay

Time Does Not Bring Relief

Time does not bring relief; you all have lied
Who told me time would ease me of my pain!
I miss him in the weeping of the rain;
I want him at the shrinking of the tide;

The old snows melt from every mountain-side, 5
And last year's leaves are smoke in every lane;
But last year's bitter loving must remain
Heaped on my heart, and my old thoughts abide.
There are a hundred places where I fear
To go,—so with his memory they brim. 10
And entering with relief some quiet place
Where never fell his foot or shone his face
I say, "There is no memory of him here!"
And so stand stricken, so remembering him.

[1917]

First Fig

My candle burns at both ends;
It will not last the night;
But ah, my foes, and oh, my friends—
It gives a lovely light!

[1920]

Second Fig

Safe upon the solid rock the ugly houses stand:
Come and see my shining palace built upon the sand!

[1920]

Recuerdo*

We were very tired, we were very merry—
We had gone back and forth all night on the ferry.
It was bare and bright, and smelled like a stable—
But we looked into a fire, we leaned across a table,

*Spanish, "I remember."

We lay on a hill-top underneath the moon; *5*
And the whistles kept blowing, and the dawn came soon.

We were very tried, we were very merry—
We had gone back and forth all night on the ferry;
And you ate an apple, and I ate a pear,
From a dozen of each we had bought somewhere; *10*
And the sky went wan, and the wind came cold,
And the sun rose dripping, a bucketful of gold.

We were very tired, we were very merry,
We had gone back and forth all night on the ferry.
We hailed, "Good morrow, mother!" to a shawl-covered head, *15*
And bought a morning paper, which neither of us read;
And she wept, "God bless you!" for the apples and pears,
And we gave her all our money but our subway fares.

[1920]

Passer Mortuus Est*

Death devours all lovely things:
  Lesbia with her sparrow
Shares the darkness,—presently
  Every bed is narrow.

Unremembered as old rain *5*
  Dries the sheer libation;
And the little petulant hand
  Is an annotation.

After all, my erstwhile dear,
  My no longer cherished, *10*
Need we say it was not love,
  Just because it perished?

[1921]

*Latin, "The sparrow is dead." The Roman poet Catullus (84?–54 BC) wrote a mock elegy bewailing that his beloved Lesbia's pet sparrow had died. The nickname "Lesbia" did not have any gay associations in Catullus's time.

What Lips My Lips Have Kissed

What lips my lips have kissed, and where, and why,
I have forgotten, and what arms have lain
Under my head till morning; but the rain
Is full of ghosts tonight, that tap and sigh
Upon the glass and listen for reply, *5*
And in my heart there sits a quiet pain
For unremembered lads that not again
Will turn to me at midnight with a cry.
Thus in the winter stands the lonely tree,
Nor knows what birds have vanished one by one, *10*
Yet knows its boughs more silent than before:
I cannot say what loves have come and gone,
I only know that summer sang in me
A little while, that in me sings no more.

[1923]

Perhaps the most influential war poet of the twentieth century, **Wilfred Owen** *(1893–1918) was born in Shropshire, England. His father was a railway stationmaster. After Owen failed to get a scholarship to attend London University, he worked as a lay assistant to the vicar of Dunsden and as an English tutor in Bordeaux, France. Owen enlisted to fight in World War I, and became a lieutenant in the Manchester Regiment. The horrors of war quickly took their toll on Owen. He was declared "unfit to command troops" and was admitted to the Craiglockhart War Hospital in Edinburgh. From then until he returned to battle the following autumn, Owen edited the hospital journal,* Hydra, *and met Siegfried Sassoon, the person who would have the most profound influence on Owen's poetry. It was during this time that Owen composed nearly all of the poems for which he is remembered. Owen rejoined his regiment in France and was awarded the Military Cross. On November 4, 1918—only one week before the armistice—Owen was killed leading his troops across the Sambre Canal. Siegfried Sassoon edited his* Poems *posthumously in 1920.*

Wilfred Owen

Anthem for Doomed Youth

What passing-bells for these who die as cattle?
    Only the monstrous anger of the guns.
    Only the stuttering rifles' rapid rattle
Can patter out their hasty orisons.
No mockeries now for them; no prayers nor bells, *5*
    Nor any voice of mourning save the choirs,—
The shrill, demented choirs of wailing shells;
    And bugles calling for them from sad shires.

What candles may be held to speed them all?
    Not in the hands of boys, but in their eyes *10*
Shall shine the holy glimmers of good-byes.
    The pallor of girls' brows shall be their pall;
Their flowers the tenderness of patient minds,
And each slow dusk a drawing-down of blinds.

[1920]

Dulce et Decorum Est

Bent double, like old beggars under sacks,
Knock-kneed, coughing like hags, we cursed through sludge,
Till on the haunting flares we turned our backs
And towards our distant rest began to trudge.
Men marched asleep. Many had lost their boots *5*
But limped on, blood-shod. All went lame; all blind;
Drunk with fatigue; deaf even to the hoots
Of tired, outstripped Five-Nines° that dropped behind.

Gas! GAS! Quick, boys!—An ecstasy of fumbling,
Fitting the clumsy helmets just in time; *10*
But someone still was yelling out and stumbling
And flound'ring like a man in fire or lime . . .

8 *Five-Nines*: Greman howitzers which often fired shells containing poison gas.

Dim, through the misty panes and thick green light,
As under a green sea, I saw him drowning.

In all my dreams, before my helpless sight, *15*
He plunges at me, guttering, choking, drowning.

If in some smothering dreams you too could pace
Behind the wagon that we flung him in,
And watch the white eyes writhing in his face,
His hanging face, like a devil's sick of sin; *20*
If you could hear, at every jolt, the blood
Come gargling from the froth-corrupted lungs,
Obscene as cancer, bitter as the cud
Of vile, incurable sores on innocent tongues,—
My friend, you would not tell with such high zest *25*
To children ardent for some desperate glory,
The old Lie: Dulce et decorum est
Pro patria mori.°

[1920]

27–28 *Dulce et . . . mori*: from the Latin poet Horace, "It is sweet and fitting to die for one's country."

Futility

Move him into the sun—
Gently its touch awoke him once,
At home, whispering of fields unsown.
Always it woke him, even in France,
Until this morning and this snow. *5*
If anything might rouse him now
The kind old sun will know.

Think how it wakes the seeds,—
Woke, once, the clays of a cold star.
Are limbs, so dear-achieved, are sides, *10*
Full-nerved—still warm—too hard to stir?
Was it for this the clay grew tall?
—O what made fatuous sunbeams toil
To break earth's sleep at all?

[1920]

Strange Meeting

It seemed that out of battle I escaped
Down some profound dull tunnel, long since scooped
Through granites which titanic wars had groined.
Yet also there encumbered sleepers groaned,
Too fast in thought or death to be bestirred. *5*
Then, as I probed them, one sprang up, and stared
With piteous recognition in fixed eyes,
Lifting distressful hands as if to bless.
And by his smile, I knew that sullen hall,
By his dead smile I knew we stood in Hell. *10*
With a thousand pains that vision's face was grained;
Yet no blood reached there from the upper ground,
And no guns thumped, or down the flues made moan.
"Strange friend," I said, "here is no cause to mourn."
"None," said that other, "save the undone years, *15*
The hopelessness. Whatever hope is yours,
Was my life also; I went hunting wild
After the wildest beauty in the world,
Which lies not calm in eyes, or braided hair,
But mocks the steady running of the hour, *20*
And if it grieves, grieves richlier than here.
For of my glee might many men have laughed,
And of my weeping something had been left,
Which must die now. I mean the truth untold,
The pity of war, the pity war distilled. *25*
Now men will go content with what we spoiled,
Or, discontent, boil bloody, and be spilled.
They will be swift with swiftness of the tigress.
None will break ranks, though nations trek from progress.
Courage was mine, and I had mystery, *30*
Wisdom was mine, and I had mastery:
To miss the march of this retreating world
Into vain citadels that are not walled.
Then, when much blood had clogged their chariot-wheels,
I would go up and wash them from sweet wells, *35*
Even with truths that lie too deep for taint.
I would have poured my spirit without stint

But not through wounds; not on the cess of war.
Foreheads of men have bled where no wounds were.
I am the enemy you killed, my friend. *40*
I knew you in this dark: for so you frowned
Yesterday through me as you jabbed and killed.
I parried; but my hands were loath and cold.
Let us sleep now. . . ."

[1920]

E.[dward] E.[stlin] ***Cummings*** *(1894–1962) was born in Cambridge, Massachusetts, the son of a Harvard professor who became a Unitarian minister. Having decided at age 8 to be a poet, Cummings produced a poem a day for 14 years, training himself in traditional forms and slowly becoming acquainted with the work of his modernist contemporaries. At Harvard he studied Greek and other languages, then joined the Norton-Harjes Ambulance Corps and sailed for France in 1917. Cummings was arrested that year for suspicion of treason and sent to a detention center in Normandy. He wrote a memoir about the imprisonment,* The Enormous Room *(1922). Due to his father's adamant protests, Cummings was released after only three months. With America entering the war, however, he was immediately drafted into the U.S. Army and served six months in training camp. After the armistice, he returned to New York City, summering at the family retreat in New Hampshire. With the exception of one year of teaching at Harvard, Cummings pursued no other career for the rest of his life than painting and writing. He received numerous honors for his work, including the Bollingen Prize in 1958.*

E. E. Cummings

Buffalo Bill 's*

Buffalo Bill 's
defunct
          who used to

*William Cody (1846–1917) became known as "Buffalo Bill" after slaughtering thousands of buffalo for the Kansas Pacific Railroad. Later in life he enacted fictionalized versions of his exploits all over the world in his famous *Wild West Show*.

ride a watersmooth-silver
stallion *5*
and break onetwothreefourfive pigeonsjustlikethat
Jesus

he was a handsome man
and what i want to know is
how do you like your blueeyed boy *10*
Mister Death

[1923]

next to of course god america i

"next to of course god america i
love you land of the pilgrims' and so forth oh
say can you see by the dawn's early my
country 'tis of centuries come and go
and are no more what of it we should worry *5*
in every language even deafanddumb
thy sons acclaim your glorious name by gorry
by jingo by gee by gosh by gum
why talk of beauty what could be more beautiful than these heroic happy dead *10*
who rushed like lions to the roaring slaughter
they did not stop to think they died instead
then shall the voice of liberty be mute?"

He spoke. And drank rapidly a glass of water

[1926]

somewhere i have never travelled,gladly beyond

somewhere i have never travelled,gladly beyond
any experience,your eyes have their silence:
in your most frail gesture are things which enclose me,
or which i cannot touch because they are too near

your slightest look easily will unclose me *5*
though i have closed myself as fingers,
you open always petal by petal myself as Spring opens
(touching skilfully,mysteriously)her first rose

or if your wish be to close me,i and
my life will shut very beautifully,suddenly, *10*
as when the heart of this flower imagines
the snow carefully everywhere descending;

nothing which we are to perceive in this world equals
the power of your intense fragility:whose texture
compels me with the colour of its countries, *15*
rendering death and forever with each breathing

(i do not know what it is about you that closes
and opens;only something in me understands
the voice of your eyes is deeper than all roses)
nobody,not even the rain,has such small hands *20*

[1931]

may i feel said he

may i feel said he
(i'll squeal said she
just once said he)
it's fun said she

(may i touch said he *5*
how much said she
a lot said he)
why not said she

(let's go said he
not too far said she *10*
what's too far said he
where you are said she)

may i stay said he
(which way said she
like this said he *15*
if you kiss said she

may i move said he
is it love said she)
if you're willing said he
(but you're killing said she *20*

but it's life said he
but your wife said she
now said he)
ow said she

(tiptop said he *25*
don't stop said she
oh no said he)
go slow said she

(cccome?said he
ummm said she) *30*
you're divine!said he
(you are Mine said she)

[1935]

anyone lived in a pretty how town

anyone lived in a pretty how town
(with up so floating many bells down)
spring summer autumn winter
he sang his didn't he danced his did.

Women and men(both little and small) 5
cared for anyone not at all
they sowed their isn't they reaped their same
sun moon stars rain

children guessed(but only a few
and down they forgot as up they grew 10
autumn winter spring summer)
that noone loved him more by more

when by now and tree by leaf
she laughed his joy she cried his grief
bird by snow and stir by still 15
anyone's any was all to her

someones married their everyones
laughed their cryings and did their dance
(sleep wake hope and then)they
said their nevers they slept their dream 20

stars rain sun moon
(and only the snow can begin to explain
how children are apt to forget to remember
with up so floating many bells down)

one day anyone died i guess 25
(and noone stooped to kiss his face)
busy folk buried them side by side
little by little and was by was

all by all and deep by deep
and more by more they dream their sleep 30
noone and anyone earth by april
wish by spirit and if by yes.

Women and men(both dong and ding)
summer autumn winter spring
reaped their sowing and went their came 35
sun moon stars rain

[1940]

pity this busy monster,manunkind

pity this busy monster,manunkind,

not. Progress is a comfortable disease:
your victim(death and life safely beyond)

plays with the bigness of his littleness
—electrons deify one razorblade 5
into a mountainrange;lenses extend

unwish through curving wherewhen till unwish
returns on its unself.
A world of made
is not a world of born—pity poor flesh

and trees,poor stars and stones,but never this 10
fine specimen of hypermagical

ultraomnipotence. We doctors know

a hopeless case if—listen:there's a hell
of a good universe next door;let's go

[1944]

***Robert Graves** (1895–1985) was born in Wimbledon, England, the son of the poet and folklorist Alfred Perceval Graves. Although he won a scholarship to school, he opted instead to join the Royal Welch Fusiliers in World War I. He met the poet Siegfried Sassoon in France, where Graves was so badly wounded he was supposed dead. During the war he published his* *first collection,* Over the Brazier *(1916), and married Nancy Nicholson. Graves met the American poet Laura Riding in 1926, and she became his lover and literary collaborator for 14 years. Living with Graves and his wife, Riding once attempted suicide by jumping from their third-story window. After nursing her for a few months—at which point Graves's wife and children left him—the poet moved with Riding to Majorca, Spain, where they ran their Seizin Press. When the Spanish Civil War broke out, Riding and Graves left Spain, eventually moving to America in 1939 and parting ways. He remarried and returned to Majorca after World War II with his new family. Graves is remembered today for his war memoir,* Good-bye to All That *(1929), and his historical novel,* I, Claudius *(1934). He received the Queen's Gold Medal for poetry in 1968.*

Robert Graves

The Cool Web

Children are dumb to say how hot the day is,
How hot the scent is of the summer rose,
How dreadful the black wastes of evening sky,
How dreadful the tall soldiers drumming by.

But we have speech, to chill the angry day, *5*
And speech, to dull the rose's cruel scent.
We spell away the overhanging night,
We spell away the soldiers and the fright.

There's a cool web of language winds us in,
Retreat from too much joy or too much fear: *10*
We grow sea-green at last and coldly die
In brininess and volubility.

But if we let our tongues lose self-possession,
Throwing off language and its watery clasp
Before our death, instead of when death comes, *15*
Facing the wide glare of the children's day,
Facing the rose, the dark sky and the drums,
We shall go mad no doubt and die that way.

[1927]

Down, Wanton, Down!

Down, wanton, down! Have you no shame
That at the whisper of Love's name,
Or Beauty's, presto! up you raise
Your angry head and stand at gaze?

Poor bombard-captain, sworn to reach *5*
The ravelin and effect a breach—
Indifferent what you storm or why,
So be that in the breach you die!

Love may be blind, but Love at least
Knows what is man and what mere beast; *10*
Or Beauty wayward, but requires
More delicacy from her squires.

Tell me, my witless, whose one boast
Could be your staunchness at the post,
When were you made a man of parts *15*
To think fine and profess the arts?

Will many-gifted Beauty come
Bowing to your bald rule of thumb,
Or Love swear loyalty to your crown?
Be gone, have done! Down, wanton, down! *20*

[1933]

To Juan at the Winter Solstice

There is one story and one story only
That will prove worth your telling,
Whether as learned bard or gifted child;
To it all lines or lesser gauds belong
That startle with their shining *5*
Such common stories as they stray into.

Is it of trees you tell, their months and virtues,
Or strange beasts that beset you,
Of birds that croak at you the Triple will?
Or of the Zodiac and how slow it turns *10*
Below the Boreal Crown,
Prison of all true kings that ever reigned?

Water to water, ark again to ark,
From woman back to woman:
So each new victim treads unfalteringly *15*
The never altered circuit of his fate,
Bringing twelve peers as witness
Both to his starry rise and starry fall.

Or is it of the Virgin's silver beauty,
All fish below the thighs? *20*
She in her left hand bears a leafy quince;
When with her right she crooks a finger, smiling,
How may the King hold back?
Royally then he barters life for love.

Or of the undying snake from chaos hatched, *25*
Whose coils contain the ocean,
Into whose chops with naked sword he springs,
Then in black water, tangled by the reeds,
Battles three days and nights,
To be spewed up beside her scalloped shore? *30*

Much snow is falling, winds roar hollowly,
The owl hoots from the elder,
Fear in your heart cries to the loving-cup:
Sorrow to sorrow as the sparks fly upward.
The log groans and confesses: *35*
There is one story and one story only.

Dwell on her graciousness, dwell on her smiling,
Do not forget what flowers
The great boar trampled down in ivy time.
Her brow was creamy as the crested wave, *40*
Her sea-grey eyes were wild
But nothing promised that is not performed.

[1945]

Counting the Beats

You, love, and I,
(He whispers) you and I,
And if no more than only you and I
What care you or I?

Counting the beats, *5*
Counting the slow heart beats,
The bleeding to death of time in slow heart beats,
Wakeful they lie.

Cloudless day,
Night, and a cloudless day, *10*
Yet the huge storm will burst upon their heads one day
From a bitter sky.

Where shall we be,
(She whispers) where shall we be,
When death strikes home, O where then shall we be *15*
Who were you and I?

Not there but here,
(He whispers) only here,
As we are, here, together, now and here,
Always you and I. *20*

Counting the beats,
Counting the slow heart beats,
The bleeding to death of time in slow heart beats,
Wakeful they lie.

[1959]

Born in Livermore Falls, Maine, **Louise Bogan** *(1897–1970) grew up in various mill towns around New England. Her parents' marriage was turbulent, frequented by infidelity and dramatic confrontations. Bogan started writing poetry while attending the Girls' Latin School in Boston, where she received an excellent classical education. Radcliffe offered her a scholarship, but Bogan instead opted to marry an Army corporal who* *was soon transferred to Panama. She gave birth to a daughter there, though she left her husband and returned to the United States. He died of pneumonia in 1920 and Bogan remarried. She published her first book of poems,* Body of This Death *(1923), and became an influential critic. In spite of this success, she fell in and out of depression that was severe enough to require stays of hospitalization. After her second marriage dissolved, she had a brief affair with the young poet Theodore Roethke. Bogan served as the Consultant in Poetry to the Library of Congress in 1945, and shared the 1955 Bollingen Prize with Léonie Adams. Bogan died from a coronary occlusion.*

Louise Bogan

The Crows

The woman who has grown old
And knows desire must die,
Yet turns to love again,
Hears the crows' cry.

She is a stem long hardened, 5
A weed that no scythe mows.
The heart's laughter will be to her
The crying of the crows,

Who slide in the air with the same voice
Over what yields not, and what yields, 10
Alike in spring, and when there is only bitter
Winter-burning in the fields.

[1923]

Medusa*

I had come to the house, in a cave of trees,
Facing a sheer sky.
Everything moved,—a bell hung ready to strike,
Sun and reflection wheeled by.

*A female monster in Greek mythology, her horrific appearance could turn men into stone.

When the bare eyes were before me *5*
And the hissing hair,
Held up at a window, seen through a door.
The stiff bald eyes, the serpents on the forehead
Formed in the air.

This is a dead scene forever now. *10*
Nothing will ever stir.
The end will never brighten it more than this,
Nor the rain blur.

The water will always fall, and will not fall,
And the tipped bell make no sound. *15*
The grass will always be growing for hay
Deep on the ground.

And I shall stand here like a shadow
Under the great balanced day,
My eyes on the yellow dust, that was lifting in the wind, *20*
And does not drift away.

[1923]

Knowledge

Now that I know
How passion warms little
Of flesh in the mould,
And treasure is brittle,—

I'll lie here and learn *5*
How, over their ground,
Trees make a long shadow
And a light sound.

[1923]

Henceforth, from the Mind

Henceforth, from the mind,
For your whole joy, must spring
Such joy as you may find
In any earthly thing,
And every time and place *5*
Will take your thought for grace.

Henceforth, from the tongue,
From shallow speech alone,
Comes joy you thought, when young,
Would wring you to the bone, *10*
Would pierce you to the heart
And spoil its stop and start.

Henceforward, from the shell,
Wherein you heard, and wondered
At oceans like a bell *15*
So far from ocean sundered—
A smothered sound that sleeps
Long lost within lost deeps,

Will chime you change and hours,
The shadow of increase, *20*
Will sound you flowers
Born under troubled peace—
Henceforth, henceforth
Will echo sea and earth.

[1937]

[Harold] **Hart Crane** *(1899–1932) was born in Garrettsville, Ohio, into a home plagued with constant parental feuds and separations. Setting out for New York in 1916, Crane befriended many of the writers and artists living in Greenwich Village. While his mother supported his interests, his father relentlessly pressured the budding artist to pursue a more practical career, and for years Crane tried to balance his time and attention between each of his parents and their wishes. He worked for his father in Cleveland for a few years, finally returning to New York to finish his first collection of poems,* White Buildings *(1926). After the publication of his major work,* The Bridge *(1930), Crane moved to Mexico on a Guggenheim fellowship. He drank heavily during this time, and wrote little. Crane met Peggy Baird Cowley and with her had his first heterosexual love affair. In April 1932 he and Peggy set sail for New York City. At noon of the 27th, Crane leapt from the ship's stern and drowned.*

Hart Crane

Praise for an Urn

*In Memoriam: Ernest Nelson**

It was a kind and northern face
That mingled in such exile guise
The everlasting eyes of Pierrot°
And, of Gargantua,° the laughter.

His thoughts, delivered to me   5
From the white coverlet and pillow,
I see now, were inheritances—
Delicate riders of the storm.

The slant moon on the slanting hill
Once moved us toward presentiments   10
Of what the dead keep, living still,
And such assessments of the soul

As, perched in the crematory lobby,
The insistent clock commented on,
Touching as well upon our praise   15
Of glories proper to the time.

**Ernest Nelson*: a painter, poet, and friend of Crane's. A Swedish immigrant, Nelson was killed by a car in 1921.

3 *Pierrot*: a French clown common in pantomime. 4 *Gargantua*: a giant with an insatiable appetite, from *Gargantua and Pantagruel* (1535), a satire by François Rabelais.

Still, having in mind gold hair,
I cannot see that broken brow
And miss the dry sound of bees
Stretching across a lucid space. *20*

Scatter these well-meant idioms
Into the smoky spring that fills
The suburbs, where they will be lost.
They are no trophies of the sun.

[1926]

Chaplinesque*

We make our meek adjustments,
Contented with such random consolations
As the wind deposits
In slithered and too ample pockets.

For we can still love the world, who find *5*
A famished kitten on the step, and know
Recesses for it from the fury of the street,
Or warm torn elbow coverts.

We will sidestep, and to the final smirk
Dally the doom of that inevitable thumb *10*
That slowly chafes its puckered index toward us,
Facing the dull squint with what innocence
And what surprise!

And yet these fine collapses are not lies
More than the pirouettes of any pliant cane; *15*
Our obsequies are, in a way, no enterprise.
We can evade you, and all else but the heart:
What blame to us if the heart live on.

The game enforces smirks; but we have seen
The moon in lonely alleys make *20*
A grail of laughter of an empty ash can,
And through all sound of gaiety and quest
Have heard a kitten in the wilderness.

[1926]

*Crane was a dedicated fan of the silent film actor Charlie Chaplin.

My Grandmother's Love Letters

There are no stars tonight
But those of memory.
Yet how much room for memory there is
In the loose girdle of soft rain.

There is even room enough *5*
For the letters of my mother's mother,
Elizabeth,
That have been pressed so long
Into a corner of the roof
That they are brown and soft, *10*
And liable to melt as snow.

Over the greatness of such space
Steps must be gentle.
It is all hung by an invisible white hair.
It trembles as birch limbs webbing the air. *15*

And I ask myself:

"Are your fingers long enough to play
Old keys that are but echoes:
Is the silence strong enough
To carry back the music to its source *20*
And back to you again
As though to her?"

Yet I would lead my grandmother by the hand
Through much of what she would not understand;
And so I stumble. And the rain continues on the roof *25*
With such a sound of gently pitying laughter.

[1926]

Voyages

I

Above the fresh ruffles of the surf
Bright striped urchins flay each other with sand.
They have contrived a conquest for shell shucks,
And their fingers crumble fragments of baked weed
Gaily digging and scattering. *5*

And in answer to their treble interjections
The sun beats lightning on the waves,
The waves fold thunder on the sand;
And could they hear me I would tell them:

O brilliant kids, frisk with your dog, *10*
Fondle your shells and sticks, bleached
By time and the elements; but there is a line
You must not cross nor ever trust beyond it
Spry cordage of your bodies to caresses
Too lichen-faithful from too wide a breast. *15*
The bottom of the sea is cruel.

II

—And yet this great wink of eternity,
Of rimless floods, unfettered leewardings,
Samite° sheeted and processioned where
Her undinal° vast belly moonward bends, *20*
Laughing the wrapt inflections of our love;

Take this Sea, whose diapason knells
On scrolls of silver snowy sentences,
The sceptred terror of whose sessions rends
As her demeanors motion well or ill, *25*
All but the pieties of lovers' hands.

And onward, as bells off San Salvador
Salute the crocus lustres of the stars,
In these poinsettia meadows of her tides,—
Adagios of islands, O my Prodigal, *30*
Complete the dark confessions her veins spell.

19 *Samite*: silk interwoven with silver and gold. **20** *undinal*: like Undine, a female water spirit.

Mark how her turning shoulders wind the hours,
And hasten while her penniless rich palms
Pass superscription of bent foam and wave,—
Hasten, while they are true,—sleep, death, desire, *35*
Close round one instant in one floating flower.

Bind us in time, O Seasons clear, and awe.
O minstrel galleons of Carib fire,
Bequeath us to no earthly shore until
Is answered in the vortex of our grave *40*
The seal's wide spindrift gaze toward paradise.

III

Infinite consanguinity it bears—
This tendered theme of you that light
Retrieves from sea plains where the sky
Resigns a breast that every wave enthrones; *45*
While ribboned water lanes I wind
Are laved and scattered with no stroke
Wide from your side, whereto this hour
The sea lifts, also, reliquary hands.

And so, admitted through black swollen gates *50*
That must arrest all distance otherwise,—
Past whirling pillars and lithe pediments,
Light wrestling there incessantly with light,
Star kissing star through wave on wave unto
Your body rocking! *55*
                    and where death, if shed,
Presumes no carnage, but this single change,—
Upon the steep floor flung from dawn to dawn
The silken skilled transmemberment of song;

Permit me voyage, love, into your hands . . .

IV

Whose counted smile of hours and days, suppose *60*
I know as spectrum of the sea and pledge
Vastly now parting gulf on gulf of wings
Whose circles bridge, I know, (from palms to the severe

Chilled albatross's white immutability)
No stream of greater love advancing now *65*
Than, singing, this mortality alone
Through clay aflow immortally to you.

All fragrance irrefragably, and claim
Madly meeting logically in this hour
And region that is ours to wreathe again, *70*
Portending eyes and lips and making told
The chancel port and portion of our June—

Shall they not stem and close in our own steps
Bright staves of flowers and quills today as I
Must first be lost in fatal tides to tell? *75*

In signature of the incarnate word
The harbor shoulders to resign in mingling
Mutual blood, transpiring as foreknown
And widening noon within your breast for gathering
All bright insinuations that my years have caught *80*
For islands where must lead inviolably
Blue latitudes and levels of your eyes,—

In this expectant, still exclaim receive
The secret oar and petals of all love.

V

Meticulous, past midnight in clear rime, *85*
Infrangible and lonely, smooth as though cast
Together in one merciless white blade—
The bay estuaries fleck the hard sky limits.

—As if too brittle or too clear to touch!
The cables of our sleep so swiftly filed, *90*
Already hang, shred ends from remembered stars.
One frozen trackless smile . . . What words
Can strangle this deaf moonlight? For we

Are overtaken. Now no cry, no sword
Can fasten or deflect this tidal wedge, *95*
Slow tyranny of moonlight, moonlight loved
And changed . . . "There's

Nothing like this in the world," you say,
Knowing I cannot touch your hand and look
Too, into that godless cleft of sky *100*
Where nothing turns but dead sands flashing.

"—And never to quite understand!" No,
In all the argosy of your bright hair I dreamed
Nothing so flagless as this piracy.
But now
Draw in your head, alone and too tall here. *105*
Your eyes already in the slant of drifting foam;
Your breath sealed by the ghosts I do not know:
Draw in your head and sleep the long way home.

VI

Where icy and bright dungeons lift
Of swimmers their lost morning eyes, *110*
And ocean rivers, churning, shift
Green borders under stranger skies,

Steadily as a shell secretes
Its beating leagues of monotone,
Or as many waters trough the sun's *115*
Red kelson past the cape's wet stone;

O rivers mingling toward the sky
And harbor of the phoenix' breast
My eyes pressed black against the prow,
—Thy derelict and blinded guest *120*

Waiting, afire, what name, unspoke,
I cannot claim: let thy waves rear
More savage than the death of kings,
Some splintered garland for the seer.

Beyond siroccos harvesting *125*
The solstice thunders, crept away,
Like a cliff swinging or a sail
Flung into April's inmost day—

Creation's blithe and petalled word
To the lounged goddess when she rose *130*
Conceding dialogue with eyes
That smile unsearchable repose—

Still fervid covenant, Belle Isle,
—Unfolded floating dais before
Which rainbows twine continual hair— *135*
Belle Isle, white echo of the oar!

The imaged Word, it is, that holds
Hushed willows anchored in its glow.
It is the unbetrayable reply
Whose accent no farewell can know. *140*

[1926]

Langston Hughes *(1902–1967) was born in Joplin, Missouri. After his parents separated during his early years, he and his mother lived a life of itinerant poverty. Hughes attended high school in Cleveland where, as a senior, he wrote "The Negro Speaks of Rivers." Reluctantly supported by his father, he attended Columbia University for a year before withdrawing. He became a merchant seaman in 1923 and visited the ports of West Africa. For a time he lived in Paris, Genoa, and Rome before returning to the United States. The publication of* The Weary Blues *(1926) earned him immediate fame. By the time of his 1929 graduation from Lincoln University, Hughes was already one of the central figures of the Harlem Renaissance. He worked in fiction, drama, translation, criticism, opera libretti, memoir, cinema, song writing, and poetry. He also became a tireless promoter of African-American culture, crisscrossing the United States on speaking tours as well as compiling 28 anthologies of African-American folklore and poetry. Deeply involved in politics late in life, Hughes died in Harlem.*

Langston Hughes

Cross

My old man's a white old man
And my old mother's black.
If ever I cursed my white old man
I take my curses back.

If ever I cursed my black old mother *5*
And wished she were in hell,
I'm sorry for that evil wish
And now I wish her well.

My old man died in a fine big house.
My ma died in a shack. *10*
I wonder where I'm gonna die,
Being neither white nor black?

[1926]

I, Too

I, too, sing America.

I am the darker brother.
They send me to eat in the kitchen
When company comes,
But I laugh, *5*
And eat well,
And grow strong.

Tomorrow,
I'll be at the table
When company comes. *10*
Nobody'll dare
Say to me,
"Eat in the kitchen,"
Then.

Besides, 15
They'll see how beautiful I am
And be ashamed—

I, too, am America.

[1926]

Negro

I am a Negro:
   Black as the night is black,
   Black like the depths of my Africa.

I've been a slave:
   Caesar told me to keep his door-steps clean. 5
   I brushed the boots of Washington.

I've been a worker:
   Under my hand the pyramids arose,
   I made mortar for the Woolworth Building.

I've been a singer: 10
   All the way from Africa to Georgia
   I carried my sorrow songs.
   I made ragtime.

I've been a victim:
   The Belgians cut off my hands in the Congo.° 15
   They lynch me still in Mississippi.

I am a Negro:
   Black as the night is black,
   Black like the depths of my Africa.

[1926]

15 *The Belgians . . . Congo*: During King Leopold of Belgium's colonial rule over the Congo, failure to pay a labor tax often resulted in having a hand cut off, or even in the offender's execution.

The Negro Speaks of Rivers

I've known rivers:
I've known rivers ancient as the world and older than the
  flow of human blood in human veins.

My soul has grown deep like the rivers.

I bathed in the Euphrates when dawns were young.
I built my hut near the Congo and it lulled me to sleep. *5*
I looked upon the Nile and raised the pyramids above it.
I heard the singing of the Mississippi when Abe Lincoln
  went down to New Orleans, and I've seen its muddy
  bosom turn all golden in the sunset.

I've known rivers:
Ancient, dusky rivers.

My soul has grown deep like the rivers. *10*

[1926]

The Weary Blues

Droning a drowsy syncopated tune,
Rocking back and forth to a mellow croon,
  I heard a Negro play.
Down on Lenox Avenue° the other night
By the pale dull pallor of an old gas light *5*
  He did a lazy sway. . . .
  He did a lazy sway. . . .
To the tune o' those Weary Blues.
With his ebony hands on each ivory key
He made that poor piano moan with melody. *10*
  O Blues!

4 *Lenox Avenue*: street in New York City, now called Malcolm X. Boulevard.

Swaying to and fro on his rickety stool
He played that sad raggy tune like a musical fool.
Sweet Blues!
Coming from a black man's soul. *15*
O Blues!
In a deep song voice with a melancholy tone
I heard that Negro sing, that old piano moan—
"Ain't got nobody in all this world,
"Ain't got nobody but ma self. *20*
I's gwine to quit ma frownin'
And put ma troubles on the shelf."

Thump, thump, thump, went his foot on the floor.
He played a few chords then he sang some more—
"I got the Weary Blues *25*
And I can't be satisfied.
Got the Weary Blues
And can't be satisfied—
I ain't happy no mo'
And I wish that I had died." *30*
And far into the night he crooned that tune.
The stars went out and so did the moon.
The singer stopped playing and went to bed
While the Weary Blues echoed through his head.
He slept like a rock or a man that's dead. *35*

[1926]

Harlem

What happens to a dream deferred?

Does it dry up
like a raisin in the sun?
Or fester like a sore—
and then run? *5*
Does it stink like rotten meat?
Or crust and sugar over—
like a syrupy sweet?

Maybe it just sags
like a heavy load. 10

Or does it explode?

[1951]

Theme for English B

The instructor said,

Go home and write
a page tonight.
And let that page come out of you—
Then, it will be true. 5

I wonder if it's that simple?
I am twenty-two, colored, born in Winston-Salem.
I went to school there, then Durham, then here
to this college on the hill above Harlem.°
I am the only colored student in my class. 10
The steps from the hill lead down into Harlem,
through a park, then I cross St. Nicholas,
Eighth Avenue, Seventh, and I come to the Y,
the Harlem Branch Y, where I take the elevator
up to my room, sit down, and write this page: 15

It's not easy to know what is true for you and me
at twenty-two, my age. But I guess I'm what
I feel and see and hear, Harlem, I hear you:
hear you, hear me—we two—you, me, talk on this page.
(I hear New York, too.) Me—who? 20
Well, I like to eat, sleep, drink, and be in love.
I like to work, read, learn, and understand life.
I like a pipe for a Christmas present,
or records—Bessie,° bop, or Bach.

9 *college on the hill above Harlem*: usually thought to refer to Columbia University, where Hughes studied for a year. But the editors of Hughes's *Collected Poems* note that the institution in the poem is CCNY, City College of New York. (Please note, however, that this poem is not autobiographical. The young speaker is a character invented by the middle-aged author.) **24** *Bessie*: Bessie Smith (1898?–1937) was a popular blues singer often called the "Empress of the Blues."

I guess being colored doesn't make me not like 25
the same things other folks like who are other races.
So will my page be colored that I write?
Being me, it will not be white.
But it will be
a part of you, instructor. 30
You are white—
yet a part of me, as I am a part of you.
That's American.
Sometimes perhaps you don't want to be a part of me.
Nor do I often want to be a part of you. 35
But we are, that's true!
As I learn from you,
I guess you learn from me—
although you're older—and white—
and somewhat more free. 40

This is my page for English B.

[1951]

***Stevie Smith** (1902–1971) was born in Hull and raised in Palmers Green, a suburb north of London where she lived her entire life in the same house with her aunt. When she was very young, Smith's father had abandoned the family to work for a shipping line. Smith took a job as a secretary after high school, working for 30 years at a publishing house. During this time she began writing poems. After seeing her manuscript, a publisher recommended that she first write a novel. With characteristic wit, Smith composed a novel during work hours on the yellow paper used for carbon copies. Spiced throughout with her rejected verse,* Novel on Yellow Paper *(1936) was finished in only ten weeks. She followed that with her first collection of poems,* A Good Time Was Had By All *(1937), and soon gained notoriety for her poetry—much of which she illustrated with comic drawings. She became a famously eclectic performer of her verse later in life, often singing her poems in a strange, high voice. Smith won the Queen's Gold Medal for Poetry in 1969.*

Stevie Smith

One of Many

You are only one of many
And of small account if any,
You think about yourself too much.
This touched the child with a quick touch
And worked his mind to such a pitch 5
He threw his fellows in a ditch.
This little child
That was so mild
Is grown too wild.

Murder in the first degree, cried Old Fury, 10
Recording the verdict of the jury.

Now they are come to the execution tree.
The gallows stand wide. Ah me, ah me.

Christ died for sinners, intoned the Prison Chaplain from his
miscellany.
Weeping bitterly the little child cries: I die one of many. 15

[1938]

Mr. Over

Mr. Over is dead
He died fighting and true
And on his tombstone they wrote
Over to You.

And who pray is this You 5
To whom Mr. Over is gone?
Oh if we only knew that
We should not do wrong.

But who is this beautiful You
We all of us long for so much 10

Is he not our friend and our brother
Our father and such?

Yes he is this and much more
This is but a portion
A sea-drop in a bucket *15*
Taken from the ocean

So the voices spake
Softly above my head
And a voice in my heart cried: Follow
Where he has led *20*

And a devil's voice cried: Happy
Happy the dead.

[1950]

Not Waving but Drowning

Nobody heard him, the dead man,
But still he lay moaning:
I was much further out than you thought
And not waving but drowning.

Poor chap, he always loved larking *5*
And now he's dead
It must have been too cold for him his heart gave way,
They said.

Oh, no no no, it was too cold always
(Still the dead one lay moaning) *10*
I was much too far out all my life
And not waving but drowning.

[1957]

***Earle Birney** (1904–1995) was born in Calgary, Canada. He spent most of his childhood in the mountainous Kootenay Valley of British Columbia, which sparked an interest in mountain climbing. Birney studied at the University of British Columbia and the University of Toronto. He taught and lectured at many institutions throughout his life, among them the University of Utah, the University of California, Irvine, and for 19 years at his alma mater, British Columbia. He served in the Canadian army during World War II and was made a major. Birney married Esther Bull in 1937; they divorced after 40 years of marriage. Throughout his life, Birney traveled widely in Europe, Asia, South America, and Australia. Despite his frequent journeys, however, his poetry, prose, and dramatic works are distinctly Canadian, and present a clear and lasting portrait of his nation. His* Collected Poems *appeared in 1975. Birney had a long professional relationship with the Canadian Broadcasting Corporation, contributing radio plays, commentary, and readings for half a century. He died in Toronto at age 91.*

Earle Birney

David

I

David and I that summer cut trails on the Survey,
All week in the valley for wages, in air that was steeped
In the wail of mosquitoes, but over the sunalive week-ends
We climbed, to get from the ruck of the camp, the surly

Poker, the wrangling, the snoring under the fetid 5
Tents, and because we had joy in our lengthening coltish
Muscles, and mountains for David were made to see over,
Stairs from the valleys and steps to the sun's retreats.

II

Our first was Mount Gleam. We hiked in the long afternoon
To a curling lake and lost the lure of the faceted 10
Cone in the swell of its sprawling shoulders. Past
The inlet we grilled our bacon, the strips festooned

On a poplar prong, in the hurrying slant of the sunset.
Then the two of us rolled in the blanket while round us the cold
Pines thrust at the stars. The dawn was a floating 15
Of mists till we reached to the slopes above timber, and won

To snow like fire in the sunlight. The peak was upthrust
Like a fist in a frozen ocean of rock that swirled
Into valleys the moon could be rolled in. Remotely unfurling
Eastward the alien prairie glittered. Down through the dusty *20*

Skree on the west we descended, and David showed me
How to use the give of shale for giant incredible
Strides. I remember, before the larches' edge,
That I jumped a long green surf of juniper flowing

Away from the wind, and landed in gentian and saxifrage *25*
Spilled on the moss. Then the darkening firs
And the sudden whirring of water that knifed down a fern-hidden
Cliff and splashed unseen into mist in the shadows.

III

One Sunday on Rampart's arête° a rainsquall caught us,
And passed, and we clung by our blueing fingers and bootnails *30*
An endless hour in the sun, not daring to move
Till the ice had steamed from the slate. And David taught me

How time on a knife-edge can pass with the guessing of fragments
Remembered from poets, the naming of strata beside one,
And matching of stories from schooldays. . . . We crawled astride *35*
The peak to feast on the marching ranges flagged

By the fading shreds of the shattered stormcloud. Lingering
There it was David who spied to the south, remote,
And unmapped, a sunlit spire on Sawback, an overhang
Crooked like a talon. David named it the Finger. *40*

That day we chanced on the skull and the splayed white ribs
Of a mountain goat underneath a cliff-face, caught
On a rock. Around were the silken feathers of hawks.
And that was the first I knew that a goat could slip.

IV

And then Inglismaldie. Now I remember only *45*
The long ascent of the lonely valley, the live
Pine spirally scarred by lightning, the slicing pipe
Of invisible pika, and great prints, by the lowest

29 *arête*: a sharp, narrow mountain ridge.

Snow, of a grizzly. There it was too that David
Taught me to read the scroll of coral in limestone *50*
And the beetle-seal in the shale of ghostly trilobites,°
Letters delivered to man from the Cambrian° waves.

V

On Sundance we tried from the col° and the going was hard.
The air howled from our feet to the smudged rocks
And the papery lake below. At an outthrust we baulked *55*
Till David clung with his left to a dint in the scarp,

Lobbed the iceaxe over the rocky lip,
Slipped from his holds and hung by the quivering pick,
Twisted his long legs up into space and kicked
To the crest. Then grinning, he reached with his freckled wrist *60*

And drew me up after. We set a new time for that climb.
That day returning we found a robin gyrating
In grass, wing-broken. I caught it to tame but David
Took and killed it, and said, "Could you teach it to fly?"

VI

In August, the second attempt, we ascended The Fortress. *65*
By the forks of the Spray we caught five trout and fried them
Over a balsam fire. The woods were alive
With the vaulting of mule-deer and drenched with clouds all the
morning,

Till we burst at noon to the flashing and floating round
Of the peaks. Coming down we picked in our hats the bright *70*
And sunhot raspberries, eating them under a mighty
Spruce, while a marten moving like quicksilver scouted us.

VII

But always we talked of the Finger on Sawback, unknown
And hooked, till the first afternoon in September we slogged
Through the musky woods, past a swamp that quivered with *75*
frog-song,
And camped by a bottle-green lake. But under the cold

51 *trilobites*: marine fossils of the Paleozoic Era. 52 *Cambrian*: the first part of the Paleozoic Era.
53 *col*: a pass between two peaks, or a gap in a ridge.

Breath of the glacier sleep would not come, the moon-light
Etching the Finger. We rose and trod past the feathery
Larch, while the stars went out, and the quiet heather
Flushed, and the skyline pulsed with the surging bloom *80*

Of incredible dawn in the Rockies. David spotted
Bighorns across the moraine° and sent them leaping
With yodels the ramparts redoubled and rolled to the peaks,
And the peaks to the sun. The ice in the morning thaw

Was a gurgling world of crystal and cold blue chasms, *85*
And seracs° that shone like frozen saltgreen waves.
At the base of the Finger we tried once and failed. Then David
Edged to the west and discovered the chimney; the last

Hundred feet we fought the rock and shouldered and kneed
Our way for an hour and made it. Unroping we formed *90*
A cairn on the rotting tip. Then I turned to look north
At the glistening wedge of giant Assiniboine, heedless

Of handhold. And one foot gave. I swayed and shouted.
David turned sharp and reached out his arm and steadied me,
Turning again with a grin and his lips ready *95*
To jest. But the strain crumbled his foothold. Without

A gasp he was gone. I froze to the sound of grating
Edge-nails and fingers, the slither of stones, the lone
Second of silence, the nightmare thud. Then only
The wind and the muted beat of unknowing cascades. *100*

VIII

Somehow I worked down the fifty impossible feet
To the ledge, calling and getting no answer but echoes
Released in the cirque, and trying not to reflect
What an answer would mean. He lay still, with his lean

Young face upturned and strangely unmarred, but his legs *105*
Splayed beneath him, beside the final drop,
Six hundred feet sheer to the ice. My throat stopped
When I reached him, for he was alive. He opened his grey

Straight eyes and brokenly murmured "over . . . over."
And I, feeling beneath him a cruel fang *110*

82 *moraine*: an accumulation of stones and debris deposited by a glacier. 86 *seracs*: pointed masses of ice in a glacier.

Of the ledge thrust in his back, but not understanding,
Mumbled stupidly, "Best not to move," and spoke

Of his pain. But he said, "I can't move. . . . If only I felt
Some pain." Then my shame stung the tears to my eyes
As I crouched, and I cursed myself, but he cried, *115*
Louder, "No, Bobbie! Don't ever blame yourself.

I didn't test my foothold." He shut the lids
Of his eyes to the stare of the sky, while I moistened his lips
From our water flask and tearing my shirt into strips
I swabbed the shredded hands. But the blood slid *120*

From his side and stained the stone and the thirsting lichens,
And yet I dared not lift him up from the gore
Of the rock. Then he whispered, "Bob, I want to go over!"
This time I knew what he meant and I grasped for a lie.

And said, "I'll be back here by midnight with ropes *125*
And men from the camp and we'll cradle you out." But I knew
That the day and the night must pass and the cold dews
Of another morning before such men unknowing

The ways of mountains could win to the chimney's top.
And then, how long? And he knew . . . and the hell of hours *130*
After that, if he lived till we came, roping him out.
But I curled beside him and whispered, "The bleeding will stop.

You can last." He said only, "Perhaps. . . . For what? A wheelchair,
Bob?" His eyes brightening with fever upbraided me.
I could not look at him more and said, "Then I'll stay *135*
With you." But he did not speak, for the clouding fever.

I lay dazed and stared at the long valley,
The glistening hair of a creek on the rug stretched
By the firs, while the sun leaned round and flooded the ledge,
The moss, and David still as a broken doll. *140*

I hunched to my knees to leave, but he called and his voice
Now was sharpened with fear. "For Christ's sake push me over!
If I could move. . . . Or die. . . ." The sweat ran from his forehead,
But only his eyes moved. A hawk was buoying

Blackly its wings over the wrinkled ice. *145*
The purr of a waterfall rose and sank with the wind.
Above us climbed the last joint of the Finger
Beckoning bleakly the wide indifferent sky.

Even then in the sun it grew cold lying there. . . . And I knew
He had tested his holds. It was I who had not. . . . I looked 150
At the blood on the ledge, and the far valley. I looked
At last in his eyes. He breathed, "I'd do it for you, Bob."

IX

I will not remember how nor why I could twist
Up the wind-devilled peak, and down through the chimney's empty
Horror, and over the traverse alone. I remember 155
Only the pounding fear I would stumble on It

When I came to the grave-cold maw of the bergschrund . . . reeling
Over the sun-cankered snowbridge, shying the caves
In the névé . . . the fear, and the need to make sure It was there
On the ice, the running and falling and running, leaping 160

Of gaping greenthroated crevasses, alone and pursued
By the Finger's lengthening shadow. At last through the fanged
And blinding seracs I slid to the milky wrangling
Falls at the glacier's snout, through the rocks piled huge

On the humped moraine, and into the spectral larches, 165
Alone. By the glooming lake I sank and chilled
My mouth but I could not rest and stumbled still
To the valley, losing my way in the ragged marsh.

I was glad of the mire that covered the stains, on my ripped
Boots, of his blood, but panic was on me, the reek 170
Of the bog, the purple glimmer of toadstools obscene
In the twilight. I staggered clear to a firewaste, tripped

And fell with a shriek on my shoulder. It somehow eased
My heart to know I was hurt, but I did not faint
And I could not stop while over me hung the range 175
Of the Sawback. In blackness I searched for the trail by the creek

And found it. . . . My feet squelched a slug and horror
Rose again in my nostrils. I hurled myself
Down the path. In the woods behind some animal yelped.
Then I saw the glimmer of tents and babbled my story. 180

I said that he fell straight to the ice where they found him,
And none but the sun and incurious clouds have lingered

Around the marks of that day on the ledge of the Finger,
That day, the last of my youth, on the last of our mountains.

[1942]

From the Hazel Bough

He met a lady
    on a lazy street
hazel eyes
    and little plush feet

her legs swam by *5*
    like lovely trout
eyes were trees
    where boys leant out

hands in the dark and
    a river side *10*
round breasts rising
    with the finger's tide

she was plump as a finch
    and live as a salmon
gay as silk and *15*
    proud as a Brahmin

they winked when they met
    and laughed when they parted
never took time
    to be brokenhearted *20*

but no man sees
    where the trout lie now
or what leans out
    from the hazel bough

[1945]

Can. Hist.*

Once upon a colony
there was a land that was
almost a real
country called Canada

But people began to 5
feel
different
and no longer *Acadien*
or French
and rational 10
but *Canadien*
and *Mensch*°
and passional

Also no longer English
but Canadi*an* 15
and national
(though some were less specifically Canadian
Pacific)

After that it was fashionable 20
for a time to be Internationable

But now we are all quite
grown up & fir-
mly agreed to assert our right
not to be Amer- 25
icans perhaps
though on the other hand
not ever to be
unamerican

(except for the French 30
who still want to be *Mensch*)

[1973]

*The title is an abbreviation of Canadian History.

12 *Mensch*: Yiddish term for an admirable human being as well as German for human being.

W.[ystan] H.[ugh] Auden (1907–1973) was born in York and raised in Birmingham, England. His father was a family doctor and his mother a former nurse. He studied at Christ Church, Oxford. Faber and Faber, under the direction of T. S. Eliot, published Auden's first full-length book, Poems *(1930). Though homosexual, he married Thomas Mann's daughter in 1935 to save her from the German Nazis. Auden traveled widely—to Iceland, to Spain to witness the civil war, and to China during the Sino-Japanese War. Moving to America in 1939, Auden met the young poet Chester Kallman, who became his lifelong companion. Auden became a U.S. citizen in 1946. Two years later he won the Pulitzer Prize for* The Age of Anxiety, *and moved with Kallman to an island in the Bay of Naples. He wrote prolifically during this time, earning the Bollingen Prize and the National Book Award. In 1957 Auden settled in a summer cottage outside Vienna, Austria. Oxford made him a lecturer, and he spent winters there until his death.*

W. H. Auden

"O Where Are You Going?"

"O where are you going?" said reader to rider,
"That valley is fatal where furnaces burn,
Yonder's the midden whose odours will madden,
That gap is the grave where the tall return."

"O do you imagine," said fearer to farer, 5
"That dusk will delay on your path to the pass,
Your diligent looking discover the lacking
Your footsteps feel from granite to grass?"

"O what was that bird," said horror to hearer,
"Did you see that shape in the twisted trees? 10
Behind you swiftly the figure comes softly,
The spot on your skin is a shocking disease?"

"Out of this house"—said rider to reader
"Yours never will"—said farer to fearer
"They're looking for you"—said hearer to horror 15
As he left them there, as he left them there.

[1932]

As I Walked Out One Evening

As I walked out one evening,
  Walking down Bristol Street,
The crowds upon the pavement
  Were fields of harvest wheat.

And down by the brimming river 5
  I heard a lover sing
Under an arch of the railway:
  "Love has no ending.

"I'll love you, dear, I'll love you
  Till China and Africa meet, 10
And the river jumps over the mountain
  And the salmon sing in the street,

"I'll love you till the ocean
  Is folded and hung up to dry
And the seven stars go squawking 15
  Like geese about the sky.

"The years shall run like rabbits,
  For in my arms I hold
The Flower of the Ages,
  And the first love of the world." 20

But all the clocks in the city
  Began to whirr and chime:
"O let not Time deceive you,
  You cannot conquer Time.

"In the burrows of the Nightmare 25
  Where Justice naked is,
Time watches from the shadow
  And coughs when you would kiss.

"In headaches and in worry
  Vaguely life leaks away, 30

And Time will have his fancy
    Tomorrow or today.

"Into many a green valley
    Drifts the appalling snow;
Time breaks the threaded dances   *35*
    And the diver's brilliant bow.

"O plunge your hands in water,
    Plunge them in up to the wrist;
Stare, stare in the basin
    And wonder what you've missed.   *40*

"The glacier knocks in the cupboard,
    The desert sighs in the bed,
And the crack in the teacup opens
    A lane to the land of the dead.

"Where the beggars raffle the banknotes   *45*
    And the Giant is enchanting to Jack,
And the Lily-white Boy is a Roarer,
    And Jill goes down on her back.

"O look, look in the mirror,
    O look in your distress;   *50*
Life remains a blessing
    Although you cannot bless.

"O stand, stand at the window
    As the tears scald and start;
You shall love your crooked neighbor   *55*
    With your crooked heart."

It was late, late in the evening,
    The lovers they were gone;
The clocks had ceased their chiming,
    And the deep river ran on.   *60*

[1940]

In Memory of W. B. Yeats

(d. January 1939)

I

He disappeared in the dead of winter:
The brooks were frozen, the air-ports almost deserted,
And snow disfigured the public statues;
The mercury sank in the mouth of the dying day.
O all the instruments agree *5*
The day of his death was a dark cold day.

Far from his illness
The wolves ran on through the evergreen forests,
The peasant river was untempted by the fashionable quays;
By mourning tongues *10*
The death of the poet was kept from his poems.

But for him it was his last afternoon as himself,
An afternoon of nurses and rumours;
The provinces of his body revolted,
The squares of his mind were empty, *15*
Silence invaded the suburbs,
The current of his feeling failed: he became his admirers.

Now he is scattered among a hundred cities
And wholly given over to unfamiliar affections;
To find his happiness in another kind of wood *20*
And be punished under a foreign code of conscience.
The words of a dead man
Are modified in the guts of the living.

But in the importance and noise of to-morrow
When the brokers are roaring like beasts on the floor of the Bourse,° *25*
And the poor have the sufferings to which they are fairly accustomed,
And each in the cell of himself is almost convinced of his freedom;
A few thousand will think of this day
As one thinks of a day when one did something slightly unusual.

O all the instruments agree *30*
The day of his death was a dark cold day.

25 *Bourse*: the stock exchange in Paris.

II

You were silly like us: your gift survived it all;
The parish of rich women, physical decay,
Yourself; mad Ireland hurt you into poetry.
Now Ireland has her madness and her weather still, *35*
For poetry makes nothing happen: it survives
In the valley of its saying where executives
Would never want to tamper; it flows south
From ranches of isolation and the busy griefs,
Raw towns that we believe and die in; it survives, *40*
A way of happening, a mouth.

III

Earth, receive an honoured guest;
William Yeats is laid to rest:
Let the Irish vessel lie
Emptied of its poetry. *45*

Time that is intolerant
Of the brave and innocent,
And indifferent in a week
To a beautiful physique,

Worships language and forgives *50*
Everyone by whom it lives;
Pardons cowardice, conceit,
Lays its honours at their feet.

Time that with this strange excuse
Pardoned Kipling and his views, *55*
And will pardon Paul Claudel,
Pardons him for writing well.

In the nightmare of the dark
All the dogs of Europe bark,
And the living nations wait, *60*
Each sequestered in its hate;

Intellectual disgrace
Stares from every human face,
And the seas of pity lie
Locked and frozen in each eye. *65*

Follow, poet, follow right
To the bottom of the night,
With your unconstraining voice
Still persuade us to rejoice;

With the farming of a verse *70*
Make a vineyard of the curse,
Sing of human unsuccess
In a rapture of distress;

In the deserts of the heart
Let the healing fountain start, *75*
In the prison of his days
Teach the free man how to praise.

[1940]

Musée des Beaux Arts

About suffering they were never wrong,
The Old Masters: how well they understood
Its human position; how it takes place
While someone else is eating or opening a window or just walking
dully along;
How, when the aged are reverently, passionately waiting *5*
For the miraculous birth, there always must be
Children who did not specially want it to happen, skating
On a pond at the edge of the wood:
They never forgot
That even the dreadful martyrdom must run its course *10*
Anyhow in a corner, some untidy spot
Where the dogs go on with their doggy life and the torturer's horse
Scratches its innocent behind on a tree.

In Brueghel's *Icarus*,° for instance: how everything turns away
Quite leisurely from the disaster; the ploughman may *15*
Have heard the splash, the forsaken cry,
But for him it was not an important failure; the sun shone
As it had to on the white legs disappearing into the green

14 *Brueghel's Icarus*: a painting by the Flemish artist Peter Brueghel the Elder (1520?–1569). Icarus was the mythological son of Daedalus, who flew too close to the sun on his waxen wings and fell to his death when they melted.

Water; and the expensive delicate ship that must have seen
Something amazing, a boy falling out of the sky, *20*
Had somewhere to get to and sailed calmly on.

[1940]

September 1, 1939*

I sit in one of the dives
On Fifty-Second Street°
Uncertain and afraid
As the clever hopes expire
Of a low dishonest decade: *5*
Waves of anger and fear
Circulate over the bright
And darkened lands of the earth,
Obsessing our private lives;
The unmentionable odour of death *10*
Offends the September night.

Accurate scholarship can
Unearth the whole offence
From Luther° until now
That has driven a culture mad, *15*
Find what occurred at Linz,°
What huge imago made
A psychopathic god:
I and the public know
What all schoolchildren learn, *20*
Those to whom evil is done
Do evil in return.

Exiled Thucydides° knew
All that a speech can say
About Democracy, *25*
And what dictators do,
The elderly rubbish they talk
To an apathetic grave;

*The title is the day that Hitler invaded Poland and World War II began.

2 *Fifty-Second Street*: in New York City. **14** *Luther*: German priest Martin Luther (1483–1546), whose *95 Theses* (1517) ignited the Protestant Reformation. **16** *Linz*: town in Austria where Adolf Hitler was raised. **23** *Thucydides*: Greek historian of the fifth century B.C., whose History of the Peloponnesian War contains the famous oration by Pericles commemorating the Athenian war dead.

Analysed all in his book,
The enlightenment driven away, *30*
The habit-forming pain,
Mismanagement and grief:
We must suffer them all again.

Into this neutral air
Where blind skyscrapers use *35*
Their full height to proclaim
The strength of Collective Man,
Each language pours its vain
Competitive excuse:
But who can live for long *40*
In an euphoric dream;
Out of the mirror they stare,
Imperialism's face
And the international wrong.

Faces along the bar *45*
Cling to their average day:
The lights must never go out,
The music must always play,
All the conventions conspire
To make this fort assume *50*
The furniture of home;
Lest we should see where we are,
Lost in a haunted wood,
Children afraid of the night
Who have never been happy or good. *55*

The windiest militant trash
Important Persons shout
Is not so crude as our wish:
What mad Nijinsky wrote
About Diaghilev° *60*
Is true of the normal heart;
For the error bred in the bone
Of each woman and each man
Craves what it cannot have,

59–60 *What mad Nijinsky wrote/About Diaghilev*: Russian dancer Vaslav Nijinsky (1890–1960) wrote in his diary of the impresario Sergei Diaghilev (1872–1929): "Some politicians are hypocrites like Diaghilev, who does not want universal love, but to be loved alone. I want universal love."

Not universal love *65*
But to be loved alone.

From the conservative dark
Into the ethical life
The dense commuters come,
Repeating their morning vow, *70*
"I *will* be true to the wife,
I'll concentrate more on my work,"
And helpless governors wake
To resume their compulsory game:
Who can release them now, *75*
Who can reach the deaf,
Who can speak for the dumb?

All I have is a voice
To undo the folded lie,
The romantic lie in the brain *80*
Of the sensual man-in-the-street
And the lie of Authority
Whose buildings grope the sky:
There is no such thing as the State
And no one exists alone; *85*
Hunger allows no choice
To the citizen or the police;
We must love one another or die.

Defenceless under the night
Our world in stupor lies; *90*
Yet, dotted everywhere,
Ironic points of light
Flash out wherever the Just
Exchange their messages:
May I, composed like them *95*
Of Eros and of dust,
Beleaguered by the same
Negation and despair,
Show an affirming flame.

[1940]

Lullaby

Lay your sleeping head, my love,
Human on my faithless arm;
Time and fevers burn away
Individual beauty from
Thoughtful children, and the grave *5*
Proves the child ephemeral:
But in my arms till break of day
Let the living creature lie,
Mortal, guilty, but to me
The entirely beautiful. *10*

Soul and body have no bounds:
To lovers as they lie upon
Her tolerant enchanted slope
In their ordinary swoon,
Grave the vision Venus° sends *15*
Of supernatural sympathy,
Universal love and hope;
While an abstract insight wakes
Among the glaciers and the rocks
The hermit carnal ecstasy. *20*

Certainty, fidelity
On the stroke of midnight pass
Like vibrations of a bell
And fashionable madmen raise
Their pedantic boring cry: *25*
Every farthing° of the cost,
All the dreaded cards foretell,
Shall be paid, but from this night
Not a whisper, not a thought,
Not a kiss nor look be lost. *30*

Beauty, midnight, vision dies:
Let the winds of dawn that blow
Softly round your dreaming head
Such a day of welcome show

15 *Venus*: Roman goddess of love. **26** *farthing*: old British coin worth one fourth of a pence.

Eye and knocking heart may bless, 35
Find our mortal world enough;
Noons of dryness find you fed
By the involuntary powers,
Nights of insult let you pass
Watched by every human love. 40

[1940]

The Shield of Achilles

She looked over his shoulder
For vines and olive trees,
Marble well-governed cities,
And ships upon untamed seas,
But there on the shining metal 5
His hands had put instead
An artificial wilderness
And a sky like lead.

A plain without a feature, bare and brown,
No blade of grass, no sign of neighborhood, 10
Nothing to eat and nowhere to sit down,
Yet, congregated on its blankness, stood
An unintelligible multitude,
A million eyes, a million boots in line,
Without expression, waiting for a sign. 15

Out of the air a voice without a face
Proved by statistics that some cause was just
In tones as dry and level as the place:
No one was cheered and nothing was discussed;
Column by column in a cloud of dust 20
They marched away enduring a belief
Whose logic brought them, somewhere else, to grief.

She looked over his shoulder
For ritual pieties,
White flower-garlanded heifers, 25

Libation and sacrifice,
But there on the shining metal
Where the altar should have been,
She saw by his flickering forge-light
Quite another scene. *30*

Barbed wire enclosed an arbitrary spot
Where bored officials lounged (one cracked a joke)
And sentries sweated, for the day was hot:
A crowd of ordinary decent folk
Watched from without and neither moved nor spoke *35*
As three pale figures were led forth and bound
To three posts driven upright in the ground.

The mass and majesty of this world, all
That carries weight and always weighs the same,
Lay in the hands of others; they were small *40*
And could not hope for help and no help came:
What their foes liked to do was done, their shame
Was all the worst could wish; they lost their pride
And died as men before their bodies died.

She looked over his shoulder *45*
For athletes at their games,
Men and women in a dance
Moving their sweet limbs
Quick, quick, to music,
But there on the shining shield *50*
His hands had set no dancing-floor
But a weed-choked field.

A ragged urchin, aimless and alone,
Loitered about that vacancy; a bird
Flew up to safety from his well-aimed stone: *55*
That girls are raped, that two boys knife a third,
Were axioms to him, who'd never heard
Of any world where promises were kept
Or one could weep because another wept.

The thin-lipped armorer, *60*
Hephaestos, hobbled away;

Thetis of the shining breasts
    Cried out in dismay
At what the god had wrought
    To please her son, the strong *65*
Iron-hearted man-slaying Achilles
    Who would not live long.

[1955]

***A.**[lec] **D.**[erwent] **Hope** (1907–2000) was born in New South Wales, Australia, the son of a Presbyterian minister. Much of his childhood was spent in rural Tasmania. He studied English, philosophy, and psychology at Sydney University, graduating in 1928, then left for England to attend Oxford on scholarship, where his professors included J. R. R. Tolkien and C. S. Lewis. Returning to Australia a few years later, Hope worked for a time as a psychologist with the New South Wales Department of Labor and Industry. He married Penelope Robinson in 1937 and had three children. His first collection,* The Wandering Islands *(1955), was very well received. Hope taught at Sydney Teachers' College and University of Melbourne before settling in 1951 at Australian National University, Canberra. He retired in 1968. Hope won many honors for his poetry, including the Robert Frost Award and the Levinson Prize. He died in Canberra eight days before his ninety-third birthday.*

A. D. Hope

Australia

A Nation of trees, drab green and desolate grey
In the field uniform of modern wars,
Darkens her hills, those endless, outstretched paws
Of Sphinx demolished or stone lion worn away.

They call her a young country, but they lie: *5*
She is the last of lands, the emptiest,

A woman beyond her change of life, a breast
Still tender but within the womb is dry.

Without songs, architecture, history:
The emotions and superstitions of younger lands, 10
Her rivers of water drown among inland sands,
The river of her immense stupidity

Floods her monotonous tribes from Cairns to Perth.
In them at last the ultimate men arrive
Whose boast is not: "we live" but "we survive," 15
A type who will inhabit the dying earth.

And her five cities, like five teeming sores,
Each drains her: a vast parasite robber-state
Where second-hand Europeans pullulate
Timidly on the edge of alien shores. 20

Yet there are some like me turn gladly home
From the lush jungle of modern thought, to find
The Arabian desert of the human mind,
Hoping, if still from the deserts the prophets come,

Such savage and scarlet as no green hills dare 25
Springs in that waste, some spirit which escapes
The learned doubt, the chatter of cultured apes
Which is called civilization over there.

[1939]

The Lingam and the Yoni*

The Lingam and the Yoni
Are walking hand in glove,
O are you listening, honey?
I hear my honey-love.

The He and She our movers 5
What is it they discuss?

*Lingam and Yoni are the Sanskrit words for the male and female sex organs.

Is it the talk of Lovers?
And do they speak of us?

I hear their high palaver—
O tell me what they say! *10*
The talk goes on for ever
So deep in love are they;

So deep in thought, debating
The suburb and the street;
Time-payment calculating *15*
Upon the bedroom suite.

But ours is long division
By love's arithmetic,
Until they make provision
To buy a box of brick, *20*

A box that makes her prisoner,
That he must slave to win
To do the Lingam honour,
To keep the Yoni in.

The mortgage on tomorrow? *25*
The haemorrhage of rent?
Against the heart they borrow
At five or six per cent.

The heart has bought fulfilment
Which yet their mouths defer *30*
Until the last instalment
Upon the furniture.

No Lingam for her money
Can make up youth's arrears:
His layby on the Yoni *35*
Will not be paid in years.

And they, who keep this tally,
They count what they destroy;
While, in its secret valley
Withers the herb of joy. *40*

[1944]

The Judgement

Last Friday when the sun had set,
Under the stars the world was quiet.
I dreamed our Grand Assize was met,
And a great judge was there to try it.

I dreamed the bitter choice was past *5*
That kept our lives so long asunder;
And in my arms I held you fast,
Until that summons broke in thunder.

It filled the world and shook the sky,
Crying our names through all creation, *10*
And doomed our guilty hearts to die,
And after death proclaimed damnation.

A voice of warning and lament
For grace and mercy vainly shown us.
And naked from our bed we went, *15*
The first fresh dews of sleep upon us.

And, as towards judgement, you and I
In the cool darkness walked together,
I felt the softness of your thigh
That brushed mine like a night-bird's feather; *20*

I felt the hapless grief that rose,
And found your hand, and drew you nearer.
"Dear heart," you said and held me close,
"I weep for joy and not for terror;

"For joy that in your arms I lay *25*
At last, nor cared that all men knew it;
And Heaven cannot take away
That bliss, nor Hell itself undo it."

Then once again the voice of dread
Called our two names in solemn warning— *30*
And in my solitary bed
I woke to find the cold day dawning

Remembering, in helpless woe,
That love our bitter choice had ended,
The doom we spoke so long ago *35*
That no damnation now could mend it.

[1948]

Imperial Adam*

Imperial Adam, naked in the dew,
Felt his brown flanks and found the rib was gone.
Puzzled he turned and saw where, two and two,
The mighty spoor of Jahweh° marked the lawn.

Then he remembered through mysterious sleep *5*
The surgeon fingers probing at the bone,
The voice so far away, so rich and deep:
"It is not good for him to live alone."

Turning once more he found Man's counterpart
In tender parody breathing at his side. *10*
He knew her at first sight, he knew by heart
Her allegory of sense unsatisfied.

The pawpaw drooped its golden breasts above
Less generous than the honey of her flesh;
The innocent sunlight showed the place of love; *15*
The dew on its dark hairs winked crisp and fresh.

This plump gourd severed from his virile root,
She promised on the turf of Paradise
Delicious pulp of the forbidden fruit;
Sly as the snake she loosed her sinuous thighs, *20*

And waking, smiled up at him from the grass;
Her breasts rose softly and he heard her sigh—
From all the beasts whose pleasant task it was
In Eden to increase and multiply

*Hope's poem retells the story of Adam and Eve. For the Biblical version, see Genesis 2:18–4:1.

4 *Jahweh*: the Lord of the Old Testament. The Hebrew name of God was written as JHVH, but it was considered too sacred to say aloud. Yahweh and Jehovah are the other most common versions of the vowel-less Hebrew name.

Adam had learned the jolly deed of kind:° *25*
He took her in his arms and there and then,
Like the clean beasts, embracing from behind,
Began in joy to found the breed of men.

Then from the spurt of seed within her broke
Her terrible and triumphant female cry, *30*
Split upward by the sexual lightning stroke.
It was the beasts now who stood watching by:

The gravid elephant, the calving hind,
The breeding bitch, the she-ape big with young
Were the first gentle midwives of mankind; *35*
The teeming lioness rasped her with her tongue;

The proud vicuña nuzzled her as she slept
Lax on the grass; and Adam watching too
Saw how her dumb breasts at their ripening wept,
The great pod of her belly swelled and grew, *40*

And saw its water break, and saw, in fear,
Its quaking muscles in the act of birth,
Between her legs a pigmy face appear,
And the first murderer° lay upon the earth.

[1952]

25 *deed of kind*: the act of procreation. This particular expression is usually used to describe the mating of animals. **44** *the first murderer*: Cain, Adam and Eve's first child, who murdered his brother, Abel. See Genesis 4:1–16.

***Theodore Roethke** (1908–1963) was born in Saginaw, Michigan, where his father and uncle ran a commercial florist business. The greenhouses they owned would become an important influence on the poet's imagination. Roethke graduated from the University of Michigan in 1929 and briefly attended law school. Dissatisfied, he turned back to literature, studying again at Michigan and later at Harvard. His adult life was filled with manic episodes and nervous breakdowns, making it difficult for Roethke to keep a teaching position for long. He taught at Lafayette College in Pennsylvania, Michigan State College (now University), Pennsylvania State University, and Bennington College, before settling at the University of Washington, Seattle, in 1947. Roethke was an influential teacher whose* *students included James Wright, Richard Hugo, and Carolyn Kizer. Roethke's turbulent and depressive personality stabilized when he married a former Bennington student, Beatrice O'Connell, in 1953. The marriage was a happy one. Still in his mid-fifties, Roethke died of a heart attack in a friend's swimming pool. He won the Pulitzer Prize, the National Book Award, and the Bollingen Prize.*

Theodore Roethke

My Papa's Waltz

The whiskey on your breath
Could make a small boy dizzy;
But I hung on like death:
Such waltzing was not easy.

We romped until the pans 5
Slid from the kitchen shelf;
My mother's countenance
Could not unfrown itself.

The hand that held my wrist
Was battered on one knuckle; 10
At every step you missed
My right ear scraped a buckle.

You beat time on my head
With a palm caked hard by dirt,
Then waltzed me off to bed 15
Still clinging to your shirt.

[1948]

Elegy for Jane

My Student, Thrown by a Horse

I remember the neckcurls, limp and damp as tendrils;
And her quick look, a sidelong pickerel smile;
And how, once startled into talk, the light syllables leaped for her,

And she balanced in the delight of her thought,
A wren, happy, tail into the wind, *5*
Her song trembling the twigs and small branches.
The shade sang with her;
The leaves, their whispers turned to kissing;
And the mold sang in the bleached valleys under the rose.

Oh, when she was sad, she cast herself down into such a pure depth, *10*
Even a father could not find her:
Scraping her cheek against straw;
Stirring the clearest water.

My sparrow, you are not here,
Waiting like a fern, making a spiny shadow. *15*
The sides of wet stones cannot console me,
Nor the moss, wound with the last light.

If only I could nudge you from this sleep,
My maimed darling, my skittery pigeon.
Over this damp grave I speak the words of my love: *20*
I, with no rights in this matter,
Neither father nor lover.

[1953]

The Waking

I wake to sleep, and take my waking slow.
I feel my fate in what I cannot fear.
I learn by going where I have to go.

We think by feeling. What is there to know?
I hear my being dance from ear to ear. *5*
I wake to sleep, and take my waking slow.

Of those so close beside me, which are you?
God bless the Ground! I shall walk softly there,
And learn by going where I have to go.

Light takes the Tree; but who can tell us how? *10*
The lowly worm climbs up a winding stair;
I wake to sleep, and take my waking slow.

Great Nature has another thing to do
To you and me; so take the lively air,
And, lovely, learn by going where to go. *15*

This shaking keeps me steady. I should know.
What falls away is always. And is near.
I wake to sleep, and take my waking slow.
I learn by going where I have to go.

[1953]

I Knew a Woman

I knew a woman, lovely in her bones,
When small birds sighed, she would sigh back at them;
Ah, when she moved, she moved more ways than one:
The shapes a bright container can contain!
Of her choice virtues only gods should speak, *5*
Or English poets who grew up on Greek
(I'd have them sing in chorus, cheek to cheek).

How well her wishes went! She stroked my chin,
She taught me Turn, and Counter-turn, and Stand;
She taught me Touch, that undulant white skin; *10*
I nibbled meekly from her proffered hand;
She was the sickle; I, poor I, the rake,
Coming behind her for her pretty sake
(But what prodigious mowing we did make).

Love likes a gander, and adores a goose: *15*
Her full lips pursed, the errant note to seize;
She played it quick, she played it light and loose;
My eyes, they dazzled at her flowing knees;
Her several parts could keep a pure repose,
Or one hip quiver with a mobile nose *20*
(She moved in circles, and those circles moved).

Let seed be grass, and grass turn into hay:
I'm martyr to a motion not my own;
What's freedom for? To know eternity.
I swear she cast a shadow white as stone. *25*

But who would count eternity in days?
These old bones live to learn her wanton ways:
(I measure time by how a body sways).

[1958]

Born in Worcester, Massachusetts, **Elizabeth Bishop** *(1911–1979) spent her childhood living with various relatives in Nova Scotia and Massachusetts. Her health problems were serious enough that she had little formal education until high school, and she suffered from chronic asthma for the rest of her life. After graduation from Vassar College, she traveled abroad extensively, and shuttled between New York and Key West. On the recommendation of her friend Robert Lowell, Bishop was appointed the Poetry Consultant to the Library of Congress in 1949. Intending to sail around the world in 1951, she suffered a severe allergic reaction to the fruit of the cashew in Rio de Janeiro. A wealthy Brazilian friend, Lota de Macedo Soares, nursed her back to health, and the two women fell in love. Bishop's postponement of her trip evolved into a 15-year stay. Soares committed suicide in 1967, and three years later Bishop returned to the United States. Until her death in 1979 she taught mostly at Harvard. Bishop won the Pulitzer Prize for* North and South *in 1956.*

Elizabeth Bishop

The Fish

I caught a tremendous fish
and held him beside the boat
half out of water, with my hook
fast in a corner of his mouth.
He didn't fight. *5*
He hadn't fought at all.
He hung a grunting weight,
battered and venerable
and homely. Here and there
his brown skin hung in strips *10*
like ancient wallpaper,

and its pattern of darker brown
was like wallpaper:
shapes like full-blown roses
stained and lost through age. *15*
He was speckled with barnacles,
fine rosettes of lime,
and infested
with tiny white sea-lice,
and underneath two or three *20*
rags of green weed hung down.
While his gills were breathing in
the terrible oxygen
—the frightening gills,
fresh and crisp with blood, *25*
that can cut so badly—
I thought of the coarse white flesh
packed in like feathers,
the big bones and the little bones,
the dramatic reds and blacks *30*
of his shiny entrails,
and the pink swim-bladder
like a big peony.
I looked into his eyes
which were far larger than mine *35*
but shallower, and yellowed,
the irises backed and packed
with tarnished tinfoil
seen through the lenses
of old scratched isinglass. *40*
They shifted a little, but not
to return my stare.
—It was more like the tipping
of an object toward the light.
I admired his sullen face, *45*
the mechanism of his jaw,
and then I saw
that from his lower lip
—if you could call it a lip—
grim, wet, and weaponlike, *50*
hung five old pieces of fish-line,

or four and a wire leader
with the swivel still attached,
with all their five big hooks
grown firmly in his mouth. *55*
A green line, frayed at the end
where he broke it, two heavier lines,
and a fine black thread
still crimped from the strain and snap
when it broke and he got away. *60*
Like medals with their ribbons
frayed and wavering,
a five-haired beard of wisdom
trailing from his aching jaw.
I stared and stared *65*
and victory filled up
the little rented boat,
from the pool of bilge
where oil had spread a rainbow
around the rusted engine *70*
to the bailer rusted orange,
the sun-cracked thwarts,
the oarlocks on their strings,
the gunnels—until everything
was rainbow, rainbow, rainbow! *75*
And I let the fish go.

[1946]

Filling Station

Oh, but it is dirty!
—this little filling station,
oil-soaked, oil-permeated
to a disturbing, over-all
black translucency. *5*
Be careful with that match!

Father wears a dirty,
oil-soaked monkey suit

that cuts him under the arms,
and several quick and saucy 10
and greasy sons assist him
(it's a family filling station),
all quite thoroughly dirty.

Do they live in the station?
It has a cement porch 15
behind the pumps, and on it
a set of crushed and grease-
impregnated wickerwork;
on the wicker sofa
a dirty dog, quite comfy. 20

Some comic books provide
the only note of color—
of certain color. They lie
upon a big dim doily
draping a taboret 25
(part of the set), beside
a big hirsute begonia.

Why the extraneous plant?
Why the taboret?
Why, oh why, the doily? 30
(Embroidered in daisy stitch
with marguerites, I think,
and heavy with gray crochet.)

Somebody embroidered the doily.
Somebody waters the plant, 35
or oils it, maybe. Somebody
arranges the rows of cans
so that they softly say:
ESSO—SO—SO—SO
to high-strung automobiles. 40
Somebody loves us all.

[1965]

Questions of Travel

There are too many waterfalls here; the crowded streams
hurry too rapidly down to the sea,
and the pressure of so many clouds on the mountaintops
makes them spill over the sides in soft slow-motion,
turning to waterfalls under our very eyes. *5*
—For if those streaks, those mile-long, shiny, tearstains,
aren't waterfalls yet,
in a quick age or so, as ages go here,
they probably will be.
But if the streams and clouds keep travelling, travelling, *10*
the mountains look like the hulls of capsized ships,
slime-hung and barnacled.

Think of the long trip home.
Should we have stayed at home and thought of here?
Where should we be today? *15*
Is it right to be watching strangers in a play
in this strangest of theatres?
What childishness is it that while there's a breath of life
in our bodies, we are determined to rush
to see the sun the other way around? *20*
The tiniest green hummingbird in the world?
To stare at some inexplicable old stonework,
inexplicable and impenetrable,
at any view,
instantly seen and always, always delightful? *25*
Oh, must we dream our dreams
and have them, too?
And have we room
for one more folded sunset, still quite warm?

But surely it would have been a pity *30*
not to have seen the trees along this road,
really exaggerated in their beauty,
not to have seen them gesturing
like noble pantomimists, robed in pink.
—Not to have had to stop for gas and heard *35*
the sad, two-noted, wooden tune
of disparate wooden clogs
carelessly clacking over

a grease-stained filling-station floor.
(In another country the clogs would all be tested. *40*
Each pair there would have identical pitch.)
—A pity not to have heard
the other, less primitive music of the fat brown bird
who sings above the broken gasoline pump
in a bamboo church of Jesuit baroque: *45*
three towers, five silver crosses.
—Yes, a pity not to have pondered,
blurr'dly and inconclusively,
on what connection can exist for centuries
between the crudest wooden footwear *50*
and, careful and finicky,
the whittled fantasies of wooden cages.
—Never to have studied history in
the weak calligraphy of songbirds' cages.
—And never to have had to listen to rain *55*
so much like politicians' speeches:
two hours of unrelenting oratory
and then a sudden golden silence
in which the traveller takes a notebook, writes:

"Is it lack of imagination that makes us come *60*
to imagined places, not just stay at home?
Or could Pascal have been not entirely right
about just sitting quietly in one's room?

Continent, city, country, society:
the choice is never wide and never free. *65*
And here, or there . . . No. Should we have stayed at home,
wherever that may be?"

[1965]

One Art

The art of losing isn't hard to master;
so many things seem filled with the intent
to be lost that their loss is no disaster.

Lose something every day. Accept the fluster
of lost door keys, the hour badly spent. 5
The art of losing isn't hard to master.

Then practice losing farther, losing faster:
places, and names, and where it was you meant
to travel. None of these will bring disaster.

I lost my mother's watch. And look! my last, or 10
next-to-last, of three loved houses went.
The art of losing isn't hard to master.

I lost two cities, lovely ones. And, vaster,
some realms I owned, two rivers, a continent.
I miss them, but it wasn't a disaster. 15

—Even losing you (the joking voice, a gesture
I love) I shan't have lied. It's evident
the art of losing's not too hard to master
though it may look like (*Write* it!) like disaster.

[1976]

Robert Hayden *(1913–1980) was born Asa Bundy Sheffey, in Detroit, Michigan, to extremely poor parents who gave up their infant son to William and Sue Ellen Hayden. (His new parents renamed him.) The young boy suffered from extreme myopia, which turned him towards books and other arts. After attending Detroit City College, he joined the Federal Writers' Project. Hayden's first collection of poems,* Heart-Shape in the Dust *(1940), was published the same year he married Erma Inez Morris, a pianist. Though brought up Baptist, Hayden eventually converted to the Baha'i faith, which became a major influence on his writing. Another significant influence in Hayden's literary development was his mentorship with W. H. Auden, with whom he studied at the University of Michigan. Hayden taught briefly at Fisk University before accepting a position with the University of Michigan in 1969, where he remained until his death. Although Hayden never won any of the major literary awards, he did earn one significant honor—in 1976 Hayden became the first African American to serve as Consultant in Poetry to the Library of Congress.*

Robert Hayden

Homage to the Empress of the Blues*

Because there was a man somewhere in a candystripe silk shirt,
gracile and dangerous as a jaguar and because a woman moaned
for him in sixty-watt gloom and mourned him Faithless Love
Twotiming Love Oh Love Oh Careless Aggravating Love,

She came out on the stage in yards of pearls, emerging like *5*
a favorite scenic view, flashed her golden smile and sang.

Because grey laths began somewhere to show from underneath
torn hurdygurdy lithographs of dollfaced heaven;
and because there were those who feared alarming fists of snow
on the door and those who feared the riot-squad of statistics, *10*

She came out on the stage in ostrich feathers, beaded satin,
and shone that smile on us and sang.

[1966]

*The Empress of the Blues was a nickname for vocalist Bessie Smith (1898?–1937).

Those Winter Sundays

Sundays too my father got up early
and put his clothes on in the blueblack cold,
then with cracked hands that ached
from labor in the weekday weather made
banked fires blaze. No one ever thanked him. *5*

I'd wake and hear the cold splintering, breaking.
When the rooms were warm, he'd call,
and slowly I would rise and dress,
fearing the chronic angers of that house,

Speaking indifferently to him, *10*
who had driven out the cold

and polished my good shoes as well.
What did I know, what did I know
of love's austere and lonely offices?

[1966]

The Whipping

The old woman across the way
    is whipping the boy again
and shouting to the neighborhood
    her goodness and his wrongs.

Wildly he crashes through elephant ears, *5*
    pleads in dusty zinnias,
while she in spite of crippling fat
    pursues and corners him.

She strikes and strikes the shrilly circling
    boy till the stick breaks *10*
in her hand. His tears are rainy weather
    to woundlike memories:

My head gripped in bony vise
    of knees, the writhing struggle
to wrench free, the blows, the fear *15*
    worse than blows that hateful

Words could bring, the face that I
    no longer knew or loved . . . .
Well, it is over now, it is over,
    and the boy sobs in his room, *20*

And the woman leans muttering against
    a tree, exhausted, purged—
avenged in part for lifelong hidings
    she has had to bear.

[1966]

***John Berryman** (1914–1972) was born John Smith, Jr., in rural Oklahoma. His father was a small-town banker and a chronic business failure. When his banking career ended, he moved the family to Florida during the land boom of the 1920s to open a restaurant, which also quickly went under. Berryman's father shot himself in front of the 12-year-old boy. His mother, a schoolteacher, remarried to John Berryman, her landlord. Taking his stepfather's name, young Berryman was educated at a prep school and at Columbia University and Clare College, Cambridge. He eventually became a college professor at various universities, including Iowa, Harvard, and Princeton. Like many poets of his generation, Berryman suffered from severe emotional trauma, alcoholism, and manic depression. He was married three times. Berryman was tenured at the University of Minnesota and won several major prizes, including the Pulitzer, a National Book Award, and the Bollingen Prize. His magnum opus,* The Dream Songs *(1969), was very well received. Still, he could not escape his psychological turmoil. At age 57, he jumped to his death from a bridge in Minneapolis.*

John Berryman

from The Dream Songs

14

Life, friends, is boring. We must not say so.
After all, the sky flashes, the great sea yearns,
we ourselves flash and yearn,
and moreover my mother told me as a boy
(repeatingly) "Ever to confess you're bored 5
means you have no

Inner Resources." I conclude now I have no
inner resources, because I am heavy bored.
Peoples bore me,
literature bores me, especially great literature, 10
Henry bores me, with his plights & gripes
as bad as achilles,

who loves people and valiant art, which bores me.
And the tranquil hills, & gin, look like a drag
and somehow a dog *15*
has taken itself & its tail considerably away
into mountains or sea or sky, leaving
behind: me, wag.

22

I am the little man who smokes & smokes.
I am the girl who does know better but.
I am the king of the pool.
I am so wise I had my mouth sewn shut.
I am a government official & a goddamned fool. *5*
I am a lady who takes jokes.

I am the enemy of the mind.
I am the auto salesman and lóve you.
I am a teenage cancer, with a plan.
I am the blackt-out man. *10*
I am the woman powerful as a zoo.
I am two eyes screwed to my set, whose blind—

It is the Fourth of July.
Collect: while the dying man,
forgone by you creator, who forgives, *15*
is gasping "Thomas Jefferson still lives"
in vain, in vain, in vain.
I am Henry Pussy-cat! My whiskers fly.

29

There sat down, once, a thing on Henry's heart
só heavy, if he had a hundred years
& more, & weeping, sleepless, in all them time
Henry could not make good.
Starts again always in Henry's ears *5*
the little cough somewhere, an odour, a chime.

And there is another thing he has in mind
like a grave Sienese face a thousand years
would fail to blur the still profiled reproach of. Ghastly,
with open eyes, he attends, blind. *10*
All the bells say: too late. This is not for tears;
thinking.

But never did Henry, as he thought he did,
end anyone and hacks her body up
and hide the pieces, where they may be found. *15*
He knows: he went over everyone, & nobody's missing.
Often he reckons, in the dawn, them up.
Nobody is ever missing.

[1964]

***Weldon Kees** (1914–1955) was born in Beatrice, Nebraska, where his father owned a small hardware factory. He transferred between many universities, and attended graduate school at the University of Chicago but quickly dropped out and joined the Federal Writers' Project. Kees married his college girlfriend and lived in Denver for six years before moving to New York City, where he worked as a journalist and critic, began painting seriously, and published his first collection of poems,* The Last Man *(1943). Relocating to San Francisco, he immediately became a significant cultural presence. He made documentary and experimental films, hosted a radio program on film, and produced a popular literary cabaret. His* Poems 1947–1954 *(1954) exhibited the range of his poetic talents and was well received. Despite his constant work, Kees could barely make a living. After his 1954 divorce, he drank heavily and took both tranquilizers and stimulants. Some of his artistic endeavors failed, and he talked to friends about suicide and about starting a new life in Mexico. On July 18, 1955, his car was found abandoned—with the keys still in the ignition—on the north end of the Golden Gate Bridge. His body was never found.*

Weldon Kees

For My Daughter

Looking into my daughter's eyes I read
Beneath the innocence of morning flesh
Concealed, hintings of death she does not heed.
Coldest of winds have blown this hair, and mesh
Of seaweed snarled these miniatures of hands; *5*
The night's slow poison, tolerant and bland,
Has moved her blood. Parched years that I have seen
That may be hers appear: foul, lingering
Death in certain war, the slim legs green.
Or, fed on hate, she relishes the sting *10*
Of others' agony; perhaps the cruel
Bride of a syphilitic or a fool.
These speculations sour in the sun.
I have no daughter. I desire none.

[1943]

Robinson

The dog stops barking after Robinson has gone.
His act is over. The world is a gray world,
Not without violence, and he kicks under the grand piano,
The nightmare chase well under way.

The mirror from Mexico, stuck to the wall, *5*
Reflects nothing at all. The glass is black.
Robinson alone provides the image Robinsonian.

Which is all of the room—walls, curtains,
Shelves, bed, the tinted photograph of Robinson's first wife,
Rugs, vases, panatellas in a humidor. *10*
They would fill the room if Robinson came in.

The pages in the books are blank,
The books that Robinson has read. That is his favorite chair,

Or where the chair would be if Robinson were here.

All day the phone rings. It could be Robinson 15
Calling. It never rings when he is here.

Outside, white buildings yellow in the sun.
Outside, the birds circle continuously
Where trees are actual and take no holiday.

[1947]

Aspects of Robinson

Robinson at cards at the Algonquin;° a thin
Blue light comes down once more outside the blinds.
Gray men in overcoats are ghosts blown past the door.
The taxis streak the avenues with yellow, orange, and red.
This is Grand Central,° Mr. Robinson. 5

Robinson on a roof above the Heights;° the boats
Mourn like the lost. Water is slate, far down.
Through sounds of ice cubes dropped in glass, an osteopath,
Dressed for the links, describes an old Intourist° tour.
–Here's where old Gibbons jumped from, Robinson. 10

Robinson walking in the Park, admiring the elephant.
Robinson buying the *Tribune*, Robinson buying the *Times*. Robinson
Saying, "Hello. Yes, this is Robinson. Sunday
At five? I'd love to. Pretty well. And you?"
Robinson alone at Longchamps,° staring at the wall. 15

Robinson afraid, drunk, sobbing Robinson
In bed with a Mrs. Morse. Robinson at home;
Decisions: Toynbee or luminol?° Where the sun
Shines, Robinson in flowered trunks, eyes toward
The breakers. Where the night ends, Robinson in East Side bars. 20

1 *Algonquin*: a stylish Manhattan hotel favored by writers. 5 *Grand Central*: Grand Central Station, a major New York City train station. 6 *Heights*: Brooklyn Heights. 9 *Intourist*: the official Soviet Union tourist agency. 15 *Longchamps*: a Manhattan restaurant. 18 *Toynbee or luminol*: Arnold Toynbee (1889–1975), a British historian. Luminol was a sedative. The implication is that both can put Robinson to sleep.

Robinson in Glen plaid jacket, Scotch-grain shoes,
Black four-in-hand° and oxford button-down,
The jeweled and silent watch that winds itself, the brief-
Case, covert topcoat, clothes for spring, all covering
His sad and usual heart, dry as a winter leaf. *25*

[1954]

22 *four-in-hand*: a knot for a necktie.

Round*

"Wondrous life!" cried Marvell at Appleton House.°
Renan° admired Jesus Christ "wholeheartedly."
But here dried ferns keep falling to the floor,
And something inside my head
Flaps like a worn-out blind. Royal Cortissoz° is dead. *5*
A blow to the *Herald-Tribune*. A closet mouse
Rattles the wrapper on the breakfast food. Renan
Admired Jesus Christ "wholeheartedly."

Flaps like a worn-out blind. Cézanne°
Would break out in the quiet streets of Aix *10*
And shout, "Le monde, c'est terrible!"° Royal
Cortissoz is dead. And something inside my head
Flaps like a worn-out blind. The soil
In which the ferns are dying needs more Vigoro.°
There is no twilight on the moon, no mist or rain, *15*
No hail or snow, no life. Here in this house

Dried ferns keep falling to the floor, a mouse
Rattles the wrapper on the breakfast food. Cézanne

*A round is a type of song (like "Row, Row, Row Your Boat") in which three or four voices follow one another singing the same melody in counterpoint. Kees's poem combines different voices to achieve the same effect in words.

1 *Marvell at Appleton House*: English poet Andrew Marvell (1621–1678) wrote his famous celebration of the contemplative rural life, "The Garden," at Appleton House, a Yorkshire country manor. 2 *Renan*: Ernest Renan, a French historian (1823–1892), wrote *The Life of Jesus* (1863), a humanistic study of the origins of Christianity. 5 *Royal Cortissoz* (1869–1948), middlebrow art critic for the New York *Herald Tribune*. Presumably, the speaker of the poem has just read his obituary in the newspaper. 9 *Cezanne*: Paul Cezanne (1839–1906), the French post-Impressionist painter, who was born and died in Aix-en-Provence. 11 *Le monde, c'est terrible!*: French for "The world, it is terrible!" 14 *Vigoro*: a commercial brand of plant-food.

Would break out in the quiet streets and scream. Renan
Admired Jesus Christ "wholeheartedly." And something inside my
head *20*
Flaps like a worn-out blind. Royal Cortissoz is dead.
There is no twilight on the moon, no hail or snow.
One notes fresh desecrations of the portico.
"Wondrous life!" cried Marvell at Appleton House.

[1954]

Welsh poet, critic, playwright, and fiction writer **Dylan Thomas** *(1914–1953) was born in the seaport town of Swansea, Carmarthenshire. His father was the senior English master at the grammar school that Thomas attended as a boy. Although bright, he failed his university exams in 1931 and dropped out of school. He drifted between a number of odd jobs during his youth, including work as a reporter, actor, and reviewer. Moving to London in 1934, Thomas lived a poor bohemian lifestyle, sharing quarters with a group of other young artists and drinking heavily. Two years later he met Caitlin Macnamara in a pub and married her the following July. Thomas had built up quite a reputation—literary and otherwise—by the end of the decade. In 1950, always in search of money, Thomas launched his first of four eccentric and drunken reading tours of America. He was only 35 years old—and would be dead in four years. One night at New York's White Horse Tavern, Thomas collapsed during a drinking binge and died a few days later.*

Dylan Thomas

And Death Shall Have No Dominion

And death shall have no dominion.
Dead men naked they shall be one
With the man in the wind and the west moon;
When their bones are picked clean and the clean bones gone,

They shall have stars at elbow and foot; *5*
Though they go mad they shall be sane,
Though they sink through the sea they shall rise again;
Though lovers be lost love shall not;
And death shall have no dominion.

And death shall have no dominion. *10*
Under the windings of the sea
They lying long shall not die windily;
Twisting on racks when sinews give way,
Strapped to a wheel, yet they shall not break;
Faith in their hands shall snap in two, *15*
And the unicorn evils run them through;
Split all ends up they shan't crack;
And death shall have no dominion.

And death shall have no dominion.
No more may gulls cry at their ears *20*
Or waves break loud on the seashores;
Where blew a flower may a flower no more
Lift its head to the blows of the rain;
Though they be mad and dead as nails,
Heads of the characters hammer through daisies; *25*
Break in the sun till the sun breaks down,
And death shall have no dominion.

[1936]

Fern Hill

Now as I was young and easy under the apple boughs
About the lilting house and happy as the grass was green,
        The night above the dingle° starry,
            Time let me hail and climb
        Golden in the heydays of his eyes, *5*
And honored among wagons I was prince of the apple towns
And once below a time I lordly had the trees and leaves
            Trail with daisies and barley
        Down the rivers of the windfall light.

3 *dingle*: wooded valley

And as I was green and carefree, famous among the barns *10*
About the happy yard and singing as the farm was home,
In the sun that is young once only,
Time let me play and be
Golden in the mercy of his means,
And green and golden I was huntsman and herdsman, the calves *15*
Sang to my horn, the foxes on the hills barked clear and cold,
And the sabbath rang slowly
In the pebbles of the holy streams.

All the sun long it was running, it was lovely, the hay
Fields high as the house, the tunes from the chimneys, it was air *20*
And playing, lovely and watery
And fire green as grass.
And nightly under the simple stars
As I rode to sleep the owls were bearing the farm away,
All the moon long I heard, blessed among stables, the nightjars *25*
Flying with the ricks, and the horses
Flashing into the dark.

And then to awake, and the farm, like a wanderer white
With the dew, come back, the cock on his shoulder: it was all
Shining, it was Adam and maiden, *30*
The sky gathered again
And the sun grew round that very day.
So it must have been after the birth of the simple light
In the first, spinning place, the spellbound horses walking warm
Out of the whinnying green stable *35*
On to the fields of praise.

And honored among foxes and pheasants by the gay house
Under the new made clouds and happy as the heart was long,
In the sun born over and over,
I ran my heedless ways, *40*
My wishes raced through the house high hay
And nothing I cared, at my sky blue trades, that time allows
In all his tuneful turning so few and such morning songs
Before the children green and golden
Follow him out of grace, *45*

Nothing I cared, in the lamb white days, that time would take me
Up to the swallow thronged loft by the shadow of my hand,
        In the moon that is always rising,
            Nor that riding to sleep
        I should hear him fly with the high fields *50*
And wake to the farm forever fled from the childless land.
Oh as I was young and easy in the mercy of his means,
            Time held me green and dying
        Though I sang in my chains like the sea.

[1946]

In My Craft or Sullen Art

In my craft or sullen art
Exercised in the still night
When only the moon rages
And the lovers lie abed
With all their griefs in their arms, *5*
I labour by singing light
Not for ambition or bread
Or the strut and trade of charms
On the ivory stages
But for the common wages *10*
Of their most secret heart.

Not for the proud man apart
From the raging moon I write
On these spindrift pages
Nor for the towering dead *15*
With their nightingales and psalms
But for the lovers, their arms
Round the griefs of the ages,
Who pay no praise or wages
Nor heed my craft or art. *20*

[1946]

Do Not Go Gentle Into That Good Night

Do not go gentle into that good night,
Old age should burn and rave at close of day;
Rage, rage against the dying of the light.

Though wise men at their end know dark is right,
Because their words had forked no lightning they *5*
Do not go gentle into that good night.

Good men, the last wave by, crying how bright
Their frail deeds might have danced in a green bay,
Rage, rage against the dying of the light.

Wild men who caught and sang the sun in flight, *10*
And learn, too late, they grieved it on its way,
Do not go gentle into that good night.

Grave men, near death, who see with blinding sight
Blind eyes could blaze like meteors and be gay,
Rage, rage against the dying of the light. *15*

And you, my father, there on the sad height,
Curse, bless, me now with your fierce tears, I pray,
Do not go gentle into that good night.
Rage, rage against the dying of the light.

[1952]

Although **Gwendolyn Brooks** *(1917–2000) was born in Topeka, Kansas, she spent most of her life in Chicago. Her literary aspirations were encouraged by her parents from an early age, leading Brooks to publish widely and to spark correspondences with important African-American writers—including Langston Hughes and James Weldon Johnson—while still in high school. Brooks's first collection,* A Street in Bronzeville *(1945), won many prizes and launched the young poet into national attention. Her next book,* Annie Allen *(1949), won the Pulitzer Prize. Brooks's later work* *abandoned her earlier fondness for traditional forms and techniques in exchange for free verse based on African-American speech patterns. Not only was Brooks the first African American to win the Pulitzer, she was also the first black woman elected to the National Institute of Arts and Letters and the first appointed as Consultant in Poetry to the Library of Congress. Brooks taught at Chicago State University and New York's City College. The State of Illinois made her Poet Laureate from 1968 until her death at age 83.*

Gwendolyn Brooks
The Mother

Abortions will not let you forget.
You remember the children you got that you did not get,
The damp small pulps with a little or with no hair,
The singers and workers that never handled the air.
You will never neglect or beat *5*
Them, or silence or buy with a sweet.
You will never wind up the sucking-thumb
Or scuttle off ghosts that come.
You will never leave them, controlling your luscious sigh,
Return for a snack of them, with gobbling mother-eye. *10*

I have heard in the voices of the wind the voices of my dim killed
    children.
I have contracted. I have eased
My dim dears at the breasts they could never suck.
I have said, Sweets, if I sinned, if I seized
Your luck *15*
And your lives from your unfinished reach,
If I stole your births and your names,
Your straight baby tears and your games,
Your stilted or lovely loves, your tumults, your marriages, aches, and
    your deaths,
If I poisoned the beginnings of your breaths, *20*
Believe that even in my deliberateness I was not deliberate.
Though why should I whine,
Whine that the crime was other than mine?—

Since anyhow you are dead.
Or rather, or instead, 25
You were never made.
But that too, I am afraid,
Is faulty: oh, what shall I say, how is the truth to be said?
You were born, you had body, you died.
It is just that you never giggled or planned or cried. 30

Believe me, I loved you all.
Believe me, I knew you, though faintly, and I loved, I loved you
All.

[1945]

Sadie and Maud

Maud went to college.
Sadie stayed at home.
Sadie scraped life
With a fine-tooth comb.

She didn't leave a tangle in. 5
Her comb found every strand.
Sadie was one of the livingest chits
In all the land.

Sadie bore two babies
Under her maiden name. 10
Maud and Ma and Papa
Nearly died of shame.

When Sadie said her last so-long
Her girls struck out from home.
(Sadie had left as heritage 15
Her fine-tooth comb.)

Maud, who went to college,
Is a thin brown mouse.
She is living all alone
In this old house. 20

[1945]

The Rites for Cousin Vit

Carried her unprotesting out the door.
Kicked back the casket-stand. But it can't hold her,
That stuff and satin aiming to enfold her,
The lid's contrition nor the bolts before.
Oh oh. Too much. Too much. Even now, surmise, 5
She rises in the sunshine. There she goes,
Back to the bars she knew and the repose
In love-rooms and the things in people's eyes.
Too vital and too squeaking. Must emerge.
Even now she does the snake-hips with a hiss, 10
Slops the bad wine across her shantung, talks
Of pregnancy, guitars and bridgework, walks
In parks or alleys, comes haply on the verge
Of happiness, haply hysterics. Is.

[1949]

We Real Cool

The Pool Players.
Seven at the Golden Shovel.

We real cool. We
Left school. We

Lurk late. We
Strike straight. We

Sing sin. We 5
Thin gin. We

Jazz June. We
Die soon.

[1960]

***Charles Causley** (1917–2003) was born in the Cornish market town of Launceston, south of Exeter, England; except for six years of military service, he lived there his entire life. His father returned from World War I a consumptive invalid, dying when the boy was seven years old. From very early in his youth Causley intended to be a writer, beginning a novel at the age of nine. He attended Launceston College, though he dropped out at 15 to begin working. Causley spent seven years as a clerk in a builder's office and later worked for an electrical supply company. In 1940 he joined the Royal Navy. After the war, he returned to his hometown and entered the Peterborough Teacher's Training College, then began teaching at the same grammar school that he had attended as a boy. He would teach in Cornwall for almost 30 years. Causley was made an honorary fellow at the University of Exeter in the 1970s. He won many awards for his poetry, plays, and children's books, including the Queen's Gold Medal for Poetry and the Heywood Hill Literary Prize.*

Charles Causley

At the British War Cemetery, Bayeux

I walked where in their talking graves
And shirts of earth five thousand lay,
When history with ten feasts of fire
Had eaten the red air away.

"I am Christ's boy," I cried. "I bear *5*
In iron hands the bread, the fishes.
I hang with honey and with rose
This tidy wreck of all your wishes.

"On your geometry of sleep
The chestnut and the fir-tree fly, *10*
And lavender and marguerite
Forge with their flowers an English sky.

"Turn now towards the belling town
Your jigsaws of impossible bone,

And rising read your rank of snow 15
Accurate as death upon the stone."

About your easy heads my prayers
I said with syllables of clay.
"What gift," I asked, "shall I bring now
Before I weep and walk away?" 20

Take, they replied, *the oak and laurel.*
Take our fortune of tears and live
Like a spendthrift lover. All we ask
Is the one gift you cannot give.

[1957]

I Am the Great Sun

From a Normandy crucifix of 1632

I am the great sun, but you do not see me,
  I am your husband, but you turn away.
I am the captive, but you do not free me,
  I am the captain you will not obey.

I am the truth, but you will not believe me, 5
  I am the city where you will not stay,
I am your wife, your child, but you will leave me,
  I am that God to whom you will not pray.

I am your counsel, but you do not hear me,
  I am the lover whom you will betray, 10
I am the victor, but you do not cheer me,
  I am the holy dove whom you will slay.

I am your life, but if you will not name me,
Seal up your soul with tears, and never blame me.

[1957]

What Has Happened to Lulu?

What has happened to Lulu, mother?
    What has happened to Lu?
There's nothing in her bed but an old rag doll
    And by its side a shoe.

Why is her window wide, mother, 5
    The curtain flapping free,
And only a circle on the dusty shelf
    Where her money-box used to be?

Why do you turn your head, mother,
    And why do the tear-drops fall? 10
And why do you crumple that note on the fire
    And say it is nothing at all?

I woke to voices late last night,
    I heard an engine roar.
Why do you tell me the things I heard 15
    Were a dream and nothing more?

I heard somebody cry, mother,
    In anger or in pain,
But now I ask you why, mother,
    You say it was a gust of rain. 20

Why do you wander about as though
    You don't know what to do?
What has happened to Lulu, mother?
    What has happened to Lu?

[1970]

***Robert Lowell** (1917–1977) was born into a well-known, upper-class Boston family. His father, a naval officer, was related to the poets James Russell Lowell and Amy Lowell, while his mother traced her roots to the Mayflower. Lowell attended Harvard University and Kenyon College, where he studied under the poet John Crowe Ransom. Lowell married the* *older novelist Jean Stafford and converted to Catholicism. When he was drafted in 1943, Lowell declared himself a conscientious objector. He was promptly arrested and spent a year in prison. Lowell was not yet 30 when his first full-length collection,* Lord Weary's Castle *(1946), won the Pulitzer Prize. He was soon appointed Consultant in Poetry to the Library of Congress. These early accomplishments, however, could not keep Lowell from intense episodes of manic depression. He divorced Stafford in 1948, quickly remarried, and had various love affairs late in his life. His most accomplished books include* Life Studies *(1959) and* For the Union Dead *(1964). Despite his continuing emotional turbulence, Lowell landed a permanent position at Harvard in 1963, which he kept until his death. Lowell died of a heart attack in a New York taxi.*

Robert Lowell

Concord

Ten thousand Fords are idle here in search
Of a tradition. Over these dry sticks—
The Minute Man,° the Irish Catholics,°
The ruined bridge and Walden's° fished-out perch—
The belfry of the Unitarian Church 5
Rings out the hanging Jesus. Crucifix,
How can your whited spindling arms transfix
Mammon's unbridled industry, the lurch
For forms to harness Heraclitus' stream!
This Church is Concord—Concord where Thoreau° 10
Named all the birds without a gun to probe
Through darkness to the painted man and bow:
The death-dance of King Philip° and his scream
Whose echo girdled this imperfect globe.

[1946]

3 *Minute Man*: New England militiamen ready at short notice to fight against the British in the American Revolution. *Irish Catholics*: considered second-class citizens, especially by the British, the Irish immigrants were often blamed for protests such as the one resulting in the Boston Massacre of 1770. 4 *Walden's*: pond near Concord; setting of Thoreau's masterpiece. 10 *Thoreau*: Henry David Thoreau (1817–1862), an American poet and essayist who was born in Concord and in his lifetime was often at odds with American political and commercial life. 13 *King Philip*: The nickname Puritans gave to Metacomet, chief of the Wampanoags in New England. He fought a war against the Puritan settlers in 1675–76 and was killed in its aftermath.

Mr. Edwards and the Spider

I saw the spiders marching through the air,
Swimming from tree to tree that mildewed day
In latter August when the hay
Came creaking to the barn. But where
The wind is westerly, *5*
Where gnarled November makes the spiders fly
Into the apparitions of the sky,
They purpose nothing but their ease and die
Urgently beating east to sunrise and the sea;

What are we in the hands of the great God? *10*
It was in vain you set up thorn and briar
In battle array against the fire
And treason crackling in your blood;
For the wild thorns grow tame
And will do nothing to oppose the flame; *15*
Your lacerations tell the losing game
You play against a sickness past your cure.
How will the hands be strong? How will the heart endure?

A very little thing, a little worm,
Or hourglass-blazoned spider, it is said, *20*
Can kill a tiger. Will the dead
Hold up his mirror and affirm
To the four winds the smell
And flash of his authority? It's well
If God who holds you to the pit of hell, *25*
Much as one holds a spider, will destroy,
Baffle and dissipate your soul. As a small boy

On Windsor Marsh, I saw the spider die
When thrown into the bowels of fierce fire:
There's no long struggle, no desire *30*
To get up on its feet and fly—
It stretches out its feet
And dies. This is the sinner's last retreat;

Yes, and no strength exerted on the heat
Then sinews the abolished will, when sick 35
And full of burning, it will whistle on a brick.

But who can plumb the sinking of that soul?
Josiah Hawley, picture yourself cast
Into a brick-kiln where the blast
Fans your quick vitals to a coal— 40
If measured by a glass,
How long would it seem burning! Let there pass
A minute, ten, ten trillion; but the blaze
Is infinite, eternal: this is death,
To die and know it. This is the Black Widow, death. 45

[1946]

Skunk Hour

[for Elizabeth Bishop]

Nautilus Island's° hermit
heiress still lives through winter in her Spartan cottage;
her sheep still graze above the sea.
Her son's a bishop. Her farmer
is first selectman° in our village; 5
she's in her dotage.

Thirsting for
the hierarchic privacy
of Queen Victoria's century,
she buys up all 10
the eyesores facing her shore,
and lets them fall.

The season's ill—
we've lost our summer millionaire,
who seemed to leap from an L.L. Bean° 15
catalogue. His nine-knot yawl
was auctioned off to lobstermen.
A red fox stain covers Blue Hill.

1 *Nautilus Island*: an island near Castine, Maine, where Lowell spent many summers. 5 *selectman*: an elected town official in New England parlance. 15 *L.L. Bean*: a business in Freeport, Maine, that specializes in outdoor clothing and equipment.

And now our fairy
decorator brightens his shop for fall; 20
his fishnet's filled with orange cork,
orange, his cobbler's bench and awl;
there is no money in his work,
he'd rather marry.

One dark night, 25
my Tudor Ford climbed the hill's skull;
I watched for love-cars. Lights turned down,
they lay together, hull to hull,
where the graveyard shelves on the town. . . .
My mind's not right. 30

A car radio bleats,
"Love, O careless Love. . . ."° I hear
my ill-spirit sob in each blood cell,
as if my hand were at its throat. . . .
I myself am hell;° 35
nobody's here—

only skunks, that search
in the moonlight for a bite to eat.
They march on their soles up Main Street:
white stripes, moonstruck eyes' red fire 40
under the chalk-dry and spar spire
of the Trinitarian Church.

I stand on top
of our back steps and breathe the rich air—
a mother skunk with her column of kittens swills the garbage 45
pail.
She jabs her wedge-head in a cup
of sour cream, drops her ostrich tail,
and will not scare.

[1959]

25–36 *"One dark night . . . nobody's here—"*: Lowell said that he had St. John of the Cross's "Dark Night of the Soul" in mind when he wrote these lines. **32** *"Love, O Careless Love . . ."* a line from a folk song about seduction, murder, and suicide. **35** *I myself am hell*: Compare Milton's *Paradise Lost* (iv. 75), where Satan says, "which way I fly is hell; myself am hell."

For the Union Dead

*"Relinquunt Omnia Servare Rem Publicam."**

The old South Boston Aquarium° stands
in a Sahara of snow now. Its broken windows are boarded.
The bronze weathervane cod has lost half its scales.
The airy tanks are dry.

Once my nose crawled like a snail on the glass; *5*
my hand tingled
to burst the bubbles
drifting from the noses of the cowed, compliant fish.

My hand draws back. I often sigh still
for the dark downward and vegetating kingdom *10*
of the fish and reptile. One morning last March,
I pressed against the new barbed and galvanized

fence on the Boston Common. Behind their cage,
yellow dinosaur steamshovels were grunting
as they cropped up tons of mush and grass *15*
to gouge their underworld garage.

Parking spaces luxuriate like civic
sandpiles in the heart of Boston.
A girdle of orange, Puritan-pumpkin colored girders
braces the tingling Statehouse, *20*

shaking over the excavations, as it faces Colonel Shaw
and his bell-cheeked Negro infantry
on St. Gaudens' shaking Civil War relief,
propped by a plank splint against the garage's earthquake.

Two months after marching through Boston, *25*
half the regiment was dead;
at the dedication,
William James could almost hear the bronze Negroes breathe.

Their monument sticks like a fishbone
in the city's throat. *30*

*Latin for "They gave up everything to serve the Republic." Lowell takes this quote from the inscription on a monument to the Massachusetts 54th Regiment (the first all-black Union regiment in the Civil War) and its commander, Robert Gould Shaw (1837–1863). The bronze relief was made by the Irish American sculptor, Augustus Saint-Gaudens (1848–1907), and it stands in Boston Common. Lowell has altered the inscription slightly, from the singular "he" to the plural "they," meaning the whole regiment.

1 *South Boston Aquarium*: The poem was written during the reconstruction of the aquarium, which Lowell had known in childhood.

Its Colonel is as lean
as a compass-needle.

He has an angry wrenlike vigilance,
a greyhound's gentle tautness;
he seems to wince at pleasure, *35*
and suffocate for privacy.

He is out of bounds now. He rejoices in man's lovely,
peculiar power to choose life and die—
when he leads his black soldiers to death,
he cannot bend his back. *40*

On a thousand small town New England greens,
the old white churches hold their air
of sparse, sincere rebellion; frayed flags
quilt the graveyards of the Grand Army of the Republic.

The stone statues of the abstract Union Soldier *45*
grow slimmer and younger each year—
wasp-wasted, they doze over muskets
and muse through their sideburns . . .

Shaw's father wanted no monument
except the ditch, *50*
where his son's body was thrown
and lost with his "niggers."

The ditch is nearer.
There are no statues for the last war here;
on Boylston Street, a commercial photograph *55*
shows Hiroshima boiling

over a Mosler Safe, the "Rock of Ages"
that survived the blast. Space is nearer.
When I crouch to my television set,
the drained faces of Negro school-children rise like balloons. *60*

Colonel Shaw
is riding on his bubble,
he waits
for the blessed break.

The Aquarium is gone. Everywhere, *65*
giant finned cars nose forward like fish;
a savage servility
slides by on grease.

[1964]

Born in New York City, ***Richard Wilbur*** *(b. 1921) spent his childhood in what was then the country town of North Caldwell, New Jersey. His father was a painter who produced magazine covers and portraiture. Wilbur graduated from Amherst College, and soon married Mary Charlotte Hayes Ward. He enlisted in the army the following year and saw active duty in World War II, mostly serving as a cryptographer. Wilbur earned his MA at Harvard after the war and published his first collection,* The Beautiful Changes, *in 1947. He taught at various colleges and universities for the next four decades. Considered the most accomplished English-language translator of Molière and Racine, Wilbur also penned the lyrics for Leonard Bernstein's* Candide, *which premiered on Broadway in 1956. He has won nearly all the major poetry awards, including two Pulitzers, a National Book Award, and two Bollingen Prizes. In 1987 Wilbur was named the second United States Poet Laureate. Splitting their time between Key West and Cummington, Massachusetts, he and his wife have been married for more than 60 years.*

Richard Wilbur

The Pardon

My dog lay dead five days without a grave
In the thick of summer, hid in a clump of pine
And a jungle of grass and honeysuckle-vine.
I who had loved him while he kept alive

Went only close enough to where he was *5*
To sniff the heavy honeysuckle-smell
Twined with another odor heavier still
And hear the flies' intolerable buzz.

Well, I was ten and very much afraid.
In my kind world the dead were out of range *10*
And I could not forgive the sad or strange
In beast or man. My father took the spade

And buried him. Last night I saw the grass
Slowly divide (it was the same scene
But now it glowed a fierce and mortal green) *15*
And saw the dog emerging. I confess

I felt afraid again, but still he came
In the carnal sun, clothed in a hymn of flies,
And death was breeding in his lively eyes.
I started in to cry and call his name, *20*

Asking forgiveness of his tongueless head.
. . . I dreamt the past was never past redeeming:
But whether this was false or honest dreaming
I beg death's pardon now. And mourn the dead.

[1950]

Love Calls Us to the Things of This World

The eyes open to a cry of pulleys,
And spirited from sleep, the astounded soul
Hangs for a moment bodiless and simple
As false dawn.
Outside the open window
The morning air is all awash with angels. *5*

Some are in bed-sheets, some are in blouses,
Some are in smocks: but truly there they are.
Now they are rising together in calm swells
Of halcyon feeling, filling whatever they wear
With the deep joy of their impersonal breathing; *10*

Now they are flying in place, conveying
The terrible speed of their omnipresence, moving
And staying like white water; and now of a sudden
They swoon down into so rapt a quiet
That nobody seems to be there.
The soul shrinks *15*

From all that it is about to remember,
From the punctual rape of every blessèd day,
And cries,
"Oh, let there be nothing on earth but laundry,
Nothing but rosy hands in the rising steam
And clear dances done in the sight of heaven." *20*

Yet, as the sun acknowledges
With a warm look the world's hunks and colors,
The soul descends once more in bitter love
To accept the waking body, saying now
In a changed voice as the man yawns and rises, *25*

"Bring them down from their ruddy gallows;
Let there be clean linen for the backs of thieves;
Let lovers go fresh and sweet to be undone,
And the heaviest nuns walk in a pure floating
Of dark habits,
keeping their difficult balance." *30*

[1956]

October Maples, Portland

The leaves, though little time they have to live,
Were never so unfallen as today,
And seem to yield us through a rustled sieve
The very light from which time fell away.

A showered fire we thought forever lost *5*
Redeems the air. Where friends in passing meet,
They parley in the tongues of Pentecost.
Gold ranks of temples flank the dazzled street.

It is a light of maples, and will go;
But not before it washes eye and brain *10*
With such a tincture, such a sanguine glow
As cannot fail to leave a lasting stain.

So Mary's laundered mantle (in the tale
Which, like all pretty tales, may still be true),
Spread on the rosemary-bush, so drenched the pale *15*
Slight blooms in its irradiated hue,

They could not choose but to return in blue.

[1961]

The Writer

In her room at the prow of the house
Where light breaks, and the windows are tossed with linden,
My daughter is writing a story.

I pause in the stairwell, hearing
From her shut door a commotion of typewriter-keys *5*
Like a chain hauled over a gunwale.

Young as she is, the stuff
Of her life is a great cargo, and some of it heavy:
I wish her a lucky passage.

But now it is she who pauses, *10*
As if to reject my thought and its easy figure.
A stillness greatens, in which

The whole house seems to be thinking,
And then she is at it again with a bunched clamor
Of strokes, and again is silent. *15*

I remember the dazed starling
Which was trapped in that very room, two years ago;
How we stole in, lifted a sash

And retreated, not to affright it;
And how for a helpless hour, through the crack of the door, *20*
We watched the sleek, wild, dark

And iridescent creature
Batter against the brilliance, drop like a glove
To the hard floor, or the desk-top.

And wait then, humped and bloody, *25*
For the wits to try it again; and how our spirits
Rose when, suddenly sure,

It lifted off from a chair-back,
Beating a smooth course for the right window
And clearing the sill of the world. *30*

It is always a matter, my darling,
Of life or death, as I had forgotten. I wish
What I wished you before, but harder.

[1976]

***Philip Larkin** (1922–1985) was born and raised in Coventry, England, where his father was City Treasurer. Attending St. John's College, Oxford, he formed an important friendship with Kingsley Amis. Larkin graduated with top honors, and took a job as a librarian in the small town of Wellington in order to clear himself with the wartime Ministry of Labor. There he completed two novels in a short time, as well as* The North Ship *(1946), his first book of poems. He later moved on to work at several university libraries, finally settling at the Brynmor Jones Library in Hull where he remained from 1955 until his death 30 years later. Though Larkin did have relationships with women, he preferred to remain unmarried. He reviewed literature and jazz throughout his career. Suffering from increasing deafness, Larkin published little poetry during the last decade of his life, falling deeper into alcoholism and solitude. In 1984 he turned down the Poet Laureateship. By the time of his death, following surgery for throat cancer, Larkin was one of the most popular poets writing in English.*

Philip Larkin

Poetry of Departures

Sometimes you hear, fifth-hand,
As epitaph:
He chucked up everything
And just cleared off,
And always the voice will sound *5*
Certain you approve
This audacious, purifying,
Elemental move.

And they are right, I think.
We all hate home *10*
And having to be there:
I detest my room,
Its specially-chosen junk,
The good books, the good bed,
And my life, in perfect order: *15*
So to hear it said

He walked out on the whole crowd
Leaves me flushed and stirred,
Like *Then she undid her dress*
Or *Take that you bastard;* 20
Surely I can, if he did?
And that helps me stay
Sober and industrious.
But I'd go today,

Yes, swagger the nut-strewn roads, 25
Crouch in the fo'c'sle
Stubbly with goodness, if
It weren't so artificial,
Such a deliberate step backwards
To create an object: 30
Books; china; a life
Reprehensibly perfect.

[1955]

Days

What are days for?
Days are where we live.
They come, they wake us
Time and time over.
They are to be happy in: 5
Where can we live but days?

Ah, solving that question
Brings the priest and the doctor
In their long coats
Running over the fields. 10

[1964]

Home Is So Sad

Home is so sad. It stays as it was left,
Shaped to the comfort of the last to go
As if to win them back. Instead, bereft
Of anyone to please, it withers so,
Having no heart to put aside the theft 5

And turn again to what it started as,
A joyous shot at how things ought to be,
Long fallen wide. You can see how it was:
Look at the pictures and the cutlery.
The music in the piano stool. That vase. 10

[1964]

Reference Back

That was a pretty one, I heard you call
From the unsatisfactory hall
To the unsatisfactory room where I
Played record after record, idly,
Wasting my time at home, that you 5
Looked so much forward to.

Oliver's *Riverside Blues,*° it was. And now
I shall, I suppose, always remember how
The flock of notes those antique negroes blew
Out of Chicago air into 10
A huge remembering pre-electric horn
The year after I was born
Three decades later made this sudden bridge
From your unsatisfactory age
To my unsatisfactory prime. 15

Truly, though our element is time,
We are not suited to the long perspectives
Open at each instant of our lives.
They link us to our losses: worse,
They show us what we have as it once was, 20

7 *Oliver's* Riverside Blues: a recording by jazz bandleader King Oliver (1855?–1935).

Blindingly undiminished, just as though
By acting differently we could have kept it so.

[1964]

This Be the Verse

They fuck you up, your mum and dad.
    They may not mean to, but they do.
They fill you with the faults they had
    And add some extra, just for you.

But they were fucked up in their turn   *5*
    By fools in old-style hats and coats,
Who half the time were soppy-stern
    And half at one another's throats.

Man hands on misery to man.
    It deepens like a coastal shelf.   *10*
Get out as early as you can,
    And don't have any kids yourself.

[1971]

Born in Ilford, England, **Denise Levertov** *(1923–1997) was raised by an eclectic and culturally diverse family. Her father was a Russian Jew who became an Anglican minister, and her mother had descended from the Welsh mystic Angel Jones of Mold. Levertov and her older sister were homeschooled by their mother. During World War II, Levertov worked as a nurse in London hospitals, and published her first collection of poems,* The Double Image, *at the war's end. Gaining wide recognition for her debut—both at home and abroad—she married the American writer Mitchell Goodman in 1947 and moved with him to the United States. She became a naturalized American citizen in 1955. In her new country Levertov became associated with the Black Mountain Poets, modeling her early style after William Carlos Williams. Her work developed a strong political focus during the 1960s. Levertov taught English at Stanford University. Her late work emphasizes her conversion to Christianity, as well as ruminations on environmental and political issues. Levertov died from lymphoma in Seattle.*

Denise Levertov

The Ache of Marriage

The ache of marriage:

thigh and tongue, beloved,
are heavy with it,
it throbs in the teeth

We look for communion 5
and are turned away, beloved,
each and each

It is leviathan and we
in its belly
looking for joy, some joy 10
not to be known outside it

two by two in the ark of
the ache of it.

[1964]

Hypocrite Women

Hypocrite women, how seldom we speak
of our own doubts, while dubiously
we mother man in his doubt!

And if at Mill Valley perched in the trees
the sweet rain drifting through western air 5
a white sweating bull of a poet told us

our cunts are ugly—why didn't we
admit we have thought so too? (And
what shame? They are not for the eye!)

No, they are dark and wrinkled and hairy, 10
caves of the Moon . . .   And when a
dark humming fills us, a

coldness towards life,
we are too much women to
own to such unwomanliness. *15*

Whorishly with the psychopomp
we play and plead—and say
nothing of this later. And our dreams,

with what frivolity we have pared them
like toenails, clipped them like ends of *20*
split hair.

[1964]

O Taste and See

The world is
not with us enough.
O taste and see

the subway Bible poster said,
meaning **The Lord**, meaning *5*
if anything all that lives
to the imagination's tongue,

grief, mercy, language,
tangerine, weather, to
breathe them, bite, *10*
savor, chew, swallow, transform

into our flesh our
deaths, crossing the street, plum, quince,
living in the orchard and being

hungry, and plucking *15*
the fruit.

[1964]

Our Bodies

Our bodies, still young under
the engraved anxiety of our
faces, and innocently

more expressive than faces:
nipples, navel, and pubic hair 5
make anyway a

sort of face: or taking
the rounded shadows at
breast, buttock, balls,

the plump of my belly, the 10
hollow of your
groin, as a constellation,

how it leans from earth to
dawn in a gesture of
play and 15

wise compassion—
nothing like this
comes to pass
in eyes or wistful
mouths. 20
I have

a line or groove I love
runs down
my body from breastbone
to waist. It speaks of
eagerness, of 25
distance.
Your long back,
the sand color and
how the bones show, say

what sky after sunset
almost white 30
over a deep woods to which

rooks are homing, says.

[1964]

Louis Simpson *(b. 1923) was born in Jamaica, the second son of a lawyer and a Russian Jewish immigrant, who divorced when he was seven years old. Immigrating to America at 17, he enrolled at Columbia University but interrupted his studies to fight in World War II for the U.S. Army. Simpson was awarded the Purple Heart and left the army a sergeant, yet the trauma of war weighed heavily on him as he returned to Columbia. He suffered a nervous breakdown and was briefly hospitalized. The G.I. Bill provided the means for him to travel to France, where he studied at the Sorbonne. Returning to America, he published his first volumes of poetry, and he coedited with Donald Hall and Robert Pack the influential* New Poets of England and America *(1957). In 1959 Simpson accepted a position at the University of California, Berkeley, where he taught until 1967. His collection* At the End of the Open Road *(1963) won the Pulitzer Prize. In 1967 Simpson moved back to the northeast to teach at SUNY Stony Brook, and retired in 1993.*

Louis Simpson

Early in the Morning

Early in the morning
The dark Queen° said,
"The trumpets are warning
There's trouble ahead."
Spent with carousing, 5
With wine-soaked wits,
Antony° drowsing
Whispered, "It's
Too cold a morning
To get out of bed." 10

The army's retreating,
The fleet has fled,
Caesar° is beating
His drums through the dead.
"Antony, horses! 15
We'll get away,
Gather our forces

2 *The dark Queen*: Cleopatra, Egyptian queen. 7 *Antony*: Marc Antony, ruled with Cleopatra until defeated in 31 B.C. 13 *Caesar*: Caesar Augustus, originally Octavian, took the throne from Antony and Cleopatra to become the first Roman emperor.

For another day . . ."
"It's a cold morning,"
Antony said. *20*

Caesar Augustus
Cleared his phlegm.
"Corpses disgust us.
Cover them."
Caesar Augustus *25*
In his time lay
Dying, and just as
Cold as they,
On the cold morning
Of a cold day. *30*

[1955]

The Man Who Married Magdalene*

The man who married Magdalene
Had not forgiven her.
God might pardon every sin . . .
Love is no pardoner.

Her hands were hollow, pale, and blue, *5*
Her mouth like watered wine.
He watched to see if she were true
And waited for a sign.

It was old harlotry, he guessed,
That drained her strength away, *10*
So gladly for the dark she dressed,
So sadly for the day.

Their quarrels made her dull and weak
And soon a man might fit
A penny in the hollow cheek *15*
And never notice it.

*The title refers to Mary Magdalene, a notorious "sinner" in the Bible.

At last, as they exhausted slept,
Death granted the divorce,
And nakedly the woman leapt
Upon that narrow horse. 20

But when he woke and woke alone
He wept and would deny
The loose behavior of the bone
And the immodest thigh.

[1955]

My Father in the Night Commanding No

My father in the night commanding No
Has work to do. Smoke issues from his lips;
  He reads in silence.
The frogs are croaking and the street lamps glow.

And then my mother winds the gramophone; 5
The Bride of Lammermoor° begins to shriek—
  Or reads a story
About a prince, a castle, and a dragon.

The moon is glittering above the hill.
I stand before the gateposts of the King— 10
  So runs the story—
Of Thule,° at midnight when the mice are still.

And I have been in Thule! It has come true—
The journey and the danger of the world,
  All that there is 15
To bear and to enjoy, endure and do.

Landscapes, seascapes . . . where have I been led?
The names of cities—Paris, Venice, Rome—
  Held out their arms.
A feathered god, seductive, went ahead. 20

6 *The Bride of Lammermoor*: the soprano in Donizetti's opera, *Lucia di Lammermoor*, who sings on the recording the mother plays. 12 *Thule*: the northernmost inhabited country in the world according to legend.

Here is my house. Under a red rose tree
A child is swinging; another gravely plays.
    They are not surprised
That I am here; they were expecting me.

And yet my father sits and reads in silence, 25
My mother sheds a tear, the moon is still,
    And the dark wind
Is murmuring that nothing ever happens.

Beyond his jurisdiction as I move
Do I not prove him wrong? And yet, it's true 30
    They will not change
There, on the stage of terror and of love.

The actors in that playhouse always sit
In fixed positions—father, mother, child
    With painted eyes. 35
How sad it is to be a little puppet!

Their heads are wooden. And you once pretended
To understand them! Shake them as you will,
    They cannot speak.
Do what you will, the comedy is ended. 40

Father, why did you work? Why did you weep,
Mother? Was the story so important?
    "*Listen!*" the wind
Said to the children, and they fell asleep.

[1963]

The Unwritten Poem

You will never write the poem about Italy.
What Socrates said about love
is true of poetry—where is it?
Not in beautiful faces and distant scenery
but the one who writes and loves. 5

In your life here, on this street
where the houses from the outside
are all alike, and so are the people.
Inside, the furniture is dreadful—
floc on the walls, and huge color television. *10*

To love and write unrequited
is the poet's fate. Here you'll need
all your ardor and ingenuity.
This is the front and these are the heroes—
a life beginning with "Hi!" and ending with "So long!" *15*

You must rise to the sound of the alarm
and march to catch the 6:20—
watch as they ascend the station platform
and, grasping briefcases, pass beyond your gaze
and hurl themselves into the flames. *20*

[1983]

***Donald Justice** (b. 1925) is not only one of the preeminent living poets of the English language, he is also a composer and visual artist. Justice was born in Miami, where his father worked as a carpenter. Living in the South throughout his childhood, he studied at the University of Miami and the University of North Carolina. Justice married Jean Catherine Ross, a writer, and studied under Yvor Winters at Stanford in the late 1940s. He earned a PhD in 1954 at the University of Iowa, later returning there to teach. Remaining primarily at the Iowa Writers' Workshop for over 25 years, Justice became perhaps the most influential poetry teacher of the last half-century. His students included Mark Strand, Charles Wright, and Jorie Graham. Justice taught also at Syracuse, the University of California, and the University of Florida, Gainesville. He and his wife returned to Iowa City after retirement where he still writes, paints, and composes. Justice won the Pulitzer Prize for his* Selected Poems *(1979).*

Donald Justice

Counting the Mad

This one was put in a jacket,
This one was sent home,
This one was given bread and meat
But would eat none,
And this one cried No No No No *5*
All day long.

This one looked at the window
As though it were a wall,
This one saw things that were not there,
This one things that were, *10*
And this one cried No No No No
All day long.

This one thought himself a bird,
This one a dog,
And this one thought himself a man, *15*
An ordinary man,
And cried and cried No No No No
All day long.

[1960]

On the Death of Friends in Childhood

We shall not ever meet them bearded in heaven,
Nor sunning themselves among the bald of hell;
If anywhere, in the deserted schoolyard at twilight,
Forming a ring, perhaps, or joining hands
In games whose very names we have forgotten. *5*
Come, memory, let us seek them there in the shadows.

[1960]

Men at Forty

Men at forty
Learn to close softly
The doors to rooms they will not be
Coming back to.

At rest on a stair landing, *5*
They feel it moving
Beneath them now like the deck of a ship,
Though the swell is gentle.

And deep in mirrors
They rediscover *10*
The face of the boy as he practices tying
His father's tie there in secret,

And the face of that father,
Still warm with the mystery of lather.
They are more fathers than sons themselves now. *15*
Something is filling them, something

That is like the twilight sound
Of the crickets, immense,
Filling the woods at the foot of the slope
Behind their mortgaged houses. *20*

[1967]

Psalm and Lament

Hialeah, Florida
in memory of my mother (1897–1974)

The clocks are sorry, the clocks are very sad.
One stops, one goes on striking the wrong hours.

And the grass burns terribly in the sun,
The grass turns yellow secretly at the roots.

Now suddenly the yard chairs look empty, the sky looks empty, *5*
The sky looks vast and empty.

Out on Red Road the traffic continues; everything continues.
Nor does memory sleep; it goes on.

Out spring the butterflies of recollection,
And I think that for the first time I understand *10*

The beautiful ordinary light of this patio
And even perhaps the dark rich earth of a heart.

(The bedclothes, they say, had been pulled down.
I will not describe it. I do not want to describe it.

No, but the sheets were drenched and twisted. *15*
They were the very handkerchiefs of grief.)

Let summer come now with its schoolboy trumpets and fountains.
But the years are gone, the years are finally over.

And there is only
This long desolation of flower-bordered sidewalks *20*

That runs to the corner, turns, and goes on,
That disappears and goes on

Into the black oblivion of a neighborhood and a world
Without billboards or yesterdays.

Sometimes a sad moon comes and waters the roof tiles. *25*
But the years are gone. There are no more years.

[1987]

Born in Newark, New Jersey, **Allen Ginsberg** *(1926–1997) was the son of Louis Ginsberg, a poet and high school teacher. Ginsberg studied at Columbia University, and set out for San Francisco in 1954. He soon wrote the long poem* Howl *(1956), which was published by Lawrence Ferlinghetti's City Lights Books, with an introduction by William Carlos*

Williams. U.S. Customs seized a second printing, and Ferlinghetti was arrested for distributing obscene material. After testimonials of support from various American writers, Ginsberg and Ferlinghetti were eventually acquitted, and the Beat movement was launched into international celebrity. Ginsberg experimented widely with drugs, which he often used as a compositional tool. He declared himself a Buddhist in 1972, and began a relationship with the Naropa Institute in Boulder, Colorado, where he and poet Anne Waldman cofounded the Jack Kerouac School of Disembodied Poetics. The Fall of America *(1973) earned the National Book Award. Increasingly becoming a mainstream icon of popular culture, Ginsberg reportedly sold his papers to Stanford University for over a million dollars. He died in New York City of liver cancer.*

Allen Ginsberg

from America

America I've given you all and now I'm nothing.
America two dollars and twentyseven cents January 17, 1956.
I can't stand my own mind.
America when will we end the human war?
Go fuck yourself with your atom bomb. *5*
I don't feel good don't bother me.
I won't write my poem till I'm in my right mind.
America when will you be angelic?
When will you take off your clothes?
When will you look at yourself through the grave? *10*
When will you be worthy of your million Trotskyites?
America why are your libraries full of tears?
America when will you send your eggs to India?
I'm sick of your insane demands.
When can I go into the supermarket and buy what I need *15*
    with my good looks?
America after all it is you and I who are perfect not the next world.
Your machinery is too much for me.
You made me want to be a saint.
There must be some other way to settle this argument.
Burroughs is in Tangiers I don't think he'll come back it's sinister. *20*
Are you being sinister or is this some form of practical joke?

I'm trying to come to the point.
I refuse to give up my obsession.
America stop pushing I know what I'm doing.
America the plum blossoms are falling. *25*
I haven't read the newspapers for months, everyday somebody goes
    on trial for murder.
America I feel sentimental about the Wobblies.
America I used to be a communist when I was a kid I'm not sorry.
I smoke marijuana every chance I get.
I sit in my house for days on end and stare at the roses in the *30*
    closet.
When I go to Chinatown I get drunk and never get laid.
My mind is made up there's going to be trouble.
You should have seen me reading Marx.
My psychoanalyst thinks I'm perfectly right.
I won't say the Lord's Prayer. *35*
I have mystical visions and cosmic vibrations.
America I still haven't told you what you did to Uncle Max after
    he came over from Russia.
I'm addressing you.
Are you going to let your emotional life be run by Time Magazine?
I'm obsessed by Time Magazine. *40*
I read it every week.
Its cover stares at me every time I slink past the corner candystore.
I read it in the basement of the Berkeley Public Library.
It's always telling me about responsibility. Businessmen are serious.
    Movie producers are serious. Everybody's serious but me. *45*
It occurs to me that I am America.
I am talking to myself again.

Asia is rising against me.
I haven't got a chinaman's chance.
I'd better consider my national resources. *50*
My national resources consist of two joints of marijuana millions of
    genitals an unpublishable private literature that jetplanes 1400
    miles an hour and twentyfive-thousand mental institutions.
I say nothing about my prisons nor the millions of underprivileged
    who live in my flowerpots under the light of five hundred suns.
I have abolished the whorehouses of France, Tangiers is the next
    to go.
My ambition is to be President despite the fact that I'm a Catholic.

America how can I write a holy litany in your silly mood? *55*
I will continue like Henry Ford my strophes are as individual as his automobiles more so they're all different sexes.
America I will sell you strophes $2500 apiece $500 down on your old strophe
America free Tom Mooney
America save the Spanish Loyalists
America Sacco & Vanzetti must not die *60*
America I am the Scottsboro boys.
America when I was seven momma took me to Communist Cell meetings they sold us garbanzos a handful per ticket a ticket costs a nickel and the speeches were free everybody was angelic and sentimental about the workers it was all so sincere you have no idea what a good thing the party was in 1835 Scott Nearing was a grand old man a real mensch Mother Bloor the Silk-strikers' Ewig Weibliche made me cry I once saw the Yiddish orator Israel Amter plain. Everybody must have been a spy.
America you don't really want to go to war.
America it's them bad Russians.
Them Russians them Russians and them Chinamen. And them Russians. *65*
The Russia want to eat us alive. The Russia's power mad. She wants to take our cars from out our garages.
Her wants to grab Chicago. Her needs a Red *Reader's Digest*. Her want our auto plants in Siberia. Him big bureaucracy running our fillingstations.
That no good. Ugh. Him make Indians learn read. Him need big black niggers. Hah. Her make us all work sixteen hours a day. Help.
America this is quite serious.
America this is the impression I get from looking in the television set. *70*
America is this correct?
I'd better get right down to the job.
It's true I don't want to join the Army or turn lathes in precision parts factories, I'm nearsighted and psychopathic anyway.
America I'm putting my queer shoulder to the wheel.

[1956]

from Howl

For Carl Solomon

I

I saw the best minds of my generation destroyed by madness,
starving hysterical naked,
dragging themselves through the negro streets at dawn looking for
an angry fix,
angelheaded hipsters burning for the ancient heavenly connection
to the starry dynamo in the machinery of night,
who poverty and tatters and hollow-eyed and high sat up smoking
in the supernatural darkness of cold-water flats floating across
the tops of cities contemplating jazz,
who bared their brains to Heaven under the El and saw Moham- *5*
medan angels staggering on tenement roofs illuminated,
who passed through universities with radiant cool eyes hallucinat-
ing Arkansas and Blake-light tragedy among the scholars of war,
who were expelled from the academies for crazy & publishing
obscene odes on the windows of the skull,
who cowered in unshaven rooms in underwear, burning their money
in wastebaskets and listening to the Terror through the wall,
who got busted in their pubic beards returning through Laredo
with a belt of marijuana for New York,
who ate fire in paint hotels or drank turpentine in Paradise Alley, *10*
death, or purgatoried their torsos night after night
with dreams, with drugs, with waking nightmares, alcohol and
cock and endless balls,
incomparable blind streets of shuddering cloud and lightning in
the mind leaping toward poles of Canada & Paterson, illuminating all the motionless world of Time between,
Peyote solidities of halls, backyard green tree cemetery dawns,
wine drunkenness over the rooftops, storefront boroughs of
teahead joyride neon blinking traffic light, sun and moon and
tree vibrations in the roaring winter dusks of Brooklyn, ashcan
rantings and kind king light of mind,
who chained themselves to subways for the endless ride from
Battery to holy Bronx on benzedrine until the noise of wheels
and children brought them down shuddering mouth-wracked
and battered bleak of brain all drained of brilliance in the
drear light of Zoo,

who sank all night in submarine light of Bickford's floated out *15*
and sat through the stale beer afternoon in desolate Fugazzi's,
listening to the crack of doom on the hydrogen jukebox,
who talked continuously seventy hours from park to pad to bar to
Bellevue to museum to the Brooklyn Bridge,
a lost battalion of platonic conversationalists jumping down the
stoops off fire escapes off windowsills off Empire State out of
the moon,
yacketayakking screaming vomiting whispering facts and memories
and anecdotes and eyeball kicks and shocks of hospitals and
jails and wars,
whole intellects disgorged in total recall for seven days and nights
with brilliant eyes, meat for the Synagogue cast on the pavement,
who vanished into nowhere Zen New Jersey leaving a trail of *20*
ambiguous picture postcards of Atlantic City Hall,
suffering Eastern sweats and Tangerian bone-grinding and
migraines of China under junk-withdrawal in Newark's bleak
furnished room,
who wandered around and around at midnight in the railroad yard
wondering where to go, and went, leaving no broken hearts,
who lit cigarettes in boxcars boxcars boxcars racketing through
snow toward lonesome farms in grandfather night,
who studied Plotinus Poe St. John of the Cross telepathy and bop
kabbalah because the cosmos instinctively vibrated at their feet
in Kansas,
who loned it through the streets of Idaho seeking visionary indian *25*
angels who were visionary indian angels,
who thought they were only mad when Baltimore gleamed in
supernatural ecstasy,
who jumped in limousines with the Chinaman of Oklahoma on the
impulse of winter midnight streetlight smalltown rain,
who lounged hungry and lonesome through Houston seeking jazz
or sex or soup, and followed the brilliant Spaniard to converse
about America and Eternity, a hopeless task, and so took ship
to Africa,
who disappeared into the volcanoes of Mexico leaving behind
nothing but the shadow of dungarees and the lava and ash
of poetry scattered in fireplace Chicago,
who reappeared on the West Coast investigating the FBI in beards *30*
and shorts with big pacifist eyes sexy in their dark skin passing
out incomprehensible leaflets,

who burned cigarette holes in their arms protesting the narcotic
 tobacco haze of Capitalism,
who distributed Supercommunist pamphlets in Union Square
 weeping and undressing while the sirens of Los Alamos wailed
 them down, and wailed down Wall, and the Staten Island ferry
 also wailed,
who broke down crying in white gymnasiums naked and trembling
 before the machinery of other skeletons,
who bit detectives in the neck and shrieked with delight in police-
 cars for committing no crime but their own wild cooking
 pederasty and intoxication,
who howled on their knees in the subway and were dragged off *35*
 the roof waving genitals and manuscripts,
who let themselves be fucked in the ass by saintly motorcyclists,
 and screamed with joy,
who blew and were blown by those human seraphim, the sailors,
 caresses of Atlantic and Caribbean love,
who balled in the morning in the evenings in rosegardens and the
 grass of public parks and cemeteries scattering their semen
 freely to whomever come who may,
who hiccuped endlessly trying to giggle but wound up with a sob
 behind a partition in a Turkish Bath when the blond & naked
 angel came to pierce them with a sword,
who lost their loveboys to the three old shrews of fate the one eyed *40*
 shrew of the heterosexual dollar the one eyed shrew that winks
 out of the womb and the one eyed shrew that does nothing but
 sit on her ass and snip the intellectual golden threads of the
 craftsman's loom,
who copulated ecstatic and insatiate with a bottle of beer a sweetheart a package of cigarettes a candle and fell off the bed, and
 continued along the floor and down the hall and ended fainting
 on the wall with a vision of ultimate cunt and come eluding the
 last gyzym of consciousness,
who sweetened the snatches of a million girls trembling in the
 sunset, and were red eyed in the morning but prepared to
 sweeten the snatch of the sunrise, flashing buttocks under
 barns and naked in the lake,
who went out whoring through Colorado in myriad stolen night-
 cars, N.C., secret hero of these poems, cocksman and Adonis of
 Denver—joy to the memory of his innumerable lays of girls in
 empty lots & diner backyards, moviehouses' rickety rows, on

mountaintops in caves or with gaunt waitresses in familiar roadside lonely petticoat upliftings & especially secret gas-station solipsisms of johns, & hometown alleys too,

who faded out in vast sordid movies, were shifted in dreams, woke on a sudden Manhattan, and picked themselves up out of basements hung-over with heartless Tokay and horrors of Third Avenue iron dreams & stumbled to unemployment offices,

who walked all night with their shoes full of blood on the snowbank docks waiting for a door in the East River to open to a room full of steam-heat and opium, *45*

who created great suicidal dramas on the apartment cliff-banks of the Hudson under the wartime blue floodlight of the moon & their heads shall be crowned with laurel in oblivion,

who ate the lamb stew of the imagination or digested the crab at the muddy bottom of the rivers of Bowery,

who wept at the romance of the streets with their pushcarts full of onions and bad music,

who sat in boxes breathing in the darkness under the bridge, and rose up to build harpsichords in their lofts,

who coughed on the sixth floor of Harlem crowned with flame under the tubercular sky surrounded by orange crates of theology, *50*

who scribbled all night rocking and rolling over lofty incantations which in the yellow morning were stanzas of gibberish,

who cooked rotten animals lung heart feet tail borsht & tortillas dreaming of the pure vegetable kingdom,

who plunged themselves under meat trucks looking for an egg,

who threw their watches off the roof to cast their ballot for Eternity outside of Time, & alarm clocks fell on their heads every day for the next decade,

who cut their wrists three times successively unsuccessfully, gave up and were forced to open antique stores where they thought they were growing old and cried, *55*

who were burned alive in their innocent flannel suits on Madison Avenue amid blasts of leaden verse & the tanked-up clatter of the iron regiments of fashion & the nitroglycerine shrieks of the fairies of advertising & the mustard gas of sinister intelligent editors, or were run down by the drunken taxicabs of Absolute Reality,

who jumped off the Brooklyn Bridge this actually happened and walked away unknown and forgotten into the ghostly daze of Chinatown soup alleyways & firetrucks, not even one free beer, who sang out of their windows in despair, fell out of the subway window, jumped in the filthy Passaic, leaped on negroes, cried all over the street, danced on broken wineglasses barefoot smashed phonograph records of nostalgic European 1930s German jazz finished the whiskey and threw up groaning into the bloody toilet, moans in their ears and the blast of colossal steamwhistles,

who barreled down the highways of the past journeying to each other's hotrod-Golgotha jail-solitude watch or Birmingham jazz incarnation,

who drove crosscountry seventytwo hours to find out if I had a vision or you had a vision or he had a vision to find out Eternity, *60*

who journeyed to Denver, who died in Denver, who came back to Denver & waited in vain, who watched over Denver & brooded & loned in Denver and finally went away to find out the Time, & now Denver is lonesome for her heroes,

who fell on their knees in hopeless cathedrals praying for each other's salvation and light and breasts, until the soul illuminated its hair for a second,

who crashed through their minds in jail waiting for impossible criminals with golden heads and the charm of reality in their hearts who sang sweet blues to Alcatraz,

who retired to Mexico to cultivate a habit, or Rocky Mount to tender Buddha or Tangiers to boys or Southern Pacific to the black locomotive or Harvard to Narcissus to Woodlawn to the daisychain or grave,

who demanded sanity trials accusing the radio of hypnotism & were left with their insanity & their hands & a hung jury, *65*

who threw potato salad at CCNY lecturers on Dadaism and subsequently presented themselves on the granite steps of the madhouse with shaven heads and harlequin speech of suicide, demanding instantaneous lobotomy,

and who were given instead the concrete void of insulin Metrazol electricity hydrotherapy psychotherapy occupational therapy pingpong & amnesia,

who in humorless protest overturned only one symbolic pingpong table, resting briefly in catatonia,

returning years later truly bald except for a wig of blood, and tears and fingers, to the visible madman doom of the wards of the madtowns of the East,

Pilgrim State's Rockland's and Greystone's foetid halls, bickering with the echoes of the soul, rocking and rolling in the midnight *70*

solitude-bench dolmen-realms of love, dream of life a nightmare, bodies turned to stone as heavy as the moon,
with mother finally ******, and the last fantastic book flung out of the tenement window, and the last door closed at 4 A.M. and the last telephone slammed at the wall in reply and the last furnished room emptied down to the last piece of mental furniture, a yellow paper rose twisted on a wire hanger in the closet, and even that imaginary, nothing but a hopeful little bit of hallucination—
ah, Carl, while you are not safe I am not safe, and now you're really in the total animal soup of time—
and who therefore ran through the icy streets obsessed with a sudden flash of the alchemy of the use of the ellipsis catalogue a variable measure and the vibrating plane,
who dreamt and made incarnate gaps in Time & Space through images juxtaposed, and trapped the archangel of the soul between 2 visual images and joined the elemental verbs and set the noun and dash of consciousness together jumping with sensation of Pater Omnipotens Aeterna Deus
to recreate the syntax and measure of poor human prose and stand before you speechless and intelligent and shaking with shame, rejected yet confessing out the soul to conform to the rhythm of thought in his naked and endless head, *75*
the madman bum and angel beat in Time, unknown, yet putting down here what might be left to say in time come after death,
and rose reincarnate in the ghostly clothes of jazz in the goldhorn shadow of the band and blew the suffering of America's naked mind for love into an eli eli lamma lamma sabacthani saxophone cry that shivered the cities down to the last radio
with the absolute heart of the poem of life butchered out of their own bodies good to eat a thousand years.

[1956]

James Wright *(1927–1980) was born in the steelworks town of Martins Ferry, Ohio. His father worked in a nearby glass factory. Wright's tough, blue-collar background—fraught with economic hardship—would inform his poetry throughout his life. Wright joined the army after high school to serve with the occupation forces in Japan. He later attended Kenyon College, and married his high school classmate, Liberty Kardules. He did* *graduate work at the University of Washington under Theodore Roethke and Stanley Kunitz. W. H. Auden chose Wright's first collection,* The Green Wall *(1957), for the Yale Series of Younger Poets Prize. He landed a teaching job at the University of Minnesota, though was denied tenure due to his problems with alcohol. Wright and Liberty divorced in 1962, and he soon remarried. Finally settling in New York in 1966, Wright accepted a position at Hunter College, where he would teach for the rest of his life. In 1971 his* Collected Poems *won the Pulitzer Prize. After a battle with cancer, the 52-year-old poet died in the Bronx.*

James Wright

Saint Judas

When I went out to kill myself, I caught
A pack of hoodlums beating up a man.
Running to spare his suffering, I forgot
My name, my number, how my day began,
How soldiers milled around the garden stone *5*
And sang amusing songs; how all that day
Their javelins measured crowds; how I alone
Bargained the proper coins, and slipped away.

Banished from heaven, I found this victim beaten,
Stripped, kneed, and left to cry. Dropping my rope *10*
Aside, I ran, ignored the uniforms:
Then I remembered bread my flesh had eaten,
The kiss that ate my flesh. Flayed without hope,
I held the man for nothing in my arms.

[1959]

Autumn Begins in Martins Ferry, Ohio

In the Shreve High football stadium,
I think of Polacks nursing long beers in Tiltonsville,
And gray faces of Negroes in the blast furnace at Benwood,

And the ruptured night watchman of Wheeling Steel,
Dreaming of heroes. *5*

All the proud fathers are ashamed to go home.
Their women cluck like starved pullets,
Dying for love.

Therefore,
Their sons grow suicidally beautiful *10*
At the beginning of October,
And gallop terribly against each other's bodies.

[1963]

A Blessing

Just off the highway to Rochester, Minnesota,
Twilight bounds softly forth on the grass.
And the eyes of those two Indian ponies
Darken with kindness.
They have come gladly out of the willows *5*
To welcome my friend and me.
We step over the barbed wire into the pasture
Where they have been grazing all day, alone.
They ripple tensely, they can hardly contain their happiness
That we have come. *10*
They bow shyly as wet swans. They love each other.
There is no loneliness like theirs.
At home once more,
They begin munching the young tufts of spring in the darkness.
I would like to hold the slenderer one in my arms, *15*
For she has walked over to me
And nuzzled my left hand.
She is black and white,
Her mane falls wild on her forehead,
And the light breeze moves me to caress her long ear *20*
That is delicate as the skin over a girl's wrist.
Suddenly I realize
That if I stepped out of my body I would break
Into blossom.

[1963]

Lying in a Hammock at William Duffy's Farm in Pine Island, Minnesota

Over my head, I see the bronze butterfly,
Asleep on the black trunk,
Blowing like a leaf in green shadow.
Down the ravine behind the empty house,
The cowbells follow one another *5*
Into the distances of the afternoon.
To my right,
In a field of sunlight between two pines,
The droppings of last year's horses
Blaze up into golden stones. *10*
I lean back, as the evening darkens and comes on.
A chicken hawk floats over, looking for home.
I have wasted my life.

[1963]

***Anne Sexton** (1928–1974) was born in Newton, Massachusetts. At 19 she eloped with Alfred "Kayo" Sexton II. After giving birth to her first of two daughters, Sexton was diagnosed with postpartum depression and spent the better part of two years hospitalized. She attempted suicide after the birth of her second daughter in 1956. Sexton did not begin to write until she was 29, on the suggestion of her psychotherapist that she use poetry as a form of therapy. She enrolled in a creative writing workshop where she studied with W. D. Snodgrass and Robert Lowell, befriending Maxine Kumin, Sylvia Plath, and George Starbuck. Sexton was a popular performer on college campuses, often touring with a rock band called Her Kind. Her third collection,* Live or Die *(1966), won the Pulitzer Prize. Sexton's many successes, however, couldn't cover up a profoundly troubled personal life. In 1973 she and Kayo divorced. The next year she committed suicide by inhaling carbon monoxide in the garage of her home.*

Anne Sexton

Her Kind

I have gone out, a possessed witch,
haunting the black air, braver at night;
dreaming evil, I have done my hitch
over the plain houses, light by light:
lonely thing, twelve-fingered, out of mind. *5*
A woman like that is not a woman, quite.
I have been her kind.

I have found the warm caves in the woods,
filled them with skillets, carvings, shelves,
closets, silks, innumerable goods; *10*
fixed the suppers for the worms and the elves:
whining, rearranging the disaligned.
A woman like that is misunderstood.
I have been her kind.

I have ridden in your cart, driver, *15*
waved my nude arms at villages going by,
learning the last bright routes, survivor
where your flames still bite my thigh
and my ribs crack where your wheels wind.
A woman like that is not ashamed to die. *20*
I have been her kind.

[1960]

The Abortion

Somebody who should have been born is gone.

Just as the earth puckered its mouth,
each bud puffing out from its knot,
I changed my shoes, and then drove south.

Up past the Blue Mountains, where *5*
Pennsylvania humps on endlessly,
wearing, like a crayoned cat, its green hair,

its roads sunken in like a gray washboard;
where, in truth, the ground cracks evilly,
a dark socket from which the coal has poured, *10*

Somebody who should have been born is gone.

the grass as bristly and stout as chives,
and me wondering when the ground would break,
and me wondering how anything fragile survives;

up in Pennsylvania, I met a little man, *15*
not Rumpelstiltskin, at all, at all . . .
he took the fullness that love began.
Returning north, even the sky grew thin
like a high window looking nowhere.
The road was as flat as a sheet of tin. *20*

Somebody who should have been born is gone.

Yes, woman, such logic will lead
to loss without death. Or say what you meant,
you coward . . . this baby that I bleed.

[1962]

The Truth the Dead Know

For my mother, born March 1902, died March 1959, and my father, born February 1900, died June 1959

Gone, I say and walk from church,
refusing the stiff procession to the grave,
letting the dead ride alone in the hearse.
It is June. I am tired of being brave.

We drive to the Cape. I cultivate *5*
myself where the sun gutters from the sky,
where the sea swings in like an iron gate
and we touch. In another country people die.

My darling, the wind falls in like stones
From the whitehearted water and when we touch *10*
we enter touch entirely. No one's alone.
Men kill for this, or for as much.

And what of the dead? They lie without shoes
in their stone boats. They are more like stone
than the sea would be if it stopped. They refuse *15*
to be blessed, throat, eye and knucklebone.

[1962]

Wanting to Die

Since you ask, most days I cannot remember.
I walk in my clothing, unmarked by that voyage.
Then the almost unnameable lust returns.

Even then I have nothing against life.
I know well the grass blades you mention, *5*
the furniture you have placed under the sun.

But suicides have a special language.
Like carpenters they want to know *which tools.*
They never ask *why build.*

Twice I have so simply declared myself, *10*
have possessed the enemy, eaten the enemy,
have taken on his craft, his magic.

In this way, heavy and thoughtful,
warmer than oil or water,
I have rested, drooling at the mouth-hole. *15*

I did not think of my body at needle point.
Even the cornea and the leftover urine were gone.
Suicides have already betrayed the body.

Still-born, they don't always die,
but dazzled, they can't forget a drug so sweet *20*
that even children would look on and smile.

To thrust all that life under your tongue!—
that, all by itself, becomes a passion.
Death's a sad bone; bruised, you'd say,

and yet she waits for me, year after year, *25*
to so delicately undo an old wound,
to empty my breath from its bad prison.

Balanced there, suicides sometimes meet,
raging at the fruit, a pumped-up moon,
leaving the bread they mistook for a kiss, 30

leaving the page of the book carelessly open,
something unsaid, the phone off the hook
and the love, whatever it was, an infection.

[1966]

***Adrienne Rich** (b. 1929), born in Baltimore, had a Jewish father who was a doctor and professor and a Southern Protestant mother who had once been a serious pianist. At 22 years of age, she graduated from Radcliffe College and won the prestigious Yale Series of Younger Poets Award for her first book,* A Change of World *(1951), selected by W. H. Auden. Rich married Alfred Conrad, a Harvard economics professor, and gave birth to three children before the age of 30. After moving the family to New York in 1966 for various teaching opportunities, Rich became heavily involved in war protests and other social issues, which resulted in clear changes in the voice and focus of her writing. Her husband committed suicide in 1970. Rich has taught at many institutions, including Columbia University, City College of New York, Cornell University, and Stanford University.* Diving into the Wreck *(1973) won the National Book Award. Rich has become an important figure for feminist causes and gay rights.*

Adrienne Rich

Aunt Jennifer's Tigers

Aunt Jennifer's tigers prance across a screen,
Bright topaz denizens of a world of green.
They do not fear the men beneath the tree;
They pace in sleek chivalric certainty.

Aunt Jennifer's fingers fluttering through her wool 5
Find even the ivory needle hard to pull.

The massive weight of Uncle's wedding band
Sits heavily upon Aunt Jennifer's hand.

When Aunt is dead, her terrified hands will lie
Still ringed with ordeals she was mastered by. *10*
The tigers in the panel that she made
Will go on prancing, proud and unafraid.

[1951]

The Diamond Cutters

However legendary,
The stone is still a stone,
Though it had once resisted
The weight of Africa,
The hammer-blows of time *5*
That wear to bits of rubble
The mountain and the pebble—
But not this coldest one.

Now, you intelligence
So late dredged up from dark *10*
Upon whose smoky walls
Bison took fumbling form
Or flint was edged on flint—
Now, careful arriviste,
Delineate at will *15*
Incisions in the ice.

Be serious, because
The stone may have contempt
For too-familiar hands,
And because all you do *20*
Loses or gains by this:
Respect the adversary,
Meet it with tools refined,
And thereby set your price.

Be hard of heart, because *25*
The stone must leave your hand.

Although you liberate
Pure and expensive fires
Fit to enamor Shebas,
Keep your desire apart. *30*
Love only what you do,
And not what you have done.

Be proud, when you have set
The final spoke of flame
In that prismatic wheel, *35*
And nothing's left this day
Except to see the sun
Shine on the false and the true,
And know that Africa
Will yield you more to do. *40*

[1955]

Living in Sin

She had thought the studio would keep itself;
no dust upon the furniture of love.
Half heresy, to wish the taps less vocal,
the panes relieved of grime. A plate of pears,
a piano with a Persian shawl, a cat *5*
stalking the picturesque amusing mouse
had risen at his urging.
Not that at five each separate stair would writhe
under the milkman's tramp; that morning light
so coldly would delineate the scraps *10*
of last night's cheese and three sepulchral bottles;
that on the kitchen shelf among the saucers
a pair of beetle-eyes would fix her own—
envoy from some village in the moldings . . .
Meanwhile, he, with a yawn, *15*
sounded a dozen notes upon the keyboard,
declared it out of tune, shrugged at the mirror,
rubbed at his beard, went out for cigarettes;
while she, jeered by the minor demons,

pulled back the sheets and made the bed and found 20
a towel to dust the table-top,
and let the coffee-pot boil over on the stove.
By evening she was back in love again,
though not so wholly but throughout the night
she woke sometimes to feel the daylight coming 25
like a relentless milkman up the stairs.

[1955]

Rape

There is a cop who is both prowler and father:
he comes from your block, grew up with your brothers,
had certain ideals.
You hardly know him in his boots and silver badge,
on horseback, one hand touching his gun. 5

You hardly know him but you have to get to know him:
he has access to machinery that could kill you.
He and his stallion clop like warlords among the trash,
his ideals stand in the air, a frozen cloud
from between his unsmiling lips. 10

And so, when the time comes, you have to turn to him,
the maniac's sperm still greasing your thighs,
your mind whirling like crazy. You have to confess
to him, you are guilty of the crime
of having been forced. 15

And you see his blue eyes, the blue eyes of all the family
whom you used to know, grow narrow and glisten,
his hand types out the details
and he wants them all
but the hysteria in your voice pleases him best. 20

You hardly know him but now he thinks he knows you:
he has taken down your worst moment
on a machine and filed it in a file.
He knows, or thinks he knows, how much you imagined;
he knows, or thinks he knows, what you secretly wanted. 25

He has access to machinery that could get you put away;
and if, in the sickening light of the precinct,
and if, in the sickening light of the precinct,
your details sound like a portrait of your confessor,
will you swallow, will you deny them, will you lie your way home? 30

[1973]

***Ted Hughes** (1930–1998) was born in West Yorkshire. When Hughes was 7, the family moved south to a coal mining town, where his parents bought a news and tobacco shop. Hughes won a scholarship to Cambridge, which he delayed for two years in order to serve in the Royal Air Force. At Cambridge he met and married Sylvia Plath. Hughes published his first book,* The Hawk in the Rain *(1957), to much critical acclaim, and moved with Plath to America to teach at the University of Massachusetts in Amherst. In 1959 the couple returned to England, though the relationship soon broke up, reportedly due to Hughes's infidelities. After seven years of marriage, Plath committed suicide by inhaling gas from the kitchen oven. The woman for whom Hughes left Plath, Assia Wevill, killed herself and their daughter in the same manner six years later. Hughes suffered much criticism for his posthumous editing of Plath's work, omitting or changing material that presented him in a negative light. In 1970 Hughes remarried, to Carol Orchard. He was made Poet Laureate of England in 1984.*

Ted Hughes

The Thought-Fox

I imagine this midnight moment's forest:
Something else is alive
Beside the clock's loneliness
And this blank page where my fingers move.

Through the window I see no star: 5
Something more near
Though deeper within darkness
Is entering the loneliness:

Cold, delicately as the dark snow
A fox's nose touches twig, leaf; 10
Two eyes serve a movement, that now
And again now, and now, and now

Sets neat prints into the snow
Between trees, and warily a lame
Shadow lags by stump and in hollow 15
Of a body that is bold to come

Across clearings, an eye,
A widening deepening greenness,
Brilliantly, concentratedly,
Coming about its own business 20

Till, with a sudden sharp hot stink of fox
It enters the dark hole of the head.
The window is starless still; the clock ticks,
The page is printed.

[1957]

Hawk Roosting

I sit in the top of the wood, my eyes closed.
Inaction, no falsifying dream
Between my hooked head and hooked feet:
Or in sleep rehearse perfect kills and eat.

The convenience of the high trees! 5
The air's buoyancy and the sun's ray
Are of advantage to me;
And the earth's face upward for my inspection.

My feet are locked upon the rough bark.
It took the whole of Creation 10
To produce my foot, my each feather:
Now I hold Creation in my foot

Or fly up, and revolve it all slowly—
I kill where I please because it is all mine.
There is no sophistry in my body: 15
My manners are tearing off heads—

The allotment of death.
For the one path of my flight is direct
Through the bones of the living.
No arguments assert my right: 20

The sun is behind me.
Nothing has changed since I began.
My eye has permitted no change.
I am going to keep things like this.

[1960]

Pike

Pike, three inches long, perfect
Pike in all parts, green tigering the gold.
Killers from the egg: the malevolent aged grin.
They dance on the surface among the flies.

Or move, stunned by their own grandeur 5
Over a bed of emerald, silhouette
Of submarine delicacy and horror.
A hundred feet long in their world.

In ponds, under the heat-struck lily pads—
Gloom of their stillness: 10
Logged on last year's black leaves, watching upwards.
Or hung in an amber cavern of weeds

The jaws' hooked clamp and fangs
Not to be changed at this date;
A life subdued to its instrument; 15
The gills kneading quietly, and the pectorals.

Three we kept behind glass,
Jungled in weed: three inches, four,
And four and a half: fed fry to them—
Suddenly there were two. Finally one. 20

With a sag belly and the grin it was born with.
And indeed they spare nobody.
Two, six pounds each, over two feet long,
High and dry and dead in the willow-herb—

One jammed past its gills down the other's gullet: *25*
The outside eye stared: as a vice locks—
The same iron in this eye
Though its film shrank in death.

A pond I fished, fifty yards across,
Whose lilies and muscular tench *30*
Had outlasted every visible stone
Of the monastery that planted them—

Stilled legendary depth:
It was as deep as England. It held
Pike too immense to stir, so immense and old *35*
That past nightfall I dared not cast

But silently cast and fished
With the hair frozen on my head
For what might move, for what eye might move.
The still splashes on the dark pond, *40*

Owls hushing the floating woods
Frail on my ear against the dream
Darkness beneath night's darkness had freed,
That rose slowly towards me, watching.

[1960]

River

Fallen from heaven, lies across
The lap of his mother, broken by world.

But water will go on
Issuing from heaven

In dumbness uttering spirit brightness *5*
Through its broken mouth.

Scattered in a million pieces and buried
Its dry tombs will split, at a sign in the sky,

At a rending of veils.
It will rise, in a time after times, *10*

After swallowing death and the pit
It will return stainless

For the delivery of this world.
So the river is a god

Knee-deep among reeds, watching men, 15
Or hung by the heels down the door of a dam

It is a god, and inviolable.
Immortal. And will wash itself of all deaths.

[1983]

Derek Walcott *(b. 1930) was born and raised in St. Lucia, West Indies, by his schoolteacher mother. His father—a civil servant, poet, and artist—died soon after Walcott's birth. Walcott was interested in poetry and involved in theater from an early age. He attended St. Mary's College and the University of the West Indies in Jamaica to study English, French, and Latin. Working as a teacher for most of his twenties, he later moved to New York to study drama on a Rockefeller Fellowship. Also a prolific playwright, Walcott left for Trinidad in 1959 and founded the Little Carib Theater Workshop, which he ran for 17 years. He returned to the United States to teach at Harvard, Columbia, and, since 1985, at Boston University. He has been married and divorced three times, and has a son and two daughters. Walcott continues to divide his time between the Caribbean and America. He won the Nobel Prize for Literature in 1992, the first native Caribbean ever to achieve that honor.*

Derek Walcott

A Far Cry from Africa

A wind is ruffling the tawny pelt
Of Africa. Kikuyu, quick as flies,
Batten upon the bloodstreams of the veldt.
Corpses are scattered through a paradise.
Only the worm, colonel of carrion, cries: 5

"Waste no compassion on these separate dead!"
Statistics justify and scholars seize
The salients of colonial policy.
What is that to the white child hacked in bed?
To savages, expendable as Jews? *10*

Threshed out by beaters, the long rushes break
In a white dust of ibises whose cries
Have wheeled since civilization's dawn
From the parched river or beast-teeming plain.
The violence of beast on beast is read *15*
As natural law, but upright man
Seeks his divinity by inflicting pain.
Delirious as these worried beasts, his wars
Dance to the tightened carcass of a drum,
While he calls courage still that native dread *20*
Of the white peace contracted by the dead.

Again brutish necessity wipes its hands
Upon the napkin of a dirty cause, again
A waste of our compassion, as with Spain,
The gorilla wrestles with the superman. *25*
I who am poisoned with the blood of both,
Where shall I turn, divided to the vein?
I who have cursed
The drunken officer of British rule, how choose
Between this Africa and the English tongue I love? *30*
Betray them both, or give back what they give?
How can I face such slaughter and be cool?
How can I turn from Africa and live?

[1962]

The Virgins*

Down the dead streets of sun-stoned Frederiksted,°
the first free port° to die for tourism,
strolling at funeral pace, I am reminded

*The title of this poem refers to the Virgin Islands, a group of 100 small islands in the Caribbean.

1 *Frederiksted*: the biggest seaport in St. Croix, the largest of the American Virgin Islands. 2 *free port*: a port city where goods can be bought and sold without paying customs taxes.

of life not lost to the American dream;
but my small-islander's° simplicities 5
can't better our new empire's civilized
exchange of cameras, watches, perfumes, brandies
for the good life, so cheaply underpriced
that only the crime rate is on the rise
in streets blighted with sun, stone arches 10
and plazas blown dry by the hysteria
of rumour. A condominium drowns
in vacancy; its bargains are dusted,
but only a jewelled housefly drones
over the bargains. The roulettes spin 15
rustily to the wind—the vigorous trade°
that every morning would begin afresh
by revving up green water round the pierhead
heading for where the banks of silver thresh.

[1976]

5 *small-islander's*: Walcott was born on St. Lucia, another island in the West Indies. **16** *trade* : trade winds.

from *Midsummer*

XXVII

Certain things here are quietly American—
that chain-link fence dividing the absent roars
of the beach from the empty ball park, its holes
muttering the word umpire instead of empire;
the gray, metal light where an early pelican 5
coasts, with its engine off, over the pink fire
of a sea whose surface is as cold as Maine's.
The light warms up the sides of white, eager Cessnas°
parked at the airstrip under the freckling hills
of St. Thomas. The sheds, the brown, functional hangar, 10
are like those of the Occupation in the last war.

8 *Cessnas*: type of small aircraft.

The night left a rank smell under the casuarinas,
the villas have fenced-off beaches where the natives walk,
illegal immigrants from unlucky islands
who envy the smallest polyp its right to work. *15*
Here the wetback crab and the mollusc are citizens,
and the leaves have green cards. Bulldozers jerk
and gouge out a hill, but we all know that the dust
is industrial and must be suffered. Soon—
the sea's corrugations are sheets of zinc *20*
soldered by the sun's steady acetylene. This
drizzle that falls now is American rain,
stitching stars in the sand. My own corpuscles
are changing as fast. I fear what the migrant envies:
the starry pattern they make—the flag on the post office— *25*
the quality of the dirt, the fealty changing under my foot.

[1984]

Central America

Helicopters are cutlassing the wild bananas.
Between a nicotine thumb and forefinger
brittle faces crumble like tobacco leaves.
Children waddle in vests, their legs bowed,
little shrimps curled under their navels. *5*
The old men's teeth are stumps in a charred forest.
Their skins grate like the iguana's.
Their gaze like slate stones.
Women squat by the river's consolations
where children wade up to their knees, *10*
and a stick stirs up a twinkling of butterflies.
Up there, in the blue acres
of forest, flies circle their fathers.
In spring, in the upper provinces
of the Empire, yellow tanagers *15*
float up through the bare branches.
There is no distinction in these distances.

[1987]

***Rhina Espaillat** (b. 1932) was born in the Dominican Republic, which was then ruled by the dictator, Rafael Trujillo. Her father was part of the Dominican diplomatic mission in Washington. In 1939 they came to New York where the young Espaillat was suddenly immersed into a new language and culture. She attended New York City public schools, as she has remarked, "from grade to graduate school." Espaillat wrote poetry first in Spanish, later in English. Having published in a major journal as a high school junior, she was the youngest member ever accepted to the Poetry Society of America. In 1952 she married Alfred Moskowitz, an industrial arts teacher, and had three sons. After teaching high school in the New York area for many years, she retired in 1990 and moved with her husband to Newburyport, Massachusetts. Her first volume,* Lapsing to Grace, *appeared in 1992. Shortly thereafter she won both the Howard Nemerov and the* Sparrow *sonnet awards. Espaillat's second collection,* Where Horizons Go *(1998), won the T. S. Eliot Prize. She published* Rehearsing Absence *in 2002.*

Rhina Espaillat

Agua*

Mother, the trees you loved are dense with water,
alive with wings darting through stippled blue
of recent and imminent rain. And that old street
you mistook for water—remember?—is flowing still,
as when we walked between its banks of pickets 5
down to the river, which you knew was water
and spoke to, leaning over it last summer.

Mother, those cracks in pavement you stepped over,
avoiding water you imagined, are cradling
eddies of clover, tufted islands of moss; 10
and look how the roots of that locust are pouring into
every crevice, joining water to water,
look how its trunk is a fountain, a tower of water
out to the tips of its fussy, feathery branches.

Mother, balmy old Thales, how true your sight was 15
that pierced every disguise, uncovered the water
that links us, the current that bears us

*The title is the Spanish word for water.

from season to season, whose tide you greeted
in the mindless music you spoke, ocean departing,
returning, into whose keeping, Mother, 20
you slipped from your body's mooring and out before me.

[1998]

Bilingual/Bilingüe

My father liked them separate, one there,
one here (allá y aquí), as if aware

that words might cut in two his daughter's heart
(el corazón) and lock the alien part

to what he was—his memory, his name 5
(su nombre)—with a key he could not claim.

"English outside this door, Spanish inside,"
he said, "y basta." But who can divide

the world, the word (mundo y palabra) from
any child? I knew how to be dumb 10

and stubborn (testaruda); late, in bed,
I hoarded secret syllables I read

until my tongue (mi lengua) learned to run
where his stumbled. And still the heart was one.

I like to think he knew that, even when, 15
proud (orgulloso) of his daughter's pen,

he stood outside mis versos, half in fear
of words he loved but wanted not to hear.

[1998]

Bra

What a good fit! But the label says Honduras:
Alas, I am Union forever, yes, both breasts
and the heart between them committed to U.S. labor.

But such a splendid fit! And the label tells me
the woman who made it, bronze as the breasts now in it, 5
speaks the language I dream in; I count in Spanish

the pesos she made stitching this breast-divider:
will they go for her son's tuition, her daughter's wedding?
The thought is a lovely fit, but oh, the label!

And oh, those pesos that may be pennies, and hard-earned. 10
Was it son or daughter who made this, unschooled, unwedded?
How old? Fourteen? Ten? That fear is a tight fit.

If only the heart could be worn like the breast, divided,
nosing in two directions for news of the wide world,
sniffing here and there for justice, for mercy. 15

How burdened every choice is with politics, guilt,
expensive with duty, heavy as breasts in need of
this perfect fit whose label says Honduras.

[1998]

Bodega*

Bitter coffee, musty beans,
caramel and guava jam,
rice and sausage, nippy cheese,
saffron, anise, honey, ham,

rosemary, oregano, 5
clove, allspice and *bacalao*.°
Fifty years have blown away:
childhood falls around me now,

childhood and another place
where the tang of orange sweets 10
golden on the vendor's tray
drifts like laughter through the streets.

Memory is filament
weaving, weaving what I am:
bitter coffee, musty beans, 15
caramel and guava jam.

[2001]

*The title is the Spanish word for cellar or storeroom.
6 *bacalao*: Spanish for codfish.

***Geoffrey Hill** (b. 1932) was born in Worchester, England, to parents who attended school only until the age of 13. His father worked as village constable. A bright student, Hill won a scholarship to Keble College in Oxford, graduating First in English in 1953. While at Oxford, the young American Donald Hall published a pamphlet of Hill's poems with Fantasy Press. On the public and critical success of that slim volume, Hill began his academic career, holding teaching positions at the University of Leeds, Emmanuel College, and Cambridge University. He married Nancy Whittaker in 1956, and the couple had four children. In 1988 he moved to the United States to accept a position at Boston University, where he still teaches literature and religion. His writing has won numerous honors, including the Heinemann Award and the Whitbread Award.*

Geoffrey Hill

The Distant Fury of Battle

Grass resurrects to mask, to strangle,
Words glossed on stone, lopped stone-angel;
But the dead maintain their ground—
That there's no getting round—

Who in places vitally rest, *5*
Named, anonymous; who test
Alike the endurance of yews
Laurels, moonshine, stone, all tissues;

With whom, under licence and duress,
There are pacts made, if not peace. *10*
Union with the stone-wearing dead
Claims the born leader, the prepared

Leader, the devourers and all lean men.
Some, finally, learn to begin.
Some keep to the arrangement of love *15*
(Or similar trust) under whose auspices move

Most subjects, toward the profits of this
Combine of doves and witnesses.
Some, dug out of hot-beds, are brought bare,
Not past conceiving but past care. *20*

[1959]

from Funeral Music

3

They bespoke doomsday and they meant it by
God, their curved metal rimming the low ridge.
But few appearances are like this. Once
Every five hundred years a comet's
Over-riding stillness might reveal men *5*
In such array, livid and featureless,
With England crouched beastwise beneath it all.
"Oh, that old northern business . . ." A field
After battle utters its own sound
Which is like nothing on earth, but is earth. *10*
Blindly the questing snail, vulnerable
Mole emerge, blindly we lie down, blindly
Among carnage the most delicate souls
Tup in their marriage-blood, gasping "Jesus."

[1968]

Idylls of the King*

The pigeon purrs in the wood; the wood has gone;
dark leaves that flick to silver in the gust,
and the marsh-orchids and the heron's nest,
goldgrimy shafts and pillars of the sun.

Weightless magnificence upholds the past. *5*
Cement recesses smell of fur and bone
and berries wrinkle in the badger-run
and wiry heath-fern scatters its fresh rust.

*Part II, from "An Apology for the Revival of Christian Architecture in England."

"O clap your hands" so that the dove takes flight,
bursts through the leaves with an untidy sound, *10*
plunges its wings into the green twilight

above this long-sought and forsaken ground,
the half-built ruins of the new estate,
warheads of mushrooms round the filter-pond.

[1978]

Lachrimae Amantis*

What is there in my heart that you should sue
so fiercely for its love? What kind of care
brings you as though a stranger to my door
through the long night and in the icy dew

seeking the heart that will not harbour you, *5*
that keeps itself religiously secure?
At this dark solstice filled with frost and fire
your passion's ancient wounds must bleed anew.

So many nights the angel of my house
has fed such urgent comfort through a dream, *10*
whispered "your lord is coming, he is close"

that I have drowsed half-faithful for a time
bathed in pure tones of promise and remorse:
"tomorrow I shall wake to welcome him."

[1978]

*from *Lachrimae*, the title is Latin for "tears of a lover."

Born in Boston, ***Sylvia Plath*** *(1932–1963) grew up in Winthrop and Wellesley, Massachusetts. Plath's father, a German immigrant and professor at Boston University, died when the girl was eight years old. Plath published her first poem that same year, and published many other poems and short stories in newspapers and magazines by the time she entered Smith College. While interning at* Mademoiselle *magazine in New York, Plath suffered a breakdown and attempted suicide, resulting in six months of* *hospitalization. Having recovered, she won a Fulbright Fellowship to study at Cambridge University in England. There she met and married the poet Ted Hughes. They had two children together, though the marriage fell apart when she found that Hughes had been unfaithful. Plath completed her darkly autobiographical novel,* The Bell Jar *(1963), in only eight months, and worked on the poems that would become* Ariel *(1965). One month after* The Bell Jar *appeared in England, Plath committed suicide by gassing herself in the kitchen oven. Her* Collected Poems *(1981) posthumously won the Pulitzer Prize.*

Sylvia Plath

Metaphors

I'm a riddle in nine syllables,
An elephant, a ponderous house,
A melon strolling on two tendrils.
O red fruit, ivory, fine timbers!
This loaf's big with its yeasty rising. 5
Money's new-minted in this fat purse.
I'm a means, a stage, a cow in calf.
I've eaten a bag of green apples,
Boarded the train there's no getting off.

[1960]

Blackberrying

Nobody in the lane, and nothing, nothing but blackberries,
Blackberries on either side, though on the right mainly,
A blackberry alley, going down in hooks, and a sea
Somewhere at the end of it, heaving. Blackberries
Big as the ball of my thumb, and dumb as eyes 5
Ebon in the hedges, fat
With blue-red juices. These they squander on my fingers.
I had not asked for such a blood sisterhood; they must love me.
They accommodate themselves to my milkbottle, flattening their
sides.

Overhead go the choughs in black, cacophonous flocks— *10*
Bits of burnt paper wheeling in a blown sky.
Theirs is the only voice, protesting, protesting.
I do not think the sea will appear at all.
The high, green meadows are glowing, as if lit from within.
I come to one bush of berries so ripe it is a bush of flies, *15*
Hanging their bluegreen bellies and their wing panes in a Chinese
screen.
The honey-feast of the berries has stunned them; they believe in
heaven.
One more hook, and the berries and bushes end.

The only thing to come now is the sea.
From between two hills a sudden wind funnels at me, *20*
Slapping its phantom laundry in my face.
These hills are too green and sweet to have tasted salt.
I follow the sheep path between them. A last hook brings me
To the hills' northern face, and the face is orange rock
That looks out on nothing, nothing but a great space *25*
Of white and pewter lights, and a din like silversmiths
Beating and beating at an intractable metal.

[1961; 1971]

Daddy

You do not do, you do not do
Any more, black shoe
In which I have lived like a foot
For thirty years, poor and white,
Barely daring to breathe or Achoo. *5*

Daddy, I have had to kill you.
You died before I had time—
Marble-heavy, a bag full of God,
Ghastly statue with one grey toe
Big as a Frisco seal *10*

And a head in the freakish Atlantic
Where it pours bean green over blue

In the waters off beautiful Nauset.
I used to pray to recover you.
Ach, du.° *15*

In the German tongue, in the Polish town
Scraped flat by the roller
Of wars, wars, wars.
But the name of the town is common.
My Polack friend *20*

Says there are a dozen or two.
So I never could tell where you
Put your foot, your root,
I never could talk to you.
The tongue stuck in my jaw. *25*

It stuck in a barb wire snare.
Ich, ich, ich, ich,°
I could hardly speak.
I thought every German was you.
And the language obscene *30*

An engine, an engine
Chuffing me off like a Jew.
A Jew to Dachau, Auschwitz, Belsen.
I began to talk like a Jew.
I think I may well be a Jew. *35*

The snows of the Tyrol, the clear beer of Vienna
Are not very pure or true.
With my gypsy ancestress and my weird luck
And my Taroc pack and my Taroc pack
I may be a bit of a Jew. *40*

I have always been scared of *you*,
With your Luftwaffe, your gobbledygoo.
And your neat moustache
And your Aryan eye, bright blue.
Panzer-man, panzer-man, O You— *45*

Not God but a swastika
So black no sky could squeak through.
Every woman adores a Fascist,

15 *Ach, du*: German for "oh, you." **27** *ich…ich*: I . . . I.

The boot in the face, the brute
Brute heart of a brute like you. *50*

You stand at the blackboard, daddy,
In the picture I have of you,
A cleft in your chin instead of your foot
But no less a devil for that, no not
Any less the black man who *55*

Bit my pretty red heart in two.
I was ten when they buried you.
At twenty I tried to die
And get back, back, back to you.
I thought even the bones would do. *60*

But they pulled me out of the sack,
And they stuck me together with glue.
And then I knew what to do.
I made a model of you,
A man in black with a Meinkampf° look *65*

And a love of the rack and the screw.
And I said I do, I do.
So daddy, I'm finally through.
The black telephone's off at the root,
The voices just can't worm through. *70*

If I've killed one man, I've killed two—
The vampire who said he was you
And drank my blood for a year,
Seven years, if you want to know.
Daddy, you can lie back now. *75*

There's stake in your fat black heart
And the villagers never liked you.
They are dancing and stamping on you.
They always *knew* it was you.
Daddy, daddy, you bastard, I'm through. *80*

[1965]

65 *Meinkampf*: Adolf Hitler's autobiography was *Mein Kampf* (my struggle).

Lady Lazarus

I have done it again.
One year in every ten
I manage it—

A sort of walking miracle, my skin
Bright as a Nazi lampshade, *5*
My right foot

A paperweight,
My face a featureless, fine
Jew linen.

Peel off the napkin *10*
O my enemy.
Do I terrify?—

The nose, the eye pits, the full set of teeth?
The sour breath
Will vanish in a day. *15*

Soon, soon the flesh
The grave cave ate will be
At home on me

And I a smiling woman.
I am only thirty. *20*
And like the cat I have nine times to die.

This is Number Three.
What a trash
To annihilate each decade.

What a million filaments. *25*
The peanut-crunching crowd
Shoves in to see

Them unwrap me hand and foot—
The big strip tease.
Gentleman, ladies, *30*

These are my hands,
My knees.
I may be skin and bone,

Nevertheless, I am the same, identical woman.
The first time it happened I was ten. *35*
It was an accident.

The second time I meant
To last it out and not come back at all.
I rocked shut

As a seashell. *40*
They had to call and call
And pick the worms off me like sticky pearls.

Dying
Is an art, like everything else.
I do it exceptionally well. *45*

I do it so it feels like hell.
I do it so it feels real.
I guess you could say I've a call.

It's easy enough to do it in a cell.
It's easy enough to do it and stay put. *50*
It's the theatrical

Comeback in broad day
To the same place, the same face, the same brute
Amused shout:

"A miracle!" *55*
That knocks me out.
There is a charge

For the eyeing of my scars, there is a charge
For the hearing of my heart—
It really goes. *60*

And there is a charge, a very large charge,
For a word or a touch
Or a bit of blood

Or a piece of my hair or my clothes.
So, so, Herr Doktor. *65*
So, Herr Enemy.

I am your opus,
I am your valuable,
The pure gold baby

That melts to a shriek. *70*
I turn and burn.
Do not think I underestimate your great concern.

Ash, ash—
You poke and stir.
Flesh, bone, there is nothing there— *75*

A cake of soap,
A wedding ring,
A gold filling.

Herr God, Herr Lucifer,
Beware *80*
Beware.

Out of the ash
I rise with my red hair
And I eat men like air.

[1965]

***Seamus Heaney** (b. 1939) was born in Mossbawn in Northern Ireland, the eldest of nine children in a Catholic family. His father was a farmer and cattle-dealer. At age 12, Heaney won a scholarship to St. Columb's College in Derry, and left the family farm. From there he attended Queen's University, Belfast. He would later return to Queen's University to lecture on poetry. In 1965 he married Marie Devlin, and published his first book of poems,* Death of a Naturalist, *the next year. Through the early 1970s, Heaney taught at University of California, Berkeley, and Caryfort College in Dublin. He began teaching spring semesters at Harvard University in 1982, and was later named Boylston Professor of Rhetoric and Oratory. Oxford appointed him Professor of Poetry in 1989 for a period of five years. Heaney won the Nobel Prize for Literature in 1995. He divides his time between a home in Ireland and his teaching position at Harvard.*

Seamus Heaney

Digging

Between my finger and my thumb
The squat pen rests; snug as a gun.

Under my window, a clean rasping sound
When the spade sinks into gravelly ground:
My father, digging. I look down *5*

Till his straining rump among the flowerbeds
Bends low, comes up twenty years away
Stooping in rhythm through potato drills
Where he was digging.

The coarse boot nestled on the lug, the shaft *10*
Against the inside knee was levered firmly.
He rooted out tall tops, buried the bright edge deep
To scatter new potatoes that we picked,
Loving their cool hardness in our hands.

By God, the old man could handle a spade. *15*
Just like his old man.

My grandfather cut more turf in a day
Than any other man on Toner's bog.
Once I carried him milk in a bottle
Corked sloppily with paper. He straightened up *20*
To drink it, then fell to right away
Nicking and slicing neatly, heaving sods
Over his shoulder, going down and down
For the good turf. Digging.

The cold smell of potato mould, the squelch and slap *25*
Of soggy peat, the curt cuts of an edge
Through living roots awaken in my head.
But I've no spade to follow men like them.

Between my finger and my thumb
The squat pen rests. *30*
I'll dig with it.

[1966]

Bogland

For T. P. Flanagan

We have no prairies
To slice a big sun at evening—
Everywhere the eye concedes to
Encroaching horizon,

Is wooed into the cyclops' eye 5
Of a tarn. Our unfenced country
Is bog that keeps crusting
Between the sights of the sun.

They've taken the skeleton
Of the Great Irish Elk 10
Out of the peat, set it up,
An astounding crate full of air.

Butter sunk under
More than a hundred years
Was recovered salty and white. 15
The ground itself is kind, black butter

Melting and opening underfoot,
Missing its last definition
By millions of years.
They'll never dig coal here, 20

Only the waterlogged trunks
Of great firs, soft as pulp.
Our pioneers keep striking
Inwards and downwards,

Every layer they strip 25
Seems camped on before.
The bogholes might be Atlantic seepage.
The wet centre is bottomless.

[1969]

Limbo

Fishermen at Ballyshannon
Netted an infant last night
Along with the salmon.
An illegitimate spawning,

A small one thrown back *5*
To the waters. But I'm sure
As she stood in the shallows
Ducking him tenderly

Till the frozen knobs of her wrists
Were dead as the gravel, *10*
He was a minnow with hooks
Tearing her open.

She waded in under
The sign of her cross.
He was hauled in with the fish. *15*
Now limbo will be

A cold glitter of souls
Through some far briny zone.
Even Christ's palms, unhealed,
Smart and cannot fish there. *20*

[1972]

Punishment

I can feel the tug
of the halter at the nape
of her neck, the wind
on her naked front.

It blows her nipples *5*
to amber beads,
it shakes the frail rigging
of her ribs.

I can see her drowned
body in the bog, *10*

the weighing stone,
the floating rods and boughs.

Under which at first
she was a barked sapling
that is dug up *15*
oak-bone, brain-firkin:

her shaved head
like a stubble of black corn,
her blindfold a soiled bandage,
her noose a ring *20*

to store
the memories of love.
Little adulteress,
before they punished you

you were flaxen-haired, *25*
undernourished, and your
tar-black face was beautiful.
My poor scapegoat,

I almost love you
but would have cast, I know, *30*
the stones of silence.
I am the artful voyeur

of your brain's exposed
and darkened combs,
your muscles' webbing *35*
and all your numbered bones:

I who have stood dumb
when your betraying sisters,
cauled in tar,
wept by the railings, *40*

who would connive
in civilized outrage
yet understand the exact
and tribal, intimate revenge.

[1975]

***Louise Glück** (b. 1943) grew up on Long Island, where her Hungarian father was a successful executive. Her parents encouraged Glück and her younger sister intellectually and artistically. (Reportedly, Glück was well versed in classical mythology by age three.) Glück battled anorexia as a teenager, and left high school during her senior year for a seven-year course of intensive psychoanalysis. After matriculating at Sarah Lawrence College, Glück transferred to Columbia University. There she studied under Stanley Kunitz, her most influential mentor. Glück has taught at several institutions, including the University of Iowa, Goddard College, Harvard, Brandeis, and the Universities of California at Los Angeles, Berkeley, and Irvine. Since 1984 she has held a professorship at Williams College in Massachusetts. Glück has been married twice, and has a son from her first marriage.* The Wild Iris *(1992) received the Pulitzer Prize. In 2003 Glück was named United States Poet Laureate; her other honors include the National Book Critics Circle Award and the Bollingen Prize.*

Louise Glück

Mock Orange*

It is not the moon, I tell you.
It is these flowers
lighting the yard

I hate them.
I hate them as I hate sex, 5
the man's mouth
sealing my mouth, the man's
paralyzing body—

and the cry that always escapes,
the low, humiliating 10
premise of union—

In my mind tonight
I hear the question and pursuing answer
fused in one sound

**Mock Orange*: a shrub with white or gold flowers, sometimes quite fragrant.

that mourns and mounts and then 15
is split into the old selves,
the tired antagonisms. Do you see?
We are made fools of.
And the scent of mock orange
drifts through the window. 20

How can I rest?
How can I be content
when there is still
that odor in the world.

[1985]

The Gold Lily

As I perceive
I am dying now and know
I will not speak again, will not
survive the earth, be summoned
out of it again, not 5
a flower yet, a pine only, raw dirt
catching my ribs, I call you,
father and master: all around,
my companions are failing, thinking
you do not see. How 10
can they know you see
unless you save us?
In the summer twilight, are you
close enough to hear
your child's terror? Or 15
are you not my father,
you who raised me?

[1992]

Circe's Power*

I never turned anyone into a pig.
Some people are pigs; I make them
look like pigs.

I'm sick of your world
that lets the outside disguise the inside. 5

Your men weren't bad men;
undisciplined life
did that to them. As pigs,

under the care of
me and my ladies, they 10
sweetened right up.

Then I reversed the spell,
showing you my goodness
as well as my power. I saw

we could be happy here, 15
as men and women are
when their needs are simple. In the same breath,

I foresaw your departure,
your men with my help braving
the crying and pounding sea. You think 20

a few tears upset me? My friend,
every sorceress is
a pragmatist at heart; nobody

sees essence who can't
face limitation. If I wanted only to hold you 25

I could hold you prisoner.

[1996]

*In Homer's *Odyssey*, Circe is a Greek goddess who temporarily transformed Odysseus' men into pigs.

Reunion

When Odysseus° has returned at last
unrecognizable to Ithaca° and killed
the suitors swarming the throne room,
very delicately he signals to Telemachus°
to depart: as he stood twenty years ago, *5*
he stands now before Penelope.°
On the palace floor, wide bands of sunlight turning
from gold to red. He tells her
nothing of those years, choosing to speak instead
exclusively of small things, as would be *10*
the habit of a man and woman long together:
once she sees who he is, she will know what he's done.
And as he speaks, ah,
tenderly he touches her forearm.

[1996]

1 *Odysseus*: the hero of Homer's *Odyssey*, he was the king of Ithaca who returned home after ten years of travel. 2 *Ithaca*: island of western Greece. 4 *Telemachus*: son of Odysseus and Penelope. 6 *Penelope*: wife of Odysseus, she was made immortal by Circe.

Wendy Cope *(b. 1945) was born in Erith, Kent, in the south of England. Her father managed a department store where her mother worked as a secretary. They instilled in Cope an early love for literature by providing her with classic books and reciting great poetry aloud. After attending boarding school from age seven, Cope was the first in her family to go to college. She studied history at St. Hilda's College, Oxford (1966), and trained as a teacher at Westminster College (1967). She then taught for 14 years at primary schools in south London before leaving education to work as a freelance writer. Cope's first book of poems,* Making Cocoa for Kingsley Amis *(1986), was an immediate success and announced her as a master of satire and parody. In her two subsequent collections,* Serious Concerns *(1992) and* If I Don't Know *(2001), Cope has somewhat departed from parody towards more serious subject matter and tones, though her work has not lost its ardent humor. Cope has also worked as an editor and critic, and has written children's books.*

Wendy Cope

From June to December

1 Prelude

It wouldn't be a good idea
To let him stay.
When they knew each other better—
Not today.
But she put on her new black knickers *5*
Anyway.

2 A Serious Person

I can tell you're a serious person
And I know from the way you talk
That what goes on inside your head
Is pure as the whitest chalk. *10*

It's nice to meet serious people
And hear them explain their views:
Your concern for the rights of women
Is especially welcome news.

I'm sure you'd never exploit one; *15*
I expect you'd rather be dead;
I'm thoroughly convinced of it—
Now can we go to bed?

3 Summer Villanelle

You know exactly what to do—
Your kiss, your fingers on my thigh— *20*
I think of little else but you.

It's bliss to have a lover who,
Touching one shoulder, makes me sigh–
You know exactly what to do.

You make me happy through and through, *25*
The way the sun lights up the sky—
I think of little else but you.

I hardly sleep—an hour or two;
I can't eat much and this is why—
You know exactly what to do. *30*

The movie in my mind is blue—
As June runs into warm July
I think of little else but you.

But is it love? And is it true?
Who cares? This much I can't deny: *35*
You know exactly what to do;
I think of little else but you.

4 The Reading

In crumpled, bardic corduroy,
The poet took the stage
And read aloud his deathless verse, *40*
Page by deathless page.

I gazed at him as though intent
On every word he said.
From time to time I'd close my eyes
And smile and nod my head. *45*

He may have thought his every phrase
Sent shivers down my spine.
Perhaps I helped encourage him
To read till half past nine.

Don't ask what it was all about— *50*
I haven't got a clue.
I spent a blissful evening, lost
In carnal thoughts of you.

5 Some People

Some people like sex more than others—
You seem to like it a lot. *55*
There's nothing wrong with being innocent or high-minded
But I'm glad you're not.

6 Going Too Far

Cuddling the new telephone directory
After I found your name in it
Was going too far. *60*

It's a safe bet you're not hugging a phone book,
Wherever you are.

7 Verse for a Birthday Card

Many happy returns and good luck.
When it comes to a present, I'm stuck.
If you weren't far away *65*
On your own special day,
I could give you a really nice glass of lager.

8 Love Story

I thought you'd be a pushover;
I hoped I wouldn't hurt you.
I warned you this was just a fling *70*
And one day I'd desert you.

So kindly in your spectacles,
So solid in your jacket,
So manly in your big white car
That must have cost a packet. *75*

I grew to like you more and more—
I didn't try to hide it.
Fall in love with someone nice?—
I'd hardly ever tried it.

The course of true love didn't run *80*
Quite the way I'd planned it.
You failed to fall in love with me—
I couldn't understand it.

9 Spring Onions

Decapitating the spring onions,
She made this mental note: *85*
You can tell it's love, the real thing,
When you dream of slitting his throat.

10 I'll Be Nice

I'll be nice to you and smile—
It's easy for a man to win—
But I'll hate you all the while. *90*

I shall go the extra mile
And condone your every sin—
I'll be nice to you and smile.

You will think I like your style;
You'll believe I've given in *95*
But I'll hate you all the while.

Safe as an atomic pile,
Good as nitroglycerine,
I'll be nice to you and smile.

I'll say hypocrisy is vile *100*
And give a reassuring grin
But I'll hate you all the while.

Set against my wits and guile,
Manly strength won't save your skin.
I'll be nice to you and smile *105*
But I'll hate you all the while.

[1986]

Lonely Hearts

Can someone make my simple wish come true?
Male biker seeks female for touring fun.
Do you live in North London? Is it you?

Gay vegetarian whose friends are few,
I'm into music, Shakespeare and the sun. *5*
Can someone make my simple wish come true?

Executive in search of something new—
Perhaps bisexual woman, arty, young.
Do you live in North London? Is it you?

Successful, straight and solvent? I am too— 10
Attractive Jewish lady with a son.
Can someone make my simple wish come true?

I'm Libran, inexperienced and blue—
Need slim non-smoker, under twenty-one.
Do you live in North London? Is it you? 15

Please write (with photo) to Box 152.
Who knows where it may lead once we've begun?
Can someone make my simple wish come true?
Do you live in North London? Is it you?

[1986]

Rondeau Redoublé*

There are so many kinds of awful men—
One can't avoid them all. She often said
She'd never make the same mistake again:
She always made a new mistake instead.

The chinless type who made her feel ill-bred; 5
The practised charmer, less than charming when
He talked about the wife and kids and fled—
There are so many kinds of awful men.

The half-crazed hippy, deeply into Zen,
Whose cryptic homilies she came to dread; 10
The fervent youth who worshipped Tony Benn—
"One can't avoid them all," she often said.

The ageing banker, rich and overfed,
Who held forth on the dollar and the yen—
Though there were many more mistakes ahead, 15
She'd never make the same mistake again.

The budding poet, scribbling in his den
Odes not to her but to his pussy, Fred;
The drunk who fell asleep at nine or ten—
She always made a new mistake instead. 20

*A rondeau is a French verse form consisting of only two rhymes and usually 10–13 lines. Redoublé is the French word for doubled.

And so the gambler was at least unwed
And didn't preach or sneer or wield a pen
Or hoard his wealth or take the Scotch to bed.
She'd lived and learned and lived and learned but then
There are so many kinds. *25*

[1986]

***Kay Ryan** (b. 1945) was born Kay Petersen in San Jose, California, but was raised mostly in the small, working-class towns of the San Joaquin Valley and Mojave Desert. Her father, the son of Danish immigrants, was a well-driller and farmhand. Her mother taught elementary school briefly. Ryan completed her studies in English literature at University of California at Los Angeles, but she never took a creative writing course. She has lived in Marin County, north of San Francisco, since 1971, where she teaches basic English skills at College of Marin, a public two-year college, and occasionally at San Quentin Prison. An outsider to literary circles, Ryan was slow in establishing her literary career. Her first book,* Dragon Acts to Dragon Ends *(1983), was privately published by a subscription of friends and attracted no critical attention. Slowly and steadily her literary reputation has risen—supported by frequent appearances in the* New Yorker. *Her recent volumes,* Elephant Rocks *(1996) and* Say Uncle *(2000), have confirmed her position as one of the finest poets of her generation.*

Kay Ryan

Paired Things

Who, who had only seen wings,
could extrapolate the
skinny sticks of things
birds use for land,
the backward way they bend, *5*
the silly way they stand?
And who, only studying
birdtracks in the sand,
could think those little forks

had decamped on the wind? 10
So many paired things seem odd.
Who ever would have dreamed
the broad winged raven of despair
would quit the air and go
bandylegged upon the ground, 15
a common crow?

[1994]

Turtle

Who would be a turtle who could help it?
A barely mobile hard roll, a four-oared helmet,
she can ill afford the chances she must take
in rowing toward the grasses that she eats.
Her track is graceless, like dragging 5
a packing-case places, and almost any slope
defeats her modest hopes. Even being practical,
she's often stuck up to the axle on her way
to something edible. With everything optimal,
she skirts the ditch which would convert 10
her shell into a serving dish. She lives
below luck-level, never imagining some lottery
will change her load of pottery to wings.
Her only levity is patience,
the sport of truly chastened things. 15

[1994]

Blandeur

If it please God,
let less happen.
Even out Earth's
rondure, flatten
Eiger, blanden 5
the Grand Canyon.

Make valleys
slightly higher,
widen fissures
to arable land, *10*
remand your
terrible glaciers
and silence
their calving,
halving or doubling *15*
all geographical features
toward the mean.
Unlean against our hearts.
Withdraw your grandeur
from these parts. *20*

[2000]

Chemise

What would the self
disrobed look like,
the form undraped?
There is a flimsy cloth
we can't take off— *5*
some last chemise
we can't escape—
a hope more intimate
than paint
to please. *10*

[2000]

Credits

W. H. Auden, "O Where Are You Going," Copyright 1934 and renewed 1962 by W.H. Auden from *Collected Poems* by W.H. Auden. Used by permission of Random House, Inc. "As I Walked Out One Evening," "In memory of W.B. Yeats," "Musee des Beaux Arts," "September 1, 1939," and "A Lullaby" Copyright 1940 and renewed 1968 by W. H. Auden from *Collected Poems* by W. H. Auden. Used by permission of Random House, Inc. "The Shield of Achilles" Copyright © 1956 by W. H. Auden from *Collected Poems* by W. H. Auden. Used by permission of Random House, Inc.

Beowulf, "Grendel Attacks," "Battle with Grendel," and "Beowulf's Burial" from *Beowulf,* translated by Alan Sullivan and Timothy Murphy. Copyright © 2004 by Pearson Education, Inc.

John Berryman, "Dream Song #14," Dream Song #22," and "Dream Song #29" from *The Dream Songs* by John Berryman. Copyright © 1969 by John Berryman. Copyright renewed 1997 by Kate Donahue Berryman. Reprinted by permission of Farrar, Straus and Giroux, LLC.

Earle Birney, "David," "From the Hazel Bough," and "Can. Hist." from *The Ghost in the Wheels: Selected Poems by Earle Birney*. Used by permission, McClelland & Stewart Ltd. The Canadian Publishers.

Elizabeth Bishop, "The Fish," "Filling Station," "Questions of Travel," and "One Art" from *The Complete Poems: 1927–1979* by Elizabeth Bishop. Copyright © 1979, 1983 by Alice Helen Methfessel. Reprinted by permission of Farrar, Straus and Giroux, LLC.

Louise Bogan, "The Crows," "Henceforth, from the Mind," "Knowledge," and "Medusa" from *The Blue Estuaries* by Louise Bogan. Copyright © 1968 by Louise Bogan. Reprinted by permission of Farrar, Straus and Giroux, LLC.

Gwendolyn Brooks, "The Mother," "Sadie and Maud," "The Rites of Cousin Vit," and "We Real Cool" reprinted by consent of Brooks Permissions.

Charles Causley, "At the British War Cemetary, Bayeux," "I Am the Great Sun," and "What Has Happened to Lulu?" from *Collected Poems* by Charles Causley. Copyright © 1951 by Charles Causley. Reprinted by permission of David Higham Associates.

Geoffrey Chaucer, "General Prologue to the Canterbury Tales," "Prologue to the Wife of Bath's Tale," and "Merciless Beauty" from *Chaucer's Poetry*, edited by G. T. Donaldson. Copyright ©1975 by John Wiley & Sons. Reprinted by permission of Pearson Education, Inc.

Wendy Cope, "From June to September," "Lonely Hearts," and "Rondeau Dedoublé" from *Making Cocoa for Kingsley Amis* by Wendy Cope. Copyright 1986 by Wendy Cope. Reprinted by permission of Faber & Faber Limited.

Hart Crane, "Chaplinesque," "My Grandmother's Love Letters," and "Praise for an Urn" from *Complete Poems of Hart Crane* by Hart Crane, edited by Marc Simon. Copyright 1933, 1958, 1966 by Liveright Publishing Corporation. Copyright © 1986 by Marc Simon. Used by permission of Liveright Publishing Corporation. "Voyages I, II, III, IV, VI" from *Complete Poems of Hart Crane* by Hart

Crane, edited by Marc Simon. Copyright 1933, 1958, 1966 by Liveright Publishing Corporation.

E. E. Cummings, "Buffalo Bill's" copyright 1923, 1951, © 1991 by the Trustees for the E. E. Cummings Trust. Copyright © 1976 by George James Firmage. From *Complete Poems: 1904–1962* by E. E. Cummings, edited by George J. Firmage. Used by permission of Liveright Publishing Corporation. "Next to of course god america i" copyright 1926, 1954 © 1991 by the Trustees for the E. E. Cummings Trust. Copyright © 1985 by George James Firmage. From *Complete Poems: 1904–1962* by E. E. Cummings, edited by George J. Firmage. Used by permission of Liveright Publishing Corporation. "Somewhere I have never travelled, gladly beyond" copyright 1931, © 1959, 1991 by the Trustees for the E. E. Cummings Trust. Copyright © 1979 by George James Firmage. From *Complete Poems: 1904–1962* by E. E. Cummings, edited by George J. Firmage. Used by permission of Liveright Publishing Corporation. "May I feel said he" copyright 1935, © 1963, 1991 by the Trustees for the E. E. Cummings Trust. Copyright © 1978 by George James Firmage. From *Complete Poems: 1904–1962* by E. E. Cummings, edited by George J. Firmage. Used by permission of Liveright Publishing Corporation. "Anyone lived in a pretty how town" copyright 1940, © 1968, 1991 by the Trustees for the E. E. Cummings Trust. From *Complete Poems: 1904–1962* by E. E. Cummings, edited by George J. Firmage. Used by permission of Liveright Publishing Corporation. "Pity this busy monster, man unkind" copyright 1944, © 1972, 1991 by the Trustees for the E. E. Cummings Trust. From *Complete Poems: 1904–1962* by E. E. Cummings, edited by George J. Firmage. Used by permission of Liveright Publishing Corporation.

H.D. [Hilda Doolittle], "Garden," "Helen," "Oread," "Sea Rose," "Sea Violet," and "Storm" by H.D. (Hilda Doolittle), from *Collected Poems, 1912–1944,* copyright © 1982 by The Estate of Hilda Doolittle. Reprinted by permission of New Directions Publishing Corp.

Emily Dickinson, "I Felt a Funeral, in my Brain," "I'm Nobody! Who are you?," "I taste a liquor never brewed," "Wild Nights – Wild Nights!," "The Soul selects her own Society," "This is my letter to the World," "Because I could not stop for Death," "Tell all the Truth but tell it slant," and "Success is counted sweetest" reprinted by permission of the publishers and the Trustees of Amherst College from *The Poems of Emily Dickinson*, Thomas H. Johnson, ed., Cambridge, MA: The Belknap Press of Harvard University Press, Copyright © 1951, 1955, 1979 by the President and Fellows of Harvard College.

Rhina Espaillat, "Agua," "Bra," and "Bilingual/Bilingüe" from *Where Horizons Go: Poems by Rhina Espaillat.* Copyright © 1998 by Rhina Espaillat. Reprinted by permission of the author. "Bodega" from *Lapsing to Grace: Poems and Drawings* by Rhina Espaillat. Copyright © 1992 by Rhina Espaillat. Reprinted by permission of the author.

Robert Frost, "Mowing," "After Apple-Picking," "Mending Wall," "Birches," "The Road Not Taken," "Fire and Ice," "Nothing Gold Can Stay," "Stopping by Woods on a Snowy Evening," "Acquainted with the Night," and "Provide, Provide" copyright 1916, 1923, 1928, 1930, 1934, © 1969 by Henry Holt and Company, copyright 1936, 1944, 1951, 1956, 1958, 1962 by Robert Frost, copyright © 1964, 1967 by Lesley Frost Ballantine. Reprinted by permission of Henry Holt and Company, LLC.

Allen Ginsberg, all lines from "America" from *Collected Poems 1947–1980* by Allen Ginsberg. Copyright © 1956, 1959 by Allen Ginsberg. Reprinted by permission of HarperCollins Publishers, Inc. Part I from "Howl" from *Collected Poems 1947–1980* by Allen Ginsberg. Copyright © 1955 by Allen Ginsberg. Reprinted by permission of HarperCollins Publishers, Inc.

Robert Graves, "The Cool Web," "Down, Wanton, Down," "To Juan at the Winter Solstice," "Warning to Children," "Counting the Beats," from *Complete Poems by Robert Graves.* Reprinted by permission of Carcanet Press Limited.

Louise Gluck, "Mock Orange" from *First Four Books of Poetry* by Louise Gluck. Reprinted by permission of HarperCollins Publishers, Inc. "The Gold Lily" from *The Wild Iris* by Louise Gluck. Copyright © 1993 by Louise Gluck. Reprinted by permission of HarperCollins Publishers, Inc. "Circe's Power" and "Reunion" from *Meadowlands* by Louis Gluck. Copyright © 1996 by Louise Gluck. Reprinted by permission of HarperCollins Publishers, Inc.

Thomas Hardy, "Hap," "I Look into My Glass," "Neutral Tones," "The Darkling Thrush," "The Ruined Maid," "The Convergence of the Twain," and "Channel Firing" reprinted with permission of Scribner, an imprint of Simon & Schuster Adult Publishing Group, from *The Complete Poems of Thomas Hardy,* edited by James Gibson. Copyright © 1978 by Macmillan London, Ltd.

Robert Hayden, "Those Winter Sundays" copyright © 1966 by Robert Hayden, from *Collected Poems of Robert Hayden* by Robert Hayden, edited by Frederick Glaysher. Used by permission of Liveright Publishing Corporation. "Homage to the Empress of the Blues," "The Whipping" by Frederick Glaysher, editor. Copyright © 1966 by Robert Hayden, from *Collected Poems of Robert Hayden* by Robert Hayden, edited by Frederick Glaysher. Copyright © 1985 by Emma Hayden. Used by permission of Liveright Publishing Corporation.

Seamus Heaney, "Bogland," "Digging," "Limbo," and "Punishment" from *Opened Ground: Selected Poems 1966–1996* by Seamus Heaney. Copyright © 1998 by Seamus Heaney. Reprinted by permission of Farrar, Straus and Giroux, LLC. Canadian Rights: From *Death of a Naturalist* by Seamus Heaney. Reprinted by permission of Faber and Faber Limited.

Geoffrey Hill, "The Distant Fury of Battle," "Funeral Music (3)," "Idylls of Kings," and "Lacrimae Amantis" from *New and Selected Poems, 1952–1992* by Geoffrey Hill. Copyright © 1994 by Geoffrey Hill. Reprinted by permission of Houghton Mifflin Company. All rights reserved.

A.D. Hope, "Australia," "The Lingam and the Yoni," "The Judgement," and "Imperial Adam" reprinted from *Collected Poems* by A. D. Hope by permission of Carcanet Press Limited.

Langston Hughes, "Cross," "I, Too," "Negro," "The Negro Speaks of Rivers," "The Weary Blues," "Harlem," and "Theme for English B" from *The Collected Poems of Langston Hughes* by Langston Hughes, copyright © 1994 by The Estate of Langston Hughes. Used by permission of Alfred A. Knopf, a division of Random House, Inc.

Ted Hughes, "The Thought-Fox," "Hawk Roosting," "Pike," and "River" from *Selected Poems 1957–1994* by Ted Hughes. Copyright © 2002 by The Estate of Ted Hughes. Reprinted by permission of Farrar, Straus and Giroux, LLC. Canadian Rights: From *Selected Poems: 1957–1994* by Ted Hughes. Reprinted by permission of Faber & Faber Limited.

Robinson Jeffers, "To the Stone-Cutters" copyright 1924 & renewed 1952 by Robinson Jeffers. "Shine, Perishing Republic" copyright 1934 by Robinson Jeffers & renewed 1962 by Donnan Jeffers and Garth Jeffers, from *The Selected Poetry of Robinson Jeffers* by Robinson Jeffers. Used by permission of Random House, Inc. "Hurt Hawks" copyright 1928 and renewed 1956 by Robinson Jeffers; "Rock and Hawk" copyright 1925, 1929 & renewed 1953, © 1957 by Robinson Jeffers; "Carmel Point" copyright 1954 by Robinson Jeffers, from *Selected Poetry of Robinson Jeffers* by Robinson Jeffers. Used by permission of Random House, Inc. "Hands" by Robinson Jeffers from *The Collected Poetry of Robinson Jeffers,* edited by Tim Hunt, Volume 2, 1928–1938. Copyright © 1938, renewed 1966 by Donnan Jeffers and Garth Jeffers. All rights reserved.

Donald Justice, "Counting the Mad," "On the Death of Friends in Childhood," "Men at Forty," and "Psalm and Lament" from *New and Selected Poems* by Donald Justice, copyright © 1995 by Donald Justice. Used by permission of Alfred A. Knopf, a division of Random House, Inc.

Weldon Kees, "For My Daughter," "Robinson," "Aspects of Robinson," and "Round" reprinted from *The Collected Poems of Weldon Kees* edited by Donald

Justice by permission of the University of Nebraska Press. Copyright © 1975 by the University of Nebraska Press.

Philip Larkin, "Poetry of Departures," "Days," "Home is So Sad," "Reference Back," and "This Be the Verse," from *Collected Poems* by Philip Larkin. Copyright © 1988, 1989 by the Estate of Philip Larkin. Reprinted by permission of Farrar, Straus and Giroux. LLC. Canadian Rights: Reprinted by permission of Faber & Faber Limited.

D. H. Lawrence, "Piano," "Snake," and "Bavarian Gentians" from *The Complete Poems of D. H. Lawrence* by D. H. Lawrence, edited by V. de Sola Pinto & F. W. Roberts, copyright © 1964, 1971 by Angelo Ravagli and C. M. Weekley, Executors of the Estate of Frieda Lawrence Ravagli. Used by permission of Viking, Penguin, a division of Penguin Group (USA) Inc.

Denise Levertov, "The Ache of Marriage," "Hypocrite Women," "Our Bodies," and "O Taste and See" from *Poems 1960–1967* by Denise Levertov. Copyright © 1964, 1966 by Denise Levertov. Reprinted by permission of New Directions Publishing Corporation.

Robert Lowell, "Concord" and "Mr. Edwards and the Spider" from *Lord Weary's Castle,* copyright 1946 and renewed 1974 by Robert Lowell, reprinted by permission of Harcourt, Inc. "Skunk Hour" and "For the Union Dead" from *Collected Poems* by Robert Lowell. Copyright © 2003 by Harriet Lowell and Sheridan Lowell. Reprinted by permission of Farrar, Straus and Giroux, LLC.

Edna St. Vincent Millay, "What Lips My Lips Have Kissed and Where, and Why" by Edna St. Vincent Millay. From *Collected Poems,* HarperCollins. Copyright 1923, 1951 by Edna St. Vincent Millay and Norma Millay Ellis. All rights reserved. Reprinted by permission of Elizabeth Barnett, literary executor.

Marianne Moore, "The Fish," "Poetry," "To a Steam Roller," and "Silence" reprinted with the permission of Scribner, an imprint of Simon & Schuster Adult Publishing Group, from *Collected Poems of Marianne Moore* by Marianne Moore. Copyright 1935 by Marianne Moore, copyright © renewed 1963 by Marianne Moore and T. S. Eliot. "The Mind is an Enchanting Thing" reprinted with the permission of Scribner, an imprint of Simon & Schuster Adult Publishing Group, from *Collected Poems of Marianne Moore* by Marianne Moore. Copyright 1944 by Marianne Moore; copyright © renewed 1972 by Marianne Moore.

Wilfred Owen, "Anthem for Doomed Youth," "Dulce et Decorum Est," "Strange Meeting," and "Futility" by Wilfred Owen, from *The Collected Poems of Wilfred Owen,* copyright © 1963 by Chatto & Windus, Ltd. Reprinted by permission of New Directions Publishing Corp.

Sylvia Plath, all lines from "Blackberrying" from *Crossing the Water* by Sylvia Plath. Copyright © 1962 by Ted Hughes. This poem originally appeared in *Uncollected Poems,* Turret Books, London, and in the *Hudson Review.* Reprinted by permission of HarperCollins Publishers, Inc. All lines from "Daddy" from *Ariel* by Sylvia Plath. Copyright © 1963 by Ted Hughes. Reprinted by permission. All lines from "Lady Lazarus" from *Ariel* by Sylvia Plath. Copyright © 1963 by Ted Hughes. Reprinted by permission of HarperCollins Publishers, Inc. All lines from "Metaphors" from *Crossing the Water* by Sylvia Plath. Copyright © 1960 by Ted Hughes. Reprinted by permission of HarperCollins Publishers, Inc. Canadian rights: "Blackberrying," "Daddy," and "Lady Lazarus" from *Collected Poems* by Sylvia Plath. Reprinted by permission of Faber and Faber Ltd.

John Crowe Ransom, "Blue Girls," "Dead Boy," and "Piazza Piece" from *Selected Poems, Third Edition, Revised and Enlarged* by John Crowe Ransom, copyright 1924, 1927 by Alfred A. Knopf, Inc. and renewed 1952, 1955 by John Crowe Ransom. Used by permission of Alfred A. Knopf, a division of Random House, Inc. "Winter Remembered" from *Selected Poems, Third Edition, Revised and Enlarged* by John Crowe Ransom, copyright 1924 by Alfred A. Knopf, Inc. and renewed 1952 by John Crowe Ransom. Used by permission of Alfred A. Knopf, a division of Random House, Inc.

Theodore Roethke, "My Papa's Waltz," copyright 1942 by Hearst Magazines, Inc. "Elegy for Jane" copyright © 1950 by Theodore Roethke, "I Knew a Woman" copyright 1954 by Theodore Roethke, "The Waking" copyright 1953 by Theodore Roethke, from *The Collected Poems of Theodore Roethke* by Theodore Roethke. Used by permission of Doubleday, a division of Random House, Inc.

Kay Ryan, "Paired Things" and "Turtle" from *Flamingo Watching*, copyright © 1994 by Kay Ryan. Used by permission of Copper Beech Press. "Blandeur" and "Chemise" from *Say Uncle* by Kay Ryan. Copyright © 2000 by Kay Ryan. Used by permission of Grove/Atlantic, Inc.

Anne Sexton, "Her Kind" from *To Bedlam and Part Way Back* by Anne Sexton. Copyright © 1960 by Anne Sexton, copyright © renewed 1988 by Linda G. Sexton. Reprinted by permission of Houghton Mifflin Company. All rights reserved. "The Truth the Dead Know" and "The Abortion" from *All My Pretty Ones* by Anne Sexton. Copyright © 1962 by Anne Sexton, renewed 1990 by Linda G. Sexton. Reprinted by permission of Houghton Mifflin Company. All rights reserved. "Wanting to Die" from *Live or Die* by Anne Sexton. Copyright © 1966 by Anne Sexton, renewed 1994 by Linda G. Sexton. Reprinted by permission of Houghton Mifflin Company. All rights reserved.

Louis Simpson, "Early in the Morning," "The Man Who Married Magdalene," "My Father in the Night Commanding No," and "The Unwritten Poem" from *The Owner of the House: New Collected Poems 1940–2001*. Copyright © 2003 by Louis Simpson. Reprinted with the permission of BOA Editions, Ltd

Stevie Smith, "Mr. Over," "Not Waving but Drowning," and "One of Many" from *Collected Poems of Stevie Smith*, copyright © 1972 by Stevie Smith. Reprinted by permission of New Directions Publishing Corp.

Wallace Stevens, "The Snow Man," "The Emperor of Ice Cream," "Disillusionment of Ten O'Clock," "Sunday Morning," "Anecdote of the Jar," "Thirteen Ways of Looking at a Blackbird," and "Of Mere Being" from *The Collected Poems of Wallace Stevens* by Wallace Stevens, copyright 1954 by Wallace Stevens and renewed 1982 by Holly Stevens. Used by permission of Alfred A. Knopf, a division of Random House, Inc.

Dylan Thomas, "And death shall have no dominion," "Fern Hill," "In my craft or sullen art," and "Do Not Go Gentle Into that Good Night" from *The Poems of Dylan Thomas* by Dylan Thomas. Copyright 1943, 1945, 1946, 1952 by New Directions Publishing Corporation. Reprinted by permission of New Directions Publishing Corporation and David Higham Associates.

Derek Walcott, "A Far Cry from America" from *Collected Poems 1948–1984* by Derek Walcott. Copyright © 1986 by Derek Walcott. Reprinted by permission of Farrar, Starus and Giroux, LLC. "The Virgins" from *Sea Grapes* by Derek Walcott. Copyright © 1976 by Derek Walcott. Reprinted by permission of Farrar, Starus and Giroux, LLC. "XXVII" from *Midsummer* by Derek Walcott. Copyright © 1984 by Derek Walcott. Reprinted by permission of Farrar, Starus and Giroux, LLC. "Central America" from *The Arkansas Testament* by Derek Walcott. Copyright © 1987 by Derek Walcott. Reprinted by permission of Farrar, Starus and Giroux, LLC.

Richard Wilbur, "The Pardon" from *Ceremony and Other Poems*, copyright 1950 and renewed © 1978 by Richard Wilbur, reprinted by permission of Harcourt, Inc. "Love Calls Us to Things of This World" from *Things of This World*, copyright © 1956 and renewed 1984 by Richard Wilbur, reprinted by permission of Harcourt, Inc. "October Maples, Portland" from *Advice to a Prophet and Other Poems*, copyright © 1960 and renewed 1988 by Richard Wilbur, reprinted by permission of Harcourt, Inc. "The Writer" from *The Mind- Reader*, copyright © 1971 by Richard Wilbur, reprinted by permission of Harcourt, Inc.

William Carlos Williams, "Danse Russe," "Queen-Ann's Lace," "Spring and All," "The Red Wheelbarrow," "The Widow's Lament in Springtime," "The Yachts," and "To Waken an Old Lady" by William Carlos Williams from *Collected Poems: 1909–1939, Volume I,* copyright © 1938 by New Directions Publishing Corp. Reprinted by permission of New Directions Publishing Corp.

James Wright "Saint Judas," "Autumn Begins Martin's Ferry, Ohio," "A Blessing," and "Lying in a Hamock at William Duffy's Farm in Pine Island, Minnesota" from *Above the River: The Complete Poems* by James Wright. Reprinted by permission of Wesleyan University Press.

W. B. Yeats, "The Second Coming" reprinted with the permission of Scribner, an imprint of Simon & Schuster Adult Publishing Group, from *The Collected Works of W. B. Yeats, Volume I: The Poems,* Revised by Richard J. Finneran. Copyright 1924 by The Macmillan Company; copyright renewed 1952 by Bertha Georgie Yeats. "Leda and the Swan" and "Sailing to Byzantium" reprinted with the permission of Scribner, an imprint of Simon & Schuster Adult Publishing Group, from *The Collected Works of W. B. Yeats, Volume I: The Poems,* Revised by Richard J. Finneran. Copyright 1928 by The Macmillan Company; copyright renewed © 1956 by Bertha Georgie Yeats. "Crazy Jane Talks with the Bishop" reprinted with the permission of Scribner, an imprint of Simon & Schuster Adult Publishing Group, from *The Collected Works of W. B. Yeats, Volume I: The Poems,* Revised by Richard J. Finneran. Copyright 1933 by The Macmillan Company; copyright renewed © 1961 by Bertha Georgie Yeats.

Index of Poets, Titles, and First Lines

Additional Titles of Interest

Note to Instructors: Any of these Penguin-Putnam, Inc., titles can be packaged with this book at a special discount. Contact your local Allyn & Bacon/Longman sales representative for details on how to create a Penguin-Putnam, Inc., Value Package.

Albee, *The Three Tall Women*
Allison, *Bastard Out of Carolina*
Alvarez, *How the García Girls Lost Their Accents*
Austen, *Persuasion*
Austen, *Pride & Prejudice*
Bellow, *The Adventures of Augie March*
Boyle, *Tortilla Curtain*
Cather, *My Antonia*
Cather, *O Pioneers!*
Cervantes, *Don Quixote*
Chopin, *The Awakening*
Conrad, *Nostromo*
DeLillo, *White Noise*
Desai, *Journey to Ithaca*
Douglass, *Narrative of the Life of Frederick Douglass*
Golding, *Lord of the Flies*
Hawthorne, *The Scarlet Letter*
Homer, *Iliad*
Homer, *Odyssey*
Huang, *Madame Butterfly*
Hulme, *Bone People*
Jen, *Typical American*
Karr, *The Liar's Club*
Kerouac, *On The Road*
Kesey, *One Flew Over the Cuckoo's Nest*
King, *Misery*
Larson, *Passing*
Lavin, *In a Cafe*
Marquez, *Love in the Time of Cholera*
McBride, *The Color of Water*
Miller, *Death of a Salesman*
Molière, *Tartuffe and Other Plays*
Morrison, *Beloved*
Morrison, *The Bluest Eye*
Morrison, *Sula*
Naylor, *Women of Brewster Place*
Orwell, *1984*
Postman, *Amusing Ourselves to Death*
Rayben, *My First White Friend*
Rose, *Lives on the Boundary*
Rose, *Possible Lives: The Promise of Public*
Rushdie, *Midnight's Children*
Shakespeare, *Four Great Comedies*
Shakespeare, *Four Great Tragedies*
Shakespeare, *Four Histories*
Shakespeare, *Hamlet*
Shakespeare, *King Lear*
Shakespeare, *Macbeth*
Shakespeare, *Othello*
Shakespeare, *Twelfth Night*
Shelley, *Frankenstein*
Silko, *Ceremony*
Solzhenitsyn, *One Day in the Life of Ivan Denisovich*
Sophocles, *The Three Theban Plays*
Spence, *The Death of Woman Wang*
Steinbeck, *Grapes of Wrath*
Steinbeck, *The Pearl*
Stevenson, *Dr. Jekyll & Mr. Hyde*
Swift, *Gulliver's Travels*
Twain, *Adventures of Huckleberry Finn*
Wilde, *The Importance of Being Earnest*
Wilson, *Joe Turner's Come and Gone*
Wilson, *Fences*
Woolf, *Jacob's Room*